ADVANCE PRAISE FOR

THE GOSPEL ACCORDING TO SUPERHEROES

"My worldview and theological construct have been influenced almost as much by my comic book collection as by the Scriptures. So I enthusiastically welcome B. J. Oropeza's collection of fascinating articles on how these two seemingly disparate realms overlap and interrelate. This book is more powerful and compelling than those four-color pulps—and it provides a depth of insight with eternal ramifications. Excelsior!"

Peter Wallace, *Executive Producer of* Day 1*;*
Author of Out of the Quiet: Responding to God's Whispered Invitations

"With the steady popularity of comic books, Christians have reason to examine the comic book culture. *The Gospel According to Superheroes* takes a unique approach to understanding the history and spiritual implications of comic book heroes and stories. This book provides fascinating explanations behind the evolution of comic book trends, through the lens of its historical context and theological significance."

Barbara Nicolosi, Executive Director of ACT ONE

THE GOSPEL ACCORDING
TO SUPERHEROES

PETER LANG
New York • Washington, D.C./Baltimore • Bern
Frankfurt am Main • Berlin • Brussels • Vienna • Oxford

THE GOSPEL ACCORDING
TO SUPERHEROES

RELIGION AND POPULAR CULTURE

EDITED BY

B. J. OROPEZA

FOREWORD BY STAN LEE

PETER LANG
New York • Washington, D.C./Baltimore • Bern
Frankfurt am Main • Berlin • Brussels • Vienna • Oxford

Library of Congress Cataloging-in-Publication Data

The Gospel according to superheroes: religion and popular culture /
edited by B. J. Oropeza.
p. cm.
Includes bibliographical references and index.
1. Comic books, strips, etc.—Religious aspects. I. Oropeza, B. J.
PN6712 .G67   741.5'09—dc22   2005007317
ISBN 978-0-8204-7422-9

Bibliographic information published by **Die Deutsche Nationalbibliothek**.
Die Deutsche Nationalbibliothek lists this publication in the "Deutsche
Nationalbibliografie"; detailed bibliographic data are available
on the Internet at http://dnb.d-nb.de/.

Cover art by Matt Sheean
Cover design by Dutton & Sherman Design

The paper in this book meets the guidelines for permanence and durability
of the Committee on Production Guidelines for Book Longevity
of the Council of Library Resources.

© 2005, 2008 Peter Lang Publishing, Inc., New York
29 Broadway, 18th Floor, New York, NY 10006
www.peterlang.com

Printed in the United States of America

Table of Contents

Part One: Heroes from the Golden Age of Comic Books

Part Two: Heroes from the Silver Age of Comic Books

Part Three: Heroes from Intersecting Media—the Third Age and Beyond

List of Illustrations

Acknowledgments

In the making of this book, I would like to thank the contributors. I am privileged to have worked with such a fine group of dedicated scholars and specialists. I also wish to thank Stan Lee for taking time out of his busy schedule to write the Foreword to this book. Matt Sheean, the talented artist who designed the cover to this book, deserves a very special mention as well. Behind the scenes I would like to thank Heidi Burns, senior editor from Peter Lang Publishers, as well as Bernadette Shade and Sophie Appel, the productions coordinators.

For providing resources or other forms of assistance, I would like to thank Kurt Busiek, Robert Johnston, Peter Wallace, Erin Langhoser, Leo Partible, Roger White, Terry Mattingly, Bill Morrison, Guy Kinnear, Will Batchelor, Jason Clapp, Pat Losie, Scott Rosen, Chuck Robertson, Matthew Hogue, Michael Lucas, Rob Weiner, Francinne Valcour, Chris Belluomini, Thom Parham, Shana Huntly, James McGrath, Elizabeth Danna, Paul Schrier, Sheryl Lindsay, and Dick Pritchard.

Having children definitely helps when it comes to knowing which superheroes children enjoy—I thank Jared and Justin for their love and support. May the wonderment of what is good in the superhero legacy continue with both of you. I also would like to give a special thanks to Magda Sanchez (my mother), and her husband Henry, who assisted me with comic book resources originally collected by my deceased brother, Gus Oropeza. We collected hundreds of comics while growing up. He died of complications related to a kidney disease in November 1992. If I remember correctly, the Death of Superman was one of the topics of our final conversations. This book is dedicated in his memory.

B.J. Oropeza, *Editor*

Foreword

Know something? There's no way to predict how a mythology will get started. What has come to be known as the Marvel Mythology started quite by accident. Since you're a captive audience, I'd like to tell you about it.

Let me take you back to the early 1960s when I wrote the original scripts for what came to be known as the Marvel Universe of Superheroes. I must admit that attempting to create a mythology was the furthest thing from my mind at that time. I was just trying to write appealing stories about interesting characters with interesting powers. As you'd expect, all the heroes I created fought evil foes for the good of humankind. Each of them represented my feeling of what a superhero should be—a person who uses his power to protect good people from bad.

After Spider-Man, the Hulk, and the X-Men, by the time Thor, God of Thunder, was created, I had done so many superheroes with superpowers that I was hard pressed to think of a different kind of superhero, one that the readers hadn't seen before. That's why I decided to do a series featuring Thor. I felt it would be fun to borrow a god from mythology. I chose to play with Norse mythology in particular because people were too familiar with the Greek and Roman gods and I wanted my strip to seem really new.

The same held true for Dr. Strange. In his case I wanted a hero who could use magic as a weapon. And, of course, a Master of the Mystic Arts required evil foes to battle, the more demoniacal the better. I couldn't just have him fight ordinary gangsters or litterbugs.

Speaking of powerful villains, I really went all-out in the case of Galactus. He was so much more powerful than anyone else that he seemed to have the status of an actual demi-god. Remember, I was always trying to top myself in the creation of villains as well as heroes, and I wanted Galactus to be as powerful as possible.

Somehow, though I really wasn't making an attempt to create any sort of mythology, one started to develop on its own. The stories and characters just seemed to have struck a chord with a lot of people. Speaking of striking chords, with one glance at the essays in this book (and by the way, I love the title, "The Gospel According to Superheroes"), you will encounter scholarly insights for your philosophical, literary, truth-seeking self as to how it all came to be. And why not? Comics have been published since the 1930s and their heroes and villains have become part of our lives and our culture and, yes, even our belief systems. In fact, as I've told my friend and contributor to this book, the Rev. Dr. Chuck Robertson, I don't feel there'd ever be any disharmony in a conversation between Dr. Strange and an Episcopal priest if they chanced to meet. After all, Doc Strange believed in fighting evil and obviously a priest would feel the same.

Now, believe me, I wasn't consciously trying to inject religious themes into my stories, but the chapters in this book will clearly demonstrate how religious and mythological themes are often dramatically intertwined in comic books.

Another important point (well, important to me, anyway) is the fact that I scrupulously tried to avoid any reference to any specific organized religion. I thought of myself as "an equal opportunity writer." The only religious/philosophical themes I intentionally attempted to insert in anything I wrote could be summed up in the one code of ethics I've always tried to live by—"Do unto others as you'd have others do onto you." I feel if everyone followed that precept we'd have a Heaven here on Earth. And y'know what? I think Doc Strange, Thor, and the Silver Surfer would agree!

Excelsior!
Stan Lee

Introduction:
Superhero Myth and the
Restoration of Paradise

B. J. Oropeza

In the 1930s Adolph Hitler touted a twisted version of philosopher Friedrich Nietzsche's *übermensch*, a human who was superior to others. Meanwhile two Jewish-American teenagers named Jerry Siegel and Joe Shuster were creating a different kind of super-human. They developed their character until the concepts all came together. An infant child of noble birth needed to be evacuated from his home (much like the *Kindertransports*: the exodus of Jewish children from mainland European countries to Great Britain). This young alien and immigrant would have his Jewish-sounding name "Kal-El" changed to a more anglicized "Clark Kent." He possessed amazing strength and used his great power to fight evil and injustice—Superman (*Action Comics* #1; 1938). The Man of Steel turned into an immediate sensation.

What was so special about Superman? Action heroes already lined the newsstands through pulp fiction magazines and newspaper comic strips during the 1930s. In certain ways Superman, "The Man of Steel," mimicked the pulp hero Doc Savage, "The Man of Bronze." Also, heroes with dual identities had been previously popularized by *The Scarlet Pimpernel*, *The Mark of Zorro*, and *The Shadow*. Similarly, Flash Gordon and the Phantom dressed in circus uniform or "long underwear" prior to the hero from Krypton. Superman may have been a visitor from another planet, but this was hardly anything new in the science-fiction age of Buck Rogers and H. G. Wells's *War of the Worlds*. Moreover if Superman performed amazing feats of strength, he was not the first character of the time to do so. Popeye the Sailorman performed super feats that influenced Siegel and Shuster to create their hero with similar abilities. As well, the superpowers of a forgotten hero named Hugo Danner (from the 1930 Philip Wylie novel *Gladiator*) seemed to stamp an influential mark on the making of Superman.[1]

What then made Superman stand out as the hero *sine qua non*? Perhaps it was the winning *combination* of his fantastic powers, colorful costume, dual identity, and mission to fight crime all presented in color print through an innovative medium called the *comic book*.[2] While brave individuals who do great exploits, protect the innocent, or selflessly fight evil forces that threaten society can be traced back to much earlier times with heroes such as Odysseus, Beowulf, the Black Prince, Tezcatlipoca, Robin Hood, and Paul Bunyan, Superman helped spearhead a new genre in popular culture: the superhero in comic books. Humans always have admired and revered the hero, but the means of communicating and depicting the hero's exploits have changed. From cave paintings, to cuneiform, to oral traditions, to novels, to the comic book, the hero takes on new meaning. Only now, owing to advanced digital technology, superheroes on film are finally beginning to rival the realism portrayed in their comic book versions: hence, the new renaissance of superheroes at the box office.

In addition, a character like Superman fitted well with the spirit of the times. Siegel and Shuster portrayed their hero as otherworldly, handsome, confident, and *powerful* (apparently, everything his creators were not). For just ten pennies both children and adults could revel in the adventures of this invincible advocate; and maybe they would not feel so powerless themselves in an era when the damage of the Great Depression could still be felt, organized crime seemed beyond justice, and Nazi influence threatened the world. The common folk needed a super savior to take on the macro-evils of this world.

We can identify with Superman and the many superheroes that followed in his steps because they resemble people like *us*. A nearly omnipotent being impersonated a meek and frail nobody named Clark Kent—a human just like Siegel, Shuster, and us. In this manner superheroes tell us a lot about our aspirations; they are essentially the "childhood dream-self."[3] The mythic components that make up the superhero impact us on a deeper level. As comic historian Les Daniels notes, Siegel tapped into universally accepted mythic elements: "Superman recalled Moses, set adrift to become his people's savior, and also Jesus, sent from above to redeem the world. There are parallel stories in many cultures, but what is significant is that Siegel, working in the generally patronized medium of the comics, [unwittingly] created a secular American messiah."[4] The superhero trend began with the Man of Steel in the 1930s, but it continues to break new ground to this day.

At one time or another many youths and almost every adult in the Western world has read a superhero comic or seen at least one movie in this genre. At the peak of the early 1940s, as many as 95% of all children between the ages of 8 and 11 read comic books on a regular basis, and 25 million comics were being sold every month. In the early 1960s Marvel Comics alone reached 30 million copies per year, and in the early 1990s top comic books such as *The X-Men* and *The Amazing Spider-Man* commanded more than half a million readers. Special comic book issues distributed more than this. In 1992 Todd McFarlane's *Spawn* #1 sold over one million copies, and the story of "The Death of Superman" (beginning *Superman* #75) sold six million copies.[5] The *X-Men* #1 (second series; Oct. 1991) reached a circulation of more than seven million. The Spider-Man, Batman, and Superman movies rank among the highest box-office gross hits of all time. Comic book superheroes are part of popular culture[6]—they influence us as much as television shows, music, and fashion. In fact, they often do influence us in these ways too! For more than 70 years, our society has been inundated with television series, cartoons, toys, actions figures, toothbrushes, lunch pails, board games, electronic games, trading cards, pop songs, clothes, food, and vitamins that carry the names of Superman, Batman, Wonder Woman, Spider-Man, or some other costumed hero.[7] Make-believe role playing among young children frequently centers on pretending to be a favorite superhero, and for years this has concerned some parents due to the combative nature of such play.[8] It seems almost irresponsible that such an influential genre would be mostly ignored in academic circles until lately—perhaps this is because superhero stories have been stereotyped as mindless and juvenile entertainment.

The Relevance of the Superhero Myth in Relation to Theology

As anyone who reads comic books knows, there is far more complexity than mere "good guy" versus "bad guy" undergirding the superhero adventures. No doubt the classical image of heroes possessing incredible powers and using them for the cause of good appeals to our noble instincts for an ultimate sense of justice and retribution. This theme alone warrants an investigation into queries related to what is ultimately good, evil, and powerful. Such questions cannot be answered properly without addressing religion and theology (the latter is the study of God and how God relates to this world). Both the superhero fans and their creators are aware of this. The alluring subtitle given to *The Silver Surfer* comic book cover read, "The Mightiest Superhero of All!" (*The Silver Surfer* #16; May 1970). Yet one aficionado wrote in to Stan Lee and John Buscema (writer and artist of the series, respectively), and came to the conclusion that the cosmic-powered Surfer could not be omnipotent; there were at least three beings more powerful than he at the time—Galactus, the Watcher, and God.[9] When the Surfer temporarily runs amok by attacking the earth (attempting to get nations at enmity with each other to unite against him), the Watcher summons Reed Richards (Mr. Fantastic) to help stop the silver space rider. His wife Sue Richards (the Invisible Woman) asks, "But what … can he do… against the all-powerful Silver Surfer??" To which the Watcher replies: "all-powerful? There is only one who deserves that name! And his only weapon… is love!" (*Fantastic Four* #72; Mar. 1968). The Watcher implies that only God is Almighty and he uses his power for benevolent purposes, an observation that Stan Lee and Jack Kirby did not deny when a fan commented on this statement and drew out its implication in a letter from the Fantastic Four Fan Page (*Fantastic Four* #76).[10] Superheroes may be considered in this sense a pop-cultural implementation of religious premises, but as such they point to something greater than themselves.

We see, then, that intrigue and relevance relating superheroes and spiritual worlds has been around for quite some time. An important corollary follows from this. While the characters themselves might not always speak outwardly about religion and the Gospel, their storylines make implicit, and sometimes explicit, points about theology. In this way the superhero myths direct readers toward the interface between popular culture and religious ideas, both their similarities and differences. The investigation this book makes will foster appreciation for interdisciplinary studies related to art, film, literature, psychology, and any other discipline that might address religious or God-type questions. It stimulates the mind and spirit of the readers, whether comic fans, students, professionals, film directors, churchgoers, or seekers. It instructs the inquirer on how the biblical message and its theological/philosophical outgrowth has been revised or retold through the superhero genre.

The superhero legends venture to tap into universal mythic elements, and the theological subtexts play a major role in this. The adventurers portray in graphic images what is latent in mythology, biblical narrative, and philosophical ponderings. Binary questions related to good and evil, power and weakness, injustice and ultimate justice impact our psyche through these stories. Kurt Busiek, author of *Marvels* and the critically acclaimed *Astro City,* seems to agree: "the greatest strength of the superhero genre [is] the ease with which superheroes can be used as metaphor, as symbol, whether for the psychological transformation of adolescence, the self-image of a nation, or something else."[11] While theological/religious inquiry is not the only discipline unearthed from this genre, it remains an important one because such an investigation pursues answers to the big questions and meaning of life that affect humans at their core.

At least three foci in these heroes—the mythological, the theological, and the ideological—speak to the macro-issues of humanity and draw our attention to latent desires in our own psyche. We can perceive a prime example of how superhero stories cross over mythical, religious, and ideological boundaries in the theme of a *restored paradise.* The concept itself contains prominent subdivisions related to theology and myth: angst for a paradise lost, commissioning of a savior, the epic battle of good versus evil, and the pursuit of immortality. To this theme we now turn.

The Superhero's Plight: A Return to Eden

A composition of superhero characteristics typically identifies several common threads in the heroes. Not every superhero will have all the traits, but (using Wittgenstein language), there are enough "family resemblances" among the heroes to warrant such a list.[12]

1. Most superheroes have super powers (Batman, Rorschach, and the Punisher are important exceptions).
2. Many superheroes received their powers by accident or chance, often related to scientific misgivings (e.g., Spider-Man, Flash, Fantastic Four, Hulk, Daredevil, X-Men, Dr. Manhattan).
3. Many superheroes wear costumes and take on a change of identity or transformation when doing so (e.g., Superman, Batman, Wonder Woman, Spider-Man, Flash, Captain Marvel, Thor, Iron Man).
4. Many superheroes either have no parents or their parents are not present (e.g., Superman, Batman, Spider-Man, Sub-Mariner, Hulk, Wolverine/X-Men, Daredevil, Rorschach).
5. Many superheroes experience some great tragedy, challenge, or responsibility that functions as the incentive for their commission to become a hero (e.g., Superman, Batman, Spider-Man, Fantastic Four, Daredevil, Iron Man, the Punisher).
6. Many superheroes have an uneasy relationship with law authorities; they often will uphold justice before the law (Batman, Spider-Man, Daredevil, Sub-Mariner, Wolverine/X-Men, Silver Surfer, the Punisher).
7. Many superhero myths mimic the language of god-man mythology with traits such as noble origins, god-like powers, and savior capabilities (e.g., Superman, Wonder Woman, Thor, Captain Marvel, Silver Surfer, Green Lantern, Dr. Manhattan).

When examining the superhero genre through the lens of theology, numbers one and seven obviously play prominent roles, but also numbers three, four, and five stand out as significant because they combine mythic elements with religious yearnings. They identify something has been lost and needs to be restored; they point to inner conflicts and a sense of incompletion.

Religion phenomenologist Mircea Eliade captivated a primal archetype common throughout his study of various religions among numerous cultures around the world. Whether African tribes, Shamans, Virgil, Isaiah, or St. Francis, the need is the same. At the very beginning and end of human spiritual quests, there is a "yearning for Paradise," in which it is correct to assume "that the mystical memory of a blessedness without history haunts man from the moment he becomes aware of his situation in the cosmos."[13] The manifestations (i.e., the tales and rituals) about this myth may be different depending on culture or religion, but once the husk is removed and the kernel exposed, the story remains the same—humanity lost its original paradise and wants to be restored to it. In the western world this longing comes to us most clearly through the biblical words in Genesis: the story of the original human couple that is banished from the Garden of Eden (Genesis 1:26–3:24).

Angst for a Paradise Lost

The core of the "lost Eden" message is the same in almost every culture: Humans on earth once shared a primordial closeness with heaven in which there was open communication between the two realities.[14] Heaven could be reached by access of a tree, ladder, vine, or some other means of climbing. Then access to this tree was cut off. In essence, humanity suffered a "fall." Since then, the shamans and holy persons of the world have attempted to restore access between heaven and earth. If we turn to the biblical records, the priests, prophets, saints, and messiah represent the shamans, the way-showers of access to heaven.[15] Jesus of Nazareth is seen as the shaman *par excellence*, claiming to be "the way, the truth, and the life" and the "son of man" (*Adam* means "man" in Hebrew), and the apostles speak of Jesus as the New Adam, the restorer of paradise (John 14:6; Mark 8:27–38; Romans 5:12–21; Revelation 19–22). His early followers were known as "the Way," and his death on the cross (sometimes called a "tree") symbolized the tree of life.[16] If death was introduced by Adam as a result of his disobedience, eternal life is introduced by the New Adam.

Most superheroes suffer tragic loss: Superman, Batman, Spider-Man, Robin, and Toro all lose their parents, the Hulk loses his sanity, and Spawn his life. Yet despite their losses, or sometimes because of them, they gain a sense of great commission, forever trying to mend something that has been torn apart. Their stories present a subtle parable to humanity: We have lost our true identity and need to recover what was taken from us. Apparently somewhere deep within our psyche, we understand our status as fallen creatures. Inner discontentment cries out for something better than what it has, some ultimate sense of purpose and destiny. It should not be surprising, then, that one of today's best-sellers persists with the title, *The Purpose Driven Life: What on Earth Am I Here For?*[17] The heroes remind us of this. Despite their shortcomings, they commit to their purpose and have the power to go along with it. By protecting the weak and upholding justice, they want to restore a little bit of Eden to world, and so we admire and want to be like them. It seems written within the very fabric of Western culture, and certainly in movies and classic stories lines, that both the heroes and humans alike want a battle to fight, an adventure to live, and someone (or something) to rescue.[18]

The Commissioned Savior/Messianic Hero

Using Prometheus, Jason, Aeneas, Guatama Buddha, and Moses for exemplary models, mythologist scholar Joseph Campbell writes: "A hero ventures forth from the world of common day into a region of supernatural wonder: fabulous forces are there encountered and a decisive victory is won: the hero comes back from this mysterious adventure with the power to bestow boons on his fellow man."[19] This adventure may be structured in the pattern of an initiation "rite of passage" common in many cultures and religions throughout the world. Cultural anthropologist Victor Turner classifies the process in terms of three stages of initiation:

- Separation
- Transition or "Liminality"
- Reintegration[20]

After the hero, shaman, neophyte, or religious leader receives his or her commission, they must go through a period of transition or take a difficult journey before gaining higher status. The way is beset with obstacles, temptation, and anti-structure. Usually some god empowers or assists them on their journey. Jesus is baptized and immediately has an encounter with God who declares him as his beloved Son. Then, however, he enters a 40-day period of fasting in the wilderness where he is tempted by Satan. After he passes the test, he begins his ministry empowered by God's Spirit to cast out demons and proclaim the central message of God's kingdom invading the earth—the beginning of a restored Eden. As in virtually all traditions, saviors are sent to overcome evil and restore people to paradise. Prophecy in the Old Testament predicts this coming hero as the "anointed one" or messiah.

The superheroes normally come to an epiphany in which they are commissioned to help others and do battle against evil forces. For the Fantastic Four, it is their realization of superpowers gained through a cosmic accident that sets them on their path to use their special gifts for the benefit of humankind; for the X-Men, it is their commission to protect humans from other mutants who would desire their destruction. Neo sets his course as a savior when he determines to free human minds from the clutches of the matrix. The commission sets the specially chosen deliverers on their journey to restore paradise on earth. Whenever the heroes put on their mask or costume, they take on their savior identity and willfully go through another episode of separation, transition, and reintegration as they battle wicked menaces. They point us to the realization that society cannot eradicate evil on its own; it needs the help of a powerful yet godly redeemer.

The Apocalyptic Battle

Another mythological aspect discovered by anthropologists that spans across a wide spectrum of diverse cultures is the "Slaying the Monster." Whether in Homer, Herakles, Oedipus, Bantu Africa, or the book of Exodus, a macro-villain or actual monster seeks to devour a woman's child, spouse, or something else. The child then grows up to become a hero and slays the monster.[21] The biblical book of Revelation tells a similar story related to the messianic mission. Through symbolic pictures, the episode depicts a woman giving birth to a male child who is to rule all nations. A red dragon intends to eat her child, but he escapes the monster's clutches. Then Michael and his angels fight against the dragon and his angels in the heavens. The dragon, which is now revealed as Satan, falls defeated as a victory of chant of salvation is proclaimed by those who overcame him by the blood of the Lamb (Christ). The dragon is then cast down to earth, and tries to persecute the woman, who is protected in the wilderness until the grand finale (Revelation 12).[22] The Battle of Armageddon takes place with the return of the King of Kings who raises all believers from the dead, and defeats Satan, "the Beast" (the Antichrist), and death itself (Revelation 19–20;1 Corinthians 15:20–28). Through these images we see that Eden cannot be ultimately restored until one final, climactic battle takes place against the powers that originally spoiled the paradise.

The apocalyptic genre, often adapted from biblical prophecy in Daniel and Revelation, accounts for many of the comic book and fantasy story lines in recent years. Popular movies transform this genre on screen with "end of the world" scenarios, macro-good/heaven versus macro-evil/hell themes such as *Star Wars, The Terminator, The Stand, Lord of the Rings, The Matrix*, and the evangelical-oriented *Left Behind* series.[23] These pictures often bear striking resemblances to the stories of artist-writer Jack Kirby, who specialized in this genre with titles such as *The New Gods, The Forever People,* and *Kamandi, the Last Boy on Earth,* as well as the Galactus saga in *The Fantastic Four.* DC Comics' maxi-series *Crisis on Infinite Earths* is another prime example of epic battles.

The genre might well be considered in the vein of J. R. R. Tolkien's "eucatastophe," in which the forces of evil are decisively defeated.[24] Only through such a major battle can paradise be truly restored. Comic book creator and film producer Doug TenNapel says it well: "I'm attracted to superhero projects now because they are a way to bring a little fantasy into a real world situation… I think the superhero is a type of modern angel vs. demon genre because they exist on the periphery of our perception in amazing disguises engaged in epic conflict."[25] If humans can alleviate some of their anxieties about the future of this planet, superhero epic battles give us a sense of how to prepare for calamity, or at least they give us a future comfort in knowing that goodness will finally prevail over evil, especially if our personal world is not going too well. As J. S. Lawrence and Robert Jewett describe it, the superhero performs the function of a secular agent fulfilling a "millennial, religious expectation."[26]

Immortality in the New Eden

Why is getting back to the Garden so important? In a number of myths and cultures, the hero gains status through his victory, and the ultimate reward is immortality. Conquering death is something gods are supposed to do; an idea inherent in Western culture through the death and resurrection of the ultimate god-man, Christ. The restoration of Eden means that death, humanity's final enemy, is defeated; and communion with the Garden's creator is once again restored. The Bible begins with the creation of life and ends with all the dead restored to life (Genesis 1–3; Revelation 20–22). The rivers of the new paradise lead to God, suggesting the final fulfillment of the human heart once again sharing open communion with its creator. However, the unspoiled Garden in Genesis is not the same as the paradise in Revelation. The latter becomes a city with streets and artistic structures. In essence, the divine commission for Adam and Eve in Genesis to tend the Garden has now been completed by their progeny. The new Eden is a *cultivated* paradise.

Rising from the dead is a common theme among the superheroes (and a convenient way for authors to bring back what they hope will be marketable heroes!): The original Human Torch rises from his tomb in the earth through an atomic bomb explosion, Captain America is revived by the Avengers after being frozen for years, Jean Grey dies and rises again as the Phoenix, and Superman, Dr. Strange, Adam Warlock, Neo, Quasar, and others have "died" in some sense and come back again also.[27] Even so, permanent life seems evasive for the heroes. Neo dies twice in the Matrix trilogy, and Jean Grey dies again as the Dark Phoenix. True biblical resurrection is not simply a return from the dead (which is better classified as "resuscitation"), but a glorified transformation into something better, even as Jesus died and resurrected to die no more. The person who receives authentic eternal life in Revelation never dies again—death itself has been destroyed. Nevertheless by rising from the dead, even temporarily, the superheroes echo humanity's latent desire for life everlasting, a benefit of unfettered communion with the giver of life in the new paradise.

Hopefully I have established my point on why a book like this one is vitally relevant! All that remains is to lay out a brief history of superheroes so that the readers might have some contextual backdrop to fully benefit from their exploration of the chapters within this volume.

The Three Ages of Comic Book Superheroes

The chapters in this book are categorized into three main parts based on distinct comic book eras: the Golden Age, the Silver Age, and the Third Age. We will focus on the superheroes or teams according to the era in which they originated or have been widely influential.

Heroes from the Golden Age of Comic Books

The Golden Age of superheroes normally begins with Superman's first appearance in *Action Comics* #1 (June 1938) to the establishment of the Comic Code Authority and its first full year of implementation (1954–55). The characters in this era are often considered classical do-gooders chasing down bad guys, mad scientists, foreign spies, and Nazi criminals. Few have internal struggles, and superhero teams often get along well. Exceptions include the memorable dog fights between the Human Torch and the Sub-Mariner, and the pulp fiction–like mood of The Batman in the early days of *Detective Comics*. In our first chapter Ken Schenck will address the many faces of Superman as a mythic icon. In chapter 2 C. K. Robertson examines The Batman in light of Friedrich Nietzsche's *übermensch*.

Apart from the heroes already mentioned, DC Comics, Timely (Marvel), Fawcett, and other publishers introduced a lineup of colorful characters such as Captain Marvel, Captain America, Plastic Man, the Flash, the Green Lantern, the Green Arrow, Hawkman, the Atom, the Spectre, Starman, Hourman, the Guardian, the Sandman, Manhunter, the Shield, Blue Beetle, Captain Midnight, the Comet, Doll Man, Superboy, and Captain Marvel Junior. Female superheroes included women like Mary Marvel, the Black Canary, the Black Cat, Miss America, Liberty Belle, Hawkgirl, the Blond Phantom, Phantom Lady, Moon Girl, Sun Girl, and Sheena, Queen of the

Jungle. The most enduring heroine from this age is Wonder Woman. In our third chapter, Elizabeth Danna focuses on the Amazon queen as well as the mythological Hercules and the biblical Samson. Captain Marvel is also briefly covered in this chapter. Rob Weiner in chapter 4 will then address the superhero teams who fought against the Axis powers and Cold War adversaries: the Justice Society of America, the Young Allies, the All-Winners Squad, and the Invaders. He will also discuss Captain America during World War II and the Cold War.

During the late 1940s and early 1950s, superhero sales dropped as fans preferred buying comics about romance, horror, science fiction, cowboys, humor, and light-hearted Terry-Toons characters. For the most part comic readers had grown up and desired mature themes with more violence and sexuality. EC Comics raised the age of readership with famous titles such as *Tales from the Crypt, The Haunt of Fear, Weird Fantasy*, and *Mad*. The changes alarmed many adults who thought comics were just for kids. Psychologist Frederic Wertham sounded the alarm against comic books with his influential book, *Seduction of the Innocent*. Wertham's tirade against comics may have been partially motivated by anti-Semitism against comic publishers who were mostly Jews.[28] Although horror seemed to be what concerned many people, superheroes did not remain unscathed in Wertham's attack. He accused Batman and Robin of homoeroticism, Wonder Woman of lesbianism ("Suffering Sappho!"), and Superman of being a fascist archetype! Superheroes, it was thought, contributed to juvenile delinquency. The Comic Code Authority was then established in September 1954 to prohibit comics from depictions of vampires, ghouls, excessive violence, and disrespect for authorities such as police and government workers. The more graphic titles folded, and overall comic sales took a devastating hit. The Golden Age of comic books had come to an end.

Heroes from the Silver Age of Comic Books

DC Comics started a renaissance of superheroes beginning with revamps of Golden Age characters. *Showcase* #4 (Oct. 1956) introduced the new Flash, Barry Allen, wearing a new red costume designed by artist Carmine Infantino. The now famous suit would soon replace the memory of his earlier predecessor (Jay Garrick), as a new set of young fans called the Baby Boomers started buying comics. Comic historians consider this to be the first Silver Age superhero. This era covers 1956 to about 1985, but some end it much earlier than this. DC soon replaced Alan Scott with Hal Jordan as the new Green Lantern (*Showcase* #22; Oct. 1959), and Ray Palmer replaced Al Pratt as the new Atom (*Showcase* #34; Oct. 1961). Jack Kirby created

Challengers of the Unknown (*Showcase* #6; Feb. 1957), and Supergirl made her debut in *Action Comics* #252 (May 1959). A teen superhero group found audience with the Legion of Superheroes (*Adventure Comics* #247; 1958) but was overshadowed by the popularity of the adult team of flagship heavyweights called the Justice League of America (JLA) in *The Brave and Bold* #28 (Feb–March 1960). Soon other DC teams would follow like the original Teen Titans and Doom Patrol.

Meanwhile Stan Lee with artist Steve Ditko experimented on the first superhero in the Marvel Silver Age: Dr. Droom from *Amazing Adventures* #1 (June 1961). The hero did not make the cut, however, but he did become a prototype for the later Dr. Strange (*Strange Tales* #110; July 1963).[29] The big break for Marvel came by way of Stan Lee and Jack Kirby's *Fantastic Four* #1 (Nov. 1961). A plethora of new heroes came out in the immediate years that followed: the Hulk, Thor, Spider-Man, Iron Man, Ant-Man/Giant-Man, the Wasp, Daredevil, the X-Men, the Avengers, the Silver Age Sub-Mariner, and the Silver Age Captain America, the Silver Age Vision, the Scarlet Witch, the Black Widow, Hawkeye, and the Silver Surfer. Marvel set the tone for the Silver Age of heroes. Their origin stories mostly resulted from scientific accidents, with atomic age radiation as a prime culprit. Dr. Strange's mystic power stands in contrast to this trend. Unlike the Golden Age, these heroes had visible flaws and acted very human. The Avengers argued with one another, Daredevil was blind, Donald Blake (Thor) was crippled, Iron Man wore a pacemaker and later struggled with alcoholism, and Spider-Man was beset with all kinds of teen problems and inner conflicts. The heroes frequently fought one another, and many times they considered the Hulk and Sub-Mariner as their foes instead of friends. Fans of Marvel were not just kids; college students and adults also loved reading about these complex characters.

Scott Rosen will take us on a fantastic journey in chapter 5 by highlighting some of the most memorable creations of artist Jack Kirby in the Silver Age: the Fantastic Four, Thor, the New Gods and other Fourth World titles, and the Eternals. In chapter 6, I will focus on Marvel's most famous superhero: Spider-Man. Next, Robin Dugall will take a look at the split-personality of Bruce Banner and the Hulk in chapter 7. I will then follow up with another Stan Lee and Jack Kirby legend, the Silver Surfer, in chapter 8. Our final Silver Age superheroes, the X-Men, will be covered by Tim Perry in chapter 9. He will ponder the subject of original sin and the mutants, mostly as it relates to the supervillain Magneto.

The Silver Age already felt a transition in the late 1960s when DC experienced a sales slump in 1967 and 1968. The old superheroes needed some revision. In the years that followed, changes included Wonder Woman losing her Amazon powers, Supergirl trying on a mod wardrobe, Superman unaffected by eating kryptonite, and the Green Lantern teaming up with the socially conscious Green Arrow. At Marvel, the X-Men started wearing uniforms that stressed their individualism (e.g., Jean Grey's turned out to be a bright green miniskirt and yellow go-go boots), counterculture youths identified with the philosophical Silver Surfer, and Peter Parker faced the dilemma of joining hippie protesters at his college. Changes came about at Marvel Comics when Jack Kirby joined DC Comics in 1970, leaving the flagship Marvel comic *The Fantastic Four* after he had penciled the first 102 issues. Then a few years later, Stan Lee handed over his editorial responsibilities to Roy Thomas.

Coinciding with the cost of inflation, within several years (1969–74), comic book prices jumped from 12 to 15 to 20 and then to 25 cents. The price in 1980 would double this amount. While some might consider the period as heralding the end of the Silver Age, a growing number of comic historians suggest 1979 or 1985 as the official closing date. Bradford Wright defines the comic age from 1968 to 1979 as a time related to "Questioning Authority,"[30] and Les Daniels titles the 1970s for Marvel as a "Research and Development" stage.[31] Some give it the name "Bronze Age."[32] Several significant changes did take place during the period between 1968 and 1985.

First, Stan Lee took a risk in challenging the Comic Code Authority; a benchmark for the Silver Era. He read a letter from the Department of Health, Education, and Welfare requesting that a Marvel comic focus on anti-drug use. The experiment took place in *The Amazing Spider-Man* #96–98 (1971). Peter Parker's roommate, Harry Osborne, got hooked on drugs and overdosed. The Comic Code Authority did not approve of the story, but it went to press anyway with Lee and Marvel congratulated and the CCA looking a bit dated in light of the changing times. *The Green Lantern* included its own anti-drug message that same year (*Green Lantern* #83–86).

Second, heroes who killed their opponents might seem cliché today, but not in the 1960s. Things started changing, however, when Roy Thomas and Barry Windsor-Smith adapted *Conan the Barbarian* (#1 Oct. 1970) from the pulp character created by Robert E. Howard several decades earlier. Its popularity sparked a genre of sword and sorcery comics that made both magic and killing one's enemy vogue. *Kull the Conqueror, Red Sonja, Claw the Unconquered, Sword of Sorcery*, and similar comic titles followed, but none endured as long as Conan, which spawned a few movies in the 1980s starring Arnold Schwarzenegger. Marvel presented the barbarian's more graphic tales in black-and-white magazine format: *Savage Tales #1* (May 1971) was rated "M For The Mature Reader!" The *Savage Sword of Conan* black-and-white series followed up in 1974. Conan led the way for a different type of "hero"—one who practiced few morals and brutally slayed his enemies as a mercenary, thief, and transient.

The Punisher (first appearing in *Amazing Spider-Man* #129; 1974) was another example from the 1970s of a hero who killed his enemies instead of handing them over to proper authorities. The Punisher dressed in superhero garb and lived in a society resembling our own, unlike Conan who lived in a 10,000-year-old civilization where killing became necessary for survival. Driven by vengeance (or a "natural justice" beyond the law, as the remake movie words it) Vietnam vet Frank Castle's mission was to execute or "punish" all criminals after mobsters murdered his family. His storyline and fan following would grow tremendously in the 1980s and 1990s. Wolverine represents a third hero from the 1970s who killed his opponents. This "Weapon X," together with the other X-Men, became the avant-garde title for Marvel, birthing numerous mutant groups in the 1980s and 1990s.

Third, marketing strategies started changing with the widespread establishment of comic book shops in the 1970s and 1980s. The transition assisted in building "fan boy" culture; hardcore comic fans would visit the comic collector shop instead of the corner market store for comics. As well, Mini- and Maxi-Series collections (in which the total amount of issues for a series is limited to about a year's time or less) became more commonplace, paving the way for the graphic novel that often collected and reprinted these stories in one larger book. Will Eisner's *A Contract with God* (1978) and Stan Lee and Jack Kirby's reunion in *The Silver Surfer* (1978) were among the first graphic novels.

Fourth, comic storylines became more intricate and far less predictable. First, the new Wonder Woman lost her longtime love, Steve Trevor. Then Peter Parker's college sweetheart, Gwen Stacy, was killed by the Green Goblin. Fans protested to no avail. If a leading person could be killed off (and not come back again, as in Gwen's case), this made for unpredictable reading in the Marvel and DC Universes. Jean Grey of the X-Men, Elektra, Supergirl, and Flash would also perish by the end of the Silver Age. Alternative reality stories, such as Marvel's original *What If...?* added to the continuity and complexity of superhero myths. Marv Wolfman and George Pérez's *Crisis on Infinite Earths* killed off many of DC's heroes in alternate universes, enabling writers to start afresh with old superheroes.

Finally, new talent in writers and artists made for a new style in comic books, one that eventually replaced the Silver Age. Frank Miller took over Marvel's *Daredevil* (#158; 1979), adding realism to the art and plot with dark settings, more violence, and a less moral Matt Murdock. Some consider his remake of this character as the first "grim and gritty" superhero. British writer Alan Moore took over *The Saga of the Swamp Thing* (1984) and reworked the monster with intricate narratives that found audience with mature readers. After Flash was killed in November 1985 (*Crisis on Infinite*

Earths #8), the very hero who opened up the Silver Age, the comic world was ready for a new era.

Heroes from Intersecting Media—The Third Age and Beyond

A new beginning for comic books marks the year of 1986. Some define this age of comics as Postmodern, while others consider it the Bronze Age. I use "Third Age" to designate Part III of this book but agree that *postmodern* and *deconstruction* are terms that describe many of its characters and stories. The two most influential titles of the new era came out in 1986 with Frank Miller's *Batman: The Dark Knight Returns* and Alan Moore's *Watchmen*. Both titles typify the new breed of comics with multilayered intricacy, dark settings, and characters who take the law into their own hands. Best-selling comics in this era seem to depend as much on the reputation of the writer and artist as they do on the characters. Popular artist names include Alex Ross, Frank Miller, Todd McFarlane, John Byrne, George Pérez, John Romita Jr., Jim Lee, Michael Turner, and many others.

Although the traditional heroes of Marvel and DC still led the way during the 1980s and 1990s, a number of publishers joined the market such as America's Best Comics, Image, Vertigo, Dark Horse, and others, to create a lineup of mostly antiheroes. Mutations and bad scientific experiments still happen, but a number of the characters have been endowed with supernatural and occult powers, or fight against such powers; hence the magic motif plays prominently in the new era, as do weapons. Some of the characters come from earlier comic ages, but they became famous in the Third Age. Generally speaking, the new generation combines more violence and mature themes to make a roster of "bad boys" or just tough-looking dudes like Spawn, Cable, Blade, Wolverine, the Punisher, John Constantine, Deathlok, Deadshot, Deadman, Hellboy, Ghost Rider, Gambit, Judge Dredd, Lobo, Savage Dragon, Badger, Bishop, Preacher, Prophet, and the characters from *Sin City*. By way of contrast, a reconstruction of characters that are not so gloomy seems to be gaining ground with heroes such as the Samaritan from *Astro City*. Characters like Steel, Deadpool, and Tom Strong are reminiscent of older heroes.

New female characters stand out more in this era than the previous, but many resemble femme fatales with sexy costumes that exploit their voluptuous bodies. A sampling includes Elektra, Catwoman, Danger Girl, Tomb Raider/Lara Croft, Darkchylde, Lady Death, Witchblade, Avengelyne, Fathom, Shi, Dawn, Warrior Nun Areala, and female teams such as Femforce and DC's Birds of Prey: Oracle (once Batgirl), Black Canary II, Huntress, and (at one time) Power Girl. As one could surmise from just their titles, a number of these characters reflect a dark or magic ethos. *The Sensational She-Hulk* stands out as one example of a postmodern exception to this gloomy tenor, as does *Promethea* when it comes to a moderately proportioned female anatomy.

If the Christ-type represented in the classic hero slipped through the back door during the Third Age, it inadvertently snuck back in for the battle of Armageddon. The third era emphasizes apocalyptic motifs related to the Second Coming of Christ as depicted in the book of Revelation. An impending doomsday or post-doomsday milieu (sometimes with angelic and demonic battles) is easy to decipher in many of the stories. *Watchmen, Spawn, Eternal Warrior*, and the X-Men's "The Age of Apocalypse" stories versus their nemesis, Apocalypse (e.g., *X-Factor* #24; Jan. 1988; *X-Man* series), are only a few examples. The graphic novel *Marvels* rehashes the original Galactus "end of the world" invasion from the Fantastic Four, and *Kingdom Come* pits older superheroes against a newer amoral string, citing passages from Revelation along the way. An obsession with Armageddon made sense in the 1990s for a culture heading toward the ominous year 2000 and the Y2K computer-bug scare. While the postmodern characters in comic books are generally darker, less moral, and more violent than their predecessors, they still tap into their fans' inner hunger for completion, purpose, and the restoration of the paradise through the apocalyptic grand battle against evil incarnate. Comics with surrealistic settings or alternate worlds where the real and imagined interact and collide, typify many story lines. *Sandman* and *Animal Man* are two different examples of this.

Some of the long-standing characters like Superman, Spider-Man, and the Hulk were fragmented into multiple variations or literal clones after the mid-1980s. Robin (Dick Grayson) stars in his own series as *Nightwing*, and Timothy Drake stars in his own series as *Robin* (III). Robin II is killed by the Joker, and a female Robin, Carrie Kelley, appears in *Batman: The Dark Knight*. The old guard nevertheless received fresh facelifts with new series and revamped origins. In the second series of Superman, the Man of Steel is not quite as powerful this time around and finally marries Lois Lane. Wally West (once Kid Flash) replaces Barry Allen as the new Flash, and the Fantastic Four's second series turned Sue Storm into a high-ranking businessperson and her brother Johnny into a casino manager.

The flagship heroes from the previous eras remained top sellers, especially the X-Men and their many offshoots including titles like *The New Mutants, Alpha Flight, Excalibur, Generation X, X-Factor, X-Force,* and *Astonishing X-Men*. Incidentally, X-Mania in comic books found fresh readership with post-Baby Boomers appropriately named Generation X! Older superhero teams continue with novel incarnations such as the Legion of Superheroes/ Legionnaires, Teen Titans, Avengers, Doom Patrol, Suicide

Squad, and JLA (Justice League of America) with the Brad Meltzer–Rags Morales mini-series *Identity Crisis.*

Third Age teams include Gen13, League of Extraordinary Gentlemen, Top Ten, Suicide Squad, Youngblood, the New Warriors, the Invisibles, WildC.A.T.S, and the Authority. A story from the last of these teams allows for a parable contrasting the Silver Age. The Authority includes members who are sexually promiscuous, have alcohol and tobacco addictions, and do not think twice about savagely slaughtering their opponents. In the graphic novel *Under New Management*, this group fights against a team imitating Marvel Comic's Avengers during the Silver Age.[33] The Authority brutally kills the Avenger look-alikes, but a deeper message implies that the Silver Age characters are now passé. The more violent, amoral, and openly dysfunctional new breed of heroes have arrived, and unlike the Silver Age, they do not repress their inner problems or sexual desires, and they certainly do not refuse to kill their enemies in battle!

Multiple media intersections have taken place in the Third Age. Japanese *manga* characters have excelled with Katsuhiro Otomo's *Akira,* and popular animated series such as *Sailor Moon, Pokémon, Dragonball Z,* and *Yu-Gi-Oh* have made successful crossovers into films, electronic games, and comic book culture. The comic book shops as well as popular bookstores are gradually making more room for graphic novels, and blockbuster movies such as *Spider-Man* and *The X-Men* mark a resurgence of superheroes on film. In essence, the superheroes are not as easily associated with comic books as they once were in previous generations. Our final section of this book will focus on these issues: Heroes from Intersecting Media.

Thom Parham will address postmodern heroes in terms of deconstruction and reconstruction in chapter 10. Some of the influential titles of his focus include *The Saga of the Swamp Thing, Watchmen, The Dark Knight Returns, The Sandman, Kingdom Come, Astro City, Marvels,* revamps of Superman and Wonder Woman, and more. Before the grim and gritty heroes of the 1980s and 1990s, pulp fiction magazines of the 1930s and 1940s compiled tales of similar but less powerful vigilantes who took the law into their own hands to bring criminals to justice. They became precursors to the first superheroes in comic books. As well, newspaper comic strips presented their own collage of heroes. Through these media popular names included Doc Savage, the Shadow, the Spider, Flash Gordon, Buck Rogers, Dick Tracy, Tarzan, the Phantom, and the Spirit. Pulp magazines with science fiction and detective stories provided readers struggling in the Great Depression with their "wildest dreams and nightmares... peddled for pennies at every corner newsstand."[34] In chapter 11 Gregory Pepetone explores the pulp heroes, especially *The Shadow,* in light of gothic motifs and heroes from the biblical book of Judges.

Our final two chapters address superheroes in film. The success of the recent Spider-Man films seems twofold: It combined new film technology with better special effects (hence, more realism), and it tapped into pop culture's increasing desire to abandon the 1990s antiheroes for more pristine characters. In the post-9/11 world of the new millennium, a back-to-basics or reconstruction approach to heroes may be winning the day. One general observation is that film stories about heroes tend to be less complex than the comic versions that require fan commitment to purchasing numerous issues before understanding the entire story. Movies, if done well, tell the story quicker by condensing the superhero myths. In chapter 12 Leo Partible will explore the relationship between pop culture, theology, and heroes on the screen. Not only does his chapter give a fascinating historical overview about the influence of comic books on film and culture, but he also delves into the question of why superheroes and the fantasy genre are so popular today. In chapter 13 James McGrath then dissects one particular film trilogy, the Matrix, to draw out superhero and religious implications from the virtual reality of Neo.

While religious and spiritual insights do not always derive from Judaism or Christianity, because this book focuses on popular culture in the West, the Judeo-Christian worldview will be the primary point of theological address. We recognize, however, that in any multilayered medium, many religious and secular voices may be heard. In fact the nature of some heroes will require us to ponder other western and non-western ideas, such as Greco-Roman mythology (e.g., Wonder Woman), secular humanism (e.g., Batman), and Hinduism/Buddhism (e.g., the Matrix). Be that as it may, I wish to be up-front about my bias and that of the other contributors: we grew up in Western culture and this book reflects that upbringing.

And now, up, up, and away!

Notes

[1] E. C. Segar in 1929 launched Popeye's career in the comic strip entitled *Thimble Theatre*. On the previous characters that influenced Superman, see Jim Steranko, *The Steranko History of Comics Volume 1* (Reading, Penn.: Supergraphics Publication, 1970), 39–40; Les Daniels and Chip Kidd, *Superman: The Complete History* (San Francisco: Chronicle Books, 1998), 18.

[2] Newspaper comic strips existed prior to this date, and as far back as 1897, one book collected strips from *The Yellow Kid*. Many comic book authorities, however, consider *Famous Funnies* (1934) as the first authentic comic book sold on the newsstands.

[3] Phrase and idea adapted from Steranko, 39–40.

[4] Les Daniels and Chip Kidd, *Superman,* 19.

[5] For these statistics, see Matthew Pustz, *Comic Book Culture: Fanboys and True Believers* (Jackson: University Press of Mississippi, 2000), 26–27; Jordan Raphael and Tom Spurgeon, *Stan Lee and the Rise and Fall of the American Comic Book* (Chicago: Chicago Press Review, 2003), 124, 140; Carol Christine Mahoney, "A Content Analysis of Family Relationships in Six Superhero Comic Book Series," (M.A. Thesis; Michigan State University, 1997), 1–2; Les Daniels, *DC Comics: A Celebration of the World's Favorite Comic Book Heroes* (New York: Billboard Books, 2003), 218; Mila Bongco, *Reading Comics: Language, Culture, and the Concept of the Superhero in Comic Books* (New York & London: Garland Publishing, 2000), 192.

[6] When relating superheroes to popular culture, I am not intending to trivialize superheroes but emphasize the widespread, influential nature of superheroes over western culture. Too often comic books are put down as unsophisticated, lacking artistic quality, or not as important as other creative arts. Popularity need not be equated with mediocrity. Instructive on the evolution of superheroes in relation to complexity is Mila Bongco, *Reading Comics,* 91–100.

[7] See the many samples of such paraphernalia in Daniels, *DC Comics,* 72–75, 142–43, 180–81, 186–87, 216–17, 222–23, 244–45, 260–61.

[8] Cf. Penny Holland, *We Don't Play with Guns Here: War, Weapon, and Superhero Play in the Early Years* (Maidenhead, England: Open University Press, 2003); June Meyer, *Concerning Superhero Play* (UCFV Press Monograph Series #1; Abbotsford, B.C.: UCFV Press, 1993); Jackie Marsh, "'But I want to fly too!' Girls and Superhero Play in the Infant Room," *Gender & Education* 12/2 (June 2000), 209–20; Brenda Boyd, "Teacher Response to Superhero Play: To Ban or Not to Ban?" *Childhood Education* 74 (Fall 1997), 23–28; Marjorie Kostelnik et al., "Living with He-Man: Managing Superhero Fantasy Play" *Young Children* 41 (May 1986), 3–9; Alexis S. Tan and Kermit J. Scruggs, "Does Exposure to Comic Book Violence Lead to Aggression in Children?" *Journalism Quarterly* 57 (Winter 1980), 579–83.

[9] Letter from Jeff Mehr in "Who Speaks for the Surfer" fan mail section; *The Silver Surfer* #16 (1970).

[10] Letter from Jim Morgan, who cites 1 John 4:8 in the New Testament, "God is love," mentions other attributes of God, and then adds, "I'm glad to hear that the Bullpen Gang believes there is a God and that He is not dead as so many false religions teach." To which Lee and Kirby respond, "we appreciated your comments on the Watcher's observation. Perhaps we can never all accept the same meaning of God – but, don't you agree that mankind is far better off with than without Him?"

[11] Kurt Busiek, Introduction, *Astro City: Life in the Big City* (La Jolla, Calif.: Homage Comics/Juke Box Productions, 1996), 8.

[12] For elaboration on similar motifs, see Richard Reynolds, *Super Heroes: A Modern Mythology* (Jackson: University Press of Mississippi, 1992), 12–16; Bongco, *Reading Comics,* 100–06.

[13] Mircea Eliade, "The Yearning for Paradise in Primitive Tradition," in *Myth and Mythmaking* (ed. Henry A. Murray; New York: George Braziller, 1960), 73.

[14] In these myths there is normally a communion between animals and humans also.

[15] Eliade, 61–68.

[16] Acts 19:9, 23; 22:4; cf. 16:17; 18:25–26; 1 Peter 2:24; and Eliade (68–69) for sources from the early church fathers. I will delve into this topic again in chapter 8 when examining the Silver Surfer.

[17] Richard Warren (Grand Rapids: Zondervan, 2002).

[18] This thought is derived from John Eldredge's *Wild at Heart: Discovering the Passionate Soul of a Man* (Nashville: Nelson, 2001), a book that focuses on the current men's movement in western society. For Eldredge, the damsel in distress is what men want to rescue.

[19] Joseph Campbell, *The Hero with a Thousand Faces* 2nd ed. (Princeton, N.J.: Princeton University Press, 1968), 30–40. Campbell uses separation or departure—initiation—return, a model similar to the structure of Arnold van Gennep (1873–1957), who used *séparation* (separation), *marge* (transition), and *aggrégation* (incorporation). Cf. Arnold van Gennep, *The Rites of Passage* (London: Routledge & Kegan Paul, 1960) vii, 11.

[20] Victor Turner, *The Ritual Process: Structure and Antistructure* (Ithaca, N.Y.: Cornell University Press, 1969). For an elaborate summary of Turner's view, see my article, "Apostasy in the Wilderness: Paul's Message to the Corinthians in a State of Eschatological Liminality," *Journal for the Study of the New Testament* 75 (1999), 69–86.

[21] Cf. Clyde Kluckhohn, "Recurrent Themes in Myths and Mythmaking," in *Myth and Mythmaking,* ed. Henry A. Murray (New York: George Braziller, 1960), 51.

[22] The "woman" in the story is often identified as Israel, the Church, Jewish Christians, or the Messianic Community. The early Christians viewed their baptism as an initiation ceremony that prepared them for a lifelong journey of transition, much like the woman in the wilderness. They remain on earth sought out by Satan until their messiah returns and sets earth in order. For references and elaboration on the Christian life as a liminal journey, see my book, *Paul and Apostasy: Eschatology, Perseverance, and Falling Away in the Corinthian Congregation* (Tübingen: Mohr-Siebeck, 2000), especially chapter 4.

[23] This does not mean, however, that the *Left Behind* series is correct in its *interpretation* of Daniel and Revelation. The view that a rapture of believers will take place prior to seven years of tribulation, popularized by the *Scofield Reference Bible* and then Hal Lindsey's *Late Great Planet Earth,* is only held today by a shrinking number of very conservative theologians, mostly Americans. Problematic with this view is its tendency to influence non-scholastic readers to speculate on setting dates for the end of the world. For criticisms against date setting, see my book, *99 Reasons Why No One Knows When Christ Will Return* (Downer Grove, Ill.: InterVarsity Press, 1994). See also Paul Boyer, *When Time Shall Be No More: Prophecy Belief in Modern American Culture* (Cambridge, Mass.: The Belknap Press of Harvard University Press, 1992). For scholastic interpretations related to Revelation, Daniel, and the apocalyptic genre, see J. J. Collins, *The Apocalyptic Imagination: An*

Introduction to Jewish Apocalyptic Literature (Grand Rapids: Eerdmans, 1998); Millard Erickson, *Christian Theology* (Grand Rapids: Baker, 1985), 1149–1241.

[24] Cf. W. H. Auden, "Good and Evil in *The Lord of the Rings*," *Tolkien Journal* 3/1 (1967) 5–8; cited from John Warwick Montgomery, "Introduction: The Apologists of Euchatastophe," in *Myth, Allegory, and the Gospel: An Interpretation of J. R. R. Tolkien, C. S. Lewis, G. K. Chesterton, Charles Williams* (Minneapolis: Bethany Fellowship, 1974), 11.

[25] Doug TenNapel, interview by Leo Partible, electronic correspondence, [retrieved by Partible] 16 April 2004.

[26] J. S. Lawrence and Robert Jewett, *Myth of the American Superhero* (Grand Rapids: Eerdmans, 2002), 46 cf. 6, 22–25. They identify the restoration of paradise in terms of the "American monomyth."

[27] Cf. *Young Men* #24 (1954); *X-Men* #100–101 (1976); *Avengers* #4 (1964); *Dr. Strange* #1–5 (vol. 2; 1974); Peter Sanderson, *Marvel Universe* (New York: Harry N. Abrams, 1996) 169, 170; Daniels, *DC Comics,* 228.

[28] Cf. Arie Kaplan, "Kings of Comics Part 1: How the Jews Created the Comic Book Industry: The Golden Age (1933–1955)" *Reform Judaism* 32/1 (Fall 2003), 8–9 [Cited 14 Aug. 2004] Online: www.uahc.org/rjmag/03fall/comics.shtml.

[29] A similar try-out character for Dr. Strange appeared in *Strange Tales* #79 (Dec. 1960). Other examples included prototypes of Quicksilver (*Strange Tales* #67; Apr. 1959), Professor X (*Strange Tales* #69; June 1959/ *Amazing Adult Fantasy* #14; July 1962), Magneto (*Strange Tales* #84; May 1961/ *Incredible Hulk* #6; Mar. 1963); and the Hulk (*Journey into Mystery* #62; Nov. 1960).

[30] Bradford W. Wright, *Comic Book Nation: The Transformation of Youth Culture in America* (Baltimore: Johns Hopkins University Press, 2001), 226–53.

[31] Les Daniels, *Marvel: Five Fabulous Decades of the World's Greatest Comics* (New York: Harry N. Abrams, Inc., Publishers, 1991), 148. See also Bongco's study on this era in *Reading Comics*, 99–100, 137–42.

[32] This is how www.ebay.com online currently categorizes it. Arie Kaplan also uses the term but starts the Bronze Age in 1979: "Kings of Comics: How the Jews Transformed the Comic Book Industry Part III: The Bronze Age (1979–)," *Reform Judaism* 32/3 (2004) [Cited 14 Aug. 2004] Online: www.uahc.org/rjmag/04spring/comics.shtml.

[33] Warren Ellis, Brian Hitch, Paul Neary, Laura DePuy, *The Authority: Under New Management* (La Jolla: Wildstorm Productions/DC, 2000). The Authority also fight "God" in *Under New Management*. Jenny Sparks electrocutes the brain of this deity and kills it, breathing new meaning into the 1960's slogan, "God is dead." But this being hardly reflects Yahweh, the God in the Bible, who is "all powerful" Spirit and demonstrates love for humanity by delivering people from human oppression. If it is true that he created the universe, transcends time itself, bestows eternal life to his followers, and raises Jesus from the dead, I doubt if this God even has the capacity to die or a physical brain to electrocute!

[34] Daniels, *Marvel*, 15.

Recommended Resources

Anderson, Fenwick. "Comic Heroes: Popular Culture on a Pedestal." *Studies in Popular Culture* 9.2 (1986): 85-95.

Barker, Martin. *Comics: Ideology, Power and the Critics.* Cultural Politics. Manchester: Manchester University Press, 1989.

Benton, Mike. *The Comic Book in America: An Illustrated History.* Second Edition. Dallas: Taylor Publishing Company, 1993.

Bongco, Mila. *Reading Comics: Language, Culture, and the Concept of the Superhero in Comic Books.* New York: Garland, 2000.

Boyer, Paul. *When Time Shall Be No More: Prophecy Belief in Modern American Culture.* Cambridge, Mass.: Belknap Press of Harvard University Press, 1992.

Brewer, H. Michael. *Who Needs a Superhero? Finding Virtue, Vice, and What's Holy in the Comics.* Grand Rapids: Baker Book House, 2004.

Brown, Jeffrey A. *Black Superheroes, Milestone Comics, and Their Fans.* Jackson: University Press of Mississippi, 2001.

Campbell, Joseph. *The Hero with a Thousand Faces.* Bollingen Series 17. Second Edition. Princeton, N.J.: Princeton University Press, 1968.

Cohen, Stanley. "Messianic Motifs, American Popular Culture and the Judeo-Christian Tradition." *Journal of Religious Studies* 8 (Spring 1980): 24–34.

Collins, J. J. *The Apocalyptic Imagination: An Introduction to Jewish Apocalyptic Literature.* Second Edition. Grand Rapids: Eerdmans, 1998.

Daniels, Les. *Marvel: Five Fabulous Decades of the World's Greatest Comics.* New York: Harry N. Abrams, Inc., Publishers, 1991.

Daniels, Les. *DC Comics: A Celebration of the World's Favorite Comic Book Heroes.* New York: Watson-Guptill Publications, 2003.

Detweiler, Craig, and Taylor, Barr. *A Matrix of Meanings: Finding God in Pop Culture.* Baker, 2003.

Eliade, Mircea. "The Yearning for Paradise in Primitive Tradition." Pages 61–75 in *Myth and Mythmaking.* Edited by Henry A. Murray. New York: George Braziller, 1960.

Erickson, Millard J. *Christian Theology.* Grand Rapids: Baker, 1985.

Feiffer, Jules. *The Great Comic Book Heroes.* Reprint. Seattle: Fantagraphics Books, 2003.

Fingeroth, Danny. *Superman on the Couch: What Superheroes Really Tell Us About Ourselves and Our Society.* New York: Continuum, 2004.

Fox, Richard Wightman. *Jesus in America: Personal Savior, Cultural Hero, National Obsession.* San Francisco: HarperSanFrancisco, 2004.

Garrett, Greg. *Holy Superheroes: Exploring Faith and Spirituality in Comic Books.* Colorado Springs: NavPress, 2005.

Goulart, Ron. *Ron Goulart's Great History of Comic Books: The Definitive Illustrated History from the 1890s to the 1980s.* Chicago: McGraw-Hill/Contemporary Books, 1986.

Goulart, Ron. *The Comic Book Encyclopedia: The Ultimate Guide to Characters, Graphic Novels, Writers, and Artists in the Comic Book Universe.* New York: HarperEntertainment/HarperCollins, 2004.

Harvey, Robert C. *The Art of the Comic Book: An Aesthetic History.* Jackson: University Press of Mississippi, 1996.

Horn, Maurice, ed. *The World Encyclopedia of Comics.* 7 Vols. Broomall, Penn.: Chelsea House, 1999.

Inge, M. T. *Comics as Culture.* Jackson: University Press of Mississippi, 1990.

Jimenez, Phil, Scott Beatty, Robert Greenberger, and Dan Wallace. *The DC Comics Encyclopedia: The Definitive Guide to the Characters of the DC Universe.* New York: DK Publishing, 2004.

Jones, Gerard. *Men of Tomorrow: Geeks, Gangsters and the Birth of the Comic Book.* New York: Basic Books, 2004.

Jones, Gerard, and Will Jacobs. *The Comic Book Heroes.* Rocklin, Calif.: Prima Publishing, 1997.

Jung, Carl Gustav. *Man and His Symbols.* New York: Doubleday, 1964.

Kaplan, Arie. "Kings of Comics: How the Jews Transformed the Comic Book Industry Part I: The Golden Age (1933–1955)." *Reform Judaism* 32/1 (2003) Online: www.uahc.org/rjmag/03fall/comics.shtml.

Kaplan, Arie. "Kings of Comics: Part II: The Silver Age (1956–1978)." *Reform Judaism* 32/2 (2003) Online: www.uahc.org/rjmag/.

Kaplan, Arie. "Kings of Comics: Part III: The Bronze Age (1979–)." *Reform Judaism* 32/3 (2004) Online: www.uahc.org/rjmag/.

Kinsella, Sharon. *Adult Manga: Culture and Power in Contemporary Japanese Society.* Honolulu: University of Hawaii Press, 2000.

Klock, Geoff. *How to Read Superhero Comics and Why.* New York: Continuum Pub Group, 2002.

Kluckhohn, Clyde. "Recurrent Themes in Myths and Mythmaking." Pages 46–60 in *Myth and Mythmaking.* Edited by Henry A. Murray. New York: George Braziller, 1960.

Lawrence, J. S., and Robert Jewett. *Myth of the American Superhero.* Grand Rapids: Eerdmans, 2002.

Lee, Stan. *Origins of Marvel Comics.* New York: Simon & Schuster; 1974.

Lee, Stan. *Son of Origins of Marvel Comics.* New York: Simon & Schuster, 1975.

Mallory, Michael. *Marvel: The Characters and Their Universe.* New York: Marvel Characters, Inc./Barnes & Noble, 2002.

McAllister, Matthew P., Edward H. Sewell, and Ian Gordan, eds. *Comics & Ideology.* New York: Peter Lang Publishing, 2001.

McCloud, Scott. *Understanding Comics: The Invisible Art.* Northampton, Mass.: Kitchen Sink Press, 1993.

McCloud, Scott. *Reinventing Comics: How Imagination and Technology Are Revolutionizing an Art Form.* New York: Perennial, 2000.

Miller, John Jackson, Maggie Thompson, Peter Bickford, and Brent Frankenhoff. *The Standard Catalog of Comic Books.* Third Edition. Iola, Wis.: Krause Publications, 2004.

Montgomery, John Warwick, ed. *Myth, Allegory, and the Gospel: An Interpretation of J. R. R. Tolkien/C. S. Lewis/G. K. Chesterton/Charles Williams.* Minneapolis: Bethany Fellowship, 1974.

Nyberg, Amy Kiste. *Seal of Approval: The History of the Comics Code.* Studies in Popular Culture. Jackson: University Press of Mississippi, 1998.

Oropeza, B. J. *99 Reasons Why No One Knows When Christ Will Return.* Downers Grove, Ill.: InterVarsity Press, 1994.

Oropeza, B. J. *99 Answers to Questions About Angels, Demons, and Spiritual Warfare.* Downers Grove, Ill.: InterVarsity Press, 1997.

Overstreet, Robert M. *The Overstreet Comic Book Price Guide.* 34th Edition. New York: Random House, 2004.

Plowright, Frank, ed. *The Slings and Arrows Comic Guide.* Second Edition. London: Aurum Press, 2003.

Pojman, Louis P. *Philosophy of Religion: An Anthology.* Fourth Edition. New York: Wadsworth, 2002.

Pustz, Matthew J. *Comic Book Culture: Fanboys and True Believers.* Studies in Popular Culture. Jackson: University Press of Mississippi, 2000.

Reitberger, Reinhold, and Wolfgang Fuchs. *Comics: Anatomy of a Mass Medium.* Boston: Little Brown, 1972.

Reynolds, Richard. *Super Heroes: A Modern Mythology.* Studies in Popular Culture. Jackson: University Press of Mississippi, 1994.

Robbins, Trina. *The Great Women Superheroes.* Northampton, Mass.: Kitchen Sink Press, 1996.

Sanderson, Peter. *Marvel Universe.* New York: Harry N. Abrams, Inc., Publishers, 1996.

Schodt, Frederik L. *Manga! Manga! The World of Japanese Comics.* Tokyo/ New York: Kodansha International, 1983.

Shutt, Craig. *Baby Boomer Comics: The Wild, Wacky, Wonderful Comic Books of the 1960s!* Iola, Wis.:Krause Publications, 2003.

Simon, Joe, and Jim Simon. *The Comic Book Makers.* Lebanon, N.J.: Vanguard Productions, 2003.

Steranko, Jim. *The Steranko History of Comics.* 2 Vols. Reading, Penn.: Supergraphics, 1970.

Thompson, Don, and Dick Lupoff, editors. *The Comic-Book Book.* Second Edition. Carlstadt, N. J.: Rainbow Books/Krause Publications, 1998.

Turner, Victor. *The Ritual Process: Structure and Anti-Structure.* Chicago: Aldine Publishing Company, 1969.

Varnum, Robin, and Christina T. Gibbons. *The Language of Comics: Word and Image.* Studies in Popular Culture. Jackson: University Press of Mississippi, 2002.

Wertham, Frederic. *Seduction of the Innocent.* New York: Rinehart, 1954.

Weston, Joan. *Comic Books, Superheroes, and Boys: Superhero Comic Books in the Everyday Life of Pre-Adolescent Boys.* Dissertation: Thesis (Ph. D.) – University of California, Santa Barbara, 1999.

Wright, Bradford W. *Comic Book Nation: The Transformation of Youth Culture in America.* Baltimore: Johns Hopkins University, 2003.

Zimmerman, David A. *Comic Book Character: Unleashing the Hero in Us All.* Downers Grove, Ill.: InterVarsity Press, 2004.

Part One:

Heroes from the Golden Age of Comic Books

Figure 1 Superman has persisted as a pop culture icon ever since the Golden Age of Comics. His origin in the 1930s recalls the infancy of Moses, and his later death and return from the dead in the 1990s mimics that of Jesus. He is pictured here in church, ready to make confession to a priest (*Superman* #204:2; Vol. 2; June 2004; DC Comics; Jim Lee [pencils]; Scott Williams [inks]; Brian Azzarello [writer]).

Figure 2 The height of the Golden Age of Comics coincided with World War II. Since a number of the comic book creators were Jewish Americans who opposed Nazism, they encouraged readers to buy war bonds to support the Allies. In *World's Finest Comics* #9, Superman, Batman, and Robin throw balls at stereotyped caricatures of Axis leaders (Winter 1943; DC Comics; Jack Burnley [cover art]).

Figure 3 Superhero teams such as the All-Winners Squad—Captain America, the Sub-Mariner, the Human Torch, Toro, and Bucky—were depicted fighting against the Nazis during World War II. Allied Soldiers found a sense of moral support and patriotism when reading these comics (*All Winners* #11; Summer 1943; Timely [Marvel]; Alex Schomburg [pencils] Alex Schomburg [inks]).

Figure 4 Captain Marvel harnessed the powers of ancient heroes from Greco-Roman mythology and the Bible with his famous cry, "Shazam!" His offshoots included Mary Marvel and Captain Marvel Junior. Elvis Presley claimed Captain Marvel Jr. as one of his boyhood heroes. (*Shazam Annual* #1 [DC Comics], cover reprint of *Captain Marvel Adventures* #18; Dec. 1942; Fawcett; C. C. Beck [cover art]).

Figure 5 Wonder Woman is perhaps the best known female superhero. Her origin was derived from Greek mythology. Her wrist bands not only block bullets but also serve as a sign of submission to the goddess Aphrodite. In *Wonder Woman* #95 the Amazon princess protects boyfriend Steve Trevor from an atomic bomb explosion. Comic books often portrayed atomic angst and the threat of radiation during the Cold War (Jan. 1958; DC Comics; Ross Andru [pencils] Mike Esposito [inks]).

1

Superman: A Popular Culture Messiah

Ken Schenck

"They can be a great people, Kal-El. They wish to be. They only lack the light to show the way. For this reason above all, their capacity for good, I have sent them you, my only son." With these words, Clark Kent's "heavenly father" commissions him to begin his ministry on earth. Similar to Jesus Christ when he started his ministry, he is 30 years old.[1] His name *Kal-El* can be roughly translated as "all (that is) God" in biblical Hebrew.[2] Earth dwellers did not know his heavenly identity; they knew him as Superman.

The 1978 Superman movie portrayed Superman as a Christ or Messiah-like figure. He descended from heaven and came to earth as a child, like Jesus. He was sent by a heavenly father. He looked human, but he was so much more than human. He was the perfect man and yet godlike in his powers. Superman is not Christ, but some of the same aspects that draw humankind to Jesus have also made Superman an enduring figure in popular culture. His story also resembles the early life of Moses, whose parents send him off in a basket down the Nile in order to save him from Pharaoh, who ordered that newly born male sons of the Israelite slaves be killed. However, even this similarity echoes the early life of Jesus, whose parents flee to Egypt with the infant, escaping King Herod's edict to kill all male infants in Bethlehem. In the New Testament the early followers of Jesus believed him to be the long, awaited redeemer of God's people, just like Moses. In fact, Jesus was considered the "New Moses."[3]

Superman: A "God" to Whom We Can Relate on Earth

Sigmund Freud (1856–1939) claimed that people believe in God because they long for a god-sized "father figure" who can save them from things beyond their control.[4] Although his argument certainly does not disprove God's existence,[5] some people, no doubt, *do* believe in God for this reason.

They like the idea that there is someone out there stronger than they who is on their side. As the saying goes, "There are no atheists in fox holes."

Ancient Greek drama sometimes used the gods this way. When no human solution was possible, a god might appear to save the day. Because such a god arrived on stage by way of elaborate equipment or crane, this dramatic technique came to be known as *deus ex machina*, "god from the machine." We still use the term today when a story turns to some far-fetched solution to an impossible situation. Superman attracts many people because he is such a savior, or perhaps because we wish we could be. Just when all hope is gone someone yells out, "Look! Up in the sky! It's a bird! It's a plane! It's Superman!" Whether he is rescuing Lois Lane, Jimmy Olson, or the entire earth, Superman would not be Superman if he did not have the power and will to save.

The character of Superman has tackled many intractable problems like these for us. In the first 1938 issue of *Action Comics*, Superman stopped a wife-beater and traveled to Washington to take on corrupt government officials. He fought Nazis, criminals, and monstrous powers in comic books (e.g., *Superman, Action Comics, World's Finest Comics*), cartoons (1941–43), novels (George Lowther's *The Adventures of Superman* 1942), and radio programs (1940–51). We may question how ideal Superman's actions were in some of these portrayals, but he nonetheless represented the power to do what we cannot do. The Allies did eventually defeat the Nazis, but surely they would have welcomed a Superman in more uncertain days.

Long after the 1940s Superman would continue to tackle not only super-villains such as Lex Luthor, Mr. Mxyzptlk, Brainiac, and Bizarro, but also the problems we seem most helpless to solve here on earth. The radio adventures of Superman introduced him as a "defender of law and order; champion of equal rights; valiant, courageous fighter against the forces of hate and prejudice."[6] Superman could thus fight against racial and religious intolerance.[7] Themes like these appeared throughout the television series *The Adventures of Superman* (1951–57, starring George Reeves)[8] as well as in the cartoon *The New Adventures of Superman* of the late 1960s and *Super Friends* of the 1970s. From the movie *Superman IV: The Quest for Peace* (1987, starring Christopher Reeve) to the initial episodes of the *Justice League* animated series (2001),[9] Superman has occasionally tried to rid the world of nuclear weapons and bring about world peace.[10]

Just as Christians throughout the centuries struggle with the difficulty of balancing Christ's divinity with his humanness, so the many portrayals of Superman have varied in the amount of power they gave him. When Jerry Siegel and Joe Shuster originated the idea of Superman, they desired a character that epitomized all strong men, such as Samson and Hercules, rolled into one.[11] Jim Steranko suggests that the hero in the 1930 novel by

Philip Wylie entitled *Gladiator* (not to be confused with the more recent movie with the same name) provided a paradigm for Superman. Hugo Danner, the hero of the story, is injected by his father with "alkaline radicals" while he was still in his mother's womb. He discovered his powers at age ten, which included near impenetrability when shot by bullets, and the ability to run at high speeds and jump 40 feet high. Wylie gave an analogy pondering human abilities if given the same proportional powers of an ant or grasshopper.[12] When giving a scientific explanation for Superman's power in relation to his origin, Siegel and Shuster compared their hero's power to the ant carrying "hundreds of times" its own weight and the grasshopper jumping the proportional distance of what would be "several city blocks" in human terms.

Originally Superman could leap at least 1/8th of a mile, run faster than a speeding train, and "nothing less than a bursting shell could penetrate his skin."[13] This weaker version of Superman would leap rather than fly, and he genuinely struggled with his opponents. Later he became "faster than a speeding bullet" and "more powerful than a locomotive," and so powerful that he could move planets and fly to the center of the sun. Finding worthy opponents for Superman was quite a chore, but after World War II a mineral from Superman's home planet called kryptonite became his Achilles heel.[14] When exposed to it, Superman would turn weak, disoriented, or comatose. On radio, one of Superman's most dangerous foes was the Atom Man, a villain injected with kryptonite and created by *Der Teufel* ("the devil"), a Nazi scientist. The radiation from kryptonite symbolized the new threat of atomic radiation.

Superman writers have always struggled to balance his power with vulnerabilities like kryptonite. If Superman becomes too powerful, then the conflict that also draws us to him ceases to exist. Sometimes we need someone who is a little more human, someone with whom we can identify, someone who is made like us, but with powers greater than ours. The book of Hebrews' understanding of Christ in the New Testament captures this idea: "It was beneficial for him [the Messiah] to become like his brothers in every way" (Hebrews 2:17).

Recent television portrayals have focused much more on Superman's identification with humanity and thus have given us a much weaker "god." *Lois and Clark: The New Adventures of Superman* (1993–97) focused on Clark Kent, Superman's human alter ego, and his intriguing relationship with colleague Lois Lane as much as it did on the superpowered hero. More recently Superman seems to have almost disappeared in the Clark Kent of Warner Brothers' *Smallville* (2001–present). The teenager has powers, but he has not yet become the world's Superman. Hit songs from this same general era entitled *Kryptonite* by Three Doors Down and *Superman* by Five for

Fighting focus on Superman's weaknesses. The latter song has Superman protesting that he is "only a man in a silly red sheet," and that "even heroes have the right to bleed." This trend naturally leads us to consider a second dimension of Superman: his human side.

Superman: The Ideal Human

The philosopher Ludwig Feuerbach (1804–72) believed that human talk about God was really talk about ourselves. If we take all the ideals and aspirations of humanity and put them together, that is what we call God.[15] He would say that a person thinks about God as love because human nature values and aspires to love. God is thus a projection of all the best human ideals combined into one figure. Feuerbach, like Freud, certainly does not disprove the existence of God. Many portraits of God emphasize that God's essence is "Other," and thus beyond human understanding.[16] It is nonetheless true, however, that we often do tend to create God "in our own image." Because we cannot relate to a Being that is unknowable in essence, we picture "him" in categories we can understand.[17]

We do similar things with Jesus. Those who consider him a perfect moral example often picture him as the perfect embodiment of their own values. This phenomenon explains in part why so many different reconstructions of Jesus over the last two hundred years have taken place. A quick glance at the Religion section of the local bookstore will confirm how many different portraits of Jesus are out there today in writing.[18] This also reveals the subtle reality of the recently popular motto WWJD (What Would Jesus Do?)[19]—the answer you give to this question is mostly a projection of what you already think is the right thing to do. Because different people have different ideas to project, they will answer the question differently.

Our sense of what is good floats in a space between enduring ideals and cultural values. At any point in history it can be difficult to know which of our values will endure and which will be rejected by our children. We live out our lives with this interplay between the enduring and the passing. Thus some depictions of God and Christ have persisted throughout the ages. Others we easily spot in hindsight as "dead ends" from past generations. We see that the quest for God and Christ is greater than any individual. We need one another and a long view of history to ground ourselves in something beyond the moment. (We will have to leave the matter of *God's quest for us* for some other occasion!) It is not surprising to find that the same principle applies to how Superman has been portrayed over the multiple decades since his creation. Changing audiences have each created a Superman in their own image, according to their own ideals and fantasies. Some of these images endure, others we now recognize as the echoes of passing cultural preferences. In every case he has been a "super" man, a larger-than-life representation of the rest of us, the embodiment of our values.

Siegel and Shuster created Superman against the historical backdrop of Adolf Hitler's bid for the "Aryan" people to be a race of "supermen"— Hitler's ideal humanity. Hitler himself drew the image from a twisted reading of German philosopher Friedrich Nietzsche, who wrote of the *Übermensch* or "superman" who lived "beyond good and evil."[20] For Nietzsche, the superman was someone who impacted the course of the human race in a way that transcended the normal categories of good and evil. Such a person might have to disguise himself [*sic*] as a normal human, as a fellow-follower of the myths believed by everyone else. However, in reality this person would surpass those others who were "human, all too human," creating new "myths" for others to follow. The Superman of the comic books was probably a closer representation of Nietzsche's concept than Hitler's. Interestingly, Siegel and Shuster (both Jewish), portrayed their Superman battling the Nazis in the early 1940s.[21] In any case they seem to have adopted the name of their hero from neither Nietzsche nor Hitler but from science fiction writings that used the term. Lester Dent's pulp hero Doc Savage, "the Man of Bronze," was occasionally described as a superman.[22]

Prior to the popular comic book version, Siegel's original Superman story introduced a bald, evil human with superior mental abilities resembling more Superman's later nemeses, the Ultra-Humanite and Lex Luthor, than the benevolent hero who became famous in the comics. Indeed, in the early comic books, Superman was a little more violent than he is now. His goals were good, but he had no problem "cracking a few heads" in the process of achieving them. Before long, however, he would become a model citizen. The fact that children have frequently dominated Superman's audience is one of the factors that has always pushed his character toward the straight and narrow. Within a few years of his inception, Superman would start turning criminals over to the police for prosecution rather than serving as judge and jury himself. The Man of Steel became the ideal human of the 1950s generation, a Christ-like moral example for "one nation under God."[23]

Superman has modeled enduring values repeatedly throughout his history. Miss Tessmacher saves Superman from kryptonite in the first movie when he promises her that he will save her mother from any harm caused by Luthor. She trusts him because she knows Superman never lies. In one episode of the animated series *Justice League*, Superman hangs on chains from a wall while his enemy spits in his face and tells him how weak he is.[24] After his enemy leaves, he casually rips the chains off the wall. When asked why he did not show his strength when he was being insulted, Superman replies with an answer resembling Christ, "It's called turning the other cheek."[25] Later in this same episode Superman refuses to kill this same opponent and is even willing to sacrifice his own life for the opponent's home planet.

Superman also carries the image of passing American values along with those that appear more timeless. According to the cartoon movies of the early 1940s, Superman's quest was to "fight the never ending battle for truth and justice." This last line, though, was altered a little in both the radio series from the 1940s and the television series from the 1950s: Superman did not just fight the battle for truth and justice; he fought the battle for "truth, justice, *and the American way*." For much of his early history Superman was specifically an *American* hero who fought for American causes and embodied American values. The American bald eagle rests on his arm as he stands in front of the stars and strips on the cover of *Superman* #14 (Jan./Feb. 1942); on the cover of *Superman* #24 (Sept./Oct. 1943) he holds an American flag with the caption "America's Favorite Adventure-Strip Character." We are not too surprised to find him fighting the "Japanazis" during World War II, an American war term meant to combine the Nazis and Japanese in one word.[26] Although Superman himself did not act with prejudice in such cases, the depictions of Japanese and Germans in these cartoons and comics left something to be desired.

The phrase "the American way" in itself conjures up images of the early Cold War era in which Senator Joseph McCarthy and his associates accused countless innocent individuals of subversive political activities (1950–54). The fear driving this paranoid quest was of course the rise of communist powers in Russia and China. While Superman represented the "American way" well before McCarthy, we see in this phrase a reflection of the nationalism that has often characterized Superman.

American Christianity also has a tendency to confuse its faith with national pride. Those who clamor that America was founded as a Christian nation forget the religious conflicts that led its founders to abhor the idea of an official state religion. The establishment of a particular religion, let alone a particular form of Christianity, as a national religion has usually led to the oppression of others. In the end, an American flag on the platform of an American church is just as odd as a British flag in a British church or a German flag in a German church.

More recent portrayals of Superman have divested him of his narrow nationalism. The Superman of the *Justice League* fights for the whole planet, not just for America. In one episode of *Smallville* Clark reveals a slightly different quest from his predecessors. He tells his parents that he will go on to fight for "truth, justice, and, er, other stuff."[27] Superman has become an image of our current globalist perspective on the world.

Superman Without Sin?

At times Superman's "goodness" generates overkill from the perspective of his audiences. Human perfection simply becomes un-human and unrealistic at some point. Christians throughout the centuries have also wrestled with the humanness of Christ in the light of his divineness. On the one hand, the early Christian creeds affirm that Jesus' humanness cannot be diminished in any way.[28] Yet was it even really an option for Christ to sin if he was also God incarnate? Equally as difficult a question is whether any of us could be as perfect as Christ was in his humanness. The creeds imply that these thoughts must be possibilities if Christ was fully human like us.

The Superman movies of the late 1970s and 1980s occasionally had Superman "sin" a little to make him more human—and arguably better representative of us. In *Superman: The Movie* the Man of Steel disobeys his father Jor-El, who represents God. He violates the primary rule: "It is forbidden for you to interfere with human history," reversing time to "raise" Lois Lane from the dead. We can debate whether Superman actually lies in *Superman II*, but he certainly deceives Zod, Lex Luthor, and the other Kryptonians taking over the planet. He also goes against his parents' will by abandoning his powers; something he later regrets. In *Superman III* an attempt to fabricate kryptonite leads to an inner struggle between good and evil within him, ending in a dramatic battle between Clark Kent and Superman. Clark emerges victorious, and the good in Superman wins out.

Many of Superman's comic book fans have found the "goody-two shoes" image of Superman especially annoying. The Silver Age of Superman came to an end with the 1986 comic book series by Alan Moore: *Superman: Whatever Happened to the Man of Tomorrow?*[29] This book entailed the end of the corny, boy-scout persona of Superman from the previous era of comics.

After another reinvention of the man from Krypton in the late 1980s and early 1990s, Superman's personality became much less defined in the comics. Like his Generation X audience in that decade, this Superman (to a large degree) lacked a sense of purpose and identity. He also became much less in control of the things going on around him. On the Internet Superman Homepage, one regular contributor makes an interesting comment that may reflect the partial difficulty we sometimes have in relating to Superman. He claims that Superman writers frequently do not realize the extent to which fans read the comics as much or more for Lex Luthor, Superman's arch-enemy, than for Superman *per se*.[30] Is it possible that the good Superman cannot fully represent us and that we need the villains who oppose him to mirror other aspects of who we are?

Perhaps for some of us it is Clark Kent who bears our human image. Maybe the attraction of the Peter Parkers, the Harry Potters, and the Clark Kents of fiction has always been the idea that lurking somewhere within the unnoticed, "mild-mannered reporter" in us is something super and extraordinary. We are just waiting for the crisis when our true, secret identity will come out, and the world will hail us as savior of the day.

The Death of Superman

The skeptic Voltaire (1694–1778) predicted that Christianity would eventually die. More than two hundred years later it is still going strong by most accounts. In particular Christianity in America seems as powerful a force as it has ever been. There must be some enduring aspect to it, or it surely would have died a long time ago. Perhaps it is not entirely appropriate to compare Superman's mere 70 years to Christianity's 2000. Yet as we have already seen, elements of the Superman saga mirror those of the Christian story. Superman is not God, but he reflects God's power and goodness. He is not the Christ, but he represents a kind of ideal humanity as Christ does. Superman did not die for our sins, but he would die to save us. Arguably the greatest parable of Superman's Christ-likeness comes in *Superman II* when Superman is willing to give up his powers because of his love for Lois Lane. It is easy to hear echoes from the Christian story in the New Testament: "Although he [Christ] existed in the form of God, he did not consider equality with God something to take advantage of, but he emptied himself and took the form of a servant. He became like humans" (Philippians 2:6–7). Superman is willing to divest himself of his powers and privileges for love. Later on in the same movie, Emperor Zod will identify Superman's main weakness: "he cares."

Superman has had a few bouts with death in his brief history, but he always seems to come back—sort of a resurrection. In the late 1980s *Superman: Whatever Happened to the Man of Tomorrow?* marked a type of death for the hero so that he could be reinvented again. More recently *Superman* #200 (Second Series) has swallowed up much of Superman's history in death, leaving yet another new beginning for the Man of Steel (December 2003).[31] Superman's closest bout with death, however, came in the highly publicized *Doomsday* series of 1992.[32] It was a time when Lois Lane accepted Clark Kent's proposal of marriage and he revealed to her his secret identity (often a sign pointing to the end of a superhero or television series). On November 18, 1992, Superman died.[33] The Justice League attended his funeral, and a time of great mourning ensued.

The world was stunned. The story even made the cover of the New York magazine *Newsday*: "The Death of Superman." However, similar to the Thomas J. J. Altizer and other "God is dead" theologians of the 1960s, those who herald the demise of Superman always seem to speak too soon.[34] In the months that followed, Superman comics featured "disciples" who took up and preached his message. Four incarnations carried his torch for the months that followed: Superboy, Steel, the Eradicator, and a Cyborg Superman. For a time, comic book readers were unsure whether one of these might be the resurrected Superman. They each seemed to carry on some aspect of his persona. In the end Superman was only "mostly dead." He would rise to new life, briefly with long hair and a new costume. Two new heroes would endure beyond this period to become superheroes in their own right: Steel and the new Superboy. Both in their own way came into existence because a world without Superman was inconceivable. Steel in particular, an African-American hero, felt called to take up Superman's fallen role as a force for good in the world, to do what he could in the fight against evil.

Superman and Women

Many feminist thinkers about God and Christ have run up against the extremely male orientation of traditional Christian thought and imagery. This conundrum is not too difficult to resolve when it comes to God *the Father*. It is easy enough to recognize that God does not have genitalia if he is "spirit," as various religions including Christianity believe. If he did, he would be just like the gods of the ancient Greeks and Canaanites. The masculine imagery of God must be understood in terms of pictures or metaphors, ones in which God transcends in essential being.

However, the situation is not as simple when it comes to Christian beliefs about Jesus Christ, for he was clearly a person who lived on earth and was literally male. Feminist thinkers like Mary Daly have long argued that an exclusively masculine embodiment of God on earth cannot represent all humanity.[35] Such thinkers have sometimes turned to the Virgin Mary for an image of God on earth in feminine form. Sometimes feminists also turn to the idea of *Sophia* or Wisdom as a feminine dimension to the supreme God. Many Christians feel greatly uncomfortable or disturbed by such proposals, and thankfully a chapter on Superman does not need to solve any of these problems!

We do find some female characters in the Superman saga who provide us with various models of woman. They are probably not adequate representations for all women, but in their own way they mirror contemporary values when it comes to the interests of women. The two main candidates are Lois Lane and Lana Lang, both of whose characters have gone through variations just as Superman has. Lois Lane has always been a spunky reporter type.[36] The very fact that she was a single, working woman in the Superman media of the 1940s immediately stereotyped her as a certain *kind* of woman. Lois generally mirrors the assertive female, a symbol of woman's liberation. She represents the woman who is fully equal to man—and better than most.[37]

From the beginning Lois possessed an aggressive, slightly impetuous persona. In the 1942 cartoon movie *Volcano*, she steals Clark Kent's press pass so that she can get the scoop on an approaching eruption.[38] In *Superman II* Lois sneaks past the police and hides underneath an elevator car at the Eiffel Tower, almost placing herself in the middle of a nuclear explosion. In the Superman comics she earned a black belt in karate and serves as a member of Metropolis's Special Crime Unit.[39] She can hold her own against thugs. Her assertive nature was part and parcel of *Lois and Clark: The New Adventures of Superman*. Indeed the television series turned out to be as much about Lois as it was about Clark or Superman. In all these various contexts Lois Lane has shown herself to be as capable and empowered as any man.

From time to time the intriguing love triangle between Clark, Lois, and Superman has also fueled the plotlines of Superman media. It even convinced the Man of Steel to give up his powers in *Superman II*. The two have been married for about ten years in the comic books, although Superman revisions will no doubt start the cycle all over again. Even so, throughout each variation Lois has never abandoned her career one wit, making her and Clark a model of the two-career home.

Lana Lang represents a softer side of femininity than Lois. In the comic books she has loved Clark from the very beginning and has known his secret since the days before he left for Metropolis. Until the recent reset on Superman comics, she was married to the Vice President of the United States, Pete Ross, and had a child.[40] Nevertheless, Lana is not an un-empowered woman by any means. *Superman III* portrays her character as an allegory of a woman who first settled for less than her potential but then rises to empowerment. Lana moves on from her loser, ex-jock, ex-husband and travels to the big city where she lands a job working for the *Daily Planet*.

The Lana of *Smallville* is also no push-over. Although she has inner struggles and occasional self-doubt, she always pushes forward. She sometimes resonates the type of person who can rise to success with the support of those around her. An example of this aspect of her character appears when Lana makes a business proposal to the young Lex Luthor to preserve the Talon Theater. Initially she had only mourned the planned demolition of the building, since it was the place where her parents, now dead, had first met.[41] With a small display of confidence by Clark, however, Lana took action.

Both Lois and Lana thus represent in their own ways what woman can be in this age. While their personalities and characters differ in so many ways, neither is inferior to a man in any way. They thus give us an image of complete equality between man and woman, something the New Testament anticipates: "There is neither Jew nor Greek, neither slave nor free, neither male nor female, for you are all one in Christ Jesus" (Galatians 3:28).

Supergirl sometimes functions as another female role model, for she possesses powers similar to Superman's; but in a way, it is unfortunate that there is no Super*woman*, only a teenage Supergirl whose name reflects the subordinate nature of her identity—at least in the age when she was created.[42] She originally appeared during the Silver Age of comics in *Action Comics* #252 (1959) in a decade when pop culture turned a youthful face to teen idols instigated by rock-and-roll music and movies such as *Rebel Without a Cause*. Teen superheroes were just starting to become big sellers. Superboy's comics sold decently enough to survive the "slump years" of the 1950s, and the Legion of Super-Heroes premiered in *Adventure Comics* #247 (April 1958). The Teen Titans, Spider-Man, and the X-Men would carry this youthful trend to a higher level of success in the early 1960s.[43] Supergirl's name was Kara Zor-El; she happened to be Superman's younger cousin who also escaped the late planet Krypton and flew by rocket to earth. Superman placed her in an orphanage where the blond hero assumed the name of Linda Lee, a brunette student. Eventually she died in *Crisis on Infinite Earths* #7 (Oct. 1985), one year after actor Helen Slater played the teen heroine in the forgotten film, *Supergirl.*[44]

A different Supergirl was introduced in comic form several years after her death, and more recently Supergirl had a new appearance with red boots, white gloves, a white top that bares her midriff, and a complimentary hip-riding blue miniskirt. The evolution of Supergirl's wardrobe is a story in itself. In the late 1950s she originally wore a suit comparable to Superman's: blue with a red cape and famous logo "S" on her chest; albeit, she wore a skirt rather than tights. By the early 1970s the comic fans participated in selecting Supergirl's new wardrobe (*Adventure Comics* #397; Sept. 1970). Given the trends of the time the styles that won out included v-necks, red hot pants, and a micro mini-dress with French slits and thigh-high red boots. Some women have complained that today's "good girl" superhero art exploits the women as little more than wannabe centerfolds with back-aching breasts, tiny waists, and skintight costumes or extremely short skirts that reveal what's underneath whenever the heroine takes a tumble. The sexy costume styles of female heroes likely reflect the desires of the male-dominated comic fans and industry; albeit, in Supergirl's case, a number of female fans also participated in her wardrobe selection. In any case most women prefer Wonder Woman as a feminine role model over Supergirl.

The Myth of Superman

Rudolf Bultmann (1884–1976) was a German Christian thinker who believed that regardless of whether Christianity was literally true or not, it told a true myth about human existence. For him the resurrection of Christ pointed to the present instead of the past: It represented the possibility that we might rise from the "death" of meaningless existence to an authentic life.[45] Now many of us who claim to be Christians are still willing to believe that God literally exists and that Jesus did in fact rise from the dead in space-time history. For those who are more doubtful, however, this story still contains elements that resonate with the human soul. Here is the longing for something greater than ourselves and the sense of our own limits and impossibilities. Here is the will to survive and to vanquish mortality. Alongside the Freuds who see God as a phantom of human longing, there are also those like St. Augustine (354–430 A.D.) who believe God has built these longings into the very essence of our being: "You have made us for yourself, and our heart is restless until it finds its rest in you."[46]

In one sense Superman is a myth of our human existence. He represents all that is best in human value. He embodies our desire to overcome evil with good. His origin and character indirectly raise classic questions about what a god or human might be. If reality is measured in part by the effect something has on the world, then Superman is real. He has inspired and impacted countless lives and continues to do so. He calls us to follow his example and fight for truth and justice in the world.

Notes

[1] *Superman: The Movie* (1978). The Warner Brothers movie places the revelation of Superman at the age of 30. Clark Kent enters the Fortress of Solitude at 18 and receives instruction from his father for 12 earth years. Simple addition places Superman's emergence from the "wilderness" at a similar age to that of the New Testament Gospel of Luke for the beginning of Jesus' ministry (Luke 3:23). (The Fortress of Solitude was first introduced by Otto Binder in *Action Comics* #241 [1958].)

[2] *El* is a shorter version of *Elohiym*, which is typically translated as "God" in the Old Testament. Unhelpful in reference to Superman's earlier Hebrew name is the

rather facetious article by J. K. Brower, "The Hebrew Origins of Superman," *Biblical Archaeology Review* 5/3 (1979), 22–26.

[3] This theme is particularly strong in the Gospel of Matthew, which records Jesus's unusual birth (Moses was an unusual child); Herod's persecution of the baby Jesus (Pharaoh persecuted Moses); an escape into Egypt by Christ's parents (Moses is sent down the Nile on a boat to escape being killed); the verification God's approval of Christ's ministry through water (Moses parts the Red Sea); Christ's 40-day temptation in the wilderness (Moses spends 40 years in the wilderness); and Christ's establishing a renovated law on a mount (Moses on Mt. Sinai establishes the first law) as well as a new covenant during the Passover feast (Moses establishes the old covenant, first Passover, and Ten Commandments). These and other aspects of Christ's ministry resemble the life of Moses. See Dale C. Allison, *The New Moses: A Matthean Typology* (Edinburgh: T. & T. Clark, 1993).

[4] Sigmund Freud, *The Future of an Illusion* (New York: H. Liveright, 1928).

[5] The argument contains a genetic fallacy: The reason why someone believes something and whether that something is true are logically distinct issues.

[6] With the voice of Bud Collyer as Superman.

[7] See for instance, the "Unity House" story-line of the 1946 radio broadcasts had Superman taking a stand against the Ku Klux Klan.

[8] The show ran for 104 episodes with a Superman guest-star appearance in *I Love Lucy*.

[9] "Secret Origins," a 90-minute first episode that first aired on November 17, 2001.

[10] Interestingly, the Department of Defense actually stopped the publication of some Superman comics relating to the atom bomb in 1944, fearing the Germans might somehow conclude from them that the Americans were working on one.

[11] Jim Steranko, *The Steranko History of Comics Volume 1* (Reading, Penn.: Supergraphics Publication, 1970), 39.

[12] Steranko, 37.

[13] "The Superman Is Here!" newspaper strip; Siegel and Shuster; *Action* #1 (1938).

[14] Kryptonite first appeared on the Superman radio program (1945) before the comic book (*Superman* #61, 1949). However, several years prior to the first kryptonite story on radio, Siegel and Shuster introduced in comic format "K-Metal," a bright green substance from the planet Krypton that caused Superman pain and weakness. The story was never published, probably because Clark Kent revealed his secret identity to Lois Lane in that episode.

[15] Ludwig Feuerbach, *The Essence of Christianity* (ET; London: Kegan, Trench, Trübner, 1893).

[16] This is especially true of the so-called "negative theology" that stresses we can only know God's essence in terms of what it is *not* rather than in terms of what it *is*. The neo-orthodox theology of Karl Barth (1886–1968) similarly proceeded on the premise that we only know God because he has revealed himself (*sic*) to us.

[17] Even the reference to God as "he" is one of many metaphors meant to bring God within the scope of our understanding.

18 For a readable sketch of several approaches throughout the last two centuries, see *Who Was Jesus?* by N.T. Wright (Grand Rapids: Eerdmans, 1993).

19 The phrase originally seems to be derived from Charles Sheldon's book, *In His Steps* (Philadelphia: American Baptist Publication Society, 1898). In this book Sheldon encourages his congregation to good conduct by asking them the now famous motto.

20 Hilter's ideas came mostly from Nietzsche's work *Thus Spoke Zarathustra* (1896), although one finds the general concept throughout Nietzsche's work.

21 See, for instance, anti-Axis covers in *Superman* #13 (Nov. 1941), 17, 18, 23, 26; *Action Comics* #44, 54; *World's Finest Comics* 7.

22 Les Daniels and Chip Kidd, *Superman: The Complete History: The Life and Times of the Man of Steel* (San Francisco: Chronicle Books, 1998), 13, 18.

23 This phrase entered the Pledge of Allegiance in 1954 during the Eisenhower administration.

24 "War World": episodes aired February 24 and March 3, 2002.

25 A phrase drawn from Matthew 5:39.

26 This term first appeared in *Superman* #18. One patriotic slogan in a comic stated, "Tin Cans in the Garbage Pile Are Just a Way of Saying 'Heil!'" The Phantom Lady affirmed, "America comes first – even before Dad." Cf. Juanita Coulson, "Of (Super) Human Bondage," in *The Comic-Book Book* (Don Thompson, Dick Lupoff, eds. Carlstadt/New Rochelle: Krause, 1998), 230, 252.

27 In the episode "Red," aired February 4, 2002.

28 The Council of Chalcedon (A.D. 451) strongly affirmed this idea.

29 The comic book version appeared in *Superman* #423 and *Action Comics* #583. After this the numbers were restarted and the tale revamped to fit a new generation of Superman readers.

30 Neil Bailey, "Superman Today vs. Superman Ten Years Ago," December 21, 2003 [Cited 24 May, 2004] Online: www.supermanhomepage.com/comics/comics.php?topic=articles/today-vs-10yearsago.

31 A new Superman movie is also in the works, promising to reinvent him yet once more.

32 For an excellent reflection on this event in Superman history, see "Doomsday: Ten Years Later or Where Were You the Day Superman Died?" by Michael Bailey [Cited 24 May, 2004] Online: www.supermanhomepage.com/comics/comics.php?topic=articles/doomsday-10-years-later.

33 *Superman* #75 (second series).

34 The God is Dead controversy was so great that it made the cover of the October 22, 1965, *Time* magazine issue.

35 E.g., "After the Death of God the Father: Women's Liberation and the Transformation of Christian Consciousness," *Commonweal* (March 12, 1971), 7–11.

36 Apparently she was named after Lois Amster, a student that shy Jerry Siegel knew in school. Clark was named after the movie star Clark Gable.

37 Although in the Superman movies, some women might find Lois's almost religious awe of Superman a bit irritating. Similarly, Mila Bongco argues that Lois Lane's role "epitomizes the secondary role of women in superhero texts,

who in a typical ideological double talk, are taught to admire and desire that which rejects them." See Bongco, *Reading Comics: Language, Culture, and the Concept of the Superhero in Comic Books* (New York & London: Garland Publishing, 2000), 113.

[38] It came out 10 July, 1942.

[39] The imaginary city of Metropolis is often associated with New York City. However, the skyscrapers were patterned after Joe Shuster's hometown of Toronto (cf. Daniels and Kidd, *Superman: The Complete History*, 27).

[40] Lex Luthor, amazingly, became the president.

[41] "Kinetic" aired 26 February, 2002.

[42] A Supergirl "prototype" with short blond hair first appeared in *Superman* #123 (1958) but did not continue. A black-haired "Superwoman" appeared in *Action Comics* #156 (1951).

[43] Superboy first appeared in *More Fun Comics* #101 (Jan. 1945) before starring in *Adventure Comics* and then his own comic beginning in 1949. The first *Superboy* comic series continued until 1977. The Legion of Superheroes originally consisted of Cosmic Boy, Saturn Girl, Lightning Lad, and Superboy. The Teen Titans (originally Robin, Kid Flash, Aqualad, and then Wonder Girl) first appeared in *The Brave and Bold* #54 (July 1964) and then landed their own comic title 1966. They currently appear in a very successful animated television series.

[44] The Silver Age of comics also produced the Super "Family" that included a super-dog (Krypto), a super-cat (Streaky), and a super-horse (Comet), and even a super-monkey appearing in *Superboy* #76 (1959).

[45] Rudolph Bultmann, *Kerygma and Myth* (London: SPCK, 1953 in English).

[46] *The Confessions of St. Augustine* §1.1.

Recommended Resources

Aichele, George. "Rewriting Superman." In *Monstrous and the Unspeakable,* ed. George Aichele and Tina Pippin. Sheffield: Sheffiled Academic Press, 1997.

Beatty, Scott. *Superman: The Ultimate Guide to the Man of Steel.* New York: DK Publishing, 2002.

Brown, Harold O. J. "Refiner's Fire: Superman on the Screen: Counterfeit Myth?" *Christianity Today* 23/14 (1979): 26–27.

Cohen, Stanley. "Messianic Motifs, American Popular Culture and the Judeo-Christian Tradition." *Journal of Religious Studies* 8 (Spr. 1980): 24–34.

Daniels, Les. *DC Comics: A Celebration of the World's Favorite Comic Book Heroes.* New York: Billboard Books, 2003.

Daniels, Les, and Chip Kidd. *Superman, the Complete History: The Life and Times of the Man of Steel.* San Francisco: Chronicle Books, 1998.

Dooley, Dennis, and Gary Engle, eds. *Superman at Fifty! The Persistence of a Legend!* New York: Collier Press, 1988.

Eco, Umberto. "The Myth of Superman." In *Contemporary Literary Criticism: Modernism Through Poststructuralism,* ed. Robert Con Davis. New York: Longman, 1986.

Engle, Gary. "What Makes Superman So Darned American?" In *Living in America: A Popular Culture Reader,* ed. Patricia Y. Murray and Scott F. Covell. Mountain View, Calif.: Mayfield Publishing Company, 1998.

Galloway, John T. *The Gospel According to Superman.* Philadelphia/New York: A. J. Holman Co., 1973.

Gordon, Ian. "Nostalgia, Myth, and Ideology: Visions of Superman at the End of the 'American Century'." In *Comics & Ideology,* ed. Matthew P. McAllister, Edward H. Sewell, and Ian Gordon. New York: Peter Lang Publishing, 2001.

Grossman, Lev. "The Problem with Superman." *Time* (17 May 2004): 70–72.

Kozlovic, Anthon Karl. "Superman as Christ-Figure: The American Pop Culture Movie Messiah." *Journal of Religion and Film* 6/1 (2002) [Cited 17 May, 2004] Online: unomaha.edu/~wwjrf/superman.htm.

Maggin, Elliot S. *Superman: Last Son of Krypton.* New York: Warner Brothers, 1978.

McNair, Wesley C. "The Secret Identity of Superman: Puritanism and the American Hero." *American Baptist Quarterly* 2/1 (1983), 4–15.

Superman Homepage. [Cited 24 May, 2004] Online: www.supermanhomepage.com.

White, John Wesley. *The Man from Krypton: The Gospel According to Superman.* Minneapolis: Bethany Fellowship, 1978.

Williams, J. P. "Transformations and Projections: Constructions of Femininity in *Lois Lane*." *Studies in Popular Culture* 17.1 (1994): 45–53.

2
The True *Übermensch*: Batman as Humanistic Myth

C. K. Robertson

At five years of age, his world changed forever as he watched his father, a Lutheran minister, die before his eyes. He spent the rest of his childhood and adolescence struggling not only with personal loss, but also with constant illness. In the midst of such difficulties, it is all the more remarkable that he trained his mind like an Olympian, immersing himself in the studies of philology, poetry, and philosophy. Although the influences in his life were many—Plato and Aristotle, the German philosopher Arthur Schopenhauer, the composer Richard Wagner—it became clear from the moment he entered the scene that his own impact on the world would be unique and indelible. Praised by some, vilified by others, misunderstood by many, one thing is clear: Friedrich Nietzsche, the creator and prophet of the *übermensch*, the "overman" or "superman," can hardly be overestimated and certainly not ignored.

Less than four decades after Nietzsche's death, another young boy—no less real to many for being fictional—watched in horror as both his father and his mother were gunned down before his eyes. Driven by an indomitable will, this boy trained body and mind to human perfection, immersing himself in the studies of criminology and martial arts. The influences on his existence were many—the Shadow, Zorro, the Bat, Dracula, Leonardo da Vinci—yet it was clear from the moment he first leapt off the page that he would make a unique and indelible mark on both his fictitious universe and the real world that breathed life into his four-color form. Familiar to all, reinvented time and again, one thing is argued here: The Batman, an iconic figure in popular culture, can be understood as a prime example of Nietzsche's *übermensch*.

There Is Good, There Is Bad, and Then There Is Nietzsche

Mankind ought constantly to be striving to produce great men; this and nothing else is its duty. (Friedrich Nietzsche, *Schopenhauer as Educator*)

Friedrich Nietzsche was born on October 15, 1844 in Röcken, Prussia. It was a time of great changes for the Germanic peoples. After a devastating series of conflicts with Napoleonic France in the early years of the nineteenth century, the Congress of Vienna of 1814–15 allowed Prussia and its allies, Austria and Russia, to replace the longstanding Holy Roman Empire with a German Confederation. This Congress marked the end of an 800-year era of at least nominal centralized rule by Christian emperors. Also known as the First Reich, the Empire had been set up as an ideal mix of temporal and spiritual power, with the Church an omnipresent reality in daily life. However, resentment over ecclesiastical abuses of power and finances combined with Reformation fervor to result in the downfall of the First Reich and the rise of liberal yearnings among many. These longings ignited a revolutionary movement in 1848, one quickly extinguished by the autocrats of a new age. The yearnings, however, would not die.

Nietzsche developed an appreciation for the philosophical concepts of Arthur Schopenhauer, whom he deemed "the last German worthy of consideration."[1] Schopenhauer's *Die Welt als Wille und Vorstellung* (*The World as Will and Idea*) provided a foundation for Nietzsche's development of the concept of the "Will to Power." Schopenhauer argued that the will acts as a driving force in all forms of existence. In human beings this driving force results in dissatisfaction and suffering unless it is counterbalanced by a sense of resignation. Nietzsche went further. Considering this overarching principle of the "will to power" in light of what he perceived as the failure of Christianity to empower people, Nietzsche called for a "revaluation of all values," an overthrow of the utterly weak, "all too human" model of humanity propagated by Christianity: "At the bottom of Christianity is the rancor of the sick, instinct directed against the healthy, against health itself.... Christianity has been the greatest misfortune of mankind so far."[2] Nietzsche replaced this model with "a new table of valuations...namely that of the strong, mighty, and magnificent man, overflowing with life and elevated to his zenith, the Superman."[3]

Nowhere is the principle of the "superman" more clearly delineated than in Nietzsche's landmark and most intensely personal work, *Thus Spoke Zarathustra* (1883–85; trans. 1954). "I teach you the overman [superman]. Man is something that shall be overcome."[4] Nietzsche used the world's first great prophet, Zoroaster, or Zarathustra, to be his mouthpiece as he revealed the ways in which the prophet's descendants, the disciples of the various great religions of the West, had "failed to follow Zarathustra in the practice of examining and reexamining one's situation and formulating new distinctions."[5] Nietzsche said the prophet may indeed have been the first to create the distinctions between good and evil, but he subsequently rose above and beyond them to a new level. The religious shepherds who followed through the centuries neglected this courageous move beyond "morality," and therefore they contributed to a weak-minded, weak-willed "herd" who feared judgment in the afterlife and spoke of a Savior who could only be approached through the systems set up by the Church's shepherds. Christianity, Nietzsche pronounced, "crushed and shattered man completely and buried him as though in mud."[6] If "the Hebrew," as Nietzsche refers to Jesus, had lived longer, he would have "recanted his own teaching," for Nietzsche understood Jesus to be "noble, but not mature" at the time of his death.[7] Now, he proclaimed, had come a new age, a new opportunity for all humankind. Nietzsche said the era of the Savior had come to an end, "God is dead."[8] Now was the time of the superman!

Contrasted with the weakness of the "herd," this *übermensch* or superman is independent, strong, and, above all, healthy. He is full of intense passion but always in control of that passion, operates in the real world instead of dreaming of the afterlife, and affirms life precisely because he understands suffering and "the eternal recurrence" of events. The *übermensch* "breaks tablets and old values...writes new values on new tablets," and thereby ultimately threatens both the bad and the good alike.[9] Criminals fear him, but so do the just. Indeed, the latter loathe and dread him most, for to them the acts of criminals simply reinforce the system of justice that already exists. Such persons break laws, but in doing so fortify the system of law itself created by the shepherds. The superman, however, by nature of moving beyond the usual categories of good and evil, challenges the entire moral paradigm altogether. "It is terrible to be alone with the judge and avenger of one's own law." Thus, the just fear him, hate him, and call him "lawbreaker."

Nietzsche died in Weimar on 25 August, 1900, having been driven to madness over a decade before. Nietzsche's life came to an end even as his century came to an end, succeeded by a new age of wonders, an era in which the impossible came within humanity's grasp. Indeed, if contemporaries of Nietzsche's could step through the doorway of time into today's world—a world of satellites and supersonic airplanes and spaceships to Mars, a world of pacemakers and kidney transplants and nuclear weapons—they might well believe that the age of the *übermensch* had arrived. "Bowled over by what we could do with a car or a light switch or an automatic teller machine," to such visitors from Nietzsche's time, we might indeed appear to be "not mortals, but gods."[10]

Nietzsche's contributions to the so-called postmodern world cannot be underestimated. With his focus on the individual's internal struggle, he profoundly impacted the advances in psychology by Sigmund Freud and Carl Gustav Jung, as well as philosopher of history Oswald Spengler's theory of historical determinism, which is grounded in Nietzsche's notion of the eternal recurrence of events. Politically, of course, Adolf Hitler twisted Nietzsche's principle of the *übermensch* into a racist, genocidal agenda, although in his own lifetime, Nietzsche was clearly against all proto-Nazi thought, as he saw reflected in Wagner's works. Even as Nazism began to grow in Germany, two young boys across the ocean created a four-color hero who would be Nietzschean in name, though, as will be seen, certainly not in principle!

A Winged Figure of Vengeance

Batman came out of the darkness, out of the collective unconscious where visions of avenging angels dwell. (Les Daniels, Comics Historian)

The cover said it all. On the front of the first issue of a ten-cent comic book named *Action Comics* stood what appeared to be a man dressed in blue tights with a flowing red cape behind him, lifting a car as if it was nothing more than a paperweight while people in the foreground run in terror. For the next sixty-plus years, through comics and newspaper strips, through radio and television and film, Superman went on to become one of the most recognizable heroic icons in the world. Ironically, this brainchild of Jerry Siegel and Joe Shuster is nothing like the *übermensch* whose name he carried. For one thing, he was not even human! Rather, in words that have become familiar to children of all ages, he is a "strange visitor from another world, with powers and abilities far beyond those of mortal man." Until recent years, it was emphasized that his guise of Clark Kent, "mild-mannered reporter for a major metropolitan newspaper," was just that: a guise, a mask worn by this otherworldly being who would occasionally let us, the readers, into his cosmic joke with a simple wink at the end of a story. Of course, the wink would only come after he had done what he did best…save mortals. Here was a flying, invulnerable hero from the heavens, a celestial Savior, wrapped in the American flag, the embodiment of "truth and justice," or, as comic book writer Grant Morrison states, "the American Christ."[11]

    Siegel and Shuster's Man of Steel was clearly an exercise in wish-fulfillment for the two boys who created him and the countless boys who read about him. So many readers and radio listeners viewed themselves as real-life Clark Kents, trying desperately to capture the attention and affection of real-life Lois Lanes, but always to no avail. However, it is important to note that no matter how much wishing the audience did, they could never be Superman; they would never be able to do what he could do. Nietzsche had been clear that the *übermensch* was not an unattainable, otherworldly dream, nor a next step in evolution that was beyond human beings to achieve in this lifetime. Many young people then and now have felt they are from another planet; Superman literally was. Perhaps it is because he was the ultimate resident alien that Superman's creators quickly domesticated and Americanized him. Not unlike naturalized citizens or converts to a faith, Krypton's Last Son soon displayed a pride in, and gratitude toward, his adopted home. The ultimate outsider became the great "Boy Scout," as American as apple pie. In other words, despite the name, Siegel and Shuster's Superman was a far cry from the Nietzschean ideal of the *übermensch.*

The pressure fell on writers and artists in the nascent comic book industry to reproduce the success of Superman. One such artist was young Robert Kahn, a New York native whose father, an engraver for the *Daily News,* encouraged his son's ambition by bringing home the color comics sections.[12] Kahn, better known by the moniker Bob Kane, collaborated with cartoon strip writer Bill Finger, a fellow graduate of DeWitt Clinton High School.[13] However, even as other creators produced various imitations of Superman—only then to face lawsuits from Superman's publishers—Kane offered a different kind of hero. Although The Bat-Man (as he was initially called) would develop along a parallel path to Superman, it was immediately apparent that this was no imitation. The distinctions were visible and obvious.

Whereas Superman was draped in primary colors, the Batman's costume was set in gray and black. Whereas Superman's home turf, eventually named Metropolis, was New York in daylight, Batman's Gotham City was the Queen of Cities in dark night. Superman, the alien child who lost everything in his planet's destruction, was adopted by a kind Midwestern farmer and his wife, who instilled him with values of love and kindness; while Batman, the rich kid who had everything, lost it all in a dark alley and grew up an orphan, virtually alone. Whereas Superman's alter ego would grow up to be a mild-mannered "Everyman," the Batman's alter ego appeared only as a bored, privileged playboy. Clark Kent would forever try in vain to win the affections of Lois Lane, but Bruce Wayne was a ladies' man (and even a fiancé) who almost casually put off beautiful socialites. Superman's enemies were largely unimpressive scientists and inventors who posed little threat to the mighty extraterrestrial; yet the Batman quickly developed an unforgettable rogue's gallery full of bizarre freaks and madmen whose names became as familiar as their archenemy's (e.g., the Joker and the Penguin). Similarly, Superman's friends were helpless victims in need of timely rescues while the Batman—a loner by origin and ongoing self-description—inspired a veritable army of disciples who would adopt his dress code and tactics. In almost every way, Batman became the perfect counterpart to Superman.[14] At the same time the Batman represents what Superman, despite his name, can never be: the ultimate expression of human perfection in mind and body, the true "Superman" or *übermensch*.

Now at no time has Bob Kane, Bill Finger, or any of those associated with the Batman's creation and early development spoken of a Nietzschean influence on their work. Instead, stories abound about inspiration from a number of sources. Finger was quick to state, "Batman was written originally in the style of the pulps." These popular magazines boasted beautifully painted covers and stories full of action, drama, and suspense. According to both Finger and Kane, pulp heroes such as the Shadow and the Spider provided the most immediate influence on the Batman.[15] Kane has added the importance of film on his creation, in terms of both the film noir atmosphere of Batman's environment and the character's development. Zorro was a favorite of Kane's (and, in the comics, of Bruce Wayne's), and details such as the dual identity of a wealthy socialite and even the secret hideout's entrance through the grandfather clock owe their origin to *The Mark of Zorro* (1920). *The Bat, The Bat Whispers,* and *The Man Who Laughed* were other films that inspired Kane and Finger's work. Some of their sources were older than film and the pulps; Leonardo da Vinci's drawings of an ornithopter, a glider with bat-like wings, made such an impression on Kane that he initially drew the Batman with stiff wings that, despite Finger's suggestion to change to a billowing cape, still resonate in the cover design of the Batman's first appearance in *Detective Comics* #27 (May 1939). It is clear from many interviews conducted through the years that the Batman owed his existence to several different sources. None, however, seem to include Nietzsche.

Having said this, there are many aspects of the Batman from his earliest appearances that appear Nietzschean in substance. Perhaps in an attempt to create a hero quite different from Superman, as already seen, Kane and Finger unconsciously made their character in fact what the other was in name! It is certainly possible to argue that for Kane and Finger (as well as Gardner Fox, who began writing many of the stories early on), "the gospel according to the Batman" would be a Nietzschean message. Consider, for example, the Batman's origin. Longtime Batman writer/editor Dennis O'Neil has said that the twelve-panel story "The Batman and How He Came to Be" needed no subsequent "meddling" for a simple reason: "It is perfect."[16] That origin story contains all the elements of the Nietzschean ideal of the superman.

A young boy walks home with his parents from a movie one night, only to have a nameless thug attempt to rob them. When Bruce's father, Thomas Wayne, steps between his wife and the gunman, he is shot dead, immediately followed by Bruce's mother. "The boy's eyes are wide with terror and shock," Kane and Finger relate, "as the horrible scene is spread before him."[17] Days later, in what is narrated as a "curious and strange scene," young Bruce kneels at his bed, a lone candle burning on the bedside table. With hands clasped and a tear running down his cheek, he makes a solemn pledge: "And I swear by the spirits of my parents to avenge their deaths by spending the rest of my life warring on all criminals."[18] The scene bears all the marks of a religious conversion, although hardly a Judeo-Christian one. Absent from the boy's prayer/pledge is any mention of God; rather, he swears by his parents' spirits. There is no talk of forgiveness of one's enemies or even resignation to his loss, but instead a vow to lifelong revenge. There is not even a suggestion of devoting his life to helping others, but rather a determination to wage a private war. In *The Gay Science*, Nietzsche addresses the question of "What makes [one] heroic?" His paradoxical answer, "To go to meet simultaneously one's greatest sorrow and one's greatest hope,"[19] can be seen visually in Bruce Wayne's childhood vow. Here, tragedy once experienced is, in essence, transformed into an eternal recurrence that forever would motivate him. If indeed Nietzsche is correct that "that which does not kill me makes me stronger," then young Bruce Wayne suddenly left the world of the weak and, through his unique response to tragedy, entered a new world of the strong, the world of the *übermensch*.

Appropriately, there is not even a glimpse of anyone else in the Batman's origin, no one but the gunman, the victims, and the lone boy. In true Nietzschean fashion, the boy is alone; there is no priest, no chaplain, no angel of mercy who suddenly appears to help young Bruce. Years later, it will be explained that the orphan is aided by Alfred, the faithful butler, and later by Leslie Thompkins, a kindly woman who wraps her arms around the grieving lad. All this would appear in later renditions of the origin by writers desiring to fill in what they perceived as an obviously missing back-story.[20] In the original two-pager, however, the boy is alone, a solitary figure who intentionally and without any assistance rises above his tragic circumstances by training not only his mind but also his body: "As the years pass, Bruce Wayne prepares himself for his career. He becomes a master scientist [and] trains his body to physical perfection until he is able to perform amazing athletic feats." Nietzsche would appreciate the two panels that show this development of tragic boy into Olympian man. Healthiness of the body was a foremost consideration (a not unexpected premise, given the philosopher's own illness-ridden state): "The right place [to begin] is the body, the gesture, the diet, physiology; the rest follows from that."[21] Beyond extraordinary mental and physical health, as seen in the next panel in Batman's origin, the estate of his late father left Bruce Wayne quite wealthy, a true aristocrat. It is difficult to imagine a more accurate description of the *übermensch*.

In the case of any ordinary man, it might be expected that Bruce Wayne's story would proceed to show how he joined the ranks of the police, the military, the medical establishment, or the clergy in order to make the world a better place. Such vocational choices, of course, would not fulfill his unique and, in a sense, utterly selfish vow. In fact, making a difference in his world did not seem to be important to the orphaned lad. In a statement that could easily be drawn from Nietzsche's own pen, longtime Batman artist Dick Giordano claims: "The Batman does what he does for himself, for his needs. That society gains from his actions is incidental, an added value… but not the primary reason for his actions."[22] In *The Anti-Christ,*[23] Nietzsche asks, "What is good? All that heightens the feeling of power, the will to power, power itself in man. What is bad? All that proceeds from weakness. What is happiness? The feeling that power increases, that a resistance is overcome." Similarly, in *Zarathustra*: "The spirit of revenge, my friends, has so far been the subject of man's best reflection; and where there was suffering, one always wanted punishment, too."[24] Even so, professing the need for a disguise, Bruce Wayne adds in comics' most famous soliloquy: "'Criminals are a superstitious, cowardly lot, so my disguise must be able to strike terror into their hearts. I must be a creature of the night, black, terrible …a…a…' As if in answer, a huge bat flies in the open window! 'A bat! That's it! It's an omen. I shall become a BAT!'"[25] In *The Gay Science*, Nietzsche demands of the true hero: "You should become him who you are."[26] Bruce Wayne does just that: "Thus is born this weird figure of the dark, this avenger of evil, The Batman." Again in *The Gay Science*, Nietzsche includes a lengthy section entitled simply, *Excelsior!*

> You shall never pray again, never adore again, never again rest in endless trust; you deny yourself any stopping before ultimate wisdom, ultimate goodness, ultimate power, while unharnessing your thoughts; you have no perpetual guardian and friend for your seven solitudes…there is no avenger for you, no eventual improver…you resist any ultimate peace, you want the eternal recurrence of war and peace.[27]

In the Batman's origin, Nietzsche's words appear to leap into life. Here we see a man who is independent, strong, healthy, full of intense passion, operating in the real world, affirming life inasmuch as he understands suffering and "the eternal recurrence" of his boyhood tragedy.

Another way in which the Batman appears to rise, superman-like, to the heights of human perfection is in the way he continuously overcomes his human vulnerability. Unlike his Kryptonian counterpart, the Batman is not a "super" hero. As Jules Feiffer succinctly puts it, "If you pricked him, he bled—buckets."[28] This is evident as early as his third adventure, in *Detective* #29 (July 1939), when during a battle with Dr. Death's armed underling, Jabah, "the Batman is hit!" With "the blood still seeping from his wound," the costumed vigilante applies some of his own limited emergency medical treatment ("a pad of cotton on his bared shoulder"), before transforming into his secret identity of Bruce Wayne and seeking out his "family doctor." In what would become an ongoing dilemma for the hero, Bruce has to try to explain how he came to have a bullet wound, especially when there are no powder marks on his flesh. His flippant response, "I do funny things sometime, Doc," appears incredibly weak even for an eccentric "socialite" (*Detective Comics* #29).

This double dilemma of a need for outside medical attention without offering adequate explanation has been explored in more recent decades, from Bruce Wayne's ill-advised trip to Hugo Strange's Graytowers Clinic in the 1970s (*Detective Comics* #471) to his ill-fated romance with the beautiful Dr. Shondra Kinsolving in the 1990s. Comics painter Alex Ross has created a memorable image of a half-garbed Bruce Wayne, his bare back laced with the countless scars and cuts of a lifetime of battles. This vision of a vulnerable hero, one "who was able to take punishment and triumph in the end,"[29] has appealed to readers who tire of seeing the Kryptonian take a missile to his midsection and simply grin. As one comics historian states, "It is the Batman's ultimate vulnerability, not invulnerability, that seizes our attention, affection, and loyalty."[30] In Nietzschean terms, we might say that the Batman is one of us, while at the same time, by "overcoming his own dark passions … the irrational savage within," he has set the standard for a new kind of human being.[31]

It is not altogether surprising that the Batman in his early days experienced the Nietzschean dilemma of a struggle with "ordinary" citizens and the police. Clearly, he chose not to join the force but work as a vigilante. In the earliest issues of *Detective Comics* and *Batman,* he was depicted as a killer when necessary—strangling, shooting, throwing off a building—not unlike his pulp forebears. During a battle with one of Doctor Death's henchmen in *Detective Comics* #30 (August 1939), the Batman swung toward the hulking enemy as the latter stuck his head out of a window: "There is a sickening snap as the cossack's neck breaks under the mighty pressure of the Batman's foot." Far from displaying any remorse over the death, the masked vigilante simply says, "First Jabah, now you, … and yet Doctor Death lives on!"

It was not only criminals that appeared "scared and superstitious" upon viewing Batman, but ordinary citizens. When a crowd ran screaming in panic from his "batgyro," the Batman merely grinned (*Detective Comics* #31). Later in the same issue, a taxi driver took one look at the Batman, only to shriek, "Help! The Devil himself!" Here was a man who unnerved the police by playing by his own rules, at times even fighting them, as in *Detective Comics* #35. The police Commissioner lamented to a grinning Bruce Wayne, "That Batman. He's done it again! He's making the police department look ridiculous. I wish I could get my hands on him." When the police found the Batman with a murder victim, they automatically assumed that he himself was the killer. But later, Batman was finally being praised as "a great man" (*Detective Comics* #36; 1940). For good or for ill, this *übermensch* was being tamed and domesticated.

The Most Dangerous Man Alive

> Poor Batman was in for a hell of a makeover! (Michael Uslan, *Batman in the Fifties*)

More than almost any other fictional character of his caliber, the Batman, "weird avenger of evil" in the late 1930s, underwent such dramatic changes of both character and ethos that it is difficult to look at the Adam West depiction of the character on the 1960s television show—not to mention the George Clooney representation in the late-1990s film—and see anything substantive remaining of the Kane and Finger original. It has been said that the same is true of Superman, who was originally portrayed as a "diamond in the rough...a quick-tempered social activist" who would "gladly have bent the Miranda Laws with his bare hands."[32] Although the Man of Steel in his earliest tales, like Batman, was "chased by the law," he soon exchanged his more rebellious tendencies for what would become the "core" of his character: "Truth, Justice, and the American Way."[33] In other words any hint of the Nietzschean *übermensch* in Superman gave way to the more familiar, "canonical" definition of the character. Indeed if the two representations were placed side by side and the question was asked, "Would the true Superman please stand up," there is little doubt that, in the minds of most people, the "boy scout" would be the one to step forward. Attempts to return to a darker, harsher Man of Steel would actually feel forced and inappropriate.

With Batman, the situation is quite different. Although the case has been made that the dramatically different depictions of Gotham's defender in the decades following his "birth" have simply represented equally "valid interpretations" of the character for new eras,[34] the fact remains that something feels inherently wrong with this argument. Although Batman writer/artist Frank Miller says it in altogether subjective terms—"For me, Batman was never funny"—it is a safe bet that many of Batman's comic readers would agree with him.[35] If Superman seemed to live into his potential, it is almost as if the opposite occurred with the Batman for many years. Seeds of change were evident early on, as early as *Detective Comics* #38 (April 1940) with the introduction of Robin.

The countless kid sidekicks that would follow the Boy Wonder would all be obvious younger versions of their adult partners: Bucky and Toro (Captain America and the Human Torch), Speedy and Aqualad (Green Arrow and Aquaman), Kid Flash and Wonder Girl (Flash and Wonder Woman). Even their costumes matched or mimicked those of their mentors. They did not, however, inherit this pattern from Robin, the first of the sidekicks. Although he was orphaned by the work of criminals, like the Batman, the similarities between mentor and apprentice end there. He was never "Batboy" or "Batkid." His bright red, green, and yellow costume stood in direct contrast with the grey, black, and blue worn by the Batman. Robin's costume, like his name, had nothing to do with bats; it was explicitly stated that Robin Hood, not Batman, was the inspiration for the look and personality of the young acrobatic daredevil. It was as though the Batman himself could not be truly imitated, or more likely in the minds of his critics, *should not* be imitated.

In an early issue of the 1990s Grant Morrison/Howard Porter run of *Justice League,* Superman responds to a deadly extraterrestrial's disbelief about the Batman's abilities: "He's just one man!" The captive Man of Steel smiles grimly as he replies, "Only the most dangerous man on earth." Although Batman was not the specific target, a May 8, 1940, *Chicago Daily News* editorial written by literary critic Sterling North, entitled "A National Disgrace," lambasted comic books as a "hypodermic injection of sex and murder."[36] As Batman scholar Will Brooker notes, it is not too great a stretch of the imagination to picture parents reading about the "poison" of comic books and then flipping through the pages of *Batman* #1 (April–May 1940), only to find the hero behind a machine gun, mowing down men-turned-into-monsters; or glancing at the cover of *Detective Comics* #37 (March 1940), with a headless gangster brandishing a knife charging Batman even as the latter throws a gun-toting thug off the pier.[37] It is probably not great coincidence that the cover of the very next issue of *Detective* introduced Robin in bright primary colors, the once grim Batman smiling with paternalistic pride. Sales went up. Nietzsche would hardly have been surprised. The "eerie figure of the night" had begun to be co-opted by a religious-minded, moralistic establishment; he was becoming more likeable, less intimidating. In short, the *übermensch,* the most dangerous man on earth, was becoming "all too human."

Robin's entrée was just the beginning. For each societal reaction to Batman, the comics industry responded with a counter-reaction to tame him even further. For the remainder of the 1940s, following the published fears of parents and patriots, bizarre killers such as the Joker became clever crooks, and comic covers displayed Batman and Robin endorsing the sales of American war bonds. In the 1950s, psychologist Fredric Wertham's book, *Seduction of the Innocent,* charged comics with encouraging juvenile delinquency and made the now-famous suggestion that Batman and Robin were actually lovers who promoted the "evils" of homosexuality to young readers. In response, the world of Batman became even more "wild, wacky, and weird,"[38] with visits to other planets and battles with garish monsters. The Dynamic Duo became surrounded by a "Batman family" that included Batwoman, Bat-Girl, Bat-Hound, and even an other-dimensional imp named Bat-Mite. In the 1960s, the television show and corresponding comics made famous "Holy Deep Freeze, Batman," "Zap! Bam! Crash!" "the Batusi," and "Bat Shark Repellant." Mood was out, mod was in. Camp reigned. In Nietzschean terms, these changes should have been entirely predictable; the *übermensch* is never popular, threatening those who embrace the norm.

What is a bit more surprising, then, is the fact that the essence of the Batman's character never totally succumbed to domesticating forces. Superman's costume with its bright, primary colors was all-American. Batman's costume could be altered, ears lowered and a yellow oval placed behind the bat on his chest, but it was still the costume of a bat, still a costume of gray, black, and dark blue. Superman was a reporter, an American working man. Batman would always be the aristocrat, made more likeable but hardly relatable. Superman had loving, salt-of-the-earth Midwestern parents. Batman was surrounded by a "bat-family" but this did not change the fact that he was still and forever an orphan. It is little wonder that the television series avoided his origin altogether! Michael Uslan may be correct that there are different interpretations for different eras, but this does not mean they are equally appropriate to the essence of the character. Not all versions are "authorized" versions, even if they happen to be approved by the publisher. As Will Brooker puts it, the Batman has "transcended the role of institutional product and could survive independently...as twenty-first-century myth."[39]

The Batman Myth

> The Batman phenomenon has certain things in common with religion in that it is built around a mythology or pseudo-mythology. (Dennis O'Neil, Batman editor)

It is not only because he was the first to be created that Superman became the paradigm among superheroes, the one before whom other heroes would look in awe. Grant Morrison is correct in declaring the Man of Steel to be "the American Christ."[40] The mythical elements of his story are immediately familiar and reassuring to western readers: A father's only son is sent from the heavens to earth, sharing the life of humans while possessing remarkable abilities "far beyond those of mortal men." If he is indeed a "boy scout," then he is a boy scout of nigh-infinite power. Even after being killed by a creature appropriately named Doomsday, he would not stay dead, but instead returned as bright a beacon of hope as ever. The bold red "S" on his chest might well stand for "Savior," for that is how he is defined, as the one from the stars who comes to save.

The Batman, on the other hand, is the self-made man, the one who does not require saving. He is not the one who soars down from the heavens, but rather the one who rises up from among all-too-human people. The mythical elements in his story are of a very different kind. His tale is the ultimate humanistic myth, but not in a sentimental fashion. No, the mythology of the Batman is a mythology of the strong, the healthy, the independent.[41] This myth, wrapped up in gray and black, is about making one's destiny, not waiting for it to fall down from the sky like a rocket. It is about experiencing tragedy not once but countless times in an eternal recurrence of memory and pain. It is about integrating the tragic into one's very being, until a single individual has become what he is potentially capable, what all are potentially capable, of being. It is significant that there is no room for prayer or dependence or helplessness in the Batman's saga. The humanistic mythology that is his is about achieving the pinnacle of human perfection in this life, knowing that no one will ever truly appreciate the achievement. Against such a Nietzschean "superman," the Man of Steel, for all his power, looks weak in comparison.

No one has captured the tension, the dichotomy, between the two mythical figures better than writer/artist Frank Miller in his 1986 graphic novel collection, *The Dark Knight Returns*. In this landmark work, an aging Batman, long since retired, finds himself reborn at a time of great need. Fighting against his own body's weaknesses, he literally wills himself to press on. He allies himself with those labeled "criminals" (a particularly Nietzschean touch). Indeed, the philosopher would no doubt nod and smile at the speech the Batman gives to a group of young radicals in the final book of the series (*Batman: The Dark Knight* #4 "The Dark Knight Falls," 1986):

[On horseback, breaking a rifle with his bare hands] This is the weapon of the enemy. We do not need it. We will not use it. Our weapons are quiet, precise. In time, I will teach them to you. Tonight, you will rely on your fists...and your brains. Tonight, *we* are the law. Tonight, *I* am the law.

This unchallenged authority ("just his voice," a young female Robin notes in awe) is contrasted with the lapdog-like "Yes, sir/No, sir" replies of Superman to the American president, for whom he works personally as a kind of "secret weapon." In the operatic climax fighting against Superman, as the Batman uses every weapon in his arsenal to pummel the "invulnerable" godlike hero, the self-made man offers one last speech that would have made Nietzsche proud (*Batman: The Dark Knight* #4):

> This...is the end...for both of us....We could have changed the world. Now...look at us....I've become...a political liability...and you...you're a joke. I want you...to remember, Clark,...in all the years to come...in your most private moments...I want you to remember...my hand...at your throat. I want you...to remember...the one man who beat you...

The Batman then "dies," but it is a death he himself planned, for which he was prepared, and from which he rises to a new life, not because he has otherworldly genes, but because he has an indomitable human will and intellect.[42] Consciously or otherwise, Miller, like Kane and others, allowed the humanistic myth to reassert itself again. At the end of Miller's story, an unmasked Batman finds himself in a cave once more, training his rebel soldiers for the final battle still ahead. Comicdom's one true *übermensch* waits for the day when it can be said, as Nietzsche says at the end of *Zarathustra,* "And he left his cave, glowing and strong as a morning sun that comes out of dark mountains."

Notes

[1] From *Twilight of the Idols,* 21. Unless noted otherwise, all selections from Nietzsche's works are taken from *The Portable Nietzsche,* trans. Walter Kaufmann (1954; rpt., New York: Penguin Books, 1982).

[2] *The Antichrist,* 51.

[3] From the Introduction to Nietzsche's *Thus Spoke Zarathustra,* written by his sister, Elisabeth Förster-Nietzsche [Cited 21 February, 2004] Online: nietzsche. Thefreelibrary.com/Thus-Spake-Zarathustra/1–1. Although it is not overtly mentioned, the shadow of Nietzsche's goal called *übermensch* can be felt in most of his writings, including *The Birth of Tragedy* (1872; trans. 1966), *Beyond Good and Evil* (1886; trans. 1966), *On the Genealogy of Morals* (1887; trans. 1966), *The Antichrist* (1888; trans. 1954), and the autobiographical *Ecce Homo* (1889; trans. 1966).

[4] *Thus Spoke Zarathustra* I, 2.

[5] Robert C. Solomon and Kathleen M. Higgins, *What Nietzsche Really Said* (New York: Schocken Books, 2000), 132.

[6] *Human, All Too Human,* 114.

[7] Cf. *Zarathustra* I, "On Free Death."

[8] *Zarathustra* I, 3. "Nietzsche's increasingly polemical attacks on Christianity were intended to make people aware of the real meaning and consequences of 'the

death of God.' Nietzsche insisted that his contemporaries must take up the task of a 'revaluation of all values,' a task which had become imminent as well as urgent." Quoted in *The Cambridge Companion to Nietzsche,* Bernd Magnus and Kathleen M. Higgins, eds., (Cambridge: Cambridge University Press, 1996), 102–3.

[9] *Zarathustra* III, 26.

[10] Elliot S. Maggin, "The New Bards," *Kingdom Come* (New York: Titan, 1997), 5.

[11] Grant Morrison, *Wizard* #143 (2003), 180. Cf. my chapter, "Sorcerers and Supermen: Old Mythologies in New Guises," in James McGrath, ed., *Religion and Science Fiction* (pending publication, Albany: SUNY Press).

[12] Les Daniels, *Batman: The Complete History* (New York: DC Comics, 1999), 17.

[13] By coincidence, another Clinton High graduate also made his mark in the comics industry. Like Kahn/Kane, Stanley Lieber would enjoy a long and productive career with Marvel Comics under the now-famous name of Stan Lee.

[14] Longtime DC Comics editor Robert Greenberger asserts: "Batman represents the opposite of his predecessor, Superman. Whereas Superman has always been a light, positive hero, Batman has been grim and possessed. Their worlds rarely mesh." From "Endnotes" in *The Greatest Batman Stories Ever Told* (New York: DC Comics, 1988), 344.

[15] Dennis O'Neil later made it clear that the Batman was not simply a carbon copy of the pulp hero, The Shadow, by having Batman himself state, "Sure, I admire him...I've been inspired by him. But I'm my own man." From "The Night of the Shadow" in *Batman* #259 (December 1974).

[16] "Notes from the Batcave: An Interview with Dennis O'Neil," in Roberta E. Pearson and William Uricchio, eds., *The Many Lives of the Batman* (New York: Routledge, 1991), 24.

[17] "Notes from the Batcave," 24.

[18] "Notes from the Batcave," 24.

[19] Nietzsche, *The Gay Science,* 268.

[20] For examples of how the gaps in the Batman's origin story were filled in by creators in subsequent decades, compare Batman's origin in *Detective Comics* #33 (Nov. 1939) with "The Origin of Batman" in *Batman* # 47 (1948), "The First Batman" in *Detective Comics* #211 (1956), and "There Is No Hope in Crime Alley" in *Detective Comics* #457 (1976).

[21] *Twilight,* 47. Earlier in the same work, he actually proclaims the sick man to be a "parasite" of society and, if sick enough, "indecent to live longer" (36).

[22] From the Introduction to *The Greatest Batman Stories Ever Told* (New York: DC Comics, 1988), 8.

[23] Nietzsche, *The Anti-Christ,* 2.

[24] Book II, p. 20.

[25] Again, see *Detective Comics* #38.

[26] *The Gay Science,* 270.

[27] *The Gay Science,* 285. This title is all the more intriguing when one considers that, years later, another comics legend, Stan Lee, would make "Excelsior" his ever-ready cry.

[28] Jules Feiffer, *The Great Comic Book Heroes* (Seattle: Fantagraphics Books, 2003), 26.

[29] Rick Marschall, "Foreword," in Bob Kane, *Batman Archives,* Vol. 1 (New York: DC Comics, 1990), 6.

[30] Marschall, 6. Jules Feiffer again offers a pithy observation: "I suspect the Batman school of having healthier egos." Cf. Feiffer, *Great Comic Book Heroes,* 26.

[31] Joseph Campbell, with Bill Moyers, *The Power of Myth* (New York: Anchor, 1991; Doubleday, 1988), xiii.

[32] Mark Waid, "Introduction," *Superman in the Fifties* (New York: DC Comics, 2002), 5.

[33] Marv Wolfmann, "Reinventing the Wheel," *Superman: The Man of Steel* (New York: DC Comics, 2003). Cf. Tom Andrae, "From Menace to Messiah: The Prehistory of the Superman in Science Fiction Literature," *Discourse* #2 (Summer 1980), 84–112.

[34] Michael Uslan, "Introduction," *Batman in the Fifties* (New York: DC Comics, 2002), 6.

[35] Frank Miller, "Introduction," *Batman: Year One* (New York: DC Comics, 1988).

[36] Cited in Will Brooker, *Batman Unmasked* (New York: Continuum, 2001), 61.

[37] Brooker, 62.

[38] Uslan, "Introduction," 5.

[39] Brooker, *Batman Unmasked,* 317.

[40] Grant Morrison, *Wizard* #143 (2003), 180.

[41] Contrast Tony Stark, another crafty but tormented millionaire playboy turned superhero. Stark had a perpetual health problem: His armored suit doubled as a pacemaker to keep his heart beating after an injury. Stark resembles Wayne, but his alter ego, Iron Man, mimics the Man of Steel.

[42] Fifteen years after *The Dark Knight Returns,* Frank Miller offered his long-awaited sequel, *The Dark Knight Strikes Back* (New York: DC Comics, 2001).

Recommended Resources

Andrae, Tom. "From Menace to Messiah: The Prehistory of the Superman in Science Fiction Literature." *Discourse* 2 (Summer 1980): 84–112.

Beatty, Scott. *Batman: The Ultimate Guide to the Dark Night.* Updated Edition. New York: Dorling Kindersley, 2005.

Bongco, Mila. "Frank Miller's *The Dark Knight Returns* (1986)." In *Reading Comics: Language, Culture, and the Concept of the Superhero in Comic Books.* New York: Garland, 2000.

Brooker, Will. *Batman Unmasked: Analyzing a Cultural Icon.* New York: Continuum Pub Group, 2000.

Campbell, Joseph. *The Hero with a Thousand Faces.* Bollingen Series 17. 2d ed. Princeton, N.J.: Princeton University Press, 1968.

Campbell, Joseph, with Bill Moyers. *The Power of Myth.* New York: Anchor, 1991; Doubleday, 1988.

Daniels, Les. *Batman: The Complete History.* New York: DC Comics, 1999.

Feiffer, Jules. *The Great Comic Book Heroes.* Seattle: Fantagraphics Books, 2003.

Greenberger, Robert. *The Greatest Batman Stories Ever Told.* New York: DC Comics, 1988.

Kane, Bob. *Batman Archives, Volume 1.* New York, DC Comics, 1990.

Klock, Geoff. "The Bat and the Watchmen." Pages 25–76 in *How to Read Superhero Comics and Why.* New York: Continuum Pub Group, 2002.

Miller, Frank. *The Dark Knight Returns.* New York: DC Comics, 1986.

Nietzsche, Friedrich. *The Portable Nietzsche.* Translated by Walter Kaufmann. New York: Penguin Books, 1954; reprinted 1982.

Pearson, Roberta E. and William Uricchio, eds. *The Many Lives of the Batman.* New York: Routledge, 1991.

Robertson, C. K. "Sorcerers and Supermen: Old Mythologies in New Guises." In *Religion and Science Fiction.* James McGrath, ed. (Albany: SUNY Press, forthcoming).

Solomon, Robert C., and Kathleen M. Higgins. *What Nietzsche Really Said.* New York: Schocken Books, 2000.

Terrill, R. E. "Spectacular Repression: Sanitizing the Batman." *Critical Studies in Media Communication* 17 (2000): 493–509.

Uslan, Michael, and Bob Kane. *Batman in the Fifties.* New York: DC Comics, 2002.

3
Wonder Woman Mythology: Heroes from the Ancient World and Their Progeny

Elizabeth Danna

The ancient world did not have comic books, but they did tell stories about their own "super" heroes. Two heroes from antiquity that stand out in western culture are Samson and Herakles (Hercules). While their stories originate from the Hebrew Bible and Greek mythology, respectively, they have influenced comic book superheroes in a significant way. When creating Superman, Jerry Siegel and Joe Shuster desired a hero whose strength resembled Hercules and Samson.[1] Perhaps the choice of creating Superman with a curly lock of jet black hair hints at Samson, the ancient hero of Jewish tradition. Dell Comics developed a post-nuclear holocaust hero named the *Mighty Samson* whose strength resembled his biblical predecessor (1964–82). After Marvel Comics' success in transforming the Norse god Thor into a Silver Age superhero, Stan Lee and Jack Kirby introduced Hercules and the Olympian gods of Greek mythology (*Journey into Mystery/Thor Annual* #1; 1965). Afterward Hercules became a member of the Avengers and led the superhero team called *The Champions*, partnering with the Black Widow, Ghost Rider, and former X-Men Angel and Iceman (1975–78). Charlton Publications (1967–69) and DC Comics (1975–77) also came out with their own versions of Hercules. Captain Marvel is an heroic example owing much to both the Greek mythology of Herakles and the biblical legacy of Samson, as we shall see later.

After we examine these ancient strong men, we will turn our attention to the distaff side and look at the Amazons and then focus our primary attention on their comic-book daughter, Wonder Woman. Apart from Wonder Woman's popular feminist appeal, she may also be the best known comic book hero related to ancient mythology. The influence of Greco-Roman mythology and Jewish tradition found in the Old Testament has left its insignia on the contemporary comic book world as well as pop culture.

Hercules: Strongman of Greek Mythology

Faster than the Ceryneian doe! More powerful than the Cretan bull! Able to father fifty children by fifty different women in a single night! Long before there was Superman, there was Herakles, better known to the Romans, and to westerners, as Hercules. To the ancient Greeks, the larger-than-life Herakles was the epitome of the hero. The Roman poet Ovid wrote an account of his life, and the Greek prose writer Apollodorus wrote a longer one. The hero also appears in poems of the Greek poets Pindar and Theocritus, and in works by the Greek playwrights Sophocles and Euripides. The Greeks not only honored Herakles as a hero, but also revered him as a god.

In ancient mythology the heroes often consult a divine protector, or patron, and Herakles was no exception. His protectress was Athena, goddess of wisdom and war (she was also patron to several epic heroes). She offered advice and assistance as needed to help Herakles finish his tasks, and she led him to the underworld (a place no living mortal could go without supernatural aid) and finally to the home of the gods. She is shown in art depictions as being at his side during crucial moments.

Herakles possessed unmatched physical strength and an equally unmatched appetite for food and women. His abilities seemed to be admired by the non-Athenian Greek world. He was the son of Queen Alkmene of Tiryns and Zeus, greatest of the Olympian gods. Zeus desired the married Alkmene, but she was too faithful a wife to be seduced, so Zeus approached her in the form of her husband, Amphytryon, presently away on a military campaign. Amphytryon returned the following day, and in due time Alkmene gave birth to twins: Herakles, the offspring of her union with Zeus; and Iphicles, the result of her reunion with her husband. Of course Herakles' arrival did not go unnoticed by Zeus' wife Hera; she became his lifelong enemy because he was her husband's son by another woman. Pindar tells a tale that when Herakles was still an infant, Hera sent two large snakes into his nursery. While his brother screamed in terror, Heracles strangled the snakes, thus hinting to all that he was no ordinary child.

His emotions were as intense as his physical strength. Herakles' overreactions to small provocations often proved fatal to those around him, but his penitence was just as intense—without complaint he spent much time atoning for wrongdoings. This is the reason for his famous twelve labors. The story of the labors begins in tragedy—Herakles killed his wife and two sons in a fit of madness sent on him by Hera. When the lunacy passed Herakles wanted to kill himself, but Theseus, an Athenian hero, tried to persuade Herakles that he could not be held guilty in such a situation. Herakles could not accept this. He consulted the oracle at Delphi to ask what he should do to atone for his crime. He received his answer: He must go to his cousin King Eurystheus of Tiryns and do whatever the king asked. Eurystheus gave him twelve all-but-impossible tasks to accomplish. He completed them all, doing great exploits such as defeating the lion of Nemea with his bare hands, killing the nine-headed Hydra, getting the golden apples of Hesperides, and taking Cerberus, the three-headed dog, from Hades. In the ninth labor, Herakles was to take the belt of Hippolyta, Queen of the Amazons. Their encountered remained peaceful at first; Hippolyta welcomed Herakles and agreed to give him her belt. However, the goddess Hera interfered by making the Amazons think that Herakles intended to carry off their queen as well as her belt. They attacked Herakles' ship, and so the hero killed Hippolyta, thinking that she had ordered the attack. He fought off the other Amazons and got away with his prize.

Many other stories relate adventures about Herakles, but the ones already mentioned suffice to show his rough-and-ready nature and lower appetites, which are more characteristic of a folk hero than a lord of the nobility or epic hero. He fights mostly animals or monsters rather than humans; and in another story told by Euripides in *Alcestis*, Herakles fights with Death (*Thanatos*) and rescues Alcetis (the wife of a friend) from the dead.[2] These aspects characterize folk heroes. Herakles' heroic victories during the labors were made possible only by virtue of the tragic death of his family, and he was driven by his necessity to redeem himself from guilt. These features he holds in common with pop culture heroes such as Batman and Spider-Man.

It is also a common characteristic of heroes that they be vulnerable in at least one area. Achilles had a vulnerable heel and Meleager depended on a wooden log. Herakles could only be harmed by the blood of Nessus the Centaur. One day Herakles' second wife smeared his tunic with this blood because Nessus told her that it was a love potion to keep her husband faithful. When Herakles put on the tunic, it burned him, and the pain was so unbearable that he had a funeral pyre built for him at Mount Oeta. From the midst of the flames Herakles was taken to Olympus, home of the gods, where he was welcomed as one of them. Likewise in pop culture heroes, Superman's weakness became kryptonite and the Green Lantern's power proved helpless against the color yellow. Wonder Woman could be subdued if her bracelets were tied together or if she were unfortunate enough to get tied up by her own lasso. In biblical narrative Samson, as we shall see, kept his strength only while he retained his long hair.

Samson: He-Man of the Bible

Samson's life and great strength originate from one source: the Hebrew Bible. More specifically, the story of Samson is found in the book of Judges chapters 13–16. While there are striking similarities between Herakles and Samson, there are also some significant differences. As with Herakles, there are indications right from the beginning of Samson's life that he is destined for something unusual. Before Samson's birth, an angel appears to his mother indicating that the child is to be "a Nazirite to God from birth" (Judges 13:5). The word "Nazirite" meant someone separated or set apart for God's purposes. A Nazirite took vows to refrain from eating grapes, drinking wine, and getting haircuts. The special person was forbidden to approach a dead body (Numbers 6:1–21). In early tradition the Nazirite vows were taken for life, but later they could be taken for a specified period of time. Samson does not necessarily take the vows for himself; his mother takes them for him. An indication of Samson's distinctive status is made evident whenever the spirit of the Yahweh, Israel's God, would come upon him at various times to do great exploits (Judges 14:6, 19; 15:14). As a repetitive pattern in the book of Judges, the Israelites fall into sin by disobeying the laws that Yahweh gave them through Moses. Consequently God allows them to be conquered by their enemies until the Israelites cry out for God's help. Then he raises up a warrior judge to rescue them from oppression. Just before Samson's birth, the Philistine were the enemy, and the angel says that Samson "will begin to deliver Israel from…the Philistines" (13:5).

As a Nazirite, Samson should be in tune with what God wants, but he seems more concerned about his own agenda than God's. Whereas the other judges act against the oppressors in order to free Israel, Samson's motivations are personal—he wants revenge for injuries done to himself. Even at his death his concern as he knocks down the pillars of the Philistine temple is "that I may be avenged upon the Philistines this once for my two eyes" (Judges 16:28). Moreover, he is not very scrupulous about keeping his Nazirite vows or faithfulness to Israel. He frequently has contact with dead bodies, marries a Philistine woman (which was not lawful for Mosaic Israelites to do), sleeps with a prostitute, and gives a weeklong feast in which it is hard to believe that he does not join in on the festivities and drinking (Judges 14:1–4, 6, 9–10; 15:8, 15–16; 16:1). The only Nazirite vow that he seems to keep is not cutting his long locks (16:17; cf. 13:5). Samson is aware that his strength comes from his separation to God, which is symbolized by his hair (16:17). There is a theological point here: God can use even those who are not so perfect at fulfilling his plans. This is a comforting thought for those who serve God as best they can but frequently make mistakes.

Samson can be seen as a trickster figure who uses riddles and deception to overcome his enemies. One scholar calls him "an irresponsible practical joker."[3]   Trick and counter-trick keep the plot moving as Samson and the Philistines try to outmaneuver each other. Another scholar calls this "the trap motif."[4] Samson's inability to resist foreign women—a type of relationship which Yahweh had warned the men of Israel against (Exodus 34:16; cf. Ezra 10:10–11)—is one kind of trap. This eventually becomes his downfall when Delilah, sent by the Philistines, discovers the secret of Samson's strength, and cuts his hair accordingly. His strength departs from him and so does Yahweh his God (Judges 16:19, 20). After his hair starts growing again, however, it is a hint that God has not abandoned him after all, and the reader's hopes are raised once again (16:22).[5] The biggest trap is the last one, and it is set neither by Samson nor the Philistines. When the Philistines force their blinded prisoner Samson to perform for them, God helps Samson bring the house down—quite literally! Just when the Philistines have Samson right where they want him, Yahweh uses the strong man to destroy "all the lords of the Philistines" who were present (i.e., their nobility), as well as 3000 men and women of the common people (Judges 16:27). The Philistines had gathered to worship their god Dagon and celebrate their victory over Samson, for which they gave the credit to Dagon (16:23–25). Yahweh's action, through Samson, shows himself mightier than the Philistines' god. There is a theological point here also: God sometimes carries out his plans, even through those who have no clue what God is doing.

Similar to Herakles, Samson is more a folk hero than an epic hero: He fights with a lion, defeating the beast with his bare hands (Judges 14:6), and he shows a great appetite for food and women (14:1–3, 10–11; 16:2–4). As Athena is Herakles' patroness, Yahweh may be considered Samson's patron, and yet there is no sense in the Herakles stories that he is carrying out Athena's plans. Differently, God uses Samson to carry out his plan to deliver Israel from its oppressor (e.g., 14:4). Both heroes share a large appetite for food and women, and an emotional tendency to overreact that gets them into trouble. Both kill a lion with their bare hands, and both do menial service, Herakles to Eurystheus and Samson to the Philistines. Both make a descent into the dark, Herakles to the underworld and the blind Samson to death. Both are finally betrayed by women, and each chooses his own death. Is there a connection, then, between the Greek and the Jewish heroes? Archaeological indications suggest contact between the peoples of Palestine and the Aegean in the Late Bronze Age (i.e., 1400–1200 B.C.E.). In fact, it is possible that both stories have been influenced by the Babylonian *Epic of Gilgamesh,* written even before this time. The author of Judges, however, has anchored the Samson story firmly in ancient Judaism, both religiously and geographically (Judges 16:31; cf. 13:25).[6] Perhaps the connection is simply coincidental, or maybe it rests in our shared identity as humans, mythical patterns of thought, and our common need for heroes.

Warrior Females: The Amazon Myth

Before Zeus, I ask you, Socrates, who are these who are singing this holy song? Are they some kind of lady Heroes? (Aristophanes, *Clouds* §314–15)

Greek writers told few stories about them, but artists made many sculptures and paintings of them, indicating their importance in ancient culture. According to Greek mythology the Amazons were the daughters of Ares, god of war, and the nymph Harmony. Different sources give different places for their homeland. Homer says that they lived in Lycia and in Phrygia on the Sangarius River (*Iliad* 6.172–86; 2.811–14; 3.181–89). Other traditions place them on the Ionian coast (west Asia Minor), the foothills of the Caucasus Mountains (north of Albania), or in African Lybia. The Athenian playwright Aeschylus locates the Amazon homeland on the Thermodon River, on the north shore of the Black Sea in a city named Themiscyra (*Prometheus Bound* 415–19, 723–27). All these locations have one thing in common—they are positioned at the edge of the ancient world, for the Greeks considered the Amazons only half-civilized.

Ares aside, the Amazons worshiped Artemis, virgin goddess of the hunt, and Cybele, the Great Earth Mother. These deities were imported into Greek religion from the Near East, hence, foreign gods. Ideas of war and fertility are associated with this female clan of warriors. They are usually described as lightly armed in contrast to the heavily armed Greek hoplite soldier. They usually fought from horseback (in contrast to the hoplite), but they sometimes battled on foot. They carried a crescent-shaped, leather-covered shield, and wore a leather cap for head protection as they wielded spear, javelin, or axe. Their most famous weapon, however, was the bow. The word "Amazon" means "without a breast"; they were said to sear or remove the right breast to use the bow, though later generations of female archers would argue that practicing their sport does not require a mastectomy! It is evident that Greeks considered the Amazons to be different from themselves in manner of dress, religion, and warfare; and their country was considered an edgy part of the world where the "natural" or patriarchal order of things ran in reverse.

Most of the stories about the Amazons involve their defeat in battle against men. Herakles killed their queen and escaped from these women. Theseus raped one of them and brought her back to Athens with him. The Amazons attempted to rescue her, besieging the Acropolis before driven back. Earlier versions end with Theseus' Amazon bride negotiating a peace treaty, but later versions end with all the Amazons killed. Bellerophon also attacked and defeated them. The Greeks viewed the defeat of the Amazons as the triumph of order over chaos because patriarchy was deemed the structure that maintains order.

Wonder Woman's Mythical Origins

American psychologist and inventor of the lie detector, William Moulton Marston, wanted to create a strong female character with beauty who would appeal to "America's woman of tomorrow." In his own words, "Wonder Woman is psychological propaganda for the new type of woman who should, I believe, rule the world."[7] Marston believed that women could rule our society because they possessed more love than men, and they could use their allure to make men submit to them willingly. However, they needed more dominance and self-assertiveness. He asserted, "I have given Wonder Woman this dominant force but have kept her loving, tender, maternal and feminine in every other way."[8]

While Wonder Woman's compatriots worship the entire Greek pantheon, above all they serve Aphrodite, goddess of love and beauty. It was this goddess who instructed Queen Hippolyte to create a daughter out of clay and breathe life into her. Diana (Wonder Woman) thus represents a female Adam instead of Eve.[9] The bracelets the Amazon princess wears are a symbol of submission to the goddess of love, a visible expression indeed of what Marston called "submission to loving authority." *Sensation Comics* #1 (Jan. 1942) presented the heroine on the cover of the comic famously blocking bullets with these bracelets. Wonder Woman's magic lasso (given to her by Aphrodite), which compels anyone caught in it to obey her, is a sign of the feminine allure that women can use to influence others. Wonder Woman's lasso can be considered a visible manifestation of her powers of persuasion, and perhaps hints at Marston's controversial invention of the lie detector. It is not surprising that Marston connected all this with Aphrodite because he felt that no one would willingly submit to another's control unless there was an element of erotic pleasure in being controlled. At the beginning of her introduction in *All Star Comics* #8 (Dec. 1941), Wonder Woman is said to be "as lovely as Aphrodite—as wise as Athena—with the Speed of Mercury and the strength of Hercules."[10] Marston familiarized himself with mythology, and characters appear from the ancient Greco-Roman tales throughout the Wonder Woman comics.

Wonder Woman's mythical world is interrupted when an American pilot named Steve Trevor wrecks on Paradise Island, the home of the Amazons and Queen Hippolyte, Wonder Woman's mother. Princess Diana takes care of Trevor until he recovers. After Captain Trevor is restored back to health, Queen Hippolyte decides to send him back to the States with an Amazon

Olympic champion in order to help fight for America. The champion secretly turns out to be her daughter Diana whose fondness for Steve causes her to be an enthusiastic travel partner. She becomes nurse Diana Prince in the U.S.A., Wonder Woman's alter ego.

While there are similarities between the Amazons in *Wonder Woman* and those in the Greek myths, one difference is obvious at a glance. The scantily clad Amazons of the comic books have not surgically altered their figures to improve their archery! Another difference is that while these Amazons are skilled warriors, they have adopted the ways of peace and equality. These are the ideals that Wonder Woman has been sent to spread to the inhabitants of the "patriarch's world," as the Amazons call the region beyond their borders. The Amazons in the comic book originally live on a remote location they call Paradise Island.

Wonder Woman's early enemies included misogynist Dr. Psycho, a cat-woman named the Cheetah, and Baroness Paula von Gunther, a Nazi agent. Among the mythical pantheon, Mars (Ares) the god of war turns out to be Wonder Woman's nemesis. In George Pérez's remake of Wonder Woman in the 1980s, even prior to Diana's birth, Ares is seen as a deadly enemy of all the Amazons. It was he who incited Herakles to come against Queen Hippolyte and Amazons when they lived in the original Themyscira (*Wonder Woman* Vol. 2, #1; Feb. 1987).[11] Another ancient mythological named Circe appears prominently in the DC graphic novel *Paradise Found*.[12] The Homeric hero Odysseus describes his own encounter with Circe in *The Odyssey* 10.130–570. Circe's plan against Wonder Woman is loosely based on the plot from the *Odyssey*. When the Joker says that Circe "probably turned [the pilots of Air Force One] into pigs,"[13] this is a direct reference to the *Odyssey* 10.339–41.[14] One of Odysseus' men tells Odysseus that he avoided being enchanted by Circe because he was able to hide from her, and thus he is able to warn Odysseus of the danger (*Od.* 10.260ff). Similarly the Martian Manhunter is able to hide (by switching genders!) just long enough to inform Wonder Woman about the impending danger.[15] In the *Odyssey* Circe bewitches Odysseus' men by mixing a drug with their wine, while in *Paradise Found* the enchantment seems to be spread through the air. In both cases, men are her victims and the herb moly becomes the antidote.

There are two important differences between the *Odyssey* and *Paradise Found*, which probably arise from a distinction in the status between the women in ancient Greece and in those in the modern West. First, the Circe of *Paradise Found* is far more formidable than that of the *Odyssey*; she is a worthy opponent of Wonder Woman (whose most interesting opponents have tended to be female, right from the beginning). Certainly no ancient Greek writer could have conceived the spectacular "girl fight" that ensues between Wonder Woman and Circe. Second, the *Odyssey* does not ask about the effect of Circe's magic on women. In *Paradise Found* it is a major plot point that the magic has no effect on females. Therefore, Wonder Woman leads an army of superheroines against Circe and her villainesses. The fight between Circe and the Amazon princess ends when she dares Wonder Woman, "Just shed the lies you live with and do what you know you *want* to do! While the world watches, kill me!" Our heroine aims one final blow at Circe, but checks it, saying, "I won't let you take my *compassion* from me. I won't let you take my *ideals* away from me."[16] This refusal of brutal violence is what gives her the victory in this fight and in others. True to her origin Wonder Woman upholds peace and compassion.

Amazon Virtues

The Amazons in the comic books not only have adopted the way of peace but also reconciliation, faith, and love. In the Wonder Woman myth, Hercules invaded the Amazons before princess Diana was born. He plays a deceiver and murderer who seduces Queen Hippolyte into surrendering to him her magic girdle that provided her with strength in battle (later called the Girdle of Gaea). While she wore it, she possessed nearly invincible powers, but without it she was no match for him. Hercules and his men conquer and enslave the Amazons. When Hippolyte cries out to Aphrodite for help, the goddess of love responds but orders that all Amazons must always wear the manacles the men had chained them with (minus the chains) as a reminder that they must never serve men again. The Olympian gods punish Hercules for his attack on a race they favored. Eventually he repents of his actions and asks the Amazons for forgiveness. They pardon him and welcome him with celebration, exemplifying the virtues of forgiveness and mercy.

The idea of faith is also an important virtue in the Wonder Woman myth. The princess says that faith is the Amazons' greatest weapon, and they must use it to save the universe. Wonder Woman's own faith in the virtues of joy, hope, and love gives her the strength she needs every day to fulfill her mission of teaching those ideals.[17] Faith is also a key theme in the story *Gods of Gotham*.[18] It becomes a defensive weapon against the fear with which Ares' children assault Wonder Woman and her colleagues. Batman, as the narration points out, "believes in nothing, except himself," but he has seen the enhancement that faith in divinities brings to the lives of his friends, and wonders, "is his life any *less* bleak...for having *no* faith to cling to?"[19] His lack of belief makes him exceptionally vulnerable in the story, and he is unable to resist possession by the villain Phobos because of it.

The story ends on an inspirational note. Batman gets involved with contacting "Father Mike" to see if worshipers can go into his "Faith Center."

While nothing more is said about this Center, Father Mike's title suggests that he is a priest, which connects the Center with the Church. When Batman says that he hopes that Wonder Woman's dream of peace will come true, she answers, "*It will.* You've just got to have *faith.*" [20]

Love plays prominently in Wonder Woman as well. When challenged by Phobos, she affirms her commission on Earth: "I *forsook* my divinity...to *teach* my brothers and sisters. To *protect* them...*Is* it madness to give up the chance to live among those who I'm *sworn to save?* To know their love and to be *loved in return?*" [21] Later, "I turned my back on *godhood*...in order to claim my own destiny...as an agent of peace and change...on Earth..." [22] This reminds us of some well-known verses from the New Testament. At Mark 10:45 Jesus says, "the Son of Man came not to be served, but to serve, and to give his life as a ransom for many." In Philippians 2:6–7 the apostle Paul quotes a hymn that was sung at the time about Jesus: "although he was by nature God, he did not consider equality with God something to be grasped, but made himself nothing, taking the very nature of a servant, and was found in human form." Because of divine love for humanity, the son of God took on the form of a man, and as Paul writes in his letters, forgiveness and reconciliation are made possible by faith in the atoning death of Jesus on the cross (Romans 5; 2 Corinthians 5:14–21). Hence, in terms of reconciliation, faith, and love, Wonder Woman and Queen Hippolyte's virtues resemble those of ancient Christianity.

Wonder Woman as a Feminine Popular Culture Icon

The concept of women superheroes sometimes draws our attention to characters who are simply female counterparts to popular male heroes: Supergirl, Batgirl, Spider-Woman, She-Hulk, Mary Marvel, and Hawkgirl. Other feminine heroes may be more original, but they frequently belong to co-ed teams led by men: The Invisible Woman (Fantastic Four), the Wasp (Avengers), Saturn Girl (Legion of Superheroes), and X-Men such as Storm and Marvel Girl/Phoenix. Few would argue, however, that Wonder Woman remains the most famous female superhero in western culture, a status she has earned without the help of superhero men. [23] Like Superman and Batman, stories about her have continued unbroken since she first appeared in 1941. Indeed Wonder Woman has appeared in a number of titles apart from her own. At one point she was presented in four different titles at the same time—a feat rarely matched in comic book history. She proved that it was possible for a female comic-book character to succeed with her own title.

Yet over the decades there have been revisions of *Wonder Woman*'s image. One of these is that Wonder Woman's physical powers have been increased, until only Superman is a match for her. We wonder what Marston would make of this because a prominent theme in the early years of the heroine's comic book was that any girl could become a wonder woman if she worked and trained hard enough. Wonder Woman's real strengths nonetheless are not physical but what might be called women's strengths—compassion and the ability to win others over without the use of physical force. Of this Marston would probably approve.

During the 1950s most superhero comics folded as comic book fans turned to Horror, Westerns, Romance, Humor, and other comic genres. In this crisis period Wonder Woman's comic book often resembled more a romance than a superhero story. Diana regularly faced the dilemma that if she married Steve Trevor, she would lose her Amazon powers and not be able to fight crime and injustice. Trevor's seemingly impossible task was to eradicate evil so that Diana would marry him.[24] Be that as it may, the Amazon princess has stood the test of time while other leading ladies from the Golden Age fell by the wayside, such as Timely Comics' cat-like Miss Fury (also known as Black Fury) and Sheldon Mayer's crime-fighting Red Tornado who both preceded Wonder Woman in the comic book world.

Another crisis occurred in the late 1960s when Wonder Woman's sales went down, and a revamp seemed inevitably in order. The new Diana Prince had no Amazon powers or costume and Steve Trevor was killed off. She wore the latest fashions, and she became a martial arts heroine under the tutelage of a blind man named I-Ching (beginning with *Wonder Woman* #178; Oct. 1968). This all took place several years before *Master of Kung Fu* and *Iron Fist* popularized the genre in comics. Editor Denny O'Neil wanted to make the heroine an independent woman in the contemporary world of mortals.[25] After the rise of the Woman's Liberation Movement in the early 1970s, criticisms arose from feminist circles, most notably Gloria Steinem, that the new Wonder Woman did not have the strength of the original.[26] In July 1972 the original red, white, and blue costumed Amazon princess appears on the cover of *Ms.* magazine with the title, "Wonder Woman for President." That same year Marvel Comics introduced their own female hero to star in her own magazine: *The Cat* (Nov. 1972). (She later became Tigra of the West Coast Avengers.)[27] In 1973 the original Wonder Woman was brought back to comics in *Wonder Woman* #204 (Jan.–Feb. 1973) and in the Hanna-Barbera ABC animated series, *Super Friends*. Then Lynda Carter (former Miss World) made the Amazon princess a household icon to a new set of fans who may have never read her comic books. She appeared on screen in living rooms everywhere by starring in the Warner Brothers television series *Wonder Woman* (pilot episode 1975). The series helped pave the way for later screen heroines such as Xena, Warrior Princess, and Buffy the Vampire Slayer.[28]

DC Comics revamped Wonder Woman again, along with many of its flagship heroes, in the late 1980s. Writer-artist George Pérez determined to draw out religious themes in ancient Greek mythology, and so he brought the heroine back to her Greek roots. This second series of *Wonder Woman* sold well. In the 1990s the Amazon princess played prominently in the new JLA (*Justice League of America* #1; Jan. 1997) and in Mark Waid and Alex Ross's tale, *Kingdom Come*. Lately, she has come to life to a new generation of television viewers in the extremely popular animated version of the Justice League. She remains a cultural icon of superhero femininity.

Mythological and Biblical Legacy: The Superhero

While Wonder Woman may be the most enduring superhero empowered by the old world, she was not the first. The ancients likewise imparted their abilities to another popular hero from the Golden Age of comics—Captain Marvel. Perhaps the most recognized word related to Hebrew and Greco-Roman heroes in comic book history is Billy Batson's (or Gomer Pyle's?) famous cry "SHAZAM!" The name was originally attributed to an omniscient old man with a long beard and robe who introduced himself to young Billy in a cavern. He claimed that for 3,000 years he had been fighting the forces of evil, but now, due to his great age, he was passing on his powers to the boy. From now on whenever Billy would cry "SHAZAM!" a bolt of lightning flashed and he would be transformed into Earth's "mightiest mortal," Captain Marvel.

Fawcett Publication first introduced Captain Marvel in *Whiz Comics* (Feb. 1940) and he went on to become the Golden Age of comic's best-selling superhero. The "Big Red Cheese" also introduced characters such as Captain Marvel Jr. and Mary Marvel, and he revived again in the 1970s with DC Comics and his own television program on CBS entitled "Shazam!" (starring Michael Gray and John Davey). The magical word stood for an acrostic related to six famous gods or persons, one from the Hebrew Bible (Solomon) and five from Greco-Roman myths. Captain Marvel now possessed their powers:

Solomon: wisdom
Hercules: strength
Atlas: stamina
Zeus: power
Achilles: courage
Mercury: speed

Before he was granted all this power, little Billy had to pass through "The Seven Deadly Enemies of Man," which mimicked Dante's Seven Deadly Sins (Pride, Greed, Envy, Selfishness, Hatred, Injustice, and Slothfulness). Regarding Captain Marvel's origin story, artist and comic historian Jim Streranko writes, "The whole affair was positively theological—one began to expect the stone tablets of Moses to turn up at any moment."[29] Steranko's observation of the Captain Marvel myth raises a crucial point. There is great value in studying ancient source traditions in relation to heroes, and frequently the theological underpinnings of those traditions are inseparable from the content. Incredible gifts and wisdom are given by superbeings, whether gods of the Greek pantheon or Yahweh, the God of the Bible. The televised version of Captain Marvel emphasized this aspect. Before Billy would enter a time of conflict, the ancients (from whom he derived his powers) always gave him advice, similar to Athena counseling Hercules or God empowering Samson with his Spirit before the battle. The hero who receives the gift finds his or her source of strength through the gift giver. The hero must show himself/herself worthy of such blessing; hence, grace goes hand in hand with testings and temptation. This story line is ancient, reworked innumerable ways, but always fascinating. The amazing powers of superheroes like Wonder Woman and Captain Marvel draw our attention to this timeless wisdom. The influence of Greco-Roman mythological and biblical heroes persists to this day and is alive and well in the superhero genre.

Notes

[1] Jim Steranko, *The Steranko History of Comics Volume 1* (Reading, Penn.: Supergraphics Publication, 1970), 39.

[2] While there are a number of ancient stories and folklore about people returning from the dead, N. T. Wright points out important differences between such accounts and the resurrection of Jesus Christ. Many of the revived people, for instance, presumably come back to life only to eventually die again. This is not the same thing as a resurrection. See N. T. Wright, *Resurrection of the Son the of God* (Minneapolis: Fortress Press, 2003), 32–84.

[3] John Gray, *Joshua, Judges, Ruth* (Grand Rapids: Eerdmans, 1986), 221. For a similar view, though not quite so harsh, see J. Clinton McCann, *Judges* (Louisville, Ky.: Westminster John Knox, 2002), 103–9.

[4] Victor H. Matthews, *Judges and Ruth* (Cambridge: Cambridge University Press, 2004), 137; see also pp. 140, 144–45.

[5] Barry G. Webb, *The Book of the Judges: An Integrated Reading* (Sheffield: JSOT Press, 1987), 168–69.

[6] John Gray, *Joshua, Judges, Ruth*, 220.

[7] Les Daniels, *Wonder Woman: The Complete History* (San Francisco: Chronicle Books, 2000), 22.

[8] Daniels, *Wonder Woman,* 23.

[9] Cf. Danny Fingeroth, *Superman on the Couch* (New York: Continuum, 2004), 85. In the Genesis story, Adam was created from the dust of the earth while Eve was later created from Adam's rib (Genesis 2).

[10] In the second series of *Wonder Woman* #1 (Feb. 1987), she is given power and strength by Demeter, beauty and love by Aphrodite, wisdom by Athena, hunting skills and connection with animals by Artemis, speed and flight by Hermes, and by Hestia "fire—that it may open men's hearts to her" (1:25).

[11] In "War of the Gods" (*Wonder Woman* #58–61; 1991), for instance, Circe causes conflict between Earth's various pantheons, in the hope that the gods will eliminate each other.

[12] Published in *Wonder Woman* #171–77 (August 2001–March 2002). Phil Jimenez, Travis Moore, Brandon Badeaux, Andy Lanning *Paradise Found* (New York: DC Comics, 2003).

[13] Phil Jimenez, et al., *Paradise,* 60.

[14] It is also interesting that the first victim of Circe's spell, the Green Lantern, is turned into a stag. Shortly before meeting Circe, Odysseus kills a stag (*Od.* 10.165–70).

[15] Jimenez, *Paradise,* 96.

[16] Jimenez, *Paradise,* 158–59.

[17] Jimenez, *Paradise,* 69.

[18] Originally published as *Wonder Woman* #164–67, January–April 2001. Phil Jimenez, J. M. DeMatteis, Andy Lanning, *Gods of Gotham* (New York: DC Comics, 2001).

[19] Jimenez, *Gods,* 35.

[20] Jimenez, *Gods,* 10, 90. Faith is a negative force as well as a positive one in this story, depending on the purpose in which it is used and the object upon which it is exercised. See pp. 5, 10, 13, 89.

[21] Jimenez, *Gods,* 28.

[22] Jimenez, *Gods,* 37.

[23] This is not to say that Wonder Woman does not belong to any superhero teams; in fact, she is an important member of the Justice League, and before that she belonged to the Justice Society. Although *All Star Comics* covered the Justice Society, Wonder Woman's debut in the comic was first as a solo hero.

[24] E.g., *Wonder Woman* #96 (1958); cf. Francinne Valcour, "From Defending Democracy to Defending Domesticity: Wonder Woman in the 1950s." Paper presented at the Popular Culture Conference, San Antonio, Tex., April, 2004.

[25] Les Daniels, *DC Comics: A Celebration of the World's Favorite Comic Book Heroes* (New York: Billboard Books, 2003), 156.

[26] Daniels, *Wonder Woman,* 125–32; Daniels, *DC Comics,* 156.

[27] The Cat's own comic lasted only four issues. A couple of years earlier than the Cat, the Avenger's Black Widow went solo as a female hero and temporarily co-starred in *Amazing Adventures* #1–8 (1970–71).

28 And let us not forget cartoon heroines for younger audiences, such as the Powerpuff Girls and Kim Possible.
[29] Jim Steranko, *The Steranko History of Comics Vol. 2* (Reading, Penn.: Supergraphics Publication, 1972), 7.

Recommended Resources

Beatty, Scott, and Roger Stewart. *Wonder Woman: The Ultimate Guide to the Amazon Princess*. New York: DK Publishing, 2003.

Corley, Sarah V. "Women in the Comics." *Studies in Popular Culture* 5 (1982): 61–71.

Coulson, Juanita. "Of (Super) Human Bondage." Pages 228–55 in *The Comic-Book Book*. Edited by Don Thompson and Dick Lupoff. 2nd ed. Carlstadt, N.J.: Rainbow Books/Krause Publications, 1998.

Croal, N'Gai, and Jane Hughes. "Lara Croft, the Bit Girl." Pages 761–65 in *Signs of Life in the U.S.A.: Readings on Popular Culture for Writers*. ed. Sonia Maasik and Jack Solomon. Boston: Bedford/St. Martin's, 2003.

Daniels, Les, and Chip Kidd. *Wonder Woman: The Complete History*. San Francisco: Chronicle Books, 2000.

Horn, Maurice. *Women in the Comics*. New York/London: Chelsea House Publishers, 1977.

Jimenez, Phil, Travis Moore, Brandon Badeaux, and Andy Lanning. *Paradise Found*. New York: DC Comics, 2003.

Lay, Carol. *Wonder Woman: Mythos*. New York/London: Simon and Schuster, 2003.

Lee, Stan. *The Superhero Women*. New York: Simon & Schuster, 1977.

Marsh, Jackie. "'But I Want to Fly Too!': Girls and Superhero Play in the Infant Room." *Gender & Education* 12/2 (June 2000): 209-220.

Mavromataki, Maria. *Greek Mythology and Religion: Cosmogony, the Gods, Religious Customs, the Heroes*. Athens: Haïtalis, 1997.

McCann, J. Clinton. *Judges*. Interpretation, a Bible Commentary. Louisville, Ky.: Westminster John Knox Press, 2002.

Nock, A. D. "The Cult of Heroes." *Harvard Theological Review* 37 (1944): 141–74.

Pérez, George, Greg Potter, Len Wein, and Bruce Patterson. *Wonder Woman: Gods and Mortals*. New York: DC Comics, 2004.

Reynolds, Richard. *Super Heroes: A Modern Mythology*. Studies in Popular Culture. Jackson: University Press of Mississippi, 1994.

Robbins, Trina. *From Girls to Grrrlz: A History of Women's Comics from Teens to Zines*. San Francisco: Chronicle Books, 1999.

Robbins, Trina. *The Great Women Superheroes*. Northampton, Mass.: Kitchen Sink Press, 1996.

Robinson, Lillian S. *Wonder Women: Feminisms and Superheroes*. New York: Routledge, 2004.

Smith, Matthew J. "The Tyranny of the Melting Pot Metaphor: Wonder Woman as the Americanized Immigrant." In *Comics & Ideology*. ed. Matthew P. McAllister, Edward H. Sewell, and Ian Gordon. New York: Peter Lang Publishing, 2001.

Wood, Susan. *The Poison Maiden and the Great Bitch: Female Stereotypes in Marvel Superhero Comics*. San Bernardino, Calif.: R. Reginald/Borgo Press, 1989.

Valcour, Francinne. "From Defending Democracy to Defending Domesticity: Wonder Woman in the 1950s." Paper presented at the Popular Culture Conference; San Antonio, Tex.: April 2004.

4
"Okay, Axis, Here We Come!" Captain America and the Superhero Teams from World War II and the Cold War

Robert G. Weiner

The Golden Age of comics lasted roughly from the creation of Superman in 1938 to Fredric Wertham's crusade against comics in the mid-1950s. Significant during this time is that the West faced the perils of World War II and the Cold War. Comic books were a big business during the Allies' invasion, and even though some adults thought the magazines just for children, others became fans as well. Thousands of copies of *Superman*, *Batman*, *Captain America*, and *Captain Marvel*, among numerous titles, were shipped to Allied soldiers overseas; service personnel could transport comics easily from place to place. The military appetite for comics was huge. Illustrated stories about hero exploits helped the soldiers get over their boredom during periods of inactivity, and many of the four-color characters fought the same enemy as the servicemen. The superheroes served as tremendous morale boosters. Much could be unpackaged about the views expressed in comics toward Adolph Hitler, Hideki Tojo, the Nazis, Japan, communists, and others perceived as enemies to the Allies and the West during this era. At the same time, the birth of the atomic bomb and radiation posed new threats to the world. As well, many Judeo-Christian allegories can be derived from reading specific comic books. We will explore these facets in this chapter.[1]

Marvel is no stranger to publishing comics with a Judeo-Christian point of view. During the 1980s, the company published comics based on the lives of Saint Francis of Assisi, Pope John Paul II, and Mother Teresa. In the 1990s Marvel teamed up with Christian publisher Thomas-Nelson books for *The Easter Story*, *The Life of Christ* and adaptations of several Christian literary classics, including John Bunyan's *Pilgrim's Progress* and C. S. Lewis's *Screwtape Letters*. Marvel even created a Christian superhero comic book called *Illuminator*. While these comics varied in quality, Marvel was willing to express traditional Judeo-Christian theological values in its products.

Moreover heroes in the Marvel Universe sometimes profess religious beliefs. Kitty Pryde from the X-Men is Jewish and her Jewish creator Chris Claremont designed her so.[2] The Fantastic Four's most popular member, the Thing (Ben Grimm), has recently come to grips with his Judaic heritage,[3] and the X-Men's Nightcrawler (Kurt Wagner) is a devout Christian.[4] Marvel has never shied away from using the dark spiritual side in their characters either: Mephisto, Dracula, and the Son of Satan.[5] In fact, many of the comic creators were Jewish. They, along with other comic creators, naturally borrowed concepts from their religious and social upbringing when creating heroes. Arie Kaplan from a series in *Reform Judaism* opines that Jews practically created the comics industry.[6]

Several issues from the Silver Age *Strange Tales* #174, 176–177 featured Golem, the supernaturally endowed protector-servant made of clay from Jewish folklore. The Golem later teamed up with the Fantastic Four's the Thing in *Marvel Two-In-One* #11 (1975). Rabbi Loew conceived this legendary creature from clay during the 1500s to help the Jewish community of Prague against anti-Semitism. We can observe parallels between Superman, Captain America, and other heroes with the medieval folklore of the Golem. They are designed to see justice throughout the world, and they serve humanity, just as the Golem was designed to serve the Jews.[7]

Because a number of comic book creators were Jewish Americans, they seemed far more sensitive to the discrimination and atrocities committed against the Jewish people during the 1930s before the United States entered the Second World War. At times, this sensitivity showed up in the comic books—American superheroes were fighting Hitler even before America entered World War II. By 1941 Hitler was already despised by more than half the world and comics reflected a wave of patriotism with titles like *USA Comics, Military Comics, All American Comics, United States Marines,* and *Wings Comics.* A plethora of army comics inundated the market during World War II and the Cold War eras to highlight battles and promote patriotism: *Blackhawk, Our Army at War, Our Fighting Forces, Star Spangled War Stories, All-American Men of War, G. I. Combat, Combat Kelly, Sgt. Rock,* and *Sgt. Fury and His Howling Commandos.* There were also a number of kid-gang comics where youngsters fought criminals or Axis foes: *The Boy Commandos, Tough Kid Squad,* and the Newsboy Legion. A line of patriotic heroes included the Guardian, the Shield, Miss America, the Patriot, Blue Diamond, the Star-Spangled Kid, the Seven Soldiers of Victory, and numerous others. DC and Timely (Marvel) also made their flagship superheroes go to war. Captain America was the most famous super soldier to take on the Axis powers, and he along with other superheroes teamed up for the big battle. The Young Allies was one such team, and the All Winners Squad, the Invaders, and Liberty Legion each echo the same patriotic ideology.[8] DC Comics' Justice Society of America consisted of a group of popular Golden Age heroes who worked as a team against enemies abroad and spies within.

Comic readers in the Golden Age knew who the enemy was, as DC Comics' Superman, Batman, and Robin promoted War Bonds, battled the Axis powers, and instructed kids how to conserve material goods to help soldiers overseas. Fawcett Publications' Captain Marvel battled Captain Nazi, and Timely (Marvel) publications added dime for dime money that fans contributed to the War Department.[9] Americans felt good about buying these comics and taking part in the adventures of the fictional patriots.[10] We will now consider some of the main superheroes and groups during this unique period in comic book history.

By Land, Air, and Sea: Captain America, the Human Torch, and the Sub-Mariner Go to War

While the United States did not actually declare war until the end of 1941, comic books anticipated their entry into World War II months earlier. Captain America's first issue, dated March 1941, displayed a cover in which the patriotic hero punches Adolph Hitler. In many people's minds the Nazis already personified evil.

Joe Simon and Jack Kirby created Captain America for Marvel, a superhero that symbolized the ideology of liberty, justice, and patriotism. Jack Kirby once remarked, "Captain America was created for a time that needed noble figures."[11] Young Steve Rogers proved unfit for army duty because of his scrawny and weak physique. He thus volunteered for a top-secret military program where he drank a "super soldier" potion and transformed into the perfect fighting soldier. Unfortunately a Nazi spy infiltrated this event and killed Professor Reinstein (similar to Albert Einstein), the inventor of the formula, before he could write down its contents, and so Rogers, alias Captain America, becomes a unique fighting soldier. Captain America was the first hero that reflected a definite political agenda according to his co-creator, Joe Simon. At the beginning of 1941, while other heroes fought mobsters, evil scientists, or aliens, Simon and Kirby draped their hero in a costume that looked like the American flag, complete with a matching shield. They portrayed him fighting an actual rather than fictional enemy, thus adding realism to their stories. The following year many other American comic companies followed suit and had their heroes fighting for the United States. The Axis powers in many of these comics were portrayed with ethnic stereotypes and as bumbling fools with thick accents.[12] The irony was self-evident. Captain America and the Human Torch looked much more the part of the Master Aryan man of superior stature, while Hitler and his cohorts looked almost "sub-human." These idiotic portrayals helped reassure Allied soldiers who read the comics that the enemy was truly beatable.

Although Captain America battled a real enemy, his arch-nemesis the Red Skull was fictional. As the patriotic superhero represented all that was good, so the Red Skull became the embodiment of evil with his red color symbolizing the devil, his skull face representing death, and his Nazi emblem signifying racism and fascism. Years later it would turn out that he was even responsible for the death of Peter Parker's real parents (*Amazing Spider-Man Annual* #5; 1968).

Captain America Comics quickly became the most popular title for Timely (Marvel). Steve Rogers in his "civilian" guise became a private in the army. He gained a kid sidekick in the first issue with the camp mascot, Bucky Barnes. The very first issue contained an advertisement asking people to join the "Sentinels of Liberty" club to assist "Captain America in his wars against spies in the U.S.A." Apparently not everyone was thrilled about Captain America and the Sentinels of Liberty or enjoyed the treatment of the Führer as a blundering idiot who deserved to be beaten by the likes of a hero costumed with an American flag. Timely comics received hate mail, death threats, obscene telephone calls, and people threatening to kill Captain America and his writers. Strange people starting hanging around the Timely office in New York and slogans like "Death to the Jews" were heard. It got so bad that employees feared leaving for lunch, and so the police came out to patrol the halls and offices.[13]

Captain America aside, the other two big stars of Timely's Golden Age were the Sub Mariner and the Human Torch. Both of them premiered, along with Ka-Zar and the Angel, in Timely's first comic book entitled *Marvel Comics* #1 (October 1939).

Carl Burgos's original Human Torch appears on the cover issue. The origin tale has Professor Phineas T. Horton creating the hero as a synthetic person or android. When oxygen came into contact with the android's body, Horton's creation accidentally burst into flames. Eventually the android learned to control his fiery capabilities and attempted to blend in with humanity. He adopted the name Jim Hammond and worked for the New York police department before turning into a full-time superhero. Despite not actually being human, the Torch was in many ways very human, possessing strong emotions toward women and friends.[14] He joined the fight against the Axis powers.

Bill Everett created the Sub-Mariner, Prince Namor—a hero with pointy ears and winged ankles who lives undersea. On a 1920 expedition to the Antarctic, Namor's future father, Captain Leonard McKenzie, inadvertently bombed the undersea kingdom of the blue-skinned race of "sub-mariners." Namor's mother, Fen, spied on the expedition and fell in love with the captain. They got married before he died in an ensuing battle between the sub-mariners and humans. Because Prince Namor is hybrid human/sub-mariner, he possesses great strength, and in water he becomes nearly invulnerable; his Silver Age battles demonstrate that he can hold his own against Marvel heavyweights like the Hulk, the Thing, and Iron Man. Namor's name means "Avenging Son,"[15] but spelled backwards it reads "Roman." Classic literature's influence on the character is seen more clearly in the Silver Age: Namor is revealed to be a worshiper of Neptune and his kingdom is set in Atlantis under the Atlantic Ocean.[16]

The Sub-Mariner is one of the first genuine anti-heroes. His relationship with humans has always been filled with tension and uneasiness. He holds the human race responsible for poisoning the ocean with garbage and conducting attacks on his people.[17] Because he frequently loses his temper, often acting more out of emotion than logic, it comes as no surprise that he fights with humans quite frequently. When the Nazis started to deliberately destroy his underwater home, Namor answers Winston Churchill's call to help in the War against the Axis powers.

The first meeting between the Human Torch and the Sub-Mariner was not amicable. Fire and water make for odd bed-fellows, and the early Timely (Marvel) fans loved seeing their favorite heroes fight. The Torch and Namor became enemies and fought against each other in what many consider one of the greatest battles of all time: *The Human Torch* #5 (1941). Both of them come out about even, and they eventually form an uneasy relationship. They team up against the Nazis for the first time in *Marvel Mystery* #17 (1941; reprinted in *Invaders* #24).

The Timely Team-Up: Young Allies

Like *Captain America Comics*, Simon and Kirby created *Young Allies Comics*, which starred two kid heroes: Bucky, who was Captain America's ward, and Toro, the only youngster of the group with superpowers. Originally the sidekick for the Human Torch, Toro was born into a happy family until a train wreck took the lives of his parents. Apparently a mutant, he learned of his fire tolerating power in the presence of a circus leader and became an attraction with the traveling show until the Human Torch adopted him as his legal guardian. The Torch functions as a surrogate father to Toro; the latter referring to him as "Pappy."[18] Four everyday kids joined the two heroes: Knuckles (the tough guy); Tubby (the fat kid); Whitewash (the [politically incorrect] stereotyped Negro); and Jeff (the brainy youth). All the Young Allies were members of the Liberty Club with Bucky as its leader. The adolescent team resembled the Dead End Kids format and movie programs like *The Bowery Boys*, *East Side Kids*, and *Our Gang*/the Little Rascals. Simon himself said the idea came from the "juvenile novels about the Boy Allies he read in his youth."[19]

In the summer of 1941, the front cover of the premiere issue shows Bucky slugging the Red Skull, who collides into Hitler from the force of the blow. The Young Allies aid Agent X and Agent Zero, who have information vital to British intelligence. The Nazis want this information and send the Red Skull to kidnap Agent Zero. The British agents are ambushed by Nazis and taken prisoners. Bucky finds the passageway to the secret Nazi hideout through a graveyard, but when the Red Skull discovers the intrusion, he captures the Young Allies and nearly chokes Bucky to death in his rage. The Red Skull tells his captives, "I didn't kill you brats because I want you to witness how I torture the code message out of Agent Zero." In the end Whitewash comes to the rescue when he inadvertently pulls a lever, which frees them, but Agent X is shot as the Skull takes Agent Zero. The Young Allies promise Agent X, as he takes his dying breath, to save Agent Zero, who has the special code to save the world. Bucky rallies the rest of the Allies by saying, "Young Allies are you ready to do your duty for America and Civilization?" Everyone agrees as Toro yells "On to Berlin" (*Young Allies* #1; 1941). No doubt the comic book suggests that America needed to get more involved in the War.

In the adventures that follow, the Young Allies travel all the way to Europe. They stow away on a ship and save it from being blown up by a Nazi spy who is tailing them. As they end up in France, Tubby is upset that the place is "crawlin' with foreigners." They eventually find their way to Berlin where Hitler unthinkingly pats them on their heads during a rally stating, "my my vot nice chermun boyz."[20] When the Skull finds out that the Young Allies came to Berlin, he captures and places them in solitary confinement intending to starve them to death. With Toro's help, however, they manage to escape so that the young team ends up at the Russian front. They are arrested for listening to foreign radio blasts and sent to Siberia. Even though Russia was part of Allied Europe, Stalin is portrayed as a ruthless dictator, foreshadowing the Cold War to come.

At the Sentinels of Liberty clubhouse, Agent Zero leaves for another mission with the Young Allies not far behind, having escaped Siberia. The Red Skull captures them again but not before Jeff manages to transmit a message for help. While the Red Skull is trying to get the secret code from Agent Zero by threatening to blind him with a hot iron, the Young Allies escape. With the help of Captain America and the Human Torch, they save the agent (who turns out to be a woman). The much-valued code can now be given to all the free capitals of the world so that democracy can prevail. The end panel of the comic admonishes its readers to "rout the spies and saboteurs who overrun our nation" and urges both male and female readers to guard against any "dictatorship [that] enslaves men abroad and crushes their freedom of speech and worship...."[21] The *Young Allies* managed to run at least twenty issues of their own comic and had additional stories in Timely titles such as *Kid Komix, Amazing, Mystic,* and *Marvel Mystery Comics.*

Cold War Superhero Teams and the All Winners Squad

Just like the *Young Allies* comic book, *All Winners Comics* was first published in the summer of 1941. It frequently featured Timely's big three: the Human Torch, Sub-Mariner, and Captain America. As with many comics of that time, *All Winners* compiled various stories in an anthology format. None of them actually featured all three superheroes working together as a team until *All Winners* #19 (Fall 1946). Batman co-creator Bill Finger scripted the All Winners Squad that appeared in this issue: Captain America, the Human Torch, the Sub-Mariner, Bucky, Toro, and two lesser known heroes, Miss America and the Whizzer. Miss America started out as a backup heroine, produced by Otto Binder in *Marvel Comics* #49 (November 1943). She could fly, possessed a sixth sense that warned her of impending danger, and chased former Nazis stirring up trouble. In addition to joining the All Winners Squad, she teamed up with the Liberty Legion in the Marvel Universe. Her civilian name was Madeline Joyce and she was the longest running superheroine in Marvel comics during the 1940s. She gained her powers during a storm when she was struck with an electrical charge.[22] The Whizzer, Bob Frank, suffered a bite from a cobra during an expedition in Africa. His father gave him a transfusion with the blood of a mongoose that had killed the cobra! As an unrealistic result, Bob Frank gained super speed. The Whizzer was sort of a "low rent" version of the Flash. He and Miss America fell in love and eventually got married. They both were occasionally resurrected in the pages of *The Avengers*, believing their children were the Scarlet Witch and Quicksilver.

World War II ended one year before the All Winners Squad's formation, but the world faced new perils with the budding Cold War. "Atomic" became a mass culture phrase referring to both the immense power of the bomb and the energy that would hopefully transform the world for the better. According to historian William Savage, to many in America, "The Bomb was clear evidence that God was on our side. His gift ranked right up there with the one involving His only begotten Son."[23] Some Americans equated the bomb's power with that of God or Jesus—songs such as "Jesus Hits Like an Atom Bomb" (1949) by Louis Blanchard, and the Louvin Brothers' "Great Atomic Power" (1952), helped popularize this notion. The A-bomb was made by the hand of God, as expressed in Hawkshaw Hawkins' "When They Found Atomic Power" (1946).[24] Many Americans believed that as long as they controlled the atomic cards, the world would remain a safer, better place. However, severe tensions arose with the Soviet Union as the ever-increasing "red menace" of communist power that threatened American supremacy.

With this historical backdrop the mission of the All Winners Squad was to stop spies and saboteurs such as the master criminal ISBA plotting to take over the world. When members of the Squad decipher ISBA's code, they figure out that it stands for the "Atomic Age"—ISBA's main goal was to steal the atomic bomb. Just in the nick of time, with ISBA inside the atom smasher vacuum tube, the All Winners Squad arrives in full force to stop him. After capturing the culprit, Captain America makes a speech that sums up the sentiment of the time:

> Dictators! We've had enough of them! Atomic Power must be used for peace not wars. It must be used to make life better for all people. The coming Atomic Age is not for one man; it is for the common man for all mankind… (*All Winners Comics* 19; Fall 1946)

The subtext implies that atomic power is good for all democracies but not good for dictators like Stalin. The threat no longer involves Nazis but anyone who commands nuclear power for conquering ends. Comic book superheroes faced a new menace, though not as obvious as the Axis powers.

In comic books the fear of radiation as a result of atomic power gone wrong grew into a major subplot from the late 1940s to the early 1960s. While Captain America turned his gaze against the communists, Superman finally met his match with an alien rock from his home planet called kryptonite that emitted radiation, calling to mind the radiation of an A-bomb. Later the Silver Age Marvel heroes such as the Fantastic Four, Hulk, Spider-Man, and the X-Men all derived their origins as a result of some kind of radiation.[25] When Stan Lee and Jack Kirby created the X-Men in 1963, mutants were called Children of the Atom because of mutations occurring in experiments with radioactive materials like radium, nuclear fission, and the development of the bomb in the twentieth century.

In the next All Winners Squad story (*All Winners* #21; Winter 1946), Captain America tells the Squad about a villain named Future Man. He came from one million A.D. to conquer the twentieth-century world and possess its rich resources. His own future world had become dry and barely habitable, apparently due from some future dictator using the A-bomb. When the Squad confronts Future Man, the Human Torch and Toro put out an atomic fire started by the villain. Future Man then threatens to bring neutronic bombs from the future, but Captain America tricks him by getting the villain to travel into the past indefinitely. The Squad broke up after this tryst.

The Human Torch, Captain America, and Sub-Mariner continued in their respective magazines until the latter part of 1949. By then Horror and Science Fiction comics were outselling the superheroes. This trend continued throughout the 1950s. *Captain America Comics* became *Captain America's Weird Tales* with issue 74, and the series ended shortly thereafter. In 1954 all three heroes revived again to become defenders of freedom by fighting communists. Captain America was now known as a "Commie Smasher." These stories failed to generate much interest, and so the comic book heroes quietly died again, while at the same time Frederic Wertham's crusade against comics was in full bloom.

In the Silver Age of comics, however, atomic angst and communist adversaries would resurface with a vengeance among a new set of superheroes facing the Cold War. The Fantastic Four became superheroes when inundated with space radiation. As Americans they attempted the risky space flight in order to beat the Soviets into space (*Fantastic Four* #1; 1961). Bruce Banner became the Hulk as a result of radiation from a gamma bomb test gone wrong. The villain in this origin story? A Soviet spy named Igor had infiltrated the test sight (*The Incredible Hulk* #1; 1962). The rich playboy inventor Tony Stark became a superhero after stepping on a "booby trap" in Southeast Asia (Vietnam). A piece of shrapnel lodged near his heart. At the time, Stark was assisting soldiers with sophisticated weapons against the "Reds." When captured by the Vietcong, he was forced to build weapons for Wong Chu's camp. This allowed him time to make a pacemaker for himself out of an iron chest piece. He created an entire iron suit, broke free from his captors, and became Iron Man (*Tales to Astonish* #39; 1963). His nemeses were Wong Chu's diabolical connection, the Mandarin; and Titanium Man, a Soviet "Iron Man."[26] In the original Iron Man series, Soviet premier Kruschev is seen conspiring with Stark's enemy, the Crimson Dynamo (*Tales of Suspense* #46; 1963).

In *The Avengers* #4 (March 1964) the newly formed Marvel team (consisting of Iron Man, Thor, the Wasp, Ant-Man/Giant Man, and sometimes the Hulk) find the body of Captain America frozen in ice but very much alive after thawing out. As the story goes, Baron Zemo killed Bucky toward the end of World War II and Cap was put into suspended animation shortly thereafter. Older comic fans noticed a discrepancy: whatever happened to the "commie smasher" Captain America of 1946 to 1954? According to Marvel historian George Olshvesky, there were several distinct Captain Americas and Buckys. Captain America in the All Winners Squad reportedly turned out to be the Spirit of '76 from the British superhero group called the Crusaders (he was the only American in the group). The Spirit of '76 was eventually killed in a battle fighting an android. Then the Patriot, a former member of the Liberty Legion, became another Captain America. The superhero who fought the communists in the 1950s was yet another person whose real name is classified (as is this version's Bucky). He continued to go after communists, but became too radical (a superhero version of Senator Joseph McCarthy seeing communists everywhere); hence, the U.S. government declared this Cap and Bucky insane, placing them in cryogenic storage. In a recent graphic novel the "real" Captain America discovers that the U.S. government may have actually had him put into suspended animation on ice because they felt that he might have argued against the bombing of Japan. [27] Captain America of the Silver Age seems to be a bit disillusioned about the U.S. government.

The Invaders: World War II in Retrospect

In 1975 Marvel writer/editor Roy Thomas created the Invaders, but the idea had been brewing in his mind for years. In the mid-1960s, Thomas was instrumental in getting old superhero stories reprinted within titles such as *Fantasy Masterpieces*, *Marvel Super Heroes*, and *Marvel Tales*. He had a "concept involving super-heroes of World War Two," even though the war had been over for decades, and so he put together the core members of the Invaders, a tribute to the All Winners Squad. Captain America, Sub-Mariner, the Human Torch, and the sidekicks Bucky and Toro reunited to fight Axis Europe, with the initial cover echoing *All Winners Comics* #4 (*Giant Size Invaders* #1).[28] *The Invaders* series continued for 41 issues and one *Invaders Annual* before its cancellation in 1979. The stories take place during 1942, after the United States entered the war. In these stories, British Prime Minister Winston Churchill urged that Invaders to band together to help the Allies. He also gives them their name. Their battle cry becomes "Okay, Axis Here We Come!" which, according to Roy Thomas, was a slogan Timely occasionally used in various books.[29]

While writing the Invaders, Thomas knew with hindsight that sensitive issues related to World War II needed to be addressed, such as the concentration camps and the holocaust. The Invaders go to Warsaw, Poland, in search of Professor Goldstein's brother Jacob, a Jewish rabbi. The Axis coerced Professor Goldstein to do sabotage for them; if he refused, they would kill his brother. Issue 12 describes in historic detail the pogroms against the Jews starting in 1939. The Invaders find Goldstein's brother alive and running a bookstore. They try to get Jacob to come back with them to England, but he refuses. As they prod him about fighting back against the Nazis, Jacob replies, "Our only hope is in the patient submission to the will of God...." He tells them, "Centuries ago in Prague there was a creature which could have overcome our hated conqueror.... He was called the Golem.... [made] of living clay" (*Invaders* #12:23).

As Captain America is about to forcibly take Rabbi Jacob back to England, the Nazis attack. When the Nazis threaten some Jewish bystanders, the Invaders surrender. Jacob pleads with the Nazis to kill him instead of taking the Invaders, but rather than kill "the Jew," the Nazis are overjoyed at capturing the Allies' "greatest heroes." Jacob, using the Jewish Kabalistic texts, attempts to create a Golem to help fight the Nazis and rescue the Invaders. As he prepares the clay, almost as if God were hearing his prayers, lightning strikes the bookshop, and a hybrid Golem is born with Jacob and the clay becoming as one. The Golem rescues the Invaders from Hitler before transforming back into Jacob Goldstein. He stays in Warsaw as a protector (*Invaders* #13).

One of the most interesting stories of the whole series deals with bringing in the Asgardian god, Thor, from the Marvel Universe proper into the series in issue 32. While watching Wagner's opera, *Götterdämmerung*, Hitler comments that he "sees all the pagan pageantry... the splendor which belonged to our noble Nordic ancestors...before the spineless Christians and the hated Jew won them over to *weaker ways*." Hitler learns that with the help of a mysterious scientist, the world of Norse gods can become a reality. Through the use of a dimensional gateway, Hitler summons Thor as his champion.[30] He tries to talk Thor into fighting for the Third Reich by telling him how evil the Allies are (especially Joseph Stalin). Thor attempts to kill Stalin, whom the Invaders are asked to defend. The Invaders and Thor fight, but after Thor realizes that he was being used by the Nazis, he goes back to his dimension and wipes the Invaders' minds of his presence (*Invaders* #32:11; #33).

The Invaders gave Roy Thomas a chance to revive several obscure Golden Age Timely characters in the group called Liberty Legion. He also introduced the Kid Commandos as a tribute to the Young Allies and Boy Commandos. Thomas likewise presented the Crusaders, a British superhero team; and also Freedom's Five, a World War I superhero group that featured the hero Union Jack.[31] To keep the Marvel Universe's continuity consistent, we see the Invaders staying together after the war; not as the Invaders, but as the All Winners Squad (*What If* #4; 1977). The Nazis are portrayed in the *Invaders* quite differently than those in the original Golden Age stories. With the *Invaders* coming out thirty years after the fall of the Third Reich, Hitler and the Nazis are still ruthless and evil, but most of the buffoonery is replaced by realism. Through this comic book we observe a Jewish people protected by Golden Age superheroes and the medieval legend of Golem.

The Justice Society of America: Defenders of Democracy

The most famous World War II superhero team was the Justice Society of America (JSA). Sheldon Mayer and Gardner Fox designed the team for DC Comics under its imprint AA, or All American Comics. This became the first team that put heroes together from already existing DC titles. The Justice Society premiered in *All Star Comics* #3 (1940). Most of the stories in *All Star* followed the anthology style: The group comes together at the beginning to talk about assignments; then the members go on their own mission until the entire group comes back together again at the end. The Flash, the Spectre, the Green Lantern, the Atom, Hawkman, Sandman, Doctor Fate, and the Hourman were Justice Society's charter members. Wonder Woman joined shortly after the founding of the group. Batman, Superman, Starman, Wildcat, and Johnny Thunder also joined.

Mart Nodell and Bill Finger created the Green Lantern, alias Alan Scott. He received almost omnipotent powers when charging his ring in 24-hour intervals with the mysterious green energy from a lantern made of material from another planet (*All American Comics* #16; 1940). In the Silver Age, Hal Jordan would become the new Green Lantern (*Showcase* #22; 1959), but he ultimately turned into an apostate villain in the Third Age (*Zero Hour* series; 1994). Kyle Rayner took his place, and African-American John Stewart became another popular Green Lantern. Jerry Siegel and Bernard Baily created the Spectre beginning in *More Fun Comics* #52 (Feb. 1940). Gangsters murdered police officer Jim Corrigan and dumped his body in a river. He returned as a spirit in green cloaking and with a pasty white complexion. Like a ghost, he seemed to have unfathomable abilities, and sometimes he would scare his advocates to death. Bernard Bailey created the Hourman, alias Rex Tyler. He would swallow a pill named Miraclo, which gave him enhanced speed and the strength of ten men for one hour. The Atom, created by Bill O'Conner and Ben Flinton, was a 90-something pound weakling named Al Pratt who trained his body and became a miniature muscleman and costumed hero. Years later he gained more strength when exposed to radiation.

Gardner Fox created or co-created most of the other founding members o the JSA: Wesley Dodds, the Sandman (not to be confused with the later incarnation by Neil Gaiman), was a millionaire playboy, inventor, and CEO of a large steel corporation who uses a special "sleep" gas to bring evildoers to justice. Dr. Fate (Kent Nelson) was a junior archaeologist who reanimated Nabu, an ancient alien sorcerer. Nabu taught Nelson the mystical arts to fight his enemies. Hawkman, wealthy scientist Carter Hall, dabbled in mysticism and believed himself to be the reincarnation of Khufu, an ancient Egyptian prince. He dressed as a hawk-god and defied gravity by wearing a belt made of "ninth metal," one of his discoveries.

The Flash became the most famous superhero created by Gardner Fox. The first Flash, student Jay Garrick, accidentally inhaled fumes from the gas elements of atomic "heavy water." As a result he became the fastest man on earth, reportedly obtaining a velocity equal to the speed of light. He also possesses superhuman endurance and an energy aura that reportedly prevents him from side effects related to high speeds. He wore a red shirt and blue pants with winged boots and helmet that made him look like Greco-Roman messenger god Mercury (*Flash Comics* #1; Jan. 1940). The most memorable Flash costume, however, was red and yellow worn by the Silver Age Flash, police scientist Barry Allen (*Showcase* #4; 1956). The second Flash died sacrificing his life to destroy the Anti-Monitor's ultimate weapon in the miniseries *Crisis on Infinite Earths* (1985).[32]

By the second episode of the Justice Society (*All Star Comics* #4; March 1941) the JSA were already battling spies and saboteurs within the shores of the United States. They received a telegram to come as "patriotic Americans" to the FBI building in Washington, DC, to ferret out "Fifth Columnist" activity.[33] In the story each superhero was given a special assignment to break up organizations that were "planning ways of overthrowing America" and its freedom. When a newspaper called the *El Paso Patriot* is threatened by the "Grey Shirts" for exposing their anti-American ideology, the Sandman investigates. He confronts several Grey Shirts and explains just what the unknowing teenagers are supporting. The Sandman asks the young men to "join the army and defend America." They reply, "You showed us what dopes we were—believing the lying leader of ours." The Justice Society expose more troublemakers in the story, implying the threat of Nazi infiltration while never actually stating it. The same type of incident occurs in several other adventures—the hero exposes the group leader as a traitor to democracy and the general populace. In turn the group members do not realize they have been duped and promise to do their part to fight against spies and traitors. In *All Star* #7 (Oct.–Nov. 1941), the Justice Society raises money to help war orphans in Europe; in *All Star* #9 (Feb.–March 1942) they go to Latin America on a covert mission to weed out German and Italian spies "unofficially."

In the JSA comics Hitler tells lies to his own soldiers and lies to his public about living situations (i.e., food, religion, and weapons). He thinks of a propaganda scheme by giving Europe "something to hate... [like in Germany where] the Jews were a good subject" (*All Star Comics* #16; 1943). Hitler sends various agents into America to spread discord, setting "Gentile against Jew" and "Protestant against Catholic." With the help of young Americans who are members of the Junior Justice Society, the JSA root out the "Ratzis," making sure they get what they deserve for trying to divide America. Similar to Captain America and Bucky's Sentinels of Liberty, *All Star Comics* encouraged young readers to join the Junior Justice League where "Jew; Protestant; Gentile; Catholic...pledge to defeat...Axis propaganda...seeking to get us to fight among ourselves, so we cannot...fight...our enemies.... We are *all* Americans believing in Democracy and are resolved to do everything possible to win the war!"[34] This campaign to mobilize youth for the Junior Justice Society, and actually having the youths assist the superheroes in issue 16, not only made good business sense but also assisted in getting teenagers to join the army when they came of age.[35]

The Justice Society of America (JSA) led directly to the debut of the Justice League of America (JLA) in the *Brave and Bold* #28 (Feb.–March 1960)[36]: Superman, Batman, Wonder Woman, Green Lantern, Flash, Aquaman, and the Martian Manhunter (Jonn Jonzz) teamed up to do battle against criminals and atomic enemies in the Cold War era. The Justice League sold so well for DC Comics that competitor Martin Goodman talked with Stan Lee about making their own superhero team. Lee corroborated with Jack Kirby to produce the avant-garde for Marvel, the Fantastic Four. Both teams confirmed that the Silver Age of comics had arrived, and both persist as popular teams to this day. Many other superhero groups prospered in the Silver Age: the Legion of Superheroes (*Adventure Comics* #247; 1958), the Doom Patrol (*My Greatest Adventure* #80; 1963), and the Teen Titans (*The Brave and the Bold* #64; 1964) for DC; the Avengers (*Avengers* #1; 1963), the X-Men (*X-Men* #1; 1963), and the Defenders (*Special Marvel Edition* #1; 1971) for Marvel. In the Silver Age, superhero teams became booming business as the Cold War continued; in fact, the Silver Age collapsed before the Berlin Wall did.

Conclusion

The Justice Society of America, the Young Allies, the All Winners Squad, Captain America, and a host of other heroes were all products of the Golden Age of comics that promoted American and Allied sentiments during World War II and the Cold War. Superhero teams participated in winning the war against the personification of evil for the United States and most of the western world at that time: Hitler, Nazism, the Axis, and communist powers. Hitler himself was considered by some as the Anti-Christ or a satanic incarnation.[37] The superheroes and teams functioned as the world's saviors, defending freedom and democracy. Because America and its companions were thought to be on "God's side," comic readers could trust that the Allies would prevail in war. The Golem of Jewish folklore had become the twentieth-century superhero that now protected both Jews and Gentiles against a common enemy. One could also argue that these noble heroes resembled the Jewish messiah of apocalyptic literature coming at the end of the ages to set things right and usher the world into the kingdom of God and peace.

Notes

[1] While many comic book publishers and numerous superheroes graced the shelves of newsstands during the Golden Age, Timely (Marvel) and DC Comics have persisted in bringing to pop culture the most enduring heroes. Our focus will remain here.

[2] See Arie Kaplan, "King of Comics Part II: The Silver Age," *Reform Judaism* 32/2 (Winter 2003), 13. [Cited 15 Aug. 2004] Online: www.uahc.org/rjmag/03winter /comics.shmtl. See also the graphic novel Michael Higgins, Tom Morgan, Justin Thyme et al., *Excalibur: Weird War III* (New York: Marvel, 1990).

[3] See Mark Waid, Mike Weirgino, Karl Kesel et al, *Fantastic Four Vol. 1: Imaginauts* (New York: Marvel, 2003).

[4] Throughout Nightcrawler's tenure in the X-Men, he has always maintained his Christian outlook. At one time he was studying for the priesthood. The recent movie *X-Men 2* shows this side of the hero. Recently it has been discovered that Nightcrawler's father may have actually been Satan himself. See the graphic novel, Chuck Austen, Phillip Tan, Takeshi Miyazawa et al., *Uncanny X-Men Vol. 4: The Draco* (New York: Marvel, 2004).

[5] In fact Dracula was once worshiped mistakenly as Satan himself: cf. Steve Gerber, Marv Wolfman, Gene Colon et al., *Blade Two: Comic Adaptation* (Marvel Comics, 2002).

[6] Cf. Arie Kaplan, "Kings of Comics: How Jews Created the Comic Industry: Part I: The Golden Age," *Reform Judaism*, 32/1 (Fall 2003), 14–22, 97 [Cited 15 Aug. 2004] Online: www.uahc.org/rjmag/03fall/comics.shmtl.

[7] Cf. Kaplan. See also Michael Chabon, *The Amazing Adventures of Kavalier & Clay* (New York: Picador, 2001); Chayim Bloch, *The Golem: Legends of the Ghetto of Prague* (New York: Freedeeds Library, 1988; Micheal Rosen, *The Golem of Old Prague* (London: André Deutsch Limited, 1990). The Golem stories also resemble Mary Shelley's story of Frankenstein.

[8] Although some may regard the continuity of the Golden Age comics heroes to have no bearing on the later Marvel Universe proper, we will not make such a distinction and will consider the Golden Age as a valid source material related to the Marvel Universe. This is helpful when we examine the *Invaders*, a superhero team set in the context of World War II but created in the Silver Age.

[9] Jim Steranko, *The History of Comic Books* vol. 1 (Reading, Penn.: Supergraphics, 1970), 55.

[10] Cf. For examples of comic covers that reflect wartime patriotism in comics, see Joe Simon and Jim Simon, *The Comic Book Makers* (Lebanon, N.J.: Vanguard Productions, 2003), 44; Steranko, *History of Comic Books,* vol. 1.

[11] Joe Simon and Jim Simon, *The Comic Book Makers* (Lebanon, N.J.: Vanguard Productions, 2003), 44; Joe Simon and Jack Kirby, *Captain America: The Classic Years* vol. 1 (New York: Marvel, 1998); Ron Goulart ed., *Comics in the Golden Age*, 4 (September 1984), 4–10.

[12] Bad ethnic stereotypes prevailed even with those on the side of the Allies, as seen with African Americans such as Whitewash from the Young Allies and Asians such as Chop-Chop from Blackhawk. Unfortunately, even more recent African American heroes, such as Luke Cage, and Latino heroes, such as Skin from the X-Men spin-off Generation X, did not always escape cultural stereotyping.

[13] See Simon and Simon, Comic Book Makers, 45; Michael Chabon, *Amazing Adventures of Kavalier and Clay.*

[14] As a member of the *Invaders,* for example, he wants to give his blood to save the life of Jacqueline Fasworth (*Invaders* #11; 1976). She runs and gives Captain America a hug. The Torch is heartbroken and in a jealous rage quits the Invaders for a short time. When Toro is shot by a Nazi, the Torch burns the soldier to a smoldering cinder (*Invaders* #20; 1977); and while trying to get Toro to a doctor he declares, "If Toro dies, I'll return to Berlin and destroy Hitler even if I go down in flames with him" (*Invaders* #21).

[15] *Fantastic Four* Annual #1:2 (1963).

[16] Peter Sanderson, *Marvel Universe* (New York: Harry N. Abrams, 1996), 50.

[17] When the Sub-Mariner revived in the pages of *Fantastic Four* #4, he was appalled at the poisoning of the ocean and waged an attack on New York City.

[18] *Invaders* #22 (Nov. 1977).

[19] Ron Goulart, *The Comic Book Reader's Companion* (New York: Harper Perennial, 1993), 185.

[20] Reprinted in *Flashback Special Edition Reprint* #8 (1969), 27, 33.

[21] *Flashback Special Edition Reprint*, 34–59.

[22] See Ron Goulart, *The Comic Book Reader's Companion*: 115; Mike Benton, *The Illustrated History of Superhero Comics of the Golden Age* (Dallas: Taylor Publishing, 1992), 119.

[23] See Robert G. Weiner. "Atomic Music: Country Conservatism and Folk Discontent," *Studies in Popular Culture* (On the Culture of the American South) 19/2 (1996), 217–235; two studies which look at the impact of the atomic bomb on American culture: Bruce Franklin, *War Stars: The Superweapon and the American Imagination* (New York: Oxford University Press, 1988); and Paul Boyer, *By the Bombs Early Light: American Thought and Culture at the Dawn of the Atomic Age* (New York: Pantheon Books, 1985). For a further look at how comics were affected by the Cold War and the A-bomb, see William Savage, *Commies, Cowboys, and Jungle Queens: Comic Books and America: 1945–1954* (Hanover, N.H.: Wesleyan University Press, 1998), 15.

[24] Weiner, "Atomic Music."

[25] Toro may be the earliest mutant for the Marvel Universe. Toro's father worked with asbestos for years and his mother experimented with radium, which made them both very ill (*Invaders* #22). Even though Logan, a.k.a. Wolverine, is supposed to be the oldest X-Man and was born before Toro, there is some debate on whether he is actually a mutant. He did team up with Captain America during World War II. Cf. Bill Jemas, Joe Quesada, Paul Jenkins et al., *Origin: The True Story of Wolverine* (New York: Marvel, 2002); Jim Lee, Chris Claremont, Ann Nocenti et al., *X-Men Visionaries* (New York: Marvel, 2002).

[26] Cf. Peter Sanderson, *Marvel Universe* (New York: Harry N. Abrams, 1996), 110–12.

[27] See *What If* #4 (Aug. 1977); *Captain America* # 153–154; George Olshevsky, Tony Frutti, *The Marvel Comics Index Vol. 1. 8:A; Heroes from Tales of Suspense Book One: Captain America* (Toronto, Canada: G&T Enterprises, 1979), 4–18; Chuck Austen, John Ney Rieber, Jae Lee et al., *Captain America Vol. 3: Ice* (New York: Marvel, 2003).

[28] Roy Thomas, "Okay, Axis Here We Come—Again!" in Roy Thomas, ed., *Alter Ego: The Comic Book Artist Collection* (Raleigh, N.C.: TwoMorrows, 2001), 42–44.

[29] Thomas, 42–44; *Giant Sized Invaders*, vol. 1: 1 (June, 1975).

[30] The idea that the perfect Aryan man has roots in the Norse tradition may be quite valid considering all the pomp and pageantry of the Third Reich and fierce legends about Odin, Thor, and company. The Germans even had an auxiliary cruiser during the war called Thor: see the video *Die deutsche Wochenschau, the Weekly German Newsreel: 1943* (Chicago: International Historic Films, 1994). See also the video *Nazis: The Occult Conspiracy* (Bethesda, Md.: Discovery Channel Video, 1998); Mattias Gardell, *Gods of Blood: The Pagan Revival and White Separatism* (Durham, N.C.: Duke University Press, 2003); Cuthbert Carson Mann, *Hitler's Three Struggles: The Neo-pagan Revenge* (Evanston, Ill. : Chicago Spectrum Press, 1995);

[31] Cf. *Invaders* #5–8, 14–15, 18, 28–29; *Marvel Premiere* #29–30.

[32] There have been different versions of the Green Lantern; the Flash, the Spectre, Hawkman, the Sandman, and the Atom that have been in DC comics throughout

the years. For a more detailed explanation of the origins of these heroes, see Goulart, *The Comic Book Reader's Companion*, 9–10, 47–79, 65–66, 80–81, 83–84, 97, 151–153; Roy Thomas ed., *The All Star Companion* (Raleigh, N.C.: TwoMorrows Publishing, 2000).

[33] "Fifth Columnist" means "from within." It was used to designate any anti-American rhetoric. The term is also used for saboteurs.

[34] Roy Thomas, Gardner Fox, Sheldon Mayer et al., *All Star Comics Archive* vol. 3 (New York: DC, 1997), 238.

[35] For a detailed discussion of the Junior Justice Society of America, see Craig Delich, "Badges? We Don't Need No Stinking Badges! Unless We're Members of the Junior Justice Society of America," in Roy Thomas, *All Star Companion*, 176–181.

[36] Roy Thomas also developed the All Star Squadron in 1981, patterned after the Justice Society, to fight the Nazis. See Roy Thomas, "The Justice Society and Friends in the 1980s: From Squadron to Corporation—to Crisis," in Roy Thomas, *All Star Companion*, 198–201.

[37] For comparisons that have been made between Hitler and the Anti-Christ, see Paul Boyer, *When Time Shall Be No More: Prophecy Belief in Modern American Culture* (Cambridge, Mass.: Harvard University Press, 1992), 108, 214–16, 275; T. Mather, Ester Khubyar. *The Second Coming of the Antichrist: Adolph Hitler, the Beast from the Abyss "Whose Coming Is According to the Working of Satan"* (Mississauag, Canada: Berean Foundation, 1984).

Recommended Resources

Beatty, Scott. *The Ultimate Guide to the Justice League of America.* New York: DK Publishing, 2002.

Benton, Mike. *Superhero Comics of the Golden Age: The Illustrated History.* Dallas, Tex.: Taylor Pub.,1992.

Best, Mark T. *Secret Identities: American Masculinities and the Superhero Genre in the Fifties.* Doctoral Diss., Indiana University, 2002.

Bloch, Chayim. *The Golem: Legends of the Ghetto of Prague.* New York: Freedeeds Library, 1988.

Boyer, Paul. *By the Bombs Early Light: American Thought and Culture at the Dawn of the Atomic Age.* New York: Pantheon Books, 1985.

Brevoort, Tom, ed. *The Golden Age of Marvel Comics.* New York: Marvel Comics, 1997.

Burgos, Carl, Bill Everett, and Alex Schomburg. *Timely Presents The Human Torch.* New York: Marvel, 1999.

Chabon, Michael. *The Amazing Adventures of Kavalier and Clay.* New York: Picador, 2001.

Dixon, Chuck, Ron Marz, David Goyer. *The Justice Society Returns.* New York: DC Comics, 2003.

Feiffer, Jules. *The Great Comic Book Heroes.* New York: Bonanza, 1965.

Gold, Mike. *The Greatest 1950s Stories Ever Told.* New York: DC Comics, 1990.

Gold, Mike. *The Greatest Golden Age Stories Ever Told.* New York: DC Comics, 1990.

Goulart, Ron. *The Comic Book Reader's Companion.* New York: Harper Perennial, 1993.

Goulart, Ron. *Ron Goulart's Great History of Comic Books: The Definitive Illustrated History from the 1890s to the 1980s.* Chicago: McGraw-Hill/Contemporary Books, 1986.

Goulart, Ron. *Comic Book Culture: An Illustrated History.* Portland: Collector's Press, 2000.

Jewett, Robert, and John Shelton Lawrence. *Captain America and the Crusade Against Evil: The Dilemma of Zealous Nationalism.* Grand Rapids: Eerdmans, 2003.

Kaplan, Arie. "Kings of Comics: How Jews Created the Comic Industry: Part I: The Golden Age." *Reform Judaism,* 32/1 (Fall 2003) [Cited 15 Aug. 2004] Online: www.uahc.org/rjmag/03fall/comics.shmtl.

Kaplan, Arie. "King of Comics Part II: How Jews Created the Comic Industry: The Silver Age." *Reform Judaism* 32/2 (Fall 2003) [Cited 15 Aug. 2004] Online: www.uahc.org/rjmag/.

Pustz, Matthew J. "EC Fan-Addicts and Marvel Zombies." Pages 26–65 in *Comic Book Culture: Fanboys and True Believers.* Studies in Popular Culture. Jackson: University Press of Mississippi, 2000.

Robinson, James, and David Goyer. *JSA: Justice Be Done.* New York: DC Comics, 2000.

Savage, William. *Commies, Cowboys, and Jungle Queens: Comic Books and America: 1945–1954.* Hanover, N.H.: Wesleyan University Press, 1998.

Schelly, Bill. *The Golden Age of Comic Fandom.* Seattle: Hamster Press, 1995.

Schmidt, Peter Allon. *The History of Atomic Power and the Rise of the American Comic Book Superhero.* Master's thesis, Arizona State University, 2002.

Simon, Joe, and Jack Kirby. *Captain America: The Classic Years Volume 1.* New York: Marvel, 1998.

Simon, Joe, and Jim Simon. *The Comic Book Makers.* Lebanon, N.J.: Vanguard Productions, 2003.

Steranko, Jim. *The Steranko History of Comics.* 2 Vols. Reading, Penn.: Supergraphics, 1970.

Thomas, Roy. ed. *The All Star Companion.* Raleigh, N.C.: TwoMorrows Publishing, 2000.

Thompson, Don, Gardner Fox, and Sheldon Mayer. *All Star Comics Archive Volume 1.* New York: DC, 1991.

Thompson, Don, Richard A. Lupoff, and Dick Lupoff, eds. *All in Color for a Dime.* Iola, Wis.: Krause Publications, 1997.

Waugh, Coulton. *The Comics.* New York: Macmillan Company, 1947.

Wright, Nicky, and Joe Kubert. *The Classic Era of American Comics.* New York: McGraw-Hill/Contemporary Books, 2000.

Part Two:

Heroes from the Silver Age of Comic Books

Figure 1 The Fantastic Four was Marvel Comics' flagship superhero team during the early Silver Age. Stan Lee and Jack Kirby introduced a number of villains that became embodiments of evil, including Dr. Doom, who preceded Star Wars' Darth Vader by more than a decade (*Fantastic Four* #57; Dec. 1966; Marvel Comics; Jack Kirby [pencils] Joe Sinnott [inks]).

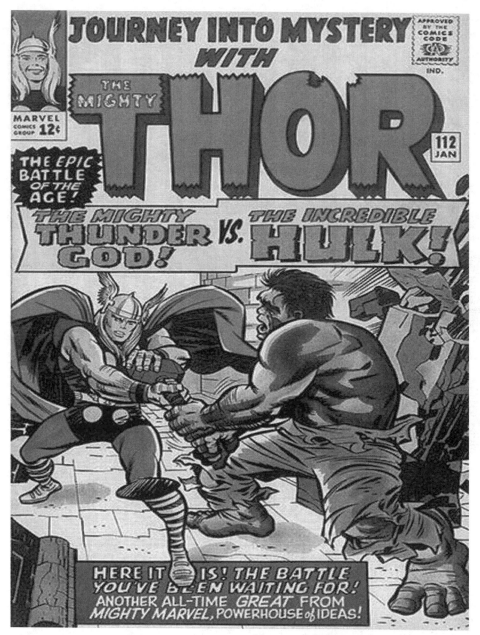

Figure 2 Stan Lee and Jack Kirby turned Thor, the mythological Norse god of thunder, into a superhero. In *Journey into Mystery* #112 he battles against another Lee–Kirby legend, the Hulk (Jan. 1965; Marvel Comics; Jack Kirby [pencils] Chic Stone [inks]). Bruce Banner struggles with inner conflicts and a monster of an alter-ego as the Hulk. His plight is a parable related to the human psyche or inner soul.

Figure 3 Peter Parker, alias Spider-Man, became a superhero because of the guilt he felt in relation to the death of his uncle, Ben Parker. After the Green Goblin murders his girlfriend, Gwen Stacy, Spider-Man almost kills the villain in a fit of rage but then realizes that he cannot cross over the moral boundary of killing his enemy (*Amazing Spider-Man* #122; June 1973; reprinted in *Marvel Tales* #99; Jan. 1979:27; Marvel Comics; Gerry Conway [script] Gil Kane [art] John Romita and T. Mortellaro [inks] Dave Hunt [colorist]).

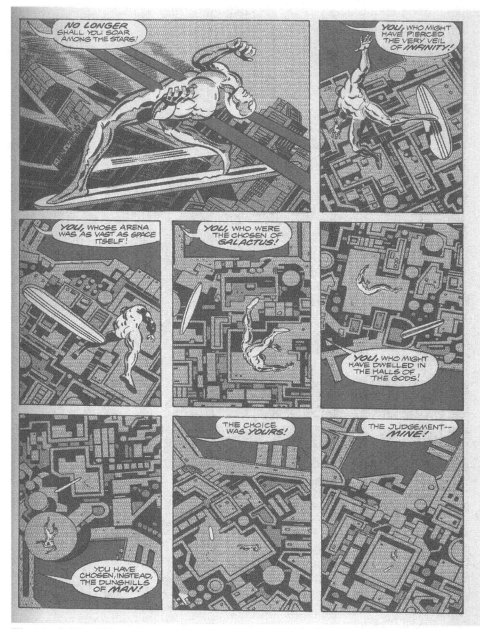

Figure 4 The Silver Surfer, a Christ-type, defends the earth against his master Galactus, who intends to devour the earth of all its energy in a doomsday tale resembling the book of Revelation. As punishment for his rebellion, Galactus takes away the Surfer's space-time flying capabilities. His descension recalls an angel falling from heaven to the earth (*The Silver Surfer* graphic novel by Stan Lee [writer] and Jack Kirby [artist]; New York: Fireside/Simon and Schuster, 1978:37).

Figure 5 Denny O'Neil and Neal Adams portrayed the Green Lantern and Green Arrow as a team that not only fought crime but also wrestled with relevant social concerns. In this issue entitled "…And Through Him Save a World!" they befriend a man resembling Jesus Christ (*Green Lantern* #89; April-May 1972; reprinted in *Green Lantern – Green Arrow* #7; Aug. 1984; DC Comics; Neal Adams, art).

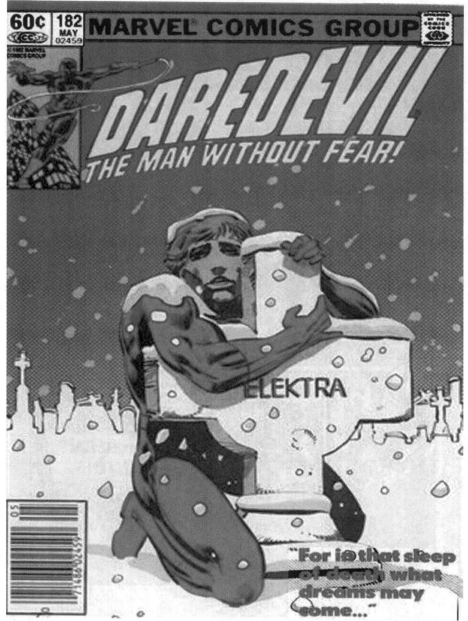

Figure 6 Frank Miller transformed Daredevil into a more realistic, religious, and yet darker hero during the late Silver Age. The comic book portrayed bleak settings and violent scenes that went beyond what was typical for the time, anticipating the Third or "Postmodern" age of comics. In this issue the blind hero grieves over his love Elektra, a heroine killed in battle against Bullseye, Daredevil's adversary (*Daredevil* #182; May, 1982; Marvel Comics; Frank Miller [pencils] Klaus Janson [inks]).

Figure 7 The X-Men gradually became an extremely popular superhero team. As mutants, the X-Men's message involves diversity and tolerance for people considered different or marginal. Magneto, another powerful mutant, becomes the X-Men's nemesis. He believes himself superior to the human race. In this graphic novel he is pictured in the background with the second X-Men team in the foreground. (*X-Men* graphic novel #5; 1982; Marvel Comics; Brent Eric Anderson [art]).

5
Gods and Fantastic Mortals:
The Superheroes of Jack Kirby

Scott Rosen

Jack Kirby has left an indelible mark on the medium of comic books. Bob Kane, who created Batman in 1939, called him "the greatest single influence in comics."[1] Comics scholar Bradford W. Wright characterized Kirby's art as "simple and direct, action-oriented and imaginative" and called him "one of the most prolific, imitated, and influential artists in the field's history."[2] He was "the master" of the ability "to delve into places both real and mythic, to leap all over the universe in needle-nosed rockets of imagination."[3] Frank Miller, who redefined Batman in 1986, emphatically assessed Kirby's importance: "Singlehandedly he developed the visual dialect, tone, and spirit of the modern superhero comic. He brought a sense of operatic drama and mythological scope to a genre that was fat, bloated, old and dying."[4]

Kirby's ability to tap into the mythic is perhaps the most salient characteristic of his work. During his long career, Kirby drew upon many religious traditions to bring a sense of awe to his creations, to elevate the lowly comic book to a cosmic scale filled with the grandeur of the gods—both old and new. In much of his voluminous output, Kirby had the uncanny ability to join the world of the divine with the world of the ordinary to create unforgettable four-color adventures that remain as classics of the genre.

Jack "King" Kirby created and co-created dozens of superheroes in a career spanning six decades. Born Jacob Kurtzberg in the predominantly Jewish Lower East Side of New York in 1917, Kirby started his career as an illustrator in 1935. Two years later Kirby met Joe Simon at Fox Comics. They forged a working alliance that lasted two decades. Together they created comic books that regularly sold millions of copies during the Golden Age of comic books. Characters like Captain America and the Young Allies for Timely Comics, the Boy Commandos and the Newsboy Legion for DC Comics, the Fly and the Shield for Archie Comics, and many others flowed from their fertile imaginations. They even created *Young Romance* (1947), the first comic book in the romance genre! But Kirby's most memorable and influential work was yet to come. In the 1960s he teamed up with Stan Lee and created a cohesive universe of comic book superheroes and villains that so revolutionized the genre that many would call the 1960s the Marvel Age of Comics. Together Lee and Kirby co-created the Fantastic Four, the Incredible Hulk, the X-Men, the Mighty Thor, and many more characters for Marvel Comics. For a decade Lee and Kirby created an unparalleled array of wondrous godlike beings, both good and evil, which still continue to populate the pages of comic books and the screens of multiplexes today. In 1970 Kirby left Marvel to work for rival DC Comics and create another crowning achievement of his long career—the Fourth World, an interrelated series of four titles containing some of Kirby's most interesting and thought-provoking work. Significantly the writing and illustration on the Fourth World comic books were not aided by his capable companions Joe Simon or Stan Lee. It was all Kirby.

The Fantastic Four: "The World's Greatest Comic Magazine!"

The Fantastic Four remains perhaps the most influential of Jack Kirby's many comic book creations. The superhero team helped define the Silver Age of comic books and paved the way for many other Marvel superheroes to follow. The caption on the cover of every issue of the *Fantastic Four*, "The World's Greatest Comic Magazine!" may not have been a pretentious claim during the years that Lee and Kirby collaborated on the series. The combination of interesting storylines with Kirby's innovative artwork at its prime (especially during the creative years of 1965–69) leaves the reader amazed at the pre-digital quality packed into a comic book that sold for only 12 cents an issue!

Like many characters of Marvel's early years, the Fantastic Four received their superpowers as the result of an accident. Peter Parker became Spider-Man as the result of a bite from a spider which was exposed to radiation in a laboratory. Bruce Banner became the Incredible Hulk after being exposed to gamma rays released at a bomb test site. Matt Murdoch became Daredevil as a result of a truck accident that caused a chemical spill; the exposure blinded him but heightened all of his other senses. In all of these origin stories, their transformation comes from the profound power of science gone awry. The notion that all humankind's ills can be cured by the promise and power of science and technology is turned on its head. In the aforementioned origin stories, the power of science cannot be completely harnessed for the betterment of humanity because its power is unpredictable. These stories, along with the other Marvel origins, suggest that scientific endeavors are to be both feared and revered: feared because their power cannot be entirely understood or explained, revered because they have the potential to create amazing beings with superhuman powers. No doubt this reflection echoed the space race and Cold War angst between the West and the former Soviet Union in the relatively new atomic age.

The origin of the Fantastic Four suggests this profound fear of science, yet their transformation also points to its promise. Their story is first told in the pages of *Fantastic Four* #1 (Nov. 1961). With a determination to beat "the Commies" to the stars, the four agree to fly a ship into space despite the danger of exposure to cosmic rays. They quarrel over their decision, yet they decide to accept the risks in order to be the first humans to attempt this feat. While on their mission they do get exposed to the deadly rays and begin to feel the effects of this understudied cosmic phenomenon. Their ship comes crashing down to Earth, and the team begins to comprehend what has happened to them.

Their transformation is both awe inspiring and terrible at the same time. Reed Richards, the leader and brains behind the flight, gains the ability to stretch his body to any size and shape his mind can imagine. Truly he is Mister Fantastic.[5] Sue Storm, Reed's fiancée,[6] can become invisible at will; she is able to project mental force fields also. She becomes the Invisible Girl (later she is called the Invisible Woman). Johnny Storm, Sue's younger brother, becomes the Human Torch—with the ability to spontaneously ignite yet not be consumed by the fire that surrounds his body. Finally, pilot Ben Grimm gains virtually boundless meta-human strength, yet his body is permanently disfigured, assuming a monstrous, orange rocky texture. Known simply as the Thing, Grimm's incredible strength makes him the most formidable member of the group. The Fantastic Four are both blessed and cursed by their transformation. They become powerful, godlike beings with the ability to harness the ancient elemental powers. Indeed they appear to embody the ancient elements themselves. Mister Fantastic's infinite fluidity parallels water. The Human Torch obviously possesses the element of fire. The Invisible Woman resembles wind—with its invisible yet undeniable power and presence, and the Thing resembles Earth itself. Yet they are at the same time changed forever, bearing the effects of their attempt to reach the heavens. Like Icarus in the ancient Greek myth, they flew too high, too close to the sun, and paid the price for their hubris.

In some significant ways the Fantastic Four resemble the early Christian Church of the book of Acts in the New Testament. Like the Fantastic Four, the early Christians received their power together. Gathered in one place on the day of Pentecost, the early Christians were filled with the Holy Spirit and began declaring the wonders of God in the languages of those assembled for the appointed feast day. Following their empowerment, they embarked on an aggressive public ministry, declaring the message of God, healing the sick, and doing battle against the evil spirits afflicting unbelievers. In the face of persecution, the mission of the early church was a phenomenal success. They proclaimed the good news that the kingdom of God was being established and that the saving work of their messiah, Jesus Christ, was available to those who believed. The early church was led by fabulously flawed individuals who worked and prayed together as a new kind of family relying on God's power residing within them. These early followers of Jesus attempted great things for God and set in motion a worldwide movement that remains today.

The Fantastic Four, however, are not proclaiming the message of biblical salvation. They are not trying to make their message known among the peoples of the earth by making converts. They are, however, establishing a new order, a new kingdom if you will, in which the fantastic is made to dwell in the lives of four ordinary individuals who argue and have occasionally fallouts with one another, but they are ultimately committed to protecting their members and the larger society from external threats. They are indeed a surrogate super-family. Significantly the Fantastic Four, along with most of the other Marvel superheroes, retained their human flaws and foibles following their amazing transformation into powerful beings. These were not the impregnable and incorruptible heroes of the Golden Age of comic books. They were fully human and fully meta-human at the same time. The Fantastic Four became godlike beings, and yet they remained entirely mortal. They exemplify that the miraculous realm of the fantastic can interrupt the lives of ordinary humans and transform them into a force for good in the world.

The members of the Fantastic Four realized very early on that they had received their powers for a higher purpose. Unlike Stan Lee and Steve Ditko's Spider-Man, who would need the murder of his beloved Uncle Ben to jolt him to use his powers for the betterment of humankind, the Fantastic Four realized almost instinctively that with great power comes great responsibility. As the leader of the group, Reed Richards makes this clear: "Listen to me, all of you! That means you too, Ben! Together we have more power than any humans have ever possessed!" Ben, in his response, speaks for the entire group: "You don't have to make a speech, big shot! We understand! We've gotta use that power to help mankind, right?" (*Fantastic Four* #1). They embraced their mission and became emissaries of good in a world plagued by constant attacks from evil forces. In so doing, it is interesting to note that they never attempted to conceal their identities. From the beginning they wore no masks nor did they attempt to live double lives under the guise of secret identities. For the first couple of issues they did not even wear costumes. They lived as public figures, well known in Marvel's fictionalized version of New York City, occupying the Baxter building, a prominent headquarters in Manhattan, emblazoned with a large number four as if it were an advertisement or a corporate sponsorship.

Lee and Kirby introduced many colorful characters into the Marvel pantheon through the *Fantastic Four*: the Silver Age Sub-Mariner, the Black Panther (the first Marvel Silver Age superhero from Africa), the Skrulls, the Kree, the Watcher, Him (Warlock), and the Molecule Man (Owen Reece), Medusa, Crystal, Black Bolt, and the rest of the Inhumans, just to name about a couple of handfuls! The cosmic-powered Silver Surfer remains the most fertile guest-hero Kirby and Lee originated in the series. In a doomsday-like epic, a giant demigod named Galactus hungers to consume the earth of all its vital energy, but his herald, the Silver Surfer turns against him to protect the earth. With the assistance of the Watcher and the Surfer, the Fantastic Four finally get Galactus to relinquish his desire to devour the planet (*Fantastic Four* #48–50; Mar.–May 1966).

The Fantastic Four faced a plethora of villains over the years, such as the Mole Man, the Red Ghost, the Puppet Master, the Mad Thinker, Kang (Rama-Tut), Psycho-Man, Dragon Man, the Frightful Four; yet one, in his embodiment of evil, stands out as the definitive foe for this superhero quartet, and perhaps for the entire Marvel Age—Dr. Doom. Lee and Kirby introduced the villain in issue #5: Victor Von Doom once studied science as a brilliant student, a classmate of Reed Richards. He turned to a fascination with sorcery, black magic, and an obsession for forbidden experiments. One night "the evil genius went too far, as he brought forth powers which even he could not control! He managed to escape with his life, although his face was badly disfigured." Forced to wear a mask to conceal his disfigurement, and expelled from school, Dr. Doom prowled "the wastelands of Tibet still seeking forbidden secrets of black magic and sorcery." Like the members of the Fantastic Four, Dr. Doom was transformed by powers he could neither fully control nor understand. Doom, however, was not a victim of the quixotic nature of scientific phenomenon; he was instead the victim of dark, supernatural forces and his own pride. Like Lucifer who was cast out of heaven only to become the dark figure known as Satan in Milton's *Paradise Lost*, Dr. Doom was removed from his position of prestige within the university and became a hideously mutilated embodiment of evil. His god became power, his intelligence sold out to evil, and his enemy was Reed Richards. Dr. Doom's character and intimidating metal mask and hood makes for an interesting comparison to a later villain in *Star Wars*: Darth Vader. His villainy made him a natural for the Fantastic Four movie produced by Ralph Winter and Avi Arad.

Other superhero teams such as DC's venerable Justice League of America and Marvel's Avengers consist of popular characters from other successful comic books. These teams provide an opportunity for readers to see their favorite individual characters interact with one another and work together to fight evil. The shared aspect of the origin of the Fantastic Four, however, sets this group apart from most other superhero teams. Kirby nonetheless had a hand in creating another interesting comic book featuring a team of four who shared a common origin and transformation. Several years before the inaugural issue of the Fantastic Four, he did a short stint for DC Comics where he created a team that would serve as a prototype for the later Marvel group. First appearing in *Showcase* #6 (Jan.–Feb. 1957), the Challengers of the Unknown consisted of a group of four accomplished men at the height of their professions: Ace Morgan, fearless jet pilot; Professor Hale, master skin diver; Red Ryan, circus daredevil; and Rocky Davis, Olympic wrestling champion. They too were fantastic among humans, but they would soon face their own mortality. As they traveled cross country in a jet piloted by Ace Morgan, their plane crashed violently to Earth. Miraculously everyone emerged unscathed from the torn and twisted metal, but each person on board changed profoundly. Seeing how close they came to death, they were each transformed by the overwhelming recognition that they were now living on borrowed time. The four decided to dedicate their lives to taking risks—to challenging the unknown—because they had faced death and lived. Together they formed "the most unique organization on earth" and accomplished an incredible array of amazing feats. Their mission was to put their lives on the line, to risk everything, in order to face whatever evil exists "in the vast darkness beyond this world" (*Challengers of the Unknown* #2; July 1958).

Thor: An Old God Becomes Superhero

In their other long-running Marvel series, Kirby and Lee adapted the ancient Norse myths to tell the story of a crippled physician transformed into a god. Initially published as the lead feature in *Journey into Mystery* #83 (Aug. 1962), *The Mighty Thor* remains Marvel's prime example of infusing a mythic tradition into the superhero genre. Unlike many other origin stories from the early 1960s, a scientific accident plays no part in the origin of Thor, although science fiction does. While vacationing in Norway, Dr. Donald Blake stumbles upon a group of Stone Men from Saturn sent to Earth as an advance team to plan an invasion. While fleeing the alien invaders, Blake discovers an ancient cane hidden in a cave. Unsuccessfully he attempts to use the cane for leverage to move a large boulder inside the cave. In a fit of anger he strikes the cane on the boulder, and in a flash of blinding light, he is transformed into Thor, the legendary god of thunder; complete with red cape, blue tights, winged helmet, and long golden locks (even before it was fashionable to be a hippie). The cane too changes into a "mighty hammer," imparting the powers of the Norse god to its bearer.

The weak and sickly Dr. Blake thus becomes Thor incarnate as long as he holds the hammer *Mjolnir*, and by striking the base of the hammer on the ground, he can assume his frail and mortal identity once again. As Thor he has the power to command thunder and lightning, and he is able to use his enchanted hammer to vanquish all who oppose him. In terms of strength he has the ability to give DC's Superman the challenge of his life. He easily defeats the Stone Men that also possess super strength and, coincidentally, resemble the Thing from the Fantastic Four.

Similar to the members of the Fantastic Four, Dr. Donald Blake quickly realizes that his newfound power is a gift to be used for the benefit of humanity. In a moment of inspiration, he declares, "I carry within this cane the greatest power ever known to mortal man! A power I shall never use, except in the cause of justice against the forces of evil!" (*Journey into Mystery* #84). While Blake's noble altruism initially presented itself as a solitary effort of a good doctor performing heroic deeds, later issues reveal that the mighty Norse god, like other Kirby creations, exists within the context of community. In fact Thor divides his time between two communities who exist to oppose evil. He is a member of the Asgardian realm, the heavenly place where Odin, the highest Norse god, rules over the entire pantheon of Norse deities. Thor's foster brother Loki, god of mischief and evil, is his perpetual adversary. Thor is also a member of the superhero team called the Avengers, an assemblage of many of Marvel's most popular superheroes who, like the Fantastic Four, fight a very public fight against a seemingly endless litany of villains and miscreants. His membership in Asgard assists in empowering him during battles; he can summon Odin and others to his aid when he is unable to act alone. His membership with the Avengers extends his power by allying him up with other like-minded heroes with complementary abilities. Both communities help him to carry out his mission of justice.

Kirby and Lee's Dr. Blake is thus a product of the union between the heavens and Earth. The rather ordinary physician becomes the embodiment of the divine in human form. This all, of course, imitates Jesus Christ who is portrayed in the New Testament as the incarnation of the living God on Earth (John 1:1–14; 10:30–33; 14:6–9; Philippians 2:5–11; Colossians 1:15–20; Titus 2:13; Hebrews 1:3–9). The similarities have their limits, however. Later in the series it turns out that prior to Blake's existence, Thor lived in Asgard but became proud, and so Odin decided that his son needed to learn a lesson in humility. He sent him to Earth in the form of Donald Blake, erasing all his prior memory as the thunder god. Eventually Odin instigated the thought in Blake's mind to vacation in Norway, where he became Thor.[7] Christian theology affirms that Jesus is fully man and fully God at the same time.

When Thor is present, however, the frail Dr. Blake disappears; and when Blake returns, the Thor persona departs. Hence his incarnation is different.

The New Gods of the Fourth World

"There came a time when the Old Gods died! The brave died with the cunning. The noble perished, locked in battle with unleashed evil! It was the last day for them! An ancient era was passing in fiery holocaust!" (*The New Gods* #1; Mar. 1971). So begins the flagship title of perhaps Kirby's loftiest and most ambitious work. Following his near decade run on the Fantastic Four and Thor at Marvel, Kirby left his many characters that he helped create and went to the distinguished competitors. At DC Comics he quickly assumed both writing and illustrating duties on a collection of titles now known as the Fourth World: *The New Gods*, *The Forever People*, *Mister Miracle*, and related stories by Kirby found in *Superman's Pal, Jimmy Olsen* (1970–72).[8] Within this series of interrelated titles, the planets of New Genesis and Apokolips are at war, a conflict that has raged for countless years. Darkseid, evil ruler of the planet Apokolips, wages war against New Genesis and has chosen Earth as his battlefield. Orion is the emissary of New Genesis who visits Earth to oppose the tyrannical rule of Darkseid. Orion does not know it, but he is actually the son of Darkseid. Orion was adopted by the ruler of New Genesis to forge an alliance of peace. It is the classic battle of good versus evil with a parallel to the Christian story of the son of God being sent to redeem humanity from the power of sin and evil.

The cosmology of the Fourth World is profoundly dualistic. Kirby pits the world of New Genesis in stark contrast to the evil world of Apokolips. New Genesis is "a world caught up in the joyful strains of life!! There are no structures on its green surface —except those which serve the cause of well being" (*New Gods* #2). Clearly New Genesis is a utopian paradise, an unspoiled Garden of Eden. Apokolips, on the other hand, is "a dismal, unclean place of great, ugly houses sheltering uglier machines. Apokolips is an armed camp where those who live with weapons rule the wretches who build them" (*New Gods* #1). Apokolips is a name apparently derived from "Apocalypse," another name for the biblical book of Revelation where it is predicted that the world as we know it will be destroyed after the Battle of Armageddon. The word has come to mean a place of total devastation and doom; an appropriate name for the world ruled by Darkseid. It is a place of death, suffering, and evil, an industrialized hell. Kirby's two worlds can actually trace their lineage back to the Old Gods (*New Gods* #7):

> In the beginning, the New Gods were formless in image and aimless in deed!!! On each of their two new worlds, their races had sprung from a survivor of the old!! The living atoms of Balduur gave nobility and strength to one!! And the Shadow Planet was saturated with the cunning and evil which was once a sorceress!!

Interestingly the Old Gods are in fact the Norse gods who animated Kirby's earlier work in *The Mighty Thor*. Balduur, the second son of Odin, was the source of New Genesis' nobility and strength while the unnamed sorceress was the reason that Apokolips, the Shadow Planet, became a place of cunning and evil. For Kirby, the contrast between good and evil had never been clearer.

Like the Fantastic Four, the New Gods may be understood within the context of mission. The transcendent power within the mythos of the Fourth World, aptly named the Source, revealed Orion's mission to him. Using imagery drawn straight from the Hebrew Bible, Kirby establishes Orion as a prophetic leader akin to Daniel or Moses, who relies upon a transcendent being for direction. Within the chamber of the Source, the transcendent equivalent of God in the Judeo-Christian tradition, Orion and Highfather witness a moving hand writing an ominous message on an ancient wall. This wall is described as New Genesis' link to the Source. It parallels in a striking manner how Yahweh, Israel's God, wrote on the wall a message to King Belshazzar that revealed the destiny of his kingdom when interpreted by Daniel the Prophet (Daniel chapter 5). Orion receives his mission: "Orion to Apokolips—then to earth—then to war!" (New Gods #1). Unlike the biblical Belshazzar, Orion's life is spared, and at the same time he is given purpose and direction. Orion's progressive mission to move from one place to another in an effort to defeat the evil rule of Darkseid resembles the progressive mission of the early Christians from the book of Acts: "But you will receive power when the Holy Spirit comes on you; and you will be my witnesses in Jerusalem, and in all Judea and Samaria, and to the ends of the earth" (Acts 1:8).

Kirby identified a story entitled "The Pact" as one of his personal favorites (*New Gods* #7). It recalls that Izaya the Inheritor, firstborn of New Genesis, became disillusioned with the endless hostility between the two warring worlds. He struck a secret alliance with the evil Darkseid to make peace. Like an activist frightened by an escalating nuclear arms race between superpowers, Izaya renounced war: "We are worse than the Old Gods! They destroyed themselves!! We destroy everything!!" In the midst of a dry wind and violent electrical storm, Izaya makes good on his conviction: "I tear off my armor! I reject this war-staff as a weapon!!! I reject the way of war!!" As the storm subsides, Izaya sees an ageless and inscrutable wall standing where he had taken his sacred vow of peace. With hands clenched he shouts at the wall, "If I am Izaya the Inheritor, what is my inheritance?" A fiery explosion engulfs the wall, and a hand of flame emerges writing the answer upon the wall: "The Source." Izaya's transformation is complete. No longer is he a warrior bearing a battle staff; he becomes instead the wise and peace-loving Highfather, bearer of the wonder staff, who is now linked to the Source. To fulfill his desire for peace, he enters into a pact involving the exchange of sons. He gives Darkseid his own son, Scott Free, who would later become Mister Miracle, the namesake of another Fourth World series. In return, Highfather adopts Orion, the son of Darkseid, as a tangible peace offering to end the terrible conflict between the two worlds.

Forever Eternals

Jack Kirby's *Forever People* centers around a group of five teenagers from Supertown, a city orbiting above the planet New Genesis. They come to Earth by means of a cosmic portal called a Boom Tube. Mark Moonrider is the leader of the group, an affable young man who can manipulate the power of nuclear fission with his megaton touch. Vykin the Black bears the Mother Box, a computer-like entity that provides guidance to the Forever People. Serifan, a resourceful lad dressed like a cowboy, wields a vast array of powerful "cosmic cartridges." Beautiful Dreamer is an attractive female with the power to induce incredible illusions, thus making her extremely powerful. Finally, there is Big Bear, who has great physical strength and a "can do" attitude. He pilots the "super cycle," a large motorcycle that transports the group on its adventures. He provides a degree of comic relief to a team that could have doubled as hippies during the time Kirby worked on the series.

The Forever People find their mission within the context of a community similar to other Kirby creations. They each have incredible gifts, but they become much more powerful and complete when they work together. Nowhere is this more evident than in the strange Mother Box ritual (*The Forever People* #1, 2, 11). The Mother Box has the power to transform the group into a unified entity. Vykin initiates the ritual by invoking the Mother Box to "unite us as one." Each member of the group then places his or her hand on the Mother Box. Together they offer the following incantation: "make us one with that life! Let him displace us. Let him enter on the power of the word—even as we vanish when the word is said" (*The Forever People* #2). This rite ends as they utter the mysterious word *taarruu*. In an instant, each of the individual members of the group disappears, and the Infinity Man appears in their place. With incomparable strength and the ability to vanquish all foes, the Infinity Man does what they could not accomplish on their own.[9]

This corporate unity reminds us of how the apostle Paul illustrates the entity of the church in the New Testament. For Paul, the members of the church are viewed collectively as the "body of Christ" (see Romans 12:3–8, 1 Corinthians 12:12–31, Ephesians 4:1–16). Each individual believer functions as a member of the body and plays a unique role in fulfilling Christ's mission to the world. Paul instructs the believers to embrace their unique spiritual gifts and to use them for the benefit of the community. Moreover he encourages every member to adopt a humble attitude in accepting those whose gifts might differ from their own. In so doing, the individual believer aspires to create unity within the body and to achieve a greater corporate strength than would be possible otherwise.

The Mother Box parallels the Ark of the Covenant—the sacred container for God's laws in the Old Testament. The Ark was, for the ancient Israelites, a mobile vessel for God's revelation on Mount Sinai and a symbol of God's presence. When Solomon built his Temple, the Ark was housed in a permanent dwelling place for God. The New Testament believers interpret the Ark as symbolically foreshadowing the redemptive work of Christ (Hebrews 8–9). It points to the time when God will dwell within the hearts and minds of his people, like miniature temples, and the collective body of those believers—the church—will work to establish his kingdom on the earth. The Mother Box of the Forever People unifies the team and provides a source of divine guidance for them. It has the power to create lasting community for those who submit to her authority.

In 1976 Kirby developed another team of super characters, this time for Marvel Comics, called *The Eternals*. The comic book followed the pattern of his earlier DC titles, but it did not enjoy as much popularity.[10] In the story, the Eternals exist as race of immortal-like heroes who were mistaken as gods by earlier civilizations on Earth. They originated as one of three species of humanity that evolved from an ancient genetic experiment done by the Celestials, a god-like race of giants who occasionally visit the earth and were responsible for a great flood that sank the ancient kingdom of Lemuria. The two other species of humanity are the Deviants and the normal humans. Ikaris and the Eternals battle against the demonic-like Kro and the Deviants who menace the human race. The story combines a pastiche of elements related to the Epic of Gilgamesh, Greco-Roman mythology, and the Bible (especially the Old Testament Book of Genesis 1–9 and the New Testament book of Revelation). In the typical Kirby fashion, "*The Eternals* is an inquiry into the nature of God," where "angels and devils [are] recast in terms of science fiction, battling for supremacy amid ordinary men and women like ourselves."[11]

Conclusion

Despite the fact that Jack Kirby's comic books are a secular form of entertainment, a great deal of spiritual truth can be gleaned from his works. The foremost is that evil is real, and it can be personified. Kirby created some of the most reprehensible bad guys ever seen in the pages of a comic book. His villains were not mere criminals seeking financial gain. They sought absolute power as supreme despots; they resemble archetypes of evil. Doctor Doom, nemesis of the Fantastic Four, can be seen as evil personified, the autocratic ruler of the fictional country of Latveria and tyrant seeking world domination. Darkseid, ruler of the fallen world of Apokolips, has been described as "one of the five-or-so superstar villains in comic book history."[12] Like the devil in the Judeo-Christian tradition, these villains function as evil incarnate, which must be opposed by that which is good. A corollary truth gleaned from Kirby's work is that evil might be best fought within a context of team effort. The Fantastic Four became superheroes together, and their powers reach their peak when they face a common enemy together. The Forever People change into a formidable force when they lose their own identity and become a corporate entity that is greater than its individual parts. Individual superpowers may be marvelous gifts to oppose the forces of darkness, but they will only be successful in defeating powerful enemies when employed within the context of community. Loners like Spider-Man and the Punisher have trouble learning this lesson.

Kirby's genius prompts his fans to believe that the amazing worlds of the gods could be experienced by ordinary mortals. His ideas populate with planet hungry demigods, philosophical space-born surfers, and disfigured tyrants bent on world domination. He did this all in a medium that had been declared dangerous and linked to juvenile delinquency in the 1950s; allegedly the lowest art form imaginable. In fact speaking of comic books as "art" or "literature" would have seemed unthinkable during Kirby's most productive years. At best comic books substituted as throwaways for genuine reading material. However, Kirby brought a cosmic grandeur to this lowly medium. He did this with a combination of skillful artistry and an incomparable reservoir of imaginative creativity. By drawing upon the spiritual insights of the biblical tradition and ancient mythology, he was able to evoke a sense of awe and wonder in his young and old readers alike— forever cementing his legacy as the king of comics.

Notes

[1] Steve Duin and Mike Richardson, *Comics, Between the Panels* (Milwaukie, Ore.: Dark Horse Comics, 1998), 263.

[2] Bradford Wright, *Comic Book Nation: The Transformation of Youth Culture in America* (Baltimore: Johns Hopkins University Press, 2001), 35.

[3] Dave Wood and Jack Kirby, *Challengers of the Unknown Archives* (New York: DC Comics, 2003), vol. 1:5.

[4] Duin and Richardson, *Comics, Between the Panels*, 260.

[5] Nevertheless Jack Cole's Plastic Man (*Police Comics* #1; 1941) and DC's Elongated Man (*Flash* #112; 1960) both preceded Mr. Fantastic as stretchy heroes.

[6] Reed and Sue Richards get married in *Fantastic Four* Annual #3 (1965). They eventually have a son named Franklin.

[7] His previous memories as the thunder god, however, were not restored right away. For a fuller synopsis of Thor's early life, see "Thor" in *The Official Handbook of the Marvel Universe S*-U, vol. 1 #11:14-15 (Nov. 1983).

[8] Kirby wrote in issues #133–39, 141–48.

[9] The TV hero team called the Power Rangers would do something similar.

[10] Some other Kirby titles in the 1970s included DC's *Kamandi: Last Boy on Earth* and Marvel's *Machine Man* and *Devil Dinosaur*.

[11] Quote from Peter Sanderson, *Marvel Universe* (New York: Harry N. Abrams, Inc., 1996), 171.

[12] Jack Kirby, *Jack Kirby's New Gods* (New York: DC Comics, 1998), 6.

Recommended Resources

Braun, Saul. "Shazam! Here Comes Captain Relevant." Pages 81–98 in *Popular Culture and the Expanding Consciousness*. Ray B. Browne, ed. New York: John Wiley & Sons, 1973.

Daniels, Les. *Marvel: Five Fabulous Decades of the World's Greatest Comics*. New York: Harry N. Abrams, Inc., Publishers, 1991.

Duin, Steve, and Mike Richardson. *Comics, Between the Panels*. Milwaukie, Ore.: Dark Horse Comics, 1998.

Kirby, Jack. *Jack Kirby's New Gods*. New York: DC Comics, 1998.

Kirby, Jack. *Jack Kirby's The Forever People*. New York: DC Comics, 1999.

Lee, Stan. *Origins of Marvel Comics*. New York: Simon & Schuster; 1974.

Lee, Stan, and George Mair. *Excelsior! The Amazing Life of Stan Lee*. New York: Fireside, 2002.

Lee, Stan, and Jack Kirby. *Essential Thor*. New York: Marvel, 2001.

Lee, Stan, and Jack Kirby. *Essential Fantastic Four*, vols. 1–4. New York: Marvel, 1998 (volume 4 forthcoming).

Lee, Stan, Jack Kirby, and John Byrne. *The Villainy of Dr. Doom*. New York: Marvel, 1999.

Reynolds, Richard. "Deciphering the Myths—Explicit Mythology: Thor." Pages 53–60 in *Super Heroes: A Modern Mythology*. Jackson: University Press of Mississippi, 1994.

Ro, Ronin. *Tales to Astonish: Jack Kirby, Stan Lee, and the American Comic Book Revolution*. New York: Bloomsbury Publishing, 2004.

Wood, Dave and Jack Kirby. *Challengers of the Unknown Archives*, vol. 1. New York: DC Comics, 2003.

6
"Behold! The Hero Has Become Like One of Us." The Perfectly Imperfect Spider-Man

B. J. Oropeza

Spider-Man was my favorite superhero when I was growing up. Apart from "Run, Jill, run," I actually learned *how* to read by reading *The Amazing Spider-Man*! I could relate to the growing pains of Peter Parker, Spidey's alias. My family just moved to a suburban neighborhood; I was the "new kid" at Toyon Elementary School, very bright, and yet the other children laughed at me my first day because I didn't know where to sit. They called me "Bozo" as a substitute for my "weird name," Brisio. Then during the class photograph, I stood with kids on the top level of stairs with two rows of children below us. Right when the cameraman took our picture, I got sick. Since it was picture day, everyone was wearing their Sunday bests. One little girl in an elegant pink dress happened to be standing exactly two levels below me. Guess where the vomit landed?

An entire generation has passed since Stan Lee and Steve Ditko presented *Amazing Fantasy* #15 (1962), the first Marvel comic to introduce Spider-Man. Since that time Spider-Man has become the most popular of Stan Lee's creations. *The Amazing Spider-Man* was the best-selling Marvel comic, rising close to 370,000 copies monthly in the late 1960s.[1] The same comic maintained over half a million subscribers 30 years later.[2] The original Spider-Man series spawned other titles such as *Marvel Tales* (reprints of *Amazing Spider-Man*), *Marvel Team-up*, *Spectacular Spider-Man*, *Web of Spider-Man*, *Spidey Super Stories*, *Spider-Man*, *Peter Parker: Spider-Man*, *Spider-Man 2099*, *Spider-Man: Chapter One*, and female versions of the hero, including *Spider-Woman* and *Spider-Girl*. The Spider-Man movie directed by Sam Raimi and starring Tobey Maguire (Columbia Pictures, 2002) grossed over $114 million its opening week and eventually commanded $800 million, scoring the ninth-highest worldwide box office hit.[3] The sequel in 2004 turned out to be a critically acclaimed box office success. The movie captured the essence of Peter Parker's manifold problems in a remake of the classic Stan Lee and John Romita story, "Spider-Man No More" (*Amazing Spider-Man* #50; 1967).

Lee affirms that Spider-Man has become so popular because he is so *human*: "He never has enough money, he's constantly beset by personal problems, and the world doesn't exactly applaud his deeds—in fact, most people tend to suspect and distrust him. In short, he's a lot like you and me."[4] Another appeal is that youth culture perpetually identifies with Peter Parker's coming of age. He receives his arachnid powers as an unpopular, puny, teenage geek. Lee discusses his creation of the character:

> For quite a while I'd been toying with the idea of doing a strip that would violate all the conventions—break all the rules. A strip that would actually feature a teenager as the star, instead of making him an (ugh!) adult hero's sidekick. A strip in which the main character would lose out as often as he'd win—in fact, more often.… Everybody knew about Superman—so the time had come for a competitor to make the scene; and what fun it would be to call him Spider-Man.[5]

We can identify with Spider-Man's humanness. Peter Parker is a troubled youth whose multiple problems get in the way of his pursuit of happiness; yet he is able to do things that average people cannot do, such as crawl on walls, spin a web, swing from building tops, and handle a gang of villains twice his size as he makes wisecracks in the heat of battle. He is just like us as Peter Parker, yet he is more powerful, more confident, and more heroic than us as Spider-Man. Maybe this is why I along with many other fans like Spidey so much. It is his imperfections clothed with amazing strength that we hold dear.

Spider-Man's story speaks volumes about teen angst. We will explore the major events of his life in relation to his problems and then ponder the Spider-Man myth in terms of guilt and redemption.

Peter Parker Angst: Living in a World That Rejects the Friendly Neighborhood Spider-Man

In the comic book version of Spider-Man, Peter Parker is a teenage budding science genius raised from early childhood by his uncle Ben and aunt May after his parents were killed overseas in a fatal accident.[6] To add to Spider-Man's realism, Stan Lee created him living in New York and growing up in the Forest Hills district. He gains his superpowers when a radioactive spider bites him at a science exhibit (unlike the genetically designed super spider in the film version). This bite forever alters the course of the teenager's history, endowing him with abilities similar to a spider: climbing walls, jumping long distances, having the proportional strength of a spider, and tingling with a "spider sense" whenever danger is about to take place.[7] Yet Peter uses his new gift for showmanship and making money. The turning point occurs when his uncle is killed by a burglar, and this sets him on a course to use his powers to combat crime.

Teen Tribulation

From the very beginning of the series, Peter Parker questions why everything turns out wrong whenever he puts on his costume. As Spider-Man he can no longer perform for money due to a loss of reputation caused by spider-bashing editorials written by J. Jonah Jameson, publisher of the *Daily Bugle*. The web-slinger is considered a public menace. He tries to join the Fantastic Four until he learns they are a nonprofit organization. He experiences public fear and misunderstanding as well as determined vengeance from his supervillain enemies. As Peter he struggles to help his aunt pay rent, and he is unable to cash an actor's check made out to "Spider-Man" without disclosing his identity. He experiences teen angst, ridicule, and rejection by his peers in high school. As in the movie, Flash Thompson, an avid supporter of Spider-Man, is Peter Parker's high-school bully.[8] It will take a few more years of education before their enmity subsides. They become uneasy friends in college, and then Flash will turn out to be Peter's best man at his wedding (*Spider-Man Annual* #21; 1987).

Above all Peter tries to help his aunt's ailing health by financially assisting with medical bills as a free-lance photographer. When he enters college and rooms with buddy Harry Osborn, Aunt May allows the villain Dr. Octopus to become her tenant, charmed by the doctor's good manners. When Peter finds out, he fights Doc Ock in front of his aunt's house, which causes her to faint when she sees the two clashing. She survives the ordeal, but her health grows weaker, and this adds to Peter's anxieties. Unlike the film *Spider-Man 2*, Aunt May originally liked Doc Ock and hated Spider-Man. She almost marries the villain until it is exposed that his motives were to seize her inheritance, a large nuclear reactor. Peter eventually develops an ulcer from all his worries (*Amazing Spider-Man* #113; 1972).[9]

Through Peter Parker we see ourselves at that awkward stage in life during teen years and young adulthood. The reader is able to empathize with him—life can be very complicated and confusing. Like the parentless Peter we struggle for a sense of belonging to some community or loved one; we yearn for acceptance, significance, and search for a life calling. Reading Spider-Man is like looking into a mirror. We can also understand why Peter questions his vocation as Spider-Man. For all his efforts to fight crime and protect his loved ones, the web-spinner cannot earn a decent living; and worse, he gets accused of being a criminal himself. Peter would not have to break dates, he would have more time to do his homework, and he would be able to take a steady job if it were not for Spider-Man. He asks himself the probing question we have all asked at one time or another: Who am I?

> Why do I do it? Why do I continue risking my life…causing a thousand unnecessary problems…a thousand heartaches and sleepless nights? Have I an insane lust for power…a need to feel more important than those around me? Or is it something deeper…more frightening? Has Spider-Man become so much a part of me that I can never lose him again? (*Amazing Spider-Man* #45:20; Feb. 1967).

Teen Heartaches: Tangled in a Web of Romances

Like most teenagers and single adults, Peter struggles to find the right person to marry.[10] The Spider-Man movies have Mary Jane as Peter Parker's love, but in the comics he falls in love with a few other women first. His famous relationships introduced an almost soap-opera feel to the superhero genre during the Silver Age of comics. His first love is Betty Brant, Jameson's secretary; she plays the Oedipal woman who happens to be a little older than Peter and looks like his deceased mother.[11] Peter wants to confide with her about his true identity as Spider-Man; but after Betty's brother dies from a stray bullet fired by a gangster fighting Spider-Man, she blames the Spider-Man's interference for his death.[12] Peter neglects his relationship with Betty due to his responsibilities as a superhero and taking care of his sick aunt; and so Betty dates Ned Leeds, a young reporter she eventually marries. He then changes into Spider-Man's nemesis called the Hobgoblin (*Amazing Spider-Man* #17–18, 30, 156, 238).

Peter then falls for Gwen Stacy, a fellow science student he meets during his first year of college. At first they do not get along as classmates, and Peter thinks this blond beauty is totally out of his league. They eventually fall in love, however, with Peter intending to marry her. Adding to his troubles, Gwen blames her father's death on Spider-Man after a battle with Doc Ock accidentally sends falling debris from a building on top of Captain George Stacy (her father). She confesses that her love for Peter, however, is stronger than her hatred of Spider-Man. At this point, Peter hates Spider-Man too for ruining his life. He intends to rid himself of his alter ego once and for all by drinking a serum that only ends up temporarily enhancing his spider powers by giving him four extra arms![13]

Gwen functions as Peter's redeemer in the series. She accepts Peter and defends him against accusations from his class peers, and she loves him unconditionally, despite his problems, lack of money, and abnormal behavior. Peter sees her as the only really good thing that has ever happened to him. No doubt she would have become a significant source of healing for Peter, if it were not for the Green Goblin, who kidnaps and kills her by knocking her off the George Washington Bridge (*Amazing Spider-Man* #121–122; 1973).[14] For years Spider-Man fans despised the death of Gwen. It in fact marked a turning point in the Marvel Universe because a leading lady was killed who had been a crucial part of the comic for many years. Gwen's death added more realism to comics, more unpredictability—the good guy did not always win in the end. Peter's redemption evaded him when Gwen died.

Nevertheless Peter's love life does have a silver lining in the original series. After several failed attempts Aunt May and neighbor Anna May Watson finally get Peter to meet Mrs. Watson's niece, Mary Jane (*Amazing Spider-Man* #42; 1966).[15] Unlike the movie, although Peter ogles over Mary Jane's beauty, he eventually thinks she is "pretty as a pumpkin seed....but just about as shallow" (#45). Then after Gwen dies and Mary Jane breaks up with boyfriend Harry Osborne, Peter starts seeing more of M.J., but the relationship is unstable. Only after a few more relationships (most notably, with Debra Whitman and the Black Cat) does Peter finally marry Mary Jane (*Amazing Spider-Man* #290-92; *Annual* #21). A live wedding in New York's Shea Stadium (1987) had two actors imitating Mary Jane and Spider-Man. M.J. helps heal Peter in a different way than Gwen—she knows he is Spider-Man and loves him anyway.

Masked Identity Angst and the Green Goblin Saga

If Peter Parker struggles with hardships and anxiety, one plausible solution would seem to be to share his burdens with those he loves. Before marrying M.J., his major obstacle to this is that he felt he could not reveal his secret identity as Spider-Man. Why did he take on a secret identity in the first place? Originally he wears a mask as a wrestler, and showman producers think it a good gimmick, but Peter keeps his identity secret as a form of insurance. Just in case his spider strength fails in the ring, he would not become a "laughing stock" (*Amazing Fantasy* #15). Early on, J. Jonah Jameson persuaded enough public notoriety against Spider-Man to offer a reward for his capture.[16] The Chameleon disguises himself as Spider-Man and commits a crime for which the web-slinger is temporarily blamed. Then Mysterio and Kraven the Hunter do likewise (*Amazing Spider-Man* #1, 13,

34). Peter fears that if his identity were revealed, Jameson would never stop harassing him until he had driven him out of town. As a result he imagined that Aunt May would suffer poverty (*Amazing Spider-Man* #4). Thus the inseparable Peter Parker/Spider-Man identity is set in place from the very beginning of the myth. The Spider-Man movies later add that his loved ones would be endangered by his enemies if he revealed his identity.[17]

Our hero suffers many close calls at being exposed.[18] Although Captain Stacy was the first friend to discover Peter's secret, he did not reveal it to anyone before he died. Peter's ultimate angst comes by way of the Green Goblin. By tracking down Spider-Man to his home (and dulling his spider sense), the Green Goblin captures Peter and then reveals himself as Norman Osborn, Harry's father (*Amazing Spider-Man* #39–40; 1966). After Spider-Man knocks out the Goblin, Osborne awakes with amnesia about the entire event. Later he suffers a relapse when his son overdoses on drugs due to his break-up with Mary Jane in the now famous saga unapproved by the Comic Code Authority: *Amazing Spider-Man* #96–98 (1971). The Goblin meets his fatal end after Gwen's death. The Goblin gets impaled by his own glider after Spider-Man dodges the impact (*Amazing Spider-Man* #122; 1973).

Continuing the saga, Harry witnessed the final battle between his father and Spider-Man and attempts to avenge his father by becoming the new Green Goblin and kidnapping Mary Jane, Aunt May, and Flash Thompson. After Spider-Man defeats him, Harry exposes Peter as Spider-Man and himself as the Green Goblin, yet the police reject both confessions, believing Harry is too young to be the Goblin and suffering from another bout with drugs (*Amazing Spider-Man* #136–37). Harry eventually gets cured of his addiction, marries Liz Allen (a high school friend of Peter and Flash), and fathers a son. He suffers relapses as the Goblin, and finally the enhancing formula that gave him the Goblin's strength poisons his system and kills him (e.g., *Amazing Spider-Man* #180; *Spectacular Spider-Man* #200).[19]

We rightly suspect that much of this tragedy in Peter's life would have been avoided had he simply revealed his identity to his loved ones at the beginning. The Messianic secret of Jesus may have worked as a strategy for Spider-Man. Jesus shunned popularity over his performing miracles. In Mark's Gospel, he repeatedly told those whom he healed in Galilee to keep his identity secret during his early ministry, not wanting to cause too much of a stir until he was ready to go to Jerusalem. Maybe Peter Parker should have done something similar. He could have revealed his hero identity to his closest friends and family while keeping it hid from outsiders, villains, and the Daily Bugle. This confession would have relieved him of much worry, and maybe, just maybe, things would have turned out differently for Norman, Harry, and Gwen.

Peter suffers from not comprehending true love, mercy, and forgiveness. If he would have confessed his true identity, his loved ones may have been troubled to hear about it, and possibly angered by knowing all the times he lied to them hoping to cover it up, but they would not have rejected him. *Amazing Spider-Man* #87 (1970) is a classic example of this. Fed up with his identity and dazed by the flu, Peter reveals himself as Spider-Man to Gwen, her father, Mary Jane, and Harry at Gwen's birthday party. Naturally they are shocked by the confession, and Gwen gets a bit hysterical, but she remains willing to see the best in Peter. After he comes to his senses, he retracts his confession and hires an impostor Spider-Man (secretly Hobie Brown, alias the Prowler, who owes Spider-Man a favor) to crash the party while Peter returns there in order to "prove" that he is not Spider-Man. In later episodes Mary Jane claims to have known all along that Peter was Spider-Man—she in fact saw Peter leave Aunt May's house as Spider-Man when his Uncle Ben died (e.g., *Amazing Spider-Man* #257; 1984). In both the comic series and film she chooses to love Peter as Spider-Man, accepting the inherent danger it may create for her. The risk of loving Peter is better for her than remaining "half alive" without him.[20] As the New Testament claims, love covers a multitude of sins (1 Peter 4:8).

New Challenges: The Clone Saga, an Alien Suit, and the "Anti-Christ"

Peter Parker's troubled journey becomes rather confusing with multiple turns in the Spider-Man comics of the 1980s and 1990s. After he finally begins settling down with Mary Jane, a new set of problems arise with the symbiotic suit and clone sagas.

Spider-Man exchanges his famous red and blues for a black and white costume. Later he discovers that the costume is a symbiotic alien, and so he gets rid of it by leading the alien to the clanging bells of a church, since the parasite is sensitive to sound (*Marvel Super Heroes: Secret Wars* #8, Dec. 1984; *Amazing Spider-Man* #252–259; May–Dec. 1984). The alien eventually binds with a reporter named Eddie Brock, who was praying in the church trying to make peace with his hatred against Spider-Man for allegedly ruining his reputation.[21] Brock becomes Spidey's nemesis, Venom (#299–300; 1988). A similar but even more vicious adversary named Carnage was birthed when a serial murder named Cletus Kasady receives superpowers via a spawn from Venom's suit (#360–63; 1992). Both villains exhibit more strength than Spider-Man, and they feel little remorse about killing their opponents. Venom became one of many grim and gritty heroes in the 1990s.

Since Venom and Carnage both originate as a result of Spider-Man's own suit, they can represent two postmodern versions of Spider-Man's

Doppelgänger, a dark mirror image of what Peter Parker could potentially become without his morals. We see a glimpse of this dark side of Peter immediately after Gwen's death. He assaults two police officers who want to question him about her death, and he commits an act of vandalism in a moment's rage (*Amazing Spider-Man* # 122, 124; 1973). Yet unlike the new heroes of the 1990s, he does not cross over the barrier of killing his enemies. His most trying restraint came in his battle with the Norman Osborn after he killed Gwen. Spidey loses control, hitting the Goblin repeatedly and saying, "You...Took...Her....Away...Filthy...Worm-eating...Scum!" Before he pulverizes the Goblin to death, he comes to his senses: "Good Lord...What in the name of heaven am I doing?" He realizes that if he had continued in his rage, he would have become a murderer just like the Green Goblin (*Amazing Spider-Man* #122).

The confusing clone saga spans over 20 years of Spider-Man comics (1975–1996). The Jackal, secretly Professor Miles Warren from Peter's university, creates a clone of both Peter Parker and Gwen Stacy before her death. The Gwen-clone meets the real Peter, but after he finds out her true identity, she leaves him, realizing that she could never have the same love Peter and the real Gwen shared. Peter's clone possesses spiderpowers and adopts the name Ben Reilly, taking his name from Uncle Ben and Aunt May's maiden name. His death was faked in *Amazing Spider-Man* #149 (1975) and he remained transient for a number of years until he returned to determine whether he or Peter was the true clone. After they conduct tests, it turned out that Peter Parker was the supposed clone and Ben the original Spider-Man! Spidey's fans were not happy about discovering that a clone had played the role of Peter Parker from 1975 to 1995. Reilly became the new Spider-Man, and Peter decided to retire his spider role by moving to Portland, Oregon, with Mary Jane.[22] Marvel experimented with this change, in part, because Peter no longer resembled the struggling teenager of his early days. He had grown older, graduated from college, married a beautiful model, and his fear of Aunt May dying was finally a thing of the past (her death, which was later revealed as fake, took place in *Amazing Spider-Man* #400). The single, financially struggling Reilly seemed better equipped for the role, but fans vehemently disagreed. Marvel complied by eventually killing off Ben Reilly, and establishing Peter again as the real Spider-Man. This scenario involved bringing back an old villain.

The clone saga finally ended with another major twist: Norman Osborn, the original Green Goblin, returned from the dead. The Goblin's serum had given him the ability to recover from his apparent death after he had killed Gwen Stacy. He escaped the morgue, moved to Europe, and had been secretly plotting against Spider-Man all these years by funding Professor Warren's clone projects. It turned out that Peter was the real Spider-Man after all; Osborn had manipulated him to believe he was not the real web-hero. In an ultimate battle symbolizing good versus evil between Spider-Man (Peter Parker and Ben Reilly) and the original Green Goblin, Reilly dies when he gets hit by the Goblin's glider (*Amazing Spider-Man* #418; *Spider-Man* #75; 1996). Here the Goblin functions as the Anti-Christ in the Spider-Man myth, and his return is appropriately entitled "Revelations." He resembles the biblical Beast of Revelation 13 who received a mortal wound, and yet revived again in a type of pseudo-resurrection to defy the Christ and persecute his people. Norman Osborn's feat resembles this. His glider originally "crucified" him, but he "rose again" after his funeral and returned in a "second coming" after a long hiatus.

If the clone saga teaches us anything, it confirms that almost nothing is certain. Characters deemed dead for years could always come back as clones, androids, or the real thing previously mistaken as dead. In the Spider-Man comics, a suspension of disbelief could only go so far. Truly the mid-1990s marked a deconstructive low point in the Spider-Man legacy. Then Marvel relaunched Spider-Man in a new and second volume series after the disappointing clone saga; most notably, *Peter Parker: Spider-Man* (1998) and a revised origin tale by John Byrne, *Spider-Man: Chapter One* (1998), to bring the web-hero back to his original commitments and struggles that made him famous in the first place. The recent Spider-Man films also present a constructive trend in the hero's myth. At the same time, through all the clones, symbiotic aliens, deconstructions, and reconstructions of Spider-Man, Uncle Ben remains the same. We have never experienced a return of Ben Parker after his death; otherwise, Spider-Man would have never become Spider-Man.

Spider-Man's Guilt

In the origin myth Peter Parker first becomes an actor after gaining his spider powers. This quickly changes when he refuses to assist a police officer in capturing a thief. Not many days later he is told by a police officer (who looks like the former officer) that his uncle, Ben Parker, has been murdered. As Spider-Man, Peter avenges his uncle's death by capturing the murderer, only to find out that the killer happens to be the thief he refused to help capture several days earlier. Peter determines that his life mission as Spider-Man would no longer involve flaunting his superpowers for fame or fortune, but it would be a secret vocation commissioned by a responsibility to use his spider capabilities to protect the innocent against evildoers. He blames himself for his uncle's death, saying, "My fault—all my fault!" The narrator (Stan Lee) at the end of *Amazing Fantasy* #15 informs the reader that Peter now becomes aware that "with great power there must come—great responsibility!"

Hence it is not fame, fortune, vengeance, altruism, or even a sense of justice that primarily motivates Spider-Man to fight crime—it is guilt. He cannot forgive himself for this tragedy. Like many flagship heroes, then, Spider-Man is an orphan attempting to resolve his commission and identity. He naturally takes this journey by himself, and when he suffers, he suffers alone. The burglar who kills Uncle Ben remains nameless, even when Spider-Man encounters him a second time, years later (*Amazing Spider-Man* #200; 1979). The villain remains nameless because this is a way that Spider-Man's own culpability for Uncle Ben's death might be stressed: "[the burglar's] function in Spider-Man's origin myth is that of a mirror."[23]

The guilt does not end with the origin story. Peter feels responsible to take care of his ailing aunt now that his uncle is dead. In what is arguably the greatest Spider-Man epic created by Stan Lee and Steve Ditko (the "Master Planner" saga), Aunt May needs a transfusion, and Peter donates his blood to her. This act of benevolence backfires when she is about to die as a result of Peter's radioactive blood in her system. He realizes that all his spider strength is helpless when it comes to healing her, but he vows to save her somehow. Although he finds a cure with the help of Dr. Curt Conners (alias the Lizard), he is unable to deliver the serum when a battle with Doc Ock that leaves him hopelessly pinned under tons of steel as an impending torrent of water begins to seep through cracks in the building. As the hero contemplates his fate, he interprets Aunt May's cure as a way to stop being "haunted" by the memory of his dead uncle. He determines that if he does not deliver the serum, he will be responsible for his aunt's death too. Gathering up all his strength, he reaffirms his commitment as Spider-Man and lifts the enormous weight off his shoulders before the water drowns him. Battling Doc Ock's henchmen with the little strength remaining in him, he escapes to deliver the serum. As he sees the doctors work on his unconscious aunt, he thinks to himself, "I've done the best I could, Aunt May! Now, there's nothing left, but prayer—!" (*Amazing Spider-Man* #33:14; 1965).[24]

After Aunt May recovers, Peter is freed from the guilt he feels about her condition, but his culpability over Uncle Ben's death remains. Plagued by constant unhappiness due to his double identity, Peter gives up his life as Spider-Man only to take it up again when he helps a watchman who is getting mugged. The man resembles Uncle Ben, and this rejuvenates Peter's call for great responsibility: "I can never fail to use the power which a mysterious destiny has seen fit to give me! No matter how unbearable the burden may be....no matter how great my personal sacrifice...I can never permit one innocent being to come to harm...because Spider-Man failed to act.... And I swear that I never will!" (*Amazing Spider-Man* #50:18; 1967).

This tension builds in the classic episodes until a new guilt plagues him through the death of Gwen and her father Captain Stacy. The web-slinger produces a chemical in his webbing that jams up Doc Octopus' brain impulse communication to his tentacles. As they fight on top of a high building, Doc Ock's tentacles go out of control, destroying part of a roof that comes crashing down on pedestrians below. A little boy looks up at the falling debris as Captain Stacy pushes the child out of the way, crying, *"Please, God—let me not be—too late!"* He saves the boy but suffers the impact himself. In his dying breath, Stacy (who has secretly known Spider-Man's identity) tells Peter to look after his daughter Gwen. Spider-Man cries out: "Why must it happen? Why? Why? First—I lost Uncle Ben.... And now— the second best friend—I've ever had! Rest easy, sir.... I'll love Gwen—and cherish her—as long as I live! But, what if she ever learns—that you died— because of—me?" (*Amazing Spider-Man* #90; 1970). Of course Spider-Man cannot entirely keep his promise: The Green Goblin kills Gwen. Spider-Man blames himself for her death because she is a victim of his double lifestyle. As the ambulance takes her away, Spider-Man says, "She's dead...and Spider-Man killed her" (*Amazing Spider-Man* #122; 1973).

What is hardly seen in a clear way is the concept of grace. Peter's problems only seem to escalate with few opportunities for relief. In the Spider-Man myth we perceive humanity trying to earn forgiveness through "good deeds," which for Peter are sacrificially attempted at the expense of happiness. Ultimately no deed ever seems good enough to pay for his guilt. Danny Fingeroth puts it well when he writes, "Spider-Man's quest is the most difficult and perilous of all the orphan quests.... Spider-Man is seeking revenge on himself. No matter how many symbolic stand-ins for the burglar he defeats, it will never be enough for him. Indeed, Peter Parker's internalization of his guilt over the perceived culpability in his uncle's death can be defined as classic neurotic behavior."[25]

The blessing of spider powers becomes Peter Parker's curse. Apart from thugs, supervillains, and a newspaper publisher who are determined to get rid of him, his school grades slip, his finances suffer, his relationships become estranged, and his loved ones endangered all as a result of his guilt-driven desire to be Spider-Man. His great responsibility becomes too overwhelming without sufficient grace or a chance to entirely redeem himself.

Spider-Man's Redemption

In the *Spider-Man* film, Peter fights villains despite his notoriety because "it's right." *Spider-Man 2* elaborates that sometimes a hero needs to give up dreams to do what is right. Courage, self-sacrifice, and dying with honor come alongside great responsibility. This brings to mind the idea of self-abandonment popularized by the Jesus saying, "He that saves his life… shall lose it; he that loses his life…shall save it" (Matthew 16:24–25; Mark 8:34–35; Luke 9:23–24; John 12:25). Why believe "it is right" to help other people? The underlying assumption seems to be the Golden Rule of Jesus: "do unto others what you would have them do to you" (Matthew 7:12), which in fact summarizes all biblical teaching.

We finally see grace triumph over guilt and angst in a significant way when Spider-Man encounters for a second time the burglar who killed Uncle Ben. After getting out of prison, the burglar, collaborating with Mysterio, kidnaps Aunt May, attempting to find out from her where an alleged fortune is hidden in the Parker home. When Spider-Man faces him, he unmasks himself and tells the thief that he has been haunted all these years by his failure to protect his uncle: "since that day I've been striving to make up for my mistake! Well, mister—maybe this is my second chance! Maybe this is the day I atone for all of Spider-Man's sins!" (*Amazing Spider-Man* #200:39; 1979). He confesses to the burglar that he hated him in an unholy manner for so many years, wanting to rip him apart "limb by limb," but what prevented him is that "if I used my power to kill you—I'd be no better than the scum you are. And if I've learned anything—it is that with great power there also comes great responsibility!" (#200:44). The episode ends with the burglar dying of a heart attack from his fear of Spider-Man.

The ordeal of being kidnapped made Aunt May stronger, bringing her and Peter closer together as she echoes a saying reminiscent of St. Paul in 1 Corinthians 13: "Love is the greatest medicine of all" (#200:46). (Aunt May is portrayed as a Christian, if we recall her praying the Lord's Prayer in the first Spider-Man film.) Peter also grew through the experience. He realized that his role as Spider-Man has augmented his sense of justice and hatred for crime. In a rare acknowledgment of God, Spider-Man says:

> At last I realize I'm the luckiest guy in the whole, wide, wonderful world! Most people wish they could help their fellow man, but this ol' web-swinger has the power to do it! Somehow, somewhere—someone with far greater power than I managed to put it all together! And I swear to be worthy—and grateful—for the rest of my life! (#200:47)

Spider-Man's great responsibility is changed at this point. No longer is it riddled with guilt but a realization that he is privileged and chosen by God to help out other people. By getting a second chance to bring his uncle's killer back to justice, he believes that he is making amends for his former negligence; and yet even this "atonement" seems misguided. It still assumes that a good deed can erase a bad deed instead of genuinely asking forgiveness and trusting in God's grace. In New Testament theology the sacrifice of Jesus on the cross becomes the perfect remedy for guilt. If Peter were a real person, he wouldn't need to make perpetual sacrifices for his mistake; Christ already paid the price for his guilt on the cross. As the New Testament affirms, salvation is by grace through faith, not by works (Ephesians 2:8–9).

But of course, without Spider-Man's guilt, we would not have him as a suffering hero calling to mind the Passion of Christ. The depictions of Spider-Man that have reached mythic proportions resemble Christ crucified. Spider-Man looks crucified with his arms spread out in *Amazing Fantasy* #15 (his origin), *Amazing Spider-Man* #1 (his first solo magazine), and *Amazing Spider-Man* # 258 (his first new costume). Moreover, the first *Spider-Man* movie has him stretched out holding a cable in one hand and Mary Jane in the other, while the Green Goblin misquotes Jesus' "suffer the children..." message (Mark 10:14, King James Version). Then in *Spider-Man 2* he stretches his arms to save the people of New York from being killed on a stray subway train, before passing out. Spider-Man mimics the role of Jesus as the suffering and sacrificial savior of humanity.

Spider-Man as the Model of Human Imperfection

When Adam and Eve fell in the Garden, God said, "Behold, the *adam* has become as one of us to know good and evil," and then God banished them from Eden (Genesis 3:22–23). By eating from the forbidden fruit, humanity gained knowledge of right and wrong, making them more like God while at the same time making them more frail and imperfect by disobeying God. The message remains the same in the Spider-Man episodes and Genesis: humanity is flawed and has lost its original communion with God. The success of Jesus was that God now ventured to become as "one of us." Born of humble origins as a frail man, utterly human; this god-man came to humanity's rescue and set people back on the path to paradise.

If Spider-Man functions as a Christ-type, he inevitably points to the human son of Mary rather than the Son of God. Spider-Man and Jesus are saviors in a differentiated sense. Though misunderstood by peers and the public, they selflessly work for the righteous cause of helping humanity. Beyond this, Peter resembles his namesake, the apostle Peter, more than Jesus. In the Gospels, Peter is the imperfect saint who tries to do what is right but constantly messes up. Unlike Jesus, both Peter Parker and St. Peter in the Gospels are harassed by guilt, lack a proper understanding of grace, and suffer as a result of their imperfections. They are *perfect* models of the blundering humans whom Christ loved and died to save.

An article in *Time* magazine reports: "It's not enough that superheroes fight our battles. We need them to suffer our heartbreaks, reflect our anxieties, embody our weaknesses."[26] If we are to relate Spider-Man and Christ, this seems best accomplished by looking at them as examples of human suffering and sacrifice. Mortals like us can identify with what is human about a savior. Jesus worked as a carpenter, grew hungry, tired, cried at the loss of loved ones, and of course, suffered and sacrificed himself for others. It is definitely in the humanity rather than deity of Christ that we see reflections of Spider-Man most clearly. Perhaps our culture needs to see more of what is human about Jesus: his life and teachings as a rabbi, his vulnerability and sufferings, his Passion. Perchance it is through his humanity that we will find a more fervent love for his deity.

Notes

[1] Jordan Raphael and Tom Spurgeon, *Stan Lee and the Rise and Fall of the American Comic Book* (Chicago: Chicago Press Review, 2003), 140. When co-creating Spider-Man (with artists Jack Kirby and Steve Ditko), Lee wanted to try a different approach than with the Fantastic Four or the Hulk. Lee decided to experiment on his new idea with a fledgling comic entitled *Amazing Fantasy,* and thus the name "Amazing" appears before Spider-Man's first comic series. Kirby drew Spider-Man too heroic-looking; Lee wanted a more human, average-looking Spider-Man, and so he chose Ditko's quirky realism as the perfect fit for his new hero. John Romita took over as artist beginning in *Amazing Spider-Man* #39 (1966). His clear drawing style made his portraits of Spider-Man the most memorable of the Silver Age. In more recent memory, Todd McFarlane's unique sketches of Spidey are reminiscent of Ditko's.

[2] Cf. Carol Christine Mahoney, "A Content Analysis of Family Relationships in Six Superhero Comic Book Series," Master's thesis, Michigan State University, 1997, 2.

[3] Steven Kotler, "A Hero's Ride," *Variety* 390/8 (April 7–13, 2003), 35.

[4] Stan Lee "Foreword," in Tom Defalco, *Spider-Man: The Ultimate Guide* (New York: Dorling Kindersley Publishing, 2001), 1.

[5] Stan Lee, *Origins of Marvel Comics* (New York: Simon & Schuster, 1974), 133–34. The novel approach to this character does not mean that Spider-Man was the very first teenage superhero. Superboy, Marvel Boy, and other teen heroes preceded him. Moreover, he was not the first spider-type hero. In the early 1940s DC worked on the Tarantula in the early issues of *Star Spangled Comics.* He was a costumed character that shot a web-gun and crawled on walls via suction cups.

[6] Peter later finds out that his parents were accused of being traitors to the U.S. As he investigates their lives, he discovers that they actually worked against the Nazi

villain called the Red Skull. They died as American spies, not traitors. Peter thus clears his parents' reputation (*Amazing Spider-Man Annual* #5; 1968).

[7] In the comic version, Parker creates his own web fluid; he does not intrinsically shoot spider webs as portrayed in the movie and *Spider-Man 2099.*

[8] In the comic series when Peter attempts to redeem himself by fighting Flash in a fair boxing match, this backfires as Flash turns to look at someone crying for help while Peter hits him. Flash gets knocked out, but the students boo Peter for an unfair hit (*Amazing Spider-Man* #8).

[9] Important issues related to the Aunt May–Doc Ock relationship include *Amazing Spider-Man Annual* #1; *Amazing Spider-Man* Vol. 1 #54, 115, 130–131.

[10] At one time he showed some fondness for Sue Richards, the Invisible Girl from the Fantastic Four before she becomes Reed Richard's wife (*Amazing Spider-Man* #8).

[11] Compare, for example, Peter's mother in *Spider-Man Annual* #5 (1968), with John Romita and Steve Ditko's sketches of Betty from 1965 to 1968.

[12] Later on, however, she comes to terms with the fact that the web-slinger actually was trying to save her life (*Amazing Spider-Man* #11; 1964).

[13] Important issues related to Peter and Gwen's relationship include *Amazing Spider-Man* #31, 37, 47, 50, 53, 59–60, 82, 90–95, 98–103.

[14] In the comic (#121) it looks like the Brooklyn Bridge; cf. Edward Gross, *Spider-Man Confidential: From Comic Icon to Hollywood Hero* (New York: Hyperion, 2002), 24.

[15] M.J. makes cameos in *Amazing Spider-Man* #15, 25, 38 (vol. 1). Unlike the movie version, which has Peter knowing her since childhood, Peter does not meet her until he is already in college.

[16] What are Jameson's motives for harassing Spider-Man? Outwardly he believes Spidey is a bad influence on young people because he is doing dangerous feats and taking the law into his own hands. He does admit that Spider-Man stories sell papers. Inwardly, however, J.J.J. hates Spider-Man because the web-slinger risks life and limb without hope of any reward; he's "brave, powerful, and unselfish," unlike Jameson who cannot respect himself and envies Spider-Man (*Amazing Spider-Man* #10). Later on it is revealed that J.J.J.'s wife was killed by a masked villain, resulting in his disdain for masked men. The city editor, Joe "Robbie" Robinson, who is sympathetic toward Spider-Man, assists as a type of conscience for Jameson. It is only when Spider-Man cures J.J.J.'s son, John Jameson, from becoming the Man-Wolf, that his father almost seems apologetic to Spider-Man (*Amazing Spider-Man* #1, 4–5, 51, 124–25).

[17] This remains the typical reason why superheroes need secret alter egos, and it has been explored recently in DC's *Identity Crisis* #1 (2004).

[18] Apart from the Green Goblin, those who discover or almost discover his secret identity include Doc Ock (#12); Aunt May, J.J.J., Spencer Smith (#25), Betty (#34), Patch/Fredrick Foswell (#46), J.J.J. (#69), M.J., Harry, and Gwen (#87), Robbie Robinson (#82), Captain Stacy (#90).

[19] See DeFalco, *Spider-Man: The Ultimate Guide,* 88–89, 129, 132–33 for a synopsis of Green Goblin stories after Norman Osborn's death.

[20] See the *Spider-Man 2* film (2004). On her alleged death bed, "Aunt May" reveals to Peter that she has known for years about his identity as Spider-Man (*Amazing Spider-Man* #400). In addition, Professor Warren, Gwen Stacy's clone, and Ned Leeds must have all known that Peter was Spider-Man (beginning in *Amazing Spider-Man* issues 142–149). Cf. also Peter Sanderson, *Marvel Universe* (New York: Harry N. Abrams, 1996), 85.

[21] Brock held a vendetta against Spider-Man because he caught a serial killer called Sin-Eater when Brock had turned in an imposter who confessed to be Sin-Eater. This reportedly cost Brock his reputation, job, and wife. For a synopsis, see DeFalco, *Ultimate Guide,* 109, 120.

[22] The clone issues are too many to mention, but some prominent ones (from 1974 to 1996) are *Amazing Spider-Man* #129, 144–51, 394; *Spectacular Spider-Man* #217; *Web of Spider-Man* #117; *Sensational Spider-Man* #1–11; *Amazing Scarlet Spider* #1–2; and *Spider-Man* #51, 75. For a synopsis of the clone saga, see DeFalco, *Ultimate Guide,* 86–87, 136–45.

[23] Sanderson, *Marvel Universe,* 78.

[24] Relevant issues related to this saga are *Amazing Spider-Man* #10, 29–33 (1964–66).

[25] Danny Fingeroth, *Superman on the Couch: What Superheroes Really Tell Us about Ourselves and Our Society* (New York: Continuum, 2004), 74–75.

[26] Andrew Arnold, Benjamin Nugent, and Heather Won Tesoriero, "Superhero Nation," *Time* 159/20 (May 20, 2002), 76–78.

Recommended Resources

DeFalco, Tom. *Spider-Man: The Ultimate Guide.* New York: Dorling Kindersley Publishing, 2001.

DeFalco, Tom. *Comics Creators on Spider-Man.* London: Titan Books, 2004.

Fingeroth, Danny. "Storm of the Orphans: Superman, Batman, and Spider-Man." In *Superman on the Couch: What Superheroes Really Tell Us about Ourselves and Our Society.* New York: Continuum, 2004.

Gross, Edward. *Spider-Man Confidential: From Comic Icon to Hollywood Hero.* New York: Hyperion, 2002.

Lee, Stan. *Origins of Marvel Comics.* New York: Simon & Schuster; 1974.

Lee, Stan, Steve Ditko, and John Romita. *The Essential Spider-Man.* 4 vols. New York: Marvel, 2002.

McFarlane, Todd, and David Michelinie. *Spider-Man vs. Venom.* New York: Marvel, 1990.

Meyer, Michaela D. E. "Utilizing Mythic Criticism in Contemporary Narrative Culture: Examining the 'Present-Absence' of Shadow Archetypes in Spider-Man." *Communication Quarterly* 51/4 (Fall 2003): 518–29.

Mondello, Salvatore. *Spider-Man: Superhero in the Liberal Tradition.* Bowling Green, Ohio: Bowling Green State University, 1976.

Sanderson, Peter. "Your Friendly Neighborhood Spider-Man." In *Marvel Universe.* New York: Harry N. Abrams, Inc., Publishers, 1996.

Stern, Roger, Tom DeFalco, Rick Leonardi, and Ron Frenz. *The Saga of the Alien Costume: Starring the Amazing Spider-Man.* New York: Marvel, 1991.

Vaz, Mark Cotta. *Behind the Mask of Spider-Man: The Secrets of the Movie.* New York: The Ballantine Publishing Group, 2002.

Vineberg, Steve. "To Kiss a Spider." *Christian Century* 119/11 (22–29 May, 2002), 48.

7
Running from or Embracing the Truth Inside You? Bruce Banner and the Hulk as a Paradigm for the Inner Self

Robin J. Dugall

Facing the truth about ourselves hurts like hell. No one with any level of sanity likes the inward journey. Even the archaic monks of Christendom had to ordain a process of circumspection as a spiritual discipline (i.e., the disciplines of Confession and Solitude), thereby challenging novices to dig deeper into the soul, the inner core of who they really are. To open the depths of our own life is one of the most frightening and sobering journeys we may ever take. Come on, admit it—if given the choice of staring into the psychoanalytic mirror or analyzing the mild neuroses of anybody else in your life, the choice would be ruthlessly obvious. You would take the path of least resistance and take an in-depth look at someone else before risking the danger of navigating through the waters of self-dissection...right? The Hulk is a superhero whose myth prompts us to the attention of deeper questions related to our own psyche: questions about identity, anger, self-deception, and grace.

The Hulk and Human Identity Crisis

> "Who am I? This or the other? Am I then, this today and the other tomorrow? Am I both at the same time? In public, a hypocrite and by myself, a contemptible, whining weakling?... Lonely questions mock me. Who I really am, you know me, I am thine, O God!" *Wer Bin Ich?* (a few stanzas from a poem by Dietrich Bonhoeffer)[1]

Who am I? It is this question and the earthy struggle epitomized in it that evolves into the story of the Hulk. Dr. Robert Bruce Banner, a nuclear scientist, becomes the green-skinned goliath as a result of heroism. He saves a young civilian named Rick Jones who happens to be at the wrong place at the wrong time when an experimental gamma bomb explodes. Banner is not so lucky, however. He gets sprayed with gamma rays from the explosion, and this turns him into the Hulk whenever he gets emotionally overdrawn. The introverted scientist becomes what he suppressed in himself; an egotistical brute who loves his own power, abhors reason, and "thinks with his fists."[2]

Unleashed by creators Stan Lee and Jack Kirby in *The Incredible Hulk* #1 (1962), the Hulk brings to mind other literary characters that battle with the depth of human existence: Dr. Jekyll/Mr. Hyde and Frankenstein.[3] Like the former, he owns a dark alter ego; like the latter, he craves acceptance but receives fear and persecution instead. He was one of the first antiheroes in the Silver Age of comic books, yet he may also echo the legend of Golem, the medieval monster of clay who was a dangerous protector of the Jewish people in Prague.[4] Lee's motive when creating the character involved his desire to have an imperfect hero with whom we could empathize. The grotesque Thing from the Fantastic Four connected with fans, and so Lee wanted to create another innovative character with bad exterior but superstrength.[5]

As the Hulk, Banner seemed to be fairly intelligent in the earliest episodes (*Incredible Hulk* #1–6; 1962–63) and in a brief stint with the superhero team called the *Avengers*. After his co-starring in *Tales to Astonish* (#60–101; 1964–68), he received his own title again (beginning with *The Incredible Hulk* #102; 1968); yet by this time his level of IQ seemed to resemble that of a child. He talks more in the comic book than in his late 1970s television series starring Lou Ferrigno or in Ang Lee's movie in 2003. And he definitely does not possess the same level of wit and articulation as that of his postmodern female counterpart, the *She-Hulk*. In any case, in his most popular mythos,[6] the Hulk is nowhere near as brilliant as Bruce Banner.

Then again, Banner's strength is nowhere near the Hulk's! When he is not running from someone or chasing something, he is attempting to contain a beast that has the propensity to destroy everything he cherishes. He has an exterior that has the ability to lift over 70 tons without breaking a sweat, powerful legs that help him jump a distance of more than 1 ½ miles, and he can resist penetration by high-impact blows from artillery shells. This leads to the green behemoth's boast, "Hulk is strongest one there is!" As sonic booms created by the slamming together of his hands often create lethal force, even so, it is nothing compared to the inferno that ravages his internal existence. Banner's life carries scars of personal tragedy, internal confusion, repressed emotions, relational meltdowns, and parental abuse. His father killed Bruce's mother, and went into fits of rage, hitting little Bruce and calling him a "monster" (e.g., *The Incredible Hulk* #312; 1985). For Banner, then, it is his psyche more than just his body that is ravaged with the intensity of a dark and terrifying journey. He is caught up in a nightmare that never seems to end.

The Bruce Banner/Hulk transformation is a paradigm for the spiritual and psychological struggle that every person faces. The dilemma of Bruce Banner summarizes the struggle of humanity—just like the Hulk, everyone possesses in the inner child a primal rage, pent-up fury, egotism, and potential for destructive mayhem. Do we run from or embrace the battle for the fulfillment of our own soul and God-sketched purpose? What does this intense warfare in the existence of every person tell us about our world and our God? Ken Gire, in his insightful book, *Windows of the Soul*, states, "our search for God and His search for us meet at the windows of our everyday experience."[7] If the soul of every living person, that inner core of who we really are, is expressed by everything we do and say, what does this mean in relation to the depth of our existence? What do the windows of our inner person show us about our lives? Any honest voyeur of comic lore eventually has to confront the reality of what this dilemma underscores in the human experience. If Bruce were listening to his life, perhaps this is what he would be hearing:

> Sin used what was good to bring about my condemnation. So we can see how terrible sin really is...the trouble is not with the law but with me because I am sold into slavery, with sin as my master. I don't understand myself at all, for I really want to do what is right, but I don't do it. Instead, I do the very thing I hate...I can't help myself, because it is sin inside of me that makes me do evil things. (Romans 7:13–20; *The Message* translation of the New Testament)

The same issues that haunt Dr. Banner as he wrestles with the green monster that lives inside of him are the issues we face—isolation, loneliness, breakdown of community, inner turmoil, and the inability to control our rage. Consequently, the soul desperately erupts. From the depth of every person emerges his or her own ability to "hulk out."

Years ago I sat across the room from a noted psychiatrist as he pronounced the verdict that I was entering into a lifelong battle with biological unipolar disorder. My first reaction was to run from the truth of my biochemistry. I would soon learn that in a skirmish between good intentions and reality, reality wins every time. As I sat squirming in my chair, I had a choice. Initially, being exposed to the reality of the medical condition of depression completely altered my world. For days, I agonized over what I had become. I told myself I would never be able to experience God's ultimate dreams for my life. Anger built inside of me to the point where I lashed out against myself, my relationships, and environment in ever increasingly barbaric ways. It was not until I sat in a stupor of mental exhaustion and spiritual bankruptcy that I was able to see clearly. My well-meaning humanity had gone awry. I could face the truth, try to run from it, anesthetize, or deny it, but I was never going to get away from it. My own "hulk" has been incarnated in me.

Escape to Fury

When my children were small, we would frequent Disneyland. It never ceased to amaze me how they would pass through the main gate and make a beeline to Fantasyland. In an atmosphere of pretend and imagination, they would leave the real world for one of flying elephants, Cheshire cats, and sleeping beauties. Nevertheless, as I have put more years under the belt of my life, I have come to the conclusion that "fantasyland" is not just a children's destination. Real-life experience demonstrates repetitively that most of us feel more comfortable living in a land of make-believe than dealing with reality. Most of us prefer to construct a world in which we are safe, the masters of our destinies, and protected from our emotional and spiritual upheavals. We wish to circumvent the perilous quest for self-understanding and transformation. As many people quip these days, "denial just isn't a river in Egypt."

In a strange sense, Bruce Banner's transformation into the Hulk becomes for him an escape route, an outlet in which he can indulge in mayhem. He can abandon reason and let his fury run wild as the rampaging monster, akin to unleashing latent desires from a Freudian "Id" or the insatiable driving "will" of Schopenhauer. As Danny Fingeroth affirms, the "Hulk personifies the anger that Batman needs a rationalization for."[8] There are times when we would like to act primitive and childish just like the Hulk; after all, he is super strong, he gets to vent out his anger, and he "smashes stuff."[9] However, living such a life is not without its dangers; it takes a huge toll on the heart and soul. When in pain and internal conflict, every individual confronts critical interior forces. In one corner of the heart is the soul's insistence upon reality and truthfulness; in the other corner, the shaming voices of condemnation that point the accusing "finger" to any imperfection and shortcoming. Often out of the desperate fear of being exposed to the world as a phony and psychological invalid comes the choice to enter the realm of self-deception. It is no wonder that many individuals out of desperation create larger-than-life personas as a means of deflecting the accusations and self-flagellation coming from their own soul. Over a process of time, human beings, dedicated to façade, become experts at the art of blaming, deflecting, anesthetizing, and avoiding their inner struggles. The fact is that modern culture has actually encouraged us to run the hard drive of our heart and spirit on the operating system of avoidance or a deflection of personal responsibility.

Even with a straight dose of reality, an honest traveler along the path of righteousness eventually comes to terms with the truth that we were created with something grander in mind. There is something in the human soul that cries out for more than meets the eye. Even so, with every personal construct comes a partnership with repression that desires to crush the vision of God, who has engineered the human life with a hunger for eternity and perfection. There is within all human beings a desire to not only commune with their Creator but understand the joy of the human experience as God originally designed. In the words of the *Qohelet*: "He (God) has also set eternity in their heart" (Ecclesiastes 3:11). When God proclaims seven times the "goodness" of his creation (Genesis 1), it is not just a revelatory comment about his nature and character but also something that denotes his purpose in creating human life. God desires us to experience his goodness, intimacy with him, inner peace, fulfillment, and fruitfulness of life. Our dilemma is how to reconcile what, in many respects, can be seen as two separate natures. One has been created by God to experience purpose and supernatural presence in the deepest levels of our psyche; the other is distorted by deception and "manufactured" by the fear, sinfulness and brokenness of our own existence. Humans are a paradox. We are cursed and blessed; we are chosen and rejected; we are favored and scorned. No wonder the apostle Paul lamented, "Wretched man that I am! Who will set me free from the body of this death?" (Romans 7:24)

Gamma Rays and the Light of Grace

The primal scream of the Hulk, as Fingeroth asserts, is essentially "the existential cry of humankind, the reason even the rich and accomplished suffer angst and depression. Is it biochemical? Is it spiritual? Whatever the reason, something is wrong. Something we can't name or define, something that a run in the park or drink or a visit to a brothel or a house of worship won't cure. It just…hurts to be alive."[10] What then is wrong with us? Maybe the inexpressible has to do with our fallenness. Our lives have been affected by "gamma exposure" to sin. Yes, our bodies took a good-sized portion of the negative brunt of that experience, but it seems that the heart and the soul were infected the most. Our tortured psyche becomes the Achilles heel of human living.

Anxiety often becomes our lot once we see our hurt, sin, and inner pain for what they really are. This has a tendency to lead us into a dark night of the soul. Every one of us wrestles with an inner disorder brought about by chronic exposure to the gamma rays of sin. Just as Dr. Banner incarnated the harsh lessons of science run amok, so our daily lives repeatedly demonstrate unmanageable fallenness. Banner's famous line, "you wouldn't like me when I'm angry" is oft repeated in his life journey; it is a line we could sheepishly recite for our own shortcomings. The paradox of the human journey is that at the precise moment of our greatest defeat, God's most glorious victory is won in the human experience. Just as Jesus Christ, the incarnate presence of the eternal creator, experienced glory through the crucible of suffering, so we also have the possibility of triumphantly emerging from the shadows of death. The New Testament calls us to look to our weaknesses, not in defeat or resignation, but as a launching pad for the grace of God to be released. The apostle Paul, in outlining his own perilous inner plight, states succinctly: "[s]o now I can boast about my weaknesses, so that the power of Christ may work through me. Since I know it is all for Christ's good, I am quite content with my weaknesses and with insults, hardships, persecutions, and calamities. For when I am weak, then I am strong" (2 Corinthians 12:9b–10; New Living Translation).

Instead of wondering what life could have been like if we had not fallen, or if we had not been exposed to "gamma rays," the biblical message tells us that the grace and mercy of God reveals itself at our point of greatest weakness. It is at the point of our emergence from the dark night of personal concealment that we experience the most profound of spiritual development. A lesson from the handbook of spiritual transformation could aptly read, "When at your deepest struggle, realize that something profoundly superior and innately more faithful to your created purpose is striving to be born." In *Dark Night of the Soul*, St. John of the Cross writes to this effect:

> The soul which God is about to lead onward is not led by His Majesty into this night of the spirit as soon as it goes forth from the aridities and trials of the first purgation and night of sense; rather it is wont to pass a long time, even years, after leaving the state of beginners, in exercising itself in that of proficients. In this latter state it is like to one that has come forth from rigorous imprisonment, it goes about the things of God with much greater freedom and satisfaction of the soul, and with more abundant and inward delight than it did at the beginning before it entered the said night.[11]

The revelation of God communicates in a clarity that even the most creative of art expression cannot match. Especially when the subject of what God can do in the midst of intense personal battle is broached, God's Word is sharp and persuasive. The book of Numbers reveals a God whose purposes of transformation in human life can occur through the testing of personal wilderness and corporate exile. Paul's letter to the Romans divulges that the vision of the divine in human experience can be accomplished through the recycling of any personality construct or persona through the filters of divine grace. The resurrection demonstrates time and again the persistence of divine sovereignty and the extent of divine love.

God is calling out to humanity, similar to how Genesis 3 describes the Creator calling the first couple: "where are you?" These words do not threaten but console. They reveal a God who is just as anxious to embrace humanity as humanity is to hide from God. Our decision of whether to run or embrace the divine wooing will reveal the depth of our desire to find victory over the battle we each face with our destructive nature. If we choose to run, we will join the Hulk. Ever since the accident transformed him into something huge and green, Bruce Banner has been a man on the run. Whether it is from General Thaddeus E. "Thunderbolt" Ross and his military force, the gamma-induced nemesis, the Leader, clandestine forces, or from the beast that lives inside of him, the Hulk/Banner has a life on the run. As the Hulk, he longs for acceptance, yet Banner struggles to accept himself. Sinners yet potential saints, many people also run and hide from the truth that presents itself to them. Frederick Buechner writes:

> The Gospel is bad news before it is good news. It is the news that man is a sinner, to use the old word, that he is evil in the imagination of his heart, that when he looks in the mirror all in a lather what he sees is at least eight parts chicken, phony, slob. That is a tragedy. But it is also the news that he is loved anyway, cherished, forgiven, bleeding to be sure, but also bled for.[12]

It appears at first glance like opposites: a man endowed with superpowers but with the intellect and temperament of a child. However, Jesus shows us the superhuman possibilities of what God can do with those who trust like a child—faith to move mountains, abilities to run and not grow weary, and passion that can change the trajectory of human history. These things are available for the tortured human soul. As terrifying as it appears at the outset, the Gospel challenges us to look inside of ourselves, not to be horrified by what we find living within, but to embrace that which the God of this universe declares redeemable. In a strange manner of speaking, that which is the most repulsive is actually that which longs to be embraced.

Slaying the Monster: Making a Saint out of the "Hulk from Within"

Like many humans, the Hulk is not really an evil person. He likes kids and animals and does not plan out the death of his enemies; but he still finds unrest. He mostly wants acceptance yet only occasionally finds it. As the Hulk, for instance, he falls for Jarella, a green princess from the subatomic world of K'ai, but the affair does not last (*Incredible Hulk* #140; 1971), and as Banner, he marries Betty Ross, daughter of the general who persecuted him when he turns into the Hulk (*Incredible Hulk* #319; 1986). Writer Peter David's treatment of the Bruce and Betty saga "has become a strangely moving metaphor for any man and woman reaching out to each other despite their own emotional scars."[13]

The Hulk need not be a paradigm of human ingenuity gone berserk; he could be a symbol of salvation and transformation through the power of the Gospel. This same message shows us how personal wounds might themselves be sources of healing. The prophet Zechariah, in an attempt to comfort the afflicted proclaimed: "and I will pour out…a spirit of grace and supplication. They will look on me, the one they have pierced, and they will mourn for him as one mourns for an only child…. If someone asks him, 'what are these wounds on your body?', he will answer, 'The wounds I was given at the house of my friends'"(Zechariah 12:10; 13:6; New American Standard Version).

The pain that permeates the depths of our spirit ultimately find their rest in Christ. As Isaiah prophesied, "by His wounds, we are healed" (Isaiah 53:4–6). Running or living in denial is an exercise in total futility. The solution to the human plight appears to be to identify and discover the supremacy of the Gospel in human existence and undergo the comfort of Christ that overflows in the midst of any occurrence. Wounds are one of God's deepest forms of intimacy.[14] They are the pathway on which the follower discovers the ultimate eternal power of an Almighty God. The battle that occurs in the depth of every human life is the passageway from which we begin to perceive life in a fresh way and respond to the world through the loving eyes of its savior.

I have often wondered about the intention of God. I have often contemplated questions regarding the origination of pain within human experience. It is very normal to ask the ultimate question: "why?" Heretically speaking, knowing what God ultimately does with problems and struggles makes me wonder if God is not the author of suffering. I don't think a good and holy God would usher in an existence of confusion and death without contradicting his own nature. A good God can do something proactive in the souls of those who have the courage to grapple with the truth of themselves; a truth that reveals a rather dark side of our souls and yet promises to make saints out of those who trust in the power of God's grace. Perhaps suffering is simply inevitable on earth. Yes, life is a battle and we must wrestle with our own "hulkness."

We do not need a God who is safe, tame, and reinforces our need to wallow in our own inadequacies and fears. To live with a God who accommodates our sin is like Bruce Banner living with the self-deception that he will suddenly awake from the nightmare of his own existence and find normalcy again. We, like Bruce Banner, must face our demons: our past failures, our emotional scars and pain, if we truly want to be healed. God will take the courageous spiritual seekers back to the scene of their exposure to death and debilitation. There they will stand at the foot of the cross. There they will choose their private "hulk" or Jesus, self-deception or reality, desperation or freedom. If only we would embrace our brokenness, we would soon realize the grace of the Gospel. It is more powerful than a thousand gamma bombs. It redeems the past and heals its wounds. It compels us to embrace instead of run from the truth.

Notes

[1] Dietrich Bonhoeffer, *Voices in the Night* (Grand Rapids: Zondervan, 1999), 45.

[2] Peter Sanderson, *Marvel Universe* (New York: Harry N. Abrams, 1996), 57.

[3] The Hulk resembles Frankenstein in color also, but sometimes our green-skinned hero takes on a shade of gray.

[4] See Arie Kaplan, "Kings of Comics: How the Jews Transformed the Comic Book Industry Part II: The Silver Age (1956–1978)," *Reform Judaism* 32/2 (2003) [Cited 14 Aug. 2004] Online: www.uahc.org/rjmag/03winter/comics.shtml.

[5] Stan Lee, *Origins of Marvel Comics* (New York: Simon and Schuster, 1974), 74–77.

[6] Like many superheroes, the Hulk has gone through transformations over the years. These changes are to numerous to address in this chapter. For more details about Hulk variations, the reader may wish to consult Tom Delfalco, *Hulk: The Incredible Guide* (New York: DK Publishing, 2003); and Sanderson, 54–67.

[7] Kenneth Gire, *Windows of the Soul* (Grand Rapids: Zondervan, 1997), 17.

[8] Danny Fingeroth, *Superman on the Couch: What Superheroes Really Tell Us about Ourselves and Our Society* (New York: Continuum, 2004), 125.

[9] Fingeroth, 124–25.

[10] Fingeroth, 126.

[11] St. John of the Cross, *Dark Night of the Soul* (ed., E. Allison Peers; New York: Image Books/ Doubleday, 1990), 44.

[12] Frederick Buechner, *Telling the Truth* (New York: Harper and Row, 1977), 7.

[13] Sanderson, *Marvel Universe*, 66–67.

[14] Mark Buchanan, *Your God Is Too Safe* (Sisters: Multnomah, 2001), 159.

Recommended Resources

Bonhoeffer, Dietrich. *Voices in the Night: The Prison Poems*. Grand Rapids: Zondervan, 1999.

Buchanan, Mark. *Your God Is Too Safe*. Sisters: Multnomah, 2001.

Buechner, Frederick. *Telling the Truth*, Harper and Row, New York, 1977.

Delfalco, Tom. *Hulk: The Incredible Guide*. New York: DK Publishing, 2003.

Fingeroth, Danny. "You Wouldn't Like Me When I'm Angry: The Hulk, Judge Dredd, and Wolverine." Pages 119–137 in *Superman on the Couch: What Superheroes Really Tell Us about Ourselves and Our Society*. New York: Continuum, 2004.

Gire, Kenneth. *Windows of the Soul*. Grand Rapids: Zondervan, 1997.

John of the Cross. *Dark Night of the Soul*. Translated and edited by E. Allison Peers. New York: Image Books/ Doubleday, 1990.

Kaplan, Arie. "Kings of Comics: How the Jews Transformed the Comic Book Industry Part II: The Silver Age (1956-1978)." *Reform Judaism* 32/2 (2003) [Cited 14 Aug. 2004] Online: www.uahc.org/rjmag/03winter/comics.shtml.

Keifer, Kit. *Marvel Encyclopedia: The Incredible Hulk*. New York: Marvel Enterprises, 2003.

Lee, Stan. *Origins of Marvel Comics*. New York: Simon and Schuster, 1974.

Lee, Stan. *Essential Hulk*. 2 vols. New York: Marvel, 2003.

Peterson, Eugene. *The Message: The Bible in Contemporary Language*. Colorado Springs, Col.: NavPress, 2002.

Sanderson, Peter. "The Antiheroes: Human Torch, Sub-Mariner, and Hulk." Pages 40–67 in *Marvel Universe*. New York: Harry N. Abrams, Inc., Publishers, 1996.

Schamus, James, John Turman, Michael France, Stan Lee, and Ang Lee. *The Hulk: The Making of the Movie Including the Complete Screenplay*. Newmarket Pictorial Moviebook Series. New York: W. W. Norton and Company, 2003.

Williams, David E. "Temper, Temper: Director of Photography Frederick Elmes, ASC Lends Dramatic Moods to the Hulk, the Big Screen Debut of a Very Angry Superhero." *American Cinematography* 84/7 (Jl 2003): 34–45.

8
The God-Man Revisited: Christology Through the Blank Eyes of the Silver Surfer

B. J. Oropeza

In the film *Breathless* (1983), Richard Gere plays a transient car thief who loves reading Silver Surfer comic books. Both the movie character and the superhero wander from place to place and believe themselves trapped on a planet of madness they did not create. Their similarities do not go much further than this because the Surfer in no way resembles a petty thief—he reflects one of the most profound examples of the god-man in the Marvel Universe. Jack Kirby originally sketched the Silver Surfer during the height of the California surfer craze in the 1960s, yet there was nothing beach-boyish about this character except for his flying space board. He emerged originally from the Galactus trilogy (*Fantastic Four* #48–50; 1965–66) and guest-starred in *The Fantastic Four* before landing his own comic book series *The Silver Surfer* (1968–1970). Since then, the Surfer has become one of Marvel's most enduring Silver Age characters, with graphic novels and later comic series bearing his name.

When creating the pivotal story, "The Coming of Galactus," Stan Lee wanted to make a villain so powerful that planets could be destroyed by him at will and regular superheroes like the Fantastic Four would seem like insects in comparison to him. The nearly omnipotent foe was named Galactus. Kirby thought up the idea of drawing a herald for this demigod: a shiny-skinned forerunner who would soar on a surfboard through space. When Lee first saw Kirby's drawings of this silver-skinned alien, he sensed something very unique about him:

> I found a certain nobility in his demeanor, an almost spiritual quality in his aspect and his bearing. In determining what his speech pattern would be, I began to imagine the way that a space-born apostle would speak. There seemed something biblically pure about our Silver Surfer, something totally selfless and magnificently innocent. As you can gather, I was tempted to imbue him with a spirit of almost religious purity.... I saw him as someone

who would graphically represent all the best, the most unselfish, qualities of intelligent life.[1]

Whereas Lee affirms the original Silver Surfer resembles an "apostle" and that which is "biblically pure," other writers have taken this concept to the next level by comparing the Surfer with Jesus Christ.[2] His myth reads like that of the Gospel of Christ, the spotless mediator between God and humans. Les Daniels writes that the Surfer represents the "highest aspirations of the Spirit."[3] The Surfer's goodness is envied by Mephisto, a satanic being who perpetually tempts the Surfer to surrender his soul to the demon, and similar to Christ as Divine Son of God, he possesses enough cosmic power to both create and destroy.

Throughout history many theologians have pondered the paradox of how Jesus Christ's Passion, his suffering and death on the cross, atones for the sins of humankind. Many affirm with St. Anselm's *Cur Deus homo* (Why God became Man) that if humans have sinned, and if God is the one who is ultimately offended by and can forgive sin, Jesus Christ the supreme god-man bridges the gap between the two parties as the perfect mediator. Still there remains some ambiguity about how this transaction takes place and how Jesus could be fully God and fully human as portrayed in the Gospels and early Christian creeds. While these mysteries may never be entirely resolved this side of eternity, pop culture superheroes might provide us a new way of viewing an old mystery. If the Silver Surfer points to divinity and yet suffers very humanly, something could be said here about the way our culture perceives the Christ of faith and the Jesus of history. The Silver Surfer myth may help us look at Christology (the study of Christ) through a fresh pair of eyes.[4]

The Passion of the Silver Surfer:
Saving the World Through Self-Sacrifice

The Galactus trilogy, arguably Stan Lee and Jack Kirby's greatest saga in the *Fantastic Four*,[5] resembled the apocalyptic doomsday described in the book of Revelation. The earth receives an omen: two suns appear instead of one, and the new sun turns the entire sky into flames as the earth dwellers panic below. The sign turns out to be an illusion created by the Watcher (Uatu), a super-alien who observes and records the cosmos but is sworn not to interfere with its species (similar to philosophical Deism). He intends to conceal the earth from being spotted by the Silver Surfer and Galactus. The Surfer possesses the power cosmic that enables him to shoot energy bolts from his hands and ride on a surfboard that travels through space at astronomical speeds. He is the herald of Galactus, a virtually omnipotent being except for one contingency—he needs to consume all the energy from planets to replenish his own. He bears no remorse about devouring the planets of lower life-forms; much the same way humans have no remorse about eating shrimp or stepping on an ant. The Surfer spots the planet Earth despite the Watcher's subterfuge, and he sends a signal to Galactus, who soon arrives ready for his terrestrial feast that would end all life on Earth.

Convinced by Alicia Masters (the Thing's blind girlfriend) that humans possess beauty and kindness, the Silver Surfer resolves to protect humanity against his master.[6] In a cosmic battle with Galactus, the Surfer unleashes his power, willing to sacrifice his life for the human race, learning "how glorious it can be to have a cause worth dying for" (*Fantastic Four* #50:7; 1966). Through the help of the Watcher, the Fantastic Four find the ultimate nullifier, a weapon that can destroy an entire galaxy or more. Mr. Fantastic threatens to trigger it unless Galactus vows not to harm Earth, and so Galactus departs after he pronounces punishment on his rebellious herald. He sentences the Surfer to life on Earth by taking away his space-time abilities and enforcing an energy barrier that would stop the shiny space rider from escaping (*Fantastic Four* #50, #60).

In a second encounter with the Fantastic Four, Galactus suffers from hunger because he cannot find a planet to consume that is relatively close to Earth. Returning to planet Earth, he searches for the Silver Surfer so that the latter might assist him in finding another planet. When he cannot locate his former herald, Galactus threatens to break his vow and consume the earth unless the Fantastic Four can locate him. The Surfer helps Galactus find another planet for consumption and then requests to be set free from Earth. His former master refuses his request by saying that it will be easy to locate the Surfer in the future as long as he is trapped on the earth. Hence the Surfer helps save the world once again at the price of his own freedom; his fate is to remain with those he saved (*Fantastic Four* # 74–77; 1968).

The earliest Silver Surfer functions as a white angelic harbinger of doom, commonly found in the biblical book of Revelation.[7] The Watcher's signs in the sky likewise recall celestial omens found in Revelation and other apocalyptic literature. There is something about major tragedies that drive people to consider their own helplessness and need for someone as powerful as God to rescue them. The Fantastic Four is no exception: Alicia "prayed" that the Surfer would turn against Galactus (*Fantastic Four* #50:12). When the Galactus saga is reworked in Kurt Busiek and Alex Ross's *Marvels* (1996), one scene has a multitude of people cramming into a church building after seeing the giant invader. During the Fantastic Four's second encounter with Galactus, Reed Richards says something similar to that of Alicia: "We'd better start praying...for a miracle!" (*Fantastic Four* #76:5). The Silver

Surfer's character develops more into a Christ-type as the plot unfolds. He comes down from the heavens to "save" the earth by self-sacrifice. Moreover, as the book of Revelation predicts Christ's Second Coming to deliver the world from Armageddon, so the Silver Surfer becomes Earth's protector from doomsday at the hand of Galactus. Later on he protects the planet against aliens called the Brotherhood of Badoon, and he saves the world again, this time from a meteor collision akin to the depiction in Revelation chapter 8 of a falling star or "great burning mountain" that impacts the earth (*The Silver Surfer* #2, 1968; #14, 1970).

When the Silver Surfer appeared in his first comic book series (1968–70), Stan Lee and artist John Buscema provided elaboration on the Surfer's origin. He formerly lived as Norrin Radd on an idyllic planet called Zenn-La. Discontent with a perfect society and perpetual pleasure, he longs for a new challenge, desiring to explore the cosmos. Essentially Radd's view of true paradise was not to be equated with his utopian society; it remained "out there" among the stars of heaven. Galactus forever changed Radd's paradise world by threatening its energy for consumption. Having faith that he could persuade the invader to spare Zenn-La, he volunteers himself as the titan's herald. Galactus accepts the offer and re-creates Norrin Radd into the Silver Surfer, giving him silvery skin for protection against space elements and a surfboard to travel the galaxies. With a god-like command, he bids the Surfer to go and span the universe, finding suitable planets for him to devour. Yet the lifelong dream for adventure is mixed with bitterness because Radd must leave his female love, Shalla Bal, behind in order to fulfill Galactus' beckonings (*The Silver Surfer* #1; 1968).

We see through his origin story that the Surfer saved his own planet long before he became Earth's savior and its guardian angel. This multiple deliverance of worlds reinforces the idea that his central myth is embedded with concepts of sacrifice and suffering, similar to Christ's Passion. Whereas the Gospels portray Jesus losing his life to save the world from sin, death, and eternal condemnation, the Surfer sacrifices himself to be Galactus' servant in order to deliver his planet Zenn-La. When it comes to Earth's inhabitants, both Christ and the Surfer forfeit themselves for people who misunderstand them. Jesus was rejected and betrayed by those he wished to save. The Surfer is feared and hated by humanity due to his cosmic power and good deeds that are wrongly interpreted as hostility toward humans. Even Spider-Man misunderstands him in their classic brawl. It is not until he sees the Surfer protect a boy while soldiers relentlessly shell him with artillery that Spidey realizes his own prejudice: "Because he was strong...because he was different...I thought he was a menace! I was guilty of acting towards him...the way others have acted...toward me!" (*The Silver Surfer* #14:20; 1970).

King of Kings? Surfer Ethics on Love vs. Power

Of all the Marvel heroes in the 1960s, the Silver Surfer is arguably the most powerful. His cosmic energy is said to be the most powerful force in the entire galaxy; it has both the ability to create and to destroy, imitating the power of a deity (*Fantastic Four* #55; 57:6; 1966). And like the god-man Jesus, the Surfer has the ability to heal those drawing near to death: He restores a male witch back to health, he cures a female victim of the Badoons, he heals Shalla Bal who gets into a flying accident, and he also heals himself after getting hit by a fatal blow from Galactus.[8]

The Surfer turns out to be a formidable match for the gods as he battles Loki, god of evil, to a stand-still (before Loki decides to quit the fight). Later he defeats Thor, taking his hammer away from him, although his victory is skewed because Loki deceptively infused the Surfer's power with his own (*The Silver Surfer* #4; Feb. 1969). When fighting in the land of the Inhumans, he considers Maximus' powerful henchmen to be "less than insects" (*The Silver Surfer* #18:5; 1970). Even the Hulk, Earth's strongest hero in the Marvel Universe, is no match for the Silver Surfer. The Surfer knocks him out with a single cosmic bolt and almost heals the green-skinned goliath of all his gamma radiation, but then the Hulk wakes up and disrupts the cosmic operation (*Tales to Astonish* #93; 1967). While in a temporarily weakened state, the Surfer is still able to decisively beat the Abomination, the Hulk's equally strong (if not stronger) nemesis (*The Silver Surfer* #12; 1969). At one point Stan Lee and John Buscema temporarily replaced the Surfer's normal cover subtitle from "Sky-Rider of the Spaceways!" to the "The Mightiest Superhero of All!" (*The Silver Surfer* #16; 1970).

Despite his unmatchable powers the gleaming space rider does not believe that "might makes right." He follows the golden rule of Christ and takes a stand similar to Reformer Martin Luther at the Diet of Worms: "So long as my life endures, so long as blood still courses through my veins, I will act as my heart and conscience dictate. I will harm no fellow being and will behave to all as I would have them behave to me."[9] Other Christ-like adages include the Surfer saying he will not "turn the other cheek" forever against Spider-Man (*The Silver Surfer* #14:12; 1970). As the Surfer unleashes a punishment on the world for making power its god and refusing to listen to reason, he cries out to heaven, "Forgive me, for what I am about to do! And grant me the strength so that I may forgive them who have driven me to do it!" The Surfer soon relents and undoes his cosmic destruction.[10]

Ironically the people of Earth fear the Silver Surfer because he possesses the very thing he despises in them—power! In fact this is the villain-vice of the entire myth. The space rider considers his own use of power to be tempered with reason, but he condemns humanity's lust for power because it leads to violence and mindless mayhem.

Before the Surfer fights his master to protect humanity, Galactus declares that power rules all; the Surfer argues instead that reason rules (*The Silver Surfer* 1978:27). Here the Surfer resembles the Greek titan Prometheus, who stole fire from heaven to assist humankind with progress and advanced thinking, while Galactus represents the powerful yet morally indifferent Zeus, punishing Prometheus for his rebellion by binding him with chains on a lonely rock for ages. For the Silver Surfer, reason overcomes power, and love is the ultimate force that can save humanity. The Surfer grieves over the human condition because "no matter what God they pray to...no matter the flag they may follow...in every land...in every clime... their goal is earthly power! When will they learn... that love is the power supreme?" (*The Silver Surfer* #16:2, 3, 5; 1970). The Surfer believes that humans have made power their god, but "power is blind and serves any who pay it homage! Only truth is constant! Only faith endures! And only love can save them!" (*The Silver Surfer* 1978:96). The Surfer then asks "where can love be found?" After sacrificing himself to be Galactus' herald once again in order to save the world, the Surfer's selfless act answers this very question as he returns to the hand that created him: "For a brief moment, the world understood that *love*, but what a *price!*" (1978:114).

Jesus speaks in terms of premonition regarding his sacrificial death in the Gospel of John. He teaches his disciples that the greatest love is demonstrated by a person who gives his life for others (John 15:13). In theology Pierre (Peter) Abélard asserted that the sacrifice of Christ shows humanity its greatest demonstration of love, and it thus becomes an exemplary model for humans to follow. While his view says little about the objective aspects of Christ's sacrifice, it nonetheless presents a subjective reason why some individuals receive Christ as Lord. Namely, Christ's death can save because it awakens a love in us that is willing to reciprocate: "In this we know love, because he [Christ] laid down his life for us" (1 John 3:16; cf. 4:19; Romans 5:8).[11] Complementing Abélard's theory, the Surfer's sacrifice on behalf of humanity demonstrates an example of how love can overcome power.

The Greatest Story Ever Told: The Incarnation
of the Second Adam in a Paradise Lost

After he is banished from space to be sentenced indefinitely on Earth, the Surfer begins an odyssey surveying his new terrain. If his homeland of Zenn-La resembles Thomas Moore's *Utopia*, and outer space represents for him the Eden of *Genesis*, the Surfer perceives Earth in terms of John Milton's *Paradise Lost*. In Milton's expansion of the Genesis creation, the angel Lucifer envies God's Son and then gathers a host of angels to rebel against the Most High. His forces are defeated and he is cast to hell, where he becomes Satan. Beelzebub, second in command of the fallen angels, suggests that Satan enslave a new being called (hu)man who lives on a beautiful paradise called Earth. Disguised as a serpent, Satan seduces Adam and Eve to disobey God, and so they are banished from their paradise. Sin, death, and calamity contaminate the world as a result of the first couple's failure, but the angelic Michael assures the despairing couple that God will forgive them. He unfolds the future from Noah to Abraham to Moses, and to the Messiah who brings about their posterity's redemption. The Silver Surfer soon discovers that something has caused a fundamental flaw in the human race. Although the earth has all the makings of a virtual paradise, he is disgusted by the fact that human greed, hatred, and violence have desecrated it.[12] Despite Earth's fundamental defects, the Surfer sees in it a God who watches over and cares for the planet. He attributes his ability to withstand the attack of Galactus as providential: "Perhaps there is another force, mightier than Galactus, that hath decreed...earth shall live!" (*The Silver Surfer* 1978:35).

From the Surfer's perspective humans are like clever children tinkering with technology too advanced for them, and so they tamper on the brink of self-destruction. Nevertheless he believes in the potential of humans to be something greater than they are. When Ardina, another herald of Galactus, attempts to convince the Surfer that humans are evil, savage, and oppressive, the Surfer points to their courage and aspirations as evidence to the contrary. He realizes that despite their many flaws, humans truly possess "a spark of divinity."[13] The space rider seems to believe that all mortal life should be respected because it was created by God: "that which is divinely created is truly divine!" (*The Silver Surfer* #6; 1969). This idea of humanity has close ties to Stoicism, Gnosticism, and Neoplatonism, which influenced early Christian traditions. In biblical texts, here we find allusions to the *imago Dei*, God creating humans in *God's image* (Genesis 1:26–27). Despite their fallen disposition, every human retains an imprint of God's nature in them; and as children of God, they are to be highly valued.

Even so, the Silver Surfer himself resembles a paradoxical blend of both the protagonist and antagonist in Milton's epic novel. First, he resembles the antagonist Lucifer, the angel of light who rebelled against his Master and falls from heaven to hell. When Galactus takes away the Surfer's ability for space travel, the Surfer falls in a ceremonious fashion from the heights of the heavens to the earth below. As he descends ever downward, Galactus declares: "You, who might have pierced the veil of infinity! You, whose arena was as vast as space itself! You, who were the chosen of Galactus!

You, who might have dwelled in the halls of the gods! You, have chosen, instead the dunghills of man!" (*The Silver Surfer* 1978:37). In this sense, the Surfer is banished from his paradise of space much like Lucifer is banished from heaven, and both stand amazed at the lowly yet beautiful Earth when they behold it. But the similarities turn on this crucial point: Lucifer becomes Satan, the embodiment of evil, while the Silver Surfer remains a symbol of purity. Second, the Surfer is patterned after the protagonist-victims Adam and Eve, the human couple who possess the seeds of greatness, God's image in themselves, and yet who are expelled from God's paradise as a result of disobedience. Much like the original couple, the Surfer despairs at the loss of his own paradise: the boundless heavens.

A superficial comparison may be drawn between Galactus and God. Galactus is supposedly transcendent in some sense, beyond the categories of good and evil. He has the ability to punish those who disobey his will, and he parrots words that are attributed to God in the book of Revelation: "I am the Then! I am the Now! I am the Yet to Be!"[14] His ethics are seriously questioned, however, in the Stan Lee and Jean Geraud Moebius story, "Parable." Galactus visits the earth again and allows himself to be worshiped as a god by a false prophet named Candell who heads a religious multitude. Galactus teaches his followers that power is all. They can live without laws because there is no sin, only pleasure. In this tale the Silver Surfer functions as the true prophet who teaches people about reason and holiness. Galactus attacks the Surfer but ruins the city in the process, and so the crowd turns against him, wanting to make the Surfer their god instead. He of course refuses to accept the role.[15] Hence while some vestiges between God and Galactus exist, the biblical Creator is far more benevolent than Galactus. Moreover God does not depend on planets for sustenance, and as the Watcher affirms, this Deity's ultimate "weapon" is "love" (*Fantastic Four* #72:13; Mar. 1968).

In Luke's Gospel, Adam is ultimately redeemed via his future posterity, the second Adam, who is Christ. The Christ emphatically calls himself the "Son of Man" (*Man* is synonymous with *Adam* in the Hebrew language), God's end-time representative, the savior of the world, and ancestor of the first Adam (e.g., Luke 3:23–38). In the New Testament book of Romans, the righteous work of Christ, as the Second Adam, frees the fallen status of humanity that resulted from the sin of the first Adam (Romans 5:12–20). Christ did what the first Adam could not do—remain obedient to God, even when dying on the cross. By overcoming the error of the first Adam, the second Adam is able to restore paradise. We might even suspect that the cross of Christ symbolically becomes the new "tree of life" that restores humanity's access to communion with its Creator. In other words the god-man's death (symbolically represented by the cross) reconciles God and humans, and his resurrection from the dead anticipates the renewed life humans will share in the new paradise. Ultimately, then, the Silver Surfer's plight calls to mind the banishment of the first Adam and the righteous act of the second. The distinction with the Surfer myth is that he resembled the sacrificial messiah *before* he resembled the banished Adam. Put differently, the Silver Surfer looked more divine when saving the earth and more human after being imprisoned on it. Trapped in a fallen paradise, he had no choice but to become more human.

At first the Silver Surfer is reluctant to use his cosmic power to transform himself into a human, comparing it to shedding an eagle's wings to become an ant, but he eventually alters his appearances and wears human attire.[16] The "god" therefore became "man" when the hero put on a human face as a "mask" and clothes for a costume! Here the Surfer winks at Christ's incarnation. Traditional Christianity teaches that Christ as God the Son, preexisted with God the Father from all eternity. Motivated by love, the Son voluntarily (and temporarily) "left" the glories of heaven to be born of a woman and grow up as the humble carpenter of Nazareth for the sake of redeeming humankind (Philippians 2:5–7; Galatians 4:4–6). Another name for this messiah is the *Word* or *Reason* (Greek *logos*). He participated in the creation of the *world* (Greek *cosmos*), became flesh and dwelt among humans, and the humans beheld his glory as Jesus, the unique Son of God (John 1:1–18; 3:16; Hebrews 1:3–8). In a nutshell, the incarnation teaches that God became man in Christ Jesus. The difference between the Silver Surfer and Jesus, according to theology, is that the latter never sheds his human identity once he puts it on: He forever remains the God-man. Moreover the latter is the true embodiment of God, with all power committed to him (Matthew 28:18). The Surfer is neither all-powerful nor "God" in an ultimate sense. When Sue Richards of the Fantastic Four considers the Surfer to be "all-powerful," the Watcher corrects her and implies that God alone deserves that title (*Fantastic Four* #72).

There are other differences also. The Surfer does not appear to be as confident about definitive answers to life's questions as Jesus. He claims to have traveled the universe, seen the birth and death of worlds, and yet, "never have I glimpsed the answer…to the riddle of the universe" (*The Silver Surfer* #1:44; 1968). Though morally pure, the Surfer is still a bit naïve, trusting villains who later betray him, such as Dr. Doom and Dr. Frankenstein (*Fantastic Four* #57–60; *The Silver Surfer* #7). Afterward, his distrust of humans festers to the point in which he wrongly believes that even the Fantastic Four have betrayed him. When he realizes his mistake and that he himself stands guilty of misunderstanding the Fantastic Four's intentions, he questions whether he was acting "too human or not human enough" (*The Silver Surfer* #15:20; 1970).

Another difference between Christ and the Surfer involves the sequence of their plights. Christ gave up the glories of "heaven" willingly; the Surfer unwillingly. Both made a sacrifice to deliver humanity, but Christ was exalted again after his sacrifice; the Surfer was punished for his. The progression of Christ's incarnation begins with:

- His glorious state in heaven (a metaphysical realm)
- His humility on Earth as a man
- His sacrifice on Earth
- His return to glory after the resurrection from the dead, followed by his second coming that will complete the restoration of the paradise lost

The Surfer's plight started with:

- His glory in the heavens (space)
- His sacrifice on Earth
- His humility on Earth
- His discovery that Earth is a paradise lost

In the original myth, the Surfer remained unsuccessful when trying to return to his former glory in outer space. He repeatedly attempts to break Galactus' energy barrier without any permanent success.[17] Indeed much of the angst in the original Silver Surfer rests on this premise. Things would not change until the hero's third series (1987–1998) when he finally escapes Earth, altering his original myth (something that was commonly done in the deconstructive 1980s and 1990s). Our hero discovers that his surfboard is what prevented him from penetrating Galactus' barrier. (In a strange sense we might say that his surfboard became the instrument of his suffering, functioning in a similar way to the cross in relation to Jesus.) The Surfer then frees Nova, another herald of Galactus, by penetrating a Skrull prison where she was held captive. He restores her to Galactus and is granted total freedom by his former master (*The Silver Surfer*, vol. 3 #1; 1987).

The Last Temptation of the Silver Surfer: Mephisto and Shalla Bal

Stan Lee and John Buscema added two prevalent characters to the Silver Surfer myth: Shalla Bal, the Silver Surfer's beloved woman from Zenn-La; and his arch-enemy, Mephisto, a Satan-like figure who calls himself the "Lord of evil," anticipates victory on the day of Armageddon, and dwells in the subterranean Stygian Sphere. This nemesis bears a name that resembles Goethe and the *Faustbuch*'s Mephistopheles, a devil who becomes Faust's servant in return for the magician making a pact with him to become his servant after death. True to his name, Mephisto tries to make a pact with the Silver Surfer.[18] He desires to possess the Surfer's immortal soul because the hero's goodness and purity poses a threat to planet Earth.[19] Fallen humanity does Mephisto's beckoning as long as it remains under the power of hate and greed. This devil unsuccessfully tempts the Surfer with riches, women, and kingship over a galactic empire in exchange for his soul. He then tempts him by making Shalla Bal appear before him. If Surfer would but serve Mephisto, he could be reunited again with Shalla Bal; if not, she would be sent back to Zenn-La. The tormented hero does the right thing, of course, and loses her again (*The Silver Surfer* #3; 1968). This plot rings of the Greco-Roman myth of Orpheus, the poet who loses his love Eurydice when she is bitten by a serpent. He travels to the underworld of Hades to bring her back to the land of the living after persuading the goddess Persephone to let her go on the condition that he would not look back. As he approaches the light of the world, he looks back and loses Eurydice again.

In another encounter Mephisto summons a ghost named the Flying Dutchman who has sold his soul to him. The ghost fights against the Surfer, but stops battling after he believes himself not "beyond redemption." The ghost renounces his pledge to serve Mephisto, who then sentences him back into limbo. When the Surfer cries for the soul of the Dutchman, the ghost says that only "a tear of forgiveness can free a lost soul…from the bondage of limbo!" (*The Silver Surfer* #8–9; 1969). The Surfer finally breaks down to accept a deal from Mephisto when the demon kidnaps his love Shalla Bal, threatens her safety, and torments the Surfer by hiding her somewhere on Earth. He breaks his pact, however, when Mephisto tries to double-cross him by intending to secretly harm Shalla Bal (*The Silver Surfer* #16–17; 1970). In the much later graphic novel *The Silver Surfer: Judgment Day* (1988), the hero temporarily forfeits his soul to Mephisto to protect innocent lives, and then Galactus becomes the ironic hero by freeing the Surfer from the demon.[20]

By making Shalla Bal the Surfer's object of desire and Mephisto his tormentor, Lee and Buscema add to the Surfer's anxiety by scrutinizing the play between moral obligation, selflessness, and the Surfer's conscience to protect Shalla Bal and others while preserving his own soul. Buscema's sketches of the Surfer depict his manifold tribulations. If Jack Kirby's drawings of the Silver Surfer emphasized him as a transcendent, muscular, and ultra-powerful, god-like being, John Buscema's Surfer looked more human with a thinner body, vulnerability, and an angst-ridden face of sorrow.

The Surfer's trial during his first encounter with Mephisto echoes the temptation of Christ in the wilderness. Mephisto tempts the Surfer three times, and Satan tempts Jesus three times: He challenges his sonship by daring him to make stones into bread after a 40-day fast, he tempts him to jump off the pinnacle of the temple, and similar to the Surfer's temptation, the devil offers Jesus all the kingdoms of the world if the Christ would bow down and worship him (Matthew 4; Luke 3). Both heroes resist their tempter's trials, valuing righteousness above worldly power. Both embody purity but are also vulnerable to temptation; albeit, biblical scripture states that Christ never sinned.[21] Because brute strength is not enough to challenge the Surfer, he must face enemies with supernatural powers or that represent symbolic embodiments of evil and fear: a devil (Mephisto), a ghost (the Flying Dutchman), a god of evil (Loki), a universal warmonger (the Overlord), a warlock prime (Sir Nigel), a monster evoked through witchcraft (the Abomination), and a man-made monster (Dr. Frankenstein's).[22] When attacking Dracula, intending to rid the world of this evil prince, the Surfer looks at a painting resembling Jesus Christ and realizes that it is not his responsibility to punish Dracula. He gets on his board and rides off, assured that "there is hope now for man" (*Tomb of Dracula* #50; 1976).

Jesus of Nazareth and the Silver Surfer

The similarities between the Silver Surfer and Jesus Christ are most evident in their roles as a sacrificial savior of the world, as a demonstration of ultimate love, as a higher being embodied in a humble state upon the earth, and as a resister of the embodiments of evil. The parallels between them break down when addressing the notions of plight, perfection, and absolute divinity. If the Silver Surfer represents Jesus, he points both in the direction of the suffering messiah from Nazareth at his first coming, and the apocalyptic liberator of the world, battling macro-evils at his second coming. His great power, heavenly ethos, selflessness, and purity directs us to a Christology from above: Jesus as the god-man. On the other hand, the Surfer's imperfections, compassion for Shalla Bal, and suffering over his predicament in a paradise lost direct us to what is more human in the hero. Thus the Silver Surfer is both god-like and human-like, pointing us again to the incarnation of Christ. The Surfer remains one of the clearest examples of the god-man in comics.

Notes

1 Stan Lee, *Son of Origins of Marvel Comics* (New York: Simon & Schuster, 1975), 206.

2 See for instance, Jean-Paul Gabilliet, "Cultural and Mythical Aspects of a Superhero: The Silver Surfer 1968–70," *Journal of Popular Culture* 28/2 (Fall 1994), 209; Bradford W. Wright, *Comic Book Nation: The Transformation of Youth Culture in America* (Baltimore: Johns Hopkins University Press, 2001), 231.

3 Les Daniels, *Marvel: Five Fabulous Decades of the World's Greatest Comics* (New York: Harry N. Abrams, Inc., Publishers, 1991), 127.

4 Because older superhero images are sometimes altered over the years, this chapter will focus primarily on the original Silver Surfer (*Fantastic Four*, vol. 1; *The Silver Surfer* vol. 1; *The Silver Surfer* [Fireside novel by Stan Lee and Jack Kirby; Simon & Schuster, 1978]) from the comic book versions popular in the 1960s and 1970s. Other series will be addressed only as needed.

5 *Fantastic Four* #48 ("The Coming of Galactus," Mar. 1966), *Fantastic Four* #49 ("If This Be Doomsday," Apr. 1966), and *Fantastic Four* #50 ("The Starling Saga of the Silver Surfer," May 1966).

6 The Silver Surfer definitely goes through a transformation in character from a seemingly cold, aloof, almost heartless space explorer to a compassionate, sensitive individual who resembles the greatest of saints. Lee and Kirby's 1978 reunion episode of *The Silver Surfer* (New York: Simon & Schuster, 1978), 19 attempts to alleviate this tension by including that before coming to Earth, while still Galactus' herald, the Surfer considered his previous existence as (the more humane) Norran Radd to be "dead"; the only mission was to serve Galactus.

7 Gabilliet recognizes this aspect along with similarities between the Surfer as a fallen angel and as Adam banished from Eden in "Cultural and mythical aspects of a Superhero," 208.

8 *The Silver Surfer* vol. 1 #12, #2, #3; *The Silver Surfer* 1978:35. However, for some reason he is unable to heal Shalla Bal a second time when she is critically injured, searching for the Surfer on Earth. He sends her back to Zenn-La, without him, to be healed by their advanced science (*The Silver Surfer* #11).

9 Stan Lee and John Buscema, *The Silver Surfer: Judgment Day* (New York: Marvel, 1988).

10 *The Silver Surfer* #3:4; 1968. On another occasion the Surfer unleashed his power against humanity intending to get them to unite against him (*Fantastic Four* #72; Mar. 1968). In this episode, his misguided motive resembles that of Ozymandias in Alan Moore's *Watchmen*.

11 I am not saying, however, that the theology of Christ's atonement is *best* explained by Abélard's view. Frankly, I do not believe that one perspective can capture all the many-faceted aspects of Christ's sacrifice. For explanations about various interpretations of the atonement, see Millard J. Erickson, *Christian Theology* (Grand Rapids: Baker Book House, 1985), 781–823; Gustaf Aulén, *Christus Victor: An Historical Study of the Three Main Types of the Idea of Atonement* (Reprint; Eugene, Ore.: Wipf & Stock, 2003).

[12] See for instance, *Fantastic Four* #55; *Fantastic Four Annual* #5; *The Silver Surfer* #10.

[13] See for example, *The Silver Surfer* 1978: 45, 61–63; *Fantastic Four* #72:20.

[14] Lee and Kirby, *The Silver Surfer*, 1978:43; Cf. Revelation 4:8. Beyond Galactus, the Marvel Universe has disclosed a number of Deity-like beings of incalculable power, such as the Watcher, Mephisto, the Stranger, Odin, Eternity, the Living Tribunal, Sise-Neg, Ego, the High Evolutionary, the Goddess, Thanos, Warlock (a clear Christ-type), Chronos, the Celestials, Eon, Elders of the Universe, Order and Chaos, the In-Betweener, and the Beyonder, a morally immature being who descended to Earth, conquers death, and speaks worlds out of existence. Owen Reece, the Molecule Man, opts for the most powerful being in the Marvel multiverse by battling the Beyonder (*Secret Wars II* #1–9; 1985–86). For the other characters, see *Strange Tales* #138 (1965); #157 (1967); #179 (1975); *Thor* #134 (1966); *Fantastic Four* #66–67 (1967); #234 (1981); *Marvel Premiere* #14 (1974); *The Silver Surfer* #5 (1969); #4 (Vol. 3; 1987); *Infinity Gauntlet* #1–6 (1991); *The Infinity Crusade* #1–6 (1993); *Marvel Superheroes: Secret Wars* #1–12 (1984–85); *Secret Wars II* #6 (1985); Cf. Peter Sanderson, "Protectors of the Universe," in *Marvel Universe* (New York: Harry N. Abrams, Inc., Publishers, 1996), 157–59, 163, 167–68.

[15] The first version came out as *The Silver Surfer* limited series #1–2 (Dec. 1988–Jan. 1989). In this postmodern tale, the Surfer also resembles a combination of secular humanism and early church fathers influenced by Neoplatonism: he believes that everyone possesses a spark of divinity and that the best faith is faith in oneself.

[16] Contrast *The Silver Surfer* #7 (1969) with *The Silver Surfer* Vol. 1 #5, 10 (1969), and then see Lee and Kirby, *The Silver Surfer* (1978:41).

[17] In the Silver Age, see for example *The Silver Surfer* #2–5, 12; *Fantastic Four* #155–57; *Incredible Hulk* #250; *The Silver Surfer* vol. 2; #1.

[18] It is later revealed that Johnny Blaze made a pact with Mephisto to cure his stepfather from cancer. He double-crosses Johnny, and binds the flaming spirit of vengeance, Zarathos, to him. Thus Johnny Blaze transforms into the fiery-skulled Ghost Rider (premiering in *Marvel Spotlight* #5; 1972).

[19] Here Mephisto seems to think like an ancient Gnostic, believing that the soul and the body can be dichotomized. The New Testament view does not make such a crass separation but sees value in both body and spirit; it is the body that will be resurrected on the final day.

[20] Stan Lee and John Buscema, *The Silver Surfer: Judgment Day* (New York: Marvel, 1988): 47–48, 60–63.

[21] E.g., 2 Corinthians 5:21; Hebrews 4:15. We will set aside the imponderable question of Christ's impeccability; whether "God the Son" was actually able to succumb to the Devil's temptation and sin against God the Father, and if so, what would be the ramifications of this. The Christian scriptures do not address this question.

[22] See *The Silver Surfer* 3, 8–9, 4, 6, 12, 12, 7 (1968–1970), respectively.

Recommended Resources

Aulén, Gustaf. *Christus Victor: An Historical Study of the Three Main Types of the Idea of Atonement.* London: SPCK, 1931; Reprint. A. G. Herber, translator. Eugene, Ore.: Wipf & Stock, 2003.

Campbell, Joseph, (with Bill Moyers). *The Power of Myth.* New York: Anchor, 1991.

Eliade, Mircea. "The Yearning for Paradise in Primitive Tradition." Pages 61–75 in *Myth and Mythmaking.* Edited by Henry A. Murray. New York: George Braziller, 1960.

Gabilliet, Jean-Paul. "Cultural and Mythical Aspects of a Superhero: The Silver Surfer 1968–1970." *Journal of Popular Culture* 28/2 (Fall 1994): 203–213.

Lee, Stan. "To Span the Spaceways." Pages 203–249 in *Son of Origins of Marvel Comics.* New York: Simon & Schuster, 1975.

Lee, Stan, and Jack Kirby. *The Silver Surfer.* (Fireside Graphic Novel) New York: Simon and Schuster, 1978.

Lee, Stan, and Jack Kirby. *Essential Fantastic Four.* Vol. 3. New York: Marvel, 1998.

Lee, Stan, and John Buscema. *Essential Silver Surfer.* New York: Marvel Comics, 1998.

Lee, Stan, and John Buscema, *The Silver Surfer: Judgment Day.* New York: Marvel, 1988.

Lee, Stan, and Jean Geraud Moebius. *The Silver Surfer.* Vol. 2 ("Parable"). New York: Marvel/Epic, 1989.

Milton, John. *Paradise Lost* (Milton's *Paradise Lost*, illustrated by Gustave Doré, edited with notes, and *A Life of Milton*, by Robert Vaughan). New York: Cassell, 1905.

Prothero, Stephen. *American Jesus: How the Son of God Became a National Icon.* New York: Holtzbrinck Publishers, 2004.

Sanderson, Peter. "Protectors of the Universe." Pages 156–177 in *Marvel Universe.* New York: Harry N. Abrams, Inc., Publishers, 1996.

Starlin, Jim, Ron Lim, and George Pérez. *Infinity Gauntlet.* New York: Marvel, 2000.

9
Mutants That Are All Too Human: The X-Men, Magneto, and Original Sin

Tim Perry

W hat would a Christian theologian find redemptive about Magneto, a character who is more villain than he is hero? While this question often expresses only good-natured ribbing, it shows awareness of the deliberately amoral and decadent characters in many recent comic books. Is there anything pious about antiheroes like Venom, Lobo, or the Punisher? Certain characters seem to be defined by their ability to transgress all social boundaries with virtual impunity. They personify Pope John Paul II's "Culture of Death" swathed in spandex. Even so, sometimes the most interesting thing about superheroes is the villains they face or the fact that a protagonist does not always act like a hero.

So then, are superhero comics and religious belief difficult horizons to merge? One report claims that only "a tiny percentage of the hundreds of characters that have appeared in comics have been attached to any particular faith."[1] The reliability of such statistics depends on what one considers as "faith" and how explicit that faith must be in the comic book. Certainly characters such as Daredevil possess Christian faith, and Ben Grimm of the Fantastic Four professes Judaism. Even the space-born Silver Surfer shows apparent admiration for Jesus Christ (*Tomb of Dracula* #50; 1976), a religious figure who also seems to be a "friend" that saves Johnny Blaze from the trap of Satan in *Ghost Rider* #9 (Vol. 1; 1975). Moreover, a comic book or movie does not need to demonstrate the hero's faith to be religiously oriented; it will suffice to uncover such meaning behind the plot or myth. The X-Men comic books and films invite interaction from a religious perspective based on their treatments of both explicit and implicit religious themes.

It seems, then, the kind of inquiry that occurs in the subsequent paragraphs is worthwhile. This conclusion is strengthened when we move from purely interpretive to theological grounds. The doctrine of the Incarnation—the assumption of human nature by the Son of God—means that no human activity, whether artistic, literary, or scientific, remains irredeemable. No work of creativity is devoid of a trace of grace that can subvert the intention of the entire work, making it a *preparatio evangelica*— a preparation for the Gospel. An example provided by another artistic medium, photography, is Andres Serrano's infamous *Piss Christ*, which portrays a crucifix suspended in a jar of urine. Although many understand this work as deliberately transgressing religious sensibilities (and either celebrate or decry it as such), some see here the profoundest portrayal of God's overcoming of sin through the compassionate embrace of humiliation and suffering in the cross of Jesus Christ. In the jar they see the transgression itself transgressed, subverted, and transformed. There is no reason that Christian literary theorists may not engage in similar re- or out-narrations of even the most morally questionable comic or character, and no reason why the subversive power of the Gospel of grace cannot extend here.

It has long been a tenet of Western Christian theology that all human beings, as Cornelius Plantiga notes, "have a biblically certified and empirically demonstrable bias toward evil. We are all both complicitous and molested by the evil of our race. We both discover evil and invent it; we both ratify and extend it."[2] This is the doctrine of "original sin." That this teaching has fallen on hard times in popular culture goes almost without saying. It is therefore ironic that some of the most interesting and attractive literary characters of past and present embody it. However much we may wish to disavow it, original sin remains in Macbeth, in Ahab, in Jack and the Hunters, and as I hope to show, in Magneto. When read through the prism of the Christian doctrine of original sin, Magneto is an all-too-human character both in his knowledge that the world is fallen and in his failure to escape its fallenness. Before examining this villain, however, we will first consider questions about human nature, some of its complexity and religious elements, as it relates to the X-Men.

Tracing the X-Men of History

In the early 1960s, the association of Stan Lee and Jack Kirby by Marvel Comics publisher, Martin Goodman inaugurated one of the most prolific creative periods in comic book history. The Fantastic Four, the Hulk, and Spider-Man, quickly distinguished the characters of Marvel Comics from the established heroes of Detective Comics (DC)—Superman, Batman, Green Lantern, and Wonder Woman. Two factors relate to both Silver Age Marvel characters and the X-Men. First, they have "scientific" origins. The Fantastic Four are ordinary humans transformed by cosmic rays; the Hulk emerges from Dr. Bruce Banner's gamma radiation exposure; and Spider-Man is

created when a radioactive spider bites Peter Parker.[3] The second is their
relative psychological complexity. Michael Lavin elaborates: "Super-hero
comics of the fifties and early sixties tended to be very formulaic, with noble,
unswerving heroes, simplistic conflicts, and often times, gimmicky plot
devices and trick endings. Little was seen of the hero's alter ego, except for
the obligatory scene where he tried to hide his secret identity from friends
and co-workers."[4] Lee and Kirby, however, created the neurotic hero. Peter
Parker's obligation to be Spider-Man—this is the classic example—arises
from his sense of guilt at the death of Ben Parker. That the X-Men titles are
no exception to the Silver Age rule is made clear by Richard Reynolds:

> The X-Men were mutants: young men and women who possessed
> extraordinary powers. These powers set them apart from the rest of
> humanity, although born as normal children to normal parents. The
> appearance of such a strain of mutants is explained as being the result of
> increased radiation in the earth's atmosphere. Mutants are therefore
> 'children of the atom'—by products of Cold War nuclear testing.[5]

The X-Men are thus products of scientific and moral miscalculation
created by the hubris of the military-industrial complexity of the United
States government. Suspicion of a "legitimate" authority grounds the X-Men
plotlines.[6] Readers meet the original team in *X-Men* #1 (1963)—Cyclops,
Beast, Angel, Iceman, and their leader, the powerful yet wheelchaired
chaired telepath, Professor Charles Xavier.[7] As the story unfolds, a
telekinetic mutant, Jean Grey, joins as the fifth "X-man," codenamed Marvel
Girl. During her induction into Professor Xavier's school, she inquires after
the mission of the X-Men, allowing him to explain that a growing number of
mutants are born every year, and "Not all of them want to help mankind!...
Some hate the human race, and wish to destroy it! Some feel that the mutants
should be the real rulers of earth! It is our job to protect mankind from those
...from the evil mutants."[8] The next panel introduces such a mutant preparing
to take over Cape Citadel: Magneto.

Dr. Bolivar Trask persuades society to believe that *all* mutants are
menaces. He reveals his powerful Sentinels (artificial intelligences designed
to destroy mutants), but he is unable to maintain control of them, and the
mechanical militia take it upon themselves to rid the world of the alleged
mutant threat (*X-Men* #14–16). The themes of prejudice and intolerance not
only call to mind the Gestapo of Hitler's Germany, but also the civil rights
movement in the United States during the 1960s, the same period that these
X-Men comics appeared on the market. The point is re-emphasized in the
remake of this X-Men story in Kurt Busiek and Alex Ross's graphic novel,
Marvels. Since the very first team, then, the X-Men myth has addressed

tolerance in relation to those who are labeled as "different" than the ruling majority. This concept repeats itself in future incarnations of the team. In the Silver Age, whether portrayed by Lee and Kirby, Roy Thomas and Neal Adams, Len Wein and Dave Cockrum, or Chris Claremont and John Byrne, the X-Men reveled in diversity, complex issues, and moral dilemmas.

The second X-Men team of the Silver Age (starting in *Giant Size X-Men* #1 and *X-Men* #94; 1975) added more complexity and characters. Scott Summers (Cyclops) is joined with Wolverine, Storm, Night Crawler, Colossus, Banshee, Thunderbird, and Sunfire, but the lineup frequently changes with other heroes coming and going, such as Phoenix, Dazzler, Kitty Pride, Havok, Polaris, Emma Frost, Rogue, and others. Their ever-changing roster and popularity led to more offshoot characters and teams that succeeded with their own series during the 1980s and 1990s: Alpha Flight, Excalibur, New Mutants, X-Force, X-Factor, X-Man, Generation X, Gambit, Deadpool, Cable, Bishop and others (not to mention X-Men clone groups from competing publishers).[9] The X-clan of heroes are not only mutants but diverse in gender, ethnicities, and nationalities. The tensions both among the characters (e.g., Jean Grey-Scott Summers-Logan [Wolverine] love triangle) and within them (e.g., the Angel-Fourth Horseman/Death-Archangel transformations of Warren Worthington) produce intricate narratives that invite the readers to suspend their disbelief.

The character of Wolverine, perhaps the most famous of the second generation of X-Men, marked a cross-over between the Silver Age and the anticipated post-1985 antiheroes. The hero always had a rebellious side, which was nothing new in the Marvel Universe, but what created moral wrinkles and a superhero dilemma was his willingness to kill his opponents, unlike other heroes of that time. Originally an opponent of the Hulk (*Incredible Hulk* #180–81; 1974), Wolverine seemed less human as a Canadian government secret weapon with an invincible adamantium skeletal structure, retractable claws, and the ability to heal himself very quickly. His humane side is seen, however, when he falls for the beautiful Mariko Yashida and battles her crimelord father in Japan (e.g., *Wolverine* #1–4 limited series; 1982). Unlike the Punisher, he retained honor and nobility despite his violent nature.

Arguably the most memorable storyline from the second X-Men group did not center on Wolverine, however, but Jean Grey. The transformation of Jean Grey from Marvel Girl to Phoenix to Dark Phoenix raised interesting dilemmas related to morality and identity. How were her erstwhile teammates who continued to love Jean Grey to oppose Dark Phoenix and her insatiable desire for power? Was she Jean Grey, the X-Men hero named Marvel Girl, or was she Dark Phoenix, one of the worst murderers in the history of comics? Jean Grey first sacrificially volunteered to pilot a ship that was bombarded with solar radiation. She died, but the combination of the radiation and her emotional trauma allowed her psionic power to harness the phoenix force, an allegedly limitless resource with the power to create and destroy through passion. This new power enabled her to raise herself from the dead as the Phoenix, appropriately named after a legendary bird whose life and death cycle was used by early church fathers as an illustration pointing to the resurrection.[10]

Her new powers also enabled her to deliver the universe from collapsing into a black hole created by the M'Krann Crystal and cracked open by the Emperor D'ken. However, due primarily to Grey's inability to contain her new powers, and without proper training, she turned into the Dark Phoenix, a force that hungered for energy at the expense of making the D'bari star flare up into a supernova and destroy a fully inhabited planet of intelligent life. Because of this genocide the Empress Lilandra of the Shi'ar Galaxy wanted to take away Grey's powers permanently. Dark Phoenix needed to be brought to justice, but the X-Men protested, hoping that Jean would stay normal. In a battle with the Shi'ar Imperial Guard, Grey lost control and became Dark Phoenix again briefly. Realizing that she could not control her power, and the danger to the universe she would cause if she reverted back to the Dark Phoenix, she took her own life, triggering a Kree energy cannon that disintegrated her (the entire narrative is found mostly in the *X-Men* #100–101, 107–108, 125, 132–38; 1976–80).

The saga carries with it implicit theological reflection related to the complexity of human nature. Grey's god-like power could not be contained because of her immaturity. She resembles a child playing with matches or a nation unable to handle its own nuclear capabilities—a violation of keeping Spider-Man's edict: with great power comes great responsibility. Even a superhero is not beyond this, and so justice and retribution almost seemed to demand that Jean Grey had to be punished for killing an entire civilization. As Adam followed Eve's rebellion in eating the forbidden fruit because he did not want to lose her (as one popular interpretation suggests), so Scott Summers refuses to face up to the consequences his lover committed as the Dark Phoenix. He loves her for better or worse.[11] Paradoxically, when in her right mind, Jean Grey functions as the savior of the world, sacrificing herself for the sake of others, and like Christ, rising from the dead. Here we see the epitome of both moral greatness and degeneracy combined in the person of Grey, an allegory for humanity itself.

Religious content in the X-Men is made explicit when looking at Kurt Wagner, the Night Crawler. His satanic appearance (blue/black with yellow eyes, pointed ears, teeth, and tail, hands and feet resembling cloven hoofs) and superpower (the ability to teleport and reappear at will, in a puff of sulfuric smoke) stand juxtaposed against his extremely devout Roman

Catholic commitment (as a priest in the making). This sharply drawn dualism also invites reflection on what defines a human being and what limits the tolerance of difference. Implicitly, the driving theme "of the *X-Men*—the isolation of mutants and their alienation from 'normal' society—can be read as a parable of the alienation of any minority."[12] When Bryan Singer, director of *X-Men* and *X2: X-Men United*, compared Professor X and Magneto with Martin Luther King Jr. and Malcom X, respectively, he placed the films (and the entire X-universe) within the realm of religious debate.[13] The issue of civil rights in the United States, like so many problems related to social justice, is essentially a religious question grounded in the worldviews of Martin Luther King's Christianity and Malcolm X's Islam. As well, Professor Xavier's teachings may be compared with Jesus instructing his followers to "turn the other cheek." Some mutants like Magneto, however, disagree with this view.[14]

Tracing the Magneto of History

From his introduction in the original *X-Men #1* to his brilliant adaptation by Sir Ian McKellen in *X-Men* and *X2* films, Magneto is driven by a singularly moral vision that injustices inflicted upon mutants must be stopped by any means necessary. This fundamentally moral nature of his motivation allows him to perpetrate great evil. In one episode he disrupts Earth's magnetic field, effectively rendering all mechanical devices inoperable (*X-Men* Vol. 2 #25); he also constructs a device designed to transform all humans into mutants (*The X-Men* movie). Geoff Klock affirms that such large-scale "social changes are a supervillain signature, manifesting when one wishes to take over the world or, alternatively, to destroy all human life.... However well intentioned, these kinds of moves almost always mark someone whom the superhero must stop...."[15] The megalomaniac deeds, however, are not what distinguish Magneto from Superman's Lex Luthor or Batman's Joker. A Silver Age villain is defined not by his actions, as much as by other reasons that Stan Lee makes plain:

> We hate to have a varlet doing evil just for the sake of being naughty. We try to indicate why he does the things he does, what made him the way he is. And, wherever possible, we may even let him exhibit some decent, likable traits. In the magic world of Marvel, not even supervillains need be all bad, just as our superheroes are rarely all good; they usually display some natural human failings even as you and I—granted, of course, that you and I are human.[16]

Dr. Doom's excessive need for control, for example, is driven by the murder of his parents, the Red Skull's fanatical devotion to Nazism comes from his self-loathing, and the original Green Goblin is created by a lethal combination of greed, a chemical explosion, and the resulting brain damage that magnified Norman Osborn's intellect and drove him to insanity.[17] Silver Age supervillains are, like all of us, caught up in a web of influencing factors that indelibly mark them and shape their conduct, and yet they are responsible for their own actions.[18]

Magneto is perhaps the most subtly drawn example of this compelling combination of moral compulsion and choice. He appears along side the X-Men in their first comic book. As far as Magneto is concerned, "The human race no longer deserves dominion over the planet earth. The day of the mutants is upon us. The first phase of my plan shall be to show my power...to make Homo Sapiens bow to Homo Superior." What follows is a standard good versus evil tale with Magneto a one-dimensional and finally unsuccessful villain. As he develops over the decades, however, a more nuanced picture emerges. At times Magneto seems open to the possibility of harmonious existence between mutants and humans. We consider his tenure as headmaster at Xavier's school: Under the alias Michael Xavier, he served as advisor to the X-Men and instructor to their junior mutant team, *The New Mutants* (#35–75). In the alternative world of "Days of Future Past," Magneto leads the X-Men when persecuted by the Sentinels (*X-Men* #141–42; 1981). At other times he advocates a policy of separation of mutants from human beings thereby ensuring the continued survival of both groups. We may think here of his assumption of government on the island of Genosha.[19] Ultimately, though, it seems that Magneto cannot escape his lust for world domination. Having created a mutant homeland on Genosha, it soon becomes a base for yet another attempt at global domination (*Uncanny X-Men* #390; *X-Men* Vol. 2 #111). Magneto's plans are undone finally by Cassandra Nova who, by controlling a group of Sentinels (artificial intelligences designed to hunt and destroy mutants), murders the 16 million inhabitants of Genosha.[20] Magneto's body, however, was not recovered from the massacre. He may well be dead, but "no matter how dead a villain seems to be...he or she always returns."[21]

Clearly Magneto is not a flat foil against which the X-Men can routinely display their superpowers. He is complex, internally divided, and at points genuinely uncertain about the best strategy for mutant betterment. Similarly, Xavier, the X-Men, and other X-characters possess ambivalence about him; in various stories they wonder whether he is an ally or antagonist.

What accounts for this complexity? We find the answer in *Magneto #0*. This graphic novel reprints two tales from Magneto's early life, "A Fire in the Night"[22] and "I Magneto,"[23] supplementing them with "Magneto

Seminar" where he becomes the focus of a university lecture.[24] Canonical status may be conferred on this book by virtue of its number: the #0 demonstrates that it is intended to be read as background to the main stories. As well, its structure is unique because Magneto becomes a university subject, a "text within a text," whose origins and actions are dissected and analyzed.

The opening panels of "A Fire in the Night" are set in Paris. In the Hotel Lutetia-Concorde, a man sleeps while a clock ticks in the background. His identity is disclosed by the familiar horned red helmet and the headline of the International Herald-Tribune: "Magneto Escapes: Worldwide Manhunt Mounted for Mutant Terrorist."[25] Magneto experiences a flood of nightmarish childhood memories that begin in Auschwitz with his rescue of a young girl, Magda, from summary execution. Although the pair flees the camp, Magda fears freezing and starving to death; she wonders why they bothered to escape given that everything she knew had perished in the gas chambers. To prevent her from lapsing into despair, Magneto counters, "You can't give up Magda! You can't give the Nazis that victory! We live, you and I. That's important, that means something, that matters!" To dispel Magda's fear, he promises, "I'll protect you now—for now and always—as I did inside the camp."[26]

The scene then shifts to a happier time in the Carpathian mountains. Magneto and Magda find work, friendship, get married, and have a daughter named Anya. However, the relative tranquility is short-lived. After a move to the Ukranian city of Vinnitsa, Magneto's mutant powers first display themselves to disastrous effect. They lead to his arrest by local police, who prevent him from rescuing Anya from a fire. Engulfed in a nihilistic rage portrayed vividly by a simple, solid black panel, Magneto strikes against his enemies with his newfound abilities. When the story resumes, surrounded by dead bodies, Magneto kneels in front of his daughter's corpse. Horrified by the tragic and senseless events, Magda flees from her husband with the words, "You're not the man I loved! You've become a monster!"[27]

Magneto awakes from the dream, calling for his wife and smelling smoke. Drawn to the window, he notices across the street a fire entrapping a mother and daughter. "I care only for my own people—homo sapiens superior—mutantkind," he muses. "They—are merely human."[28] Magneto acts nonetheless. As the two prepare to die, he now costumed but without the helmet, shields them from the fire with a magnetic field. Having returned the pair to a grateful father, he enjoins the man to tell "the world how your family was saved by Magneto. Magneto the terrorist, Magneto the super-villain, Magneto the mutant. Remember me always, M'sieu. I could have let them perish—but I chose life."[29]

Matters become more complicated in "I Magneto." The opening panels set the narrative somewhere in South America where a small band of recalcitrant Nazis dream of past and possibly future glories in an isolated fortress. An approaching man interrupts their reverie. With a smile Magneto unleashes a pulse that sunders the doors, collapses part of the fortress wall, and turns the soldiers' weapons against them. Impervious to their bullets, he searches out Hans Richter, a former member of the Waffen SS, binds his hands with rebar, and promises to give him to Israeli authorities for trial.

The next scene transports readers to Rio de Janeiro. Reading a newspaper article on Charles Xavier, the master of magnetism reflects on his long friendship with the leader of the X-Men. "Still the idealist my dear friend," he thinks, "dreaming of a world where mutants and normal humans can co-exist in peace. We hate so easily. I suspect you ask more than humanity is capable of giving."[30] The scene ends when his introspection is interrupted by Isabelle, his personal physician and companion. Although Magneto's attraction to Isabelle is curbed by a "raw wound" created by the death of Anya and the loss of Magda, the conversation tends toward physical intimacy when a knife-wielding stranger emerges from the shadows, quickly killing Isabelle. A confused Magneto is confronted by a man named Control who tells Magneto that his failure to distinguish between "our" Nazis and "theirs" will cost him his life. "The Russians are the enemy and we'll work with whoever we have to to beat 'em," he says. "If accomplishing that means turning to some of old Adolf's boys, them's the breaks. We'll use them the same way we will you muties."[31] Magneto's reply cements a destiny: "It is neither communists nor Nazis you have to fear, Control—it is we, who your short-sighted stupidity will make your foes. It is I who shall lead my people to the glory they deserve. I, Ubermensch. I, Mutant! I—Magneto!" After Magneto exacts his revenge, Control's life for Isabelle's, the narrator concludes, "And the dream dies...and the Nightmare is born."[32]

Finally, "Magneto Seminar" serves to fill gaps in the preceding narratives. Dr. Gabrielle Haller, Israel's former ambassador to Great Britain, stands behind a lectern in front of a large slide of the helmeted Magneto. She informs her audience that Magneto was born Erik Magnus Lehnsherr to gypsy parents outside Gdansk/Danzig around 1928. She then narrates Magneto's internment in Auschwitz, saying nothing of his escape but noting that he witnessed the deaths of his parents and sister. After the emergence of his mutant powers and failure to cope with Anya's death, Professor Haller documents Magneto's move to Israel, where "to save his own soul, he chose to work with survivors of the camps, and in turn, helped them regain theirs."[33] It was here that Professor Haller came under Magneto's care, which she openly admits, challenges her objectivity with respect to her subject. She wonders, "Was he a tyrannical madman placing himself above the rights of humanity or a righteous zealot fighting for a noble cause—equality for mutants?"[34]

Erik Magnus Lensherr is thus a perplexing and truly sympathetic figure, shaped profoundly by encounters with ideologically driven evil in World War II and the Cold War. As a gypsy he was interred in Auschwitz; as a mutant, he was persecuted in communist Ukraine and used by an American intelligence agency. In each case he gets victimized by a more powerful enemy, whether racially or genetically motivated. Over against this, he forms the moral thesis that will define his conduct throughout his subsequent career: Mutants must be protected from such oppression by whatever means necessary. His strategies for human-mutant relations may indeed vary from domination to separation to infrequent cooperation, but his underlying motivation does not.

This impetus allows Magneto to rationalize his own ideologically oppressive actions against humans and mutants alike. Humans are *the other* that must be assimilated, subjugated, or destroyed to ensure mutant safety and prosperity. Failing to convince Xavier and the X-Men of the righteousness of his cause, Magneto must conquer them also. He becomes what he despises: a person blinded by ideology and given to the perils of power. And despite intermittent yet genuine acts of goodness, he is incapable of deviating from his overall course for long. He is thus caught in a mimetic cycle of violence. He clearly sees and accurately names ideological oppression as evil, yet in his struggle against it, he succumbs to the same temptation—ultimate power. His mission fails as a result. Far from securing peace and safety for mutants, he succeeds only in perpetuating the cycle of violence. He is a supervillain *par excellence* that offers us a glimpse into the human soul.

The Doctrine of Original Sin

Richard Reynolds offers a clue to understanding Silver Age comic book supervillains when he writes that the "mythology underlying the [comic] text is the Old Testament…. All ['Fallen' characters] are corrupted by power, and power in the particular form of knowledge."[35] This conclusion should not startle us. The central position of the Bible is still widely accepted as the standard source for the archetypes that fire Western artistic imaginations. It is as true for comics as it is for any other artistic or literary medium. We will set aside Magneto for the moment in order to elaborate briefly the Christian doctrine of original sin. We will then test Reynolds's general conclusion with particular reference to Magneto.

The Roman Catholic theologian, Alexandre Ganoczy defines original sin as "the general imperfect state that, as a result of human sin, has been the lot of every human being since the very beginning of the species."[36] He makes three important observations. First, "original sin" denotes a state of deviation from the norm shared by every human being regardless of sex, race, nationality, or class. Second, this state is contingent upon human desire, will, decision, and action. In other words, it is not natural. It does not express God's original intention for human beings nor can it be blamed entirely upon divine, cultural, familial, or other social influences. Third, "original sin" is inescapable. Although unnatural, it nevertheless defines the human condition across time and space. "Original sin" specifies a morally deficient condition into which all humans are born, for which all humans are responsible, and from which no human can escape.

The doctrine thus summarizes a major narrative theme running throughout the Bible's Old and New Testaments, but especially Genesis 3–11 and Paul's letter to the Romans. The former narrates sin as a chaotic contagion. The virus is introduced when Adam and Eve freely disobey a divine command, resulting in the inversion of right relationships between humans and God, humans and the earth, and even among humans themselves. In subsequent chapters, the virus mutates out of control. Cain murders his brother Abel, and this act is followed by the multiple murders of Cain's descendent, Lamech. Next comes the intermarrying of "sons of God" with human women.[37] Eventually God declares that the innermost thoughts of all humans are driven to and by evil; as a result, the waters out of which the world was formed in Genesis 1 swallow it in Genesis 6. After the Flood, the building of the Tower of Babel takes place, an act of great technical capability and apparent arrogance. When read slowly, these "stories reveal the characteristics of the prototypal act of sinning: turning away from God (and thus from the source of life), greedy seizure for oneself of some good stemming from God..., refusal to obey divine commands, making an absolute of self-interest to the point of self-deification, and disregard for the boundaries laid down at creation."[38]

Turning from Genesis to Romans, we exchange Old Testament stories for doctrine. Biblical tradition-history coupled with current observations lead Paul to conclude that the human bias toward moral evil is both a structural and individual problem. In fact, he portrays it as an enslaving foreign power that "reigns" in humanity from Adam onward. Among Gentiles the disease produces idolatry, while with Jews it yields self-congratulation; either way, none is immune (Romans 1–3). Indeed sin's only analogue, both in extent and severity, is death (Romans 5:12). While it is a terminal condition in need of healing, an enslavement requiring deliverance, moral culpability is not overlooked. Not only are all in sin, but all *have* sinned and fallen short of

God's glory (Romans 3:23). The plight takes on existential overtones when Paul phrases the catastrophic situation in first-person terms: "I can will what is right, but I cannot do it. For I do not do the good I want, but the evil I do not want is what I do" (Romans 7:19b–20). The context makes it clear that sin both enslaves Paul to a certain course of actions and that his culpability for those actions persists.

This strange combination of slavery and freedom, compulsion and responsibility, is easily displayed. Take for instance the story of Jim Bob, raised in Mississippi in the 1850s.[39] Conversely, everything about his life—education, social encounters, maybe even religion—is shot through with the obviously horrible assumption of white superiority. It will inevitably shape Jim Bob as he matures. Can he help but have a racist state of mind? None of us knows for sure. Nevertheless, we persist in calling it sin because, even "if Jim Bob is not to blame for his racism, *somebody* is. Somebody in the chain of influences leading to Jim Bob's racism knew better, and this is true even if we have to follow the chain back to our first parents, who emerged good and innocent from the hands of God."[40]

Further, while all would acknowledge that traditions, assumptions, and patterns of behavior should mitigate our moral assessments of any racist actions, none would present them as an excuse. God alone may only know the "relevant degrees and even the relevant kind of blame for original and actual moral evil,"[41] but all recognize that Jim Bob himself has a share in guilt if the attitudes into which he was born spill over into actions. Plantinga correctly concludes: "We know that when we sin, we pervert, adulterate, and destroy good things. We create matrices and atmospheres of moral evil and bequeath them to our descendants. By habitual practice, we let loose a great, rolling momentum of moral and spiritual evil across generations."[42]

We may now summarize "original sin" in the following ways:

(1) It names the bias toward evil conduct that infects all human beings.
(2) It accounts for the widespread structures and acts of moral evil that mark every human culture and being.
(3) It neither prevents human beings from distinguishing between good and evil, nor is it a matter of ignorance.
(4) Accordingly, it does not absolve anyone of responsibility for his or her individual sinful actions.
(5) It can and does contaminate even good motivations and actions, allowing them to become justifications for even greater acts of moral evil.

We will show in the final section that in his exemplification of each of these, Magneto is rendered complex, sympathetic, and familiar.

Magneto and Original Sin

A catalog of examples spring to mind when we think of Magneto in the terms provided by (1) above: original sin names the bias toward evil conduct that infects everyone. Whatever his motivations, many of Magneto's actions are evil and should be named as such. Perhaps a primary example here is his refusal to distinguish among human beings. He regards all as legitimate targets, whether combatant or non-combatant, even mutants are singled out as "necessary" victims of violence for the promotion of what he conceives to be a greater good. In the *X-Men* movie, Magneto, with Mystique, Toad, and Sabretooth, hatches a plot to solve the problem of human/mutant relations once and for all by transforming humans into mutants. Thus his opponent is not an army or police force; it is human beings as human beings.

Moreover the machine he has constructed to accomplish this purpose requires an incredible amount of magnetic energy in order to operate. Fearing that the amount of power it needs will result in death, he kidnaps the X-Man Rogue, and infuses her with a measure of his powers. She will operate the machine. If she dies in the attempt, she is expendable in the service of mutant liberation. What defines Magneto's actions as evil here is not their violence. Rather, it is Magneto's refusal to discriminate between innocent and guilty persons, legitimate and illegitimate targets, that rightly earns him the label, "mutant terrorist."

Then there is consideration of (2) above: original sin accounts for a widespread moral evil that marks every human culture. This consideration prevents readers from dismissing Magneto simply as evil, for his character and conduct were themselves shaped by encounters with grave moral evil. The atrocities of Nazism, Communism, racism, xenophobia, and ideological oppression have all combined in specific ways to transform Erik Lensherr into Magneto. While we cannot excuse him, we are forced to consider his conduct's tragic nature as we reflect upon the boy in Auschwitz, the young grieving father in Vinnitsa, and the confused Nazi hunter in Brazil. Would we have acted differently faced with similar situations and capabilities? We cannot say and thus our judgment cannot be final.

Even so, no matter how well Magneto's experiences help readers to understand his later acts, (3) demands that we (and Magneto himself) name his conduct as evil. We should continue to name his moral credo, "by any means necessary" as evil, even if it seems understandable when portrayed in a certain light. Magneto acknowledges his moral culpability by rescuing the mother and daughter from the fire. He does not merely do so in a vain attempt to relive and redeem the past. Neither does he do so to atone for previous actions against both humans and mutants. Rather, he does it to signal to his enemies and to readers that there is more to his character than the actions for which he is infamous. Of course, in so acting, he accepts that the label "evil" applies at least in some sense to his conduct even in his own mind. Consequently (4), he acknowledges responsibility for his own actions, refusing to be reduced to an "explanation" of previous evil. However sympathetic a character he may be, he will not allow us to pity him.

Finally (5): Original sin pollutes even good intentions. When Magneto acts morally, the conduct is contaminated. The fire rescue is clearly as much an attempt at self-justification as it is a heroic act of altruism. His commitment to protect his family no matter the cost results, indirectly, in the death of his daughter and directly in the desertion of Magda. His commitment to the noble goal of mutant liberation blinds him to the way he has adopted the ways of his enemies.

His self-description as "Übermensch" ("superman") is deliberate. Both physically and morally, he sees himself as superior. He believes he has transcended the morality that defined the world in which he and they once lived—but has he really transcended it? His adoption of the same Nietzschean vocabulary of the superman as his erstwhile Nazi oppressors signals that far from transcending it, he has merely begun again in a recapitulation of the cycle of violence. In place of the gypsy, the Jew, and the homosexual, he believes Homo sapiens stand as "the other" to be mastered and, if necessary, erased.

Magneto knows that the world has fallen. He is well aware that his world is one in which the consequences of horrendous acts of moral evil continue to resonate long into the future. He knows also that it is good and right to act to prevent further acts of moral evil. He fails, however, in his preventive mission. He succeeds only in perpetuating the cycle of violence, only in becoming the original object of his hatred, the ideologically driven oppressor. He is right that the world needs to be saved, but wrong in believing that he is its savior. In fact, it is for these reasons that he is an attractive, sympathetic character and that we resonate with him.

In their knowledge of good and evil, their capacity for moral willing, and their failure at times to act morally, Magneto, just as the other mutants, is not "homo superior" after all. Together, they are a mirror of our own souls. They are all too human.

> He who fights against monsters should see to it that he does not become a monster in the process. And when you stare persistently into an abyss, the abyss also stares into you. (Friedrich Nietzsche, *Beyond Good and Evil*)

Notes

1 *Dallas Morning News* (August 24, 2002), as quoted in "Defenders of the Faith?" in *U.S. Catholic* (December, 2002), 5.

2 Cornelius Plantinga, *Not the Way It's Supposed to Be: A Breviary of Sin* (Grand Rapids: Eerdmans, 1995), 26.

3 The exceptions that demonstrate the rule are Thor, the Norse god of thunder (*Journey into Mystery*, #83), and Dr. Strange, Master of the Mystical Arts (*Strange Tales* #110).

4 Michael R. Lavin, "A Librarian's Guide to Marvel Comics," *Serials Review* 24 (1998), 48.

5 Reynolds, *Superheroes*, 84.

6 We find similar themes explored in the post-Vietnam Captain America books.

7 DC Comics had a similar group at the time with the Doom Patrol that first appeared in *My Greatest Adventure #80* (Jun. 1963), the same year as Marvel's X-Men first came out. The DC team originated with Dr. Niles Caulder, who was confined to a wheelchair. Robot Man, Mento, Elasti-Girl, Negative Man, and Beast Boy, comprised its members, and they all fought against the Brotherhood of Evil.

8 Stan Lee and Jack Kirby, *X-Men* #1, as reprinted in Stan Lee, *Son of Origins of Marvel Comics*, rev. ed. (New York: Marvel Comics, 1997), 25.

9 This broad scope of heroes raises the unique challenge of continuity across writers, artists, and titles. The problem of continuity is peculiar to comics in which the characters do not age even as the culture around them does. It is particularly acute with the *X-Men*, which has developed to the point that its storylines "can barely be followed by new readers unfamiliar with the vast network of unresolved tensions among a huge cast of characters." Geoff Klock, *How to Read Superhero Comics and Why* (New York: Continuum, 2002), 140.

10 See for instance, 1 Clement 25.

11 Interestingly, Grey, similar to Eve in the Garden of Eden, is nude when Summers makes his proposal (*X-Men* #136).

12 Richard Reynolds, *Superheroes: A Modern Mythology* (Jackson: University of Mississippi Press, 1992), 84.

13 As quoted in "*X-Men*: Subtext We Can't Wait to Read," *The Advocate* (6 June, 2000), 60.

14 Cf. Peter Sanderson, *Marvel Universe* (New York: Harry N. Abrams, 1996), 213. The Malcolm X/M. L. King and Christ/opponents analogies are not the only ones. Longtime *X-Men* writer and editor Chris Clarement sees in Magneto and Xavier traces of David Ben-Gurion and Menachem Begin. See Alan Foege, "The X-Men Files," in *New York Magazine* (17 July, 2000) [Cited 9 Feb. 2004] Online: www.newyorkmetro.com/nymetro/arts/features/3522/index.html. The theme of liberation has been further accentuated by the casting of outspoken gay rights activist, Sir Ian McKellen as the villain Magneto: "gays...have to decide," he says, "if they are interested in advancing gay rights politely or going out in the streets and causing a fuss. At the heart of the story [of *X-Men*], which is full

of action and special effects and wild characters, always that argument is there." Quoted in "*X-Men*: Subtext We Can't Wait to Read," 60.

[15] Klock, *How to Read Superhero Comics*, 39–40.

[16] Stan Lee, *Bring On the Bad Guys*, rev. ed. (New York: Marvel Comics, 1998), 7.

[17] Cf. Lee, *Bad Guys*, 8–80, 136–86.

[18] Indeed, the Silver Age villain may at this point display a greater narratival freedom than the hero. "Our villain," writes Lee, "has to be unique, clever, inventive, and full of fiendish surprises" (Lee, *Bad Guys,* 6).

[19] "Character Bios: Magneto" [Cited 21 Jan. 2004] Online: www.marvel.com/bios/bios.htm?id=19&family=X-MEN.

[20] See "Character Bios: Magneto," and *X-Men* vol. 2 #115–116.

[21] Klock, *How to Read Superhero Comics*, 52.

[22] The original is found in *X-Men Classic* #19.

[23] The original is found in *X-Men Classic* #12.

[24] *Magneto #0*, 25-27.

[25] *Magneto #0*: 1.

[26] *Magneto #0*: 3.

[27] *Magneto #0*: 10. Later on it turns out that Magda was pregnant and gives birth to twins, a daughter and son: Wanda (the Scarlet Witch) and Pietro (Quicksilver). When the two mutants grow up, they join Magneto as supervillains but then convert to superheroes by joining the Avengers. Cf. *X-Men* vol. 1 #4; *Avengers* vol. 1 #16; *The Official Handbook of the Marvel Universe Q-S* vol. 1 #9:3, 23.

[28] *Magneto #0*: 12.

[29] *Magneto #0*: 12.

[30] *Magneto #0*: 19.

[31] *Magneto #0*: 22.

[32] *Magneto #0*: 24.

[33] *Magneto #0*: 26.

[34] *Magneto #0*: 27.

[35] Reynolds, *Superheroes*, 24.

[36] Alexandre Ganoczy, "Original Sin," in *Handbook of Catholic Theology*, ed. Wolfgang Beinert and Francis Schüssler Fiorenza (New York: Crossroad, 1995), 513.

[37] Commentators have different views about discerning the identity of the "sons of God." Whatever the case, the passage is meant to show deviation from the divinely created order of things.

[38] Ganosczy, "Original Sin," 513.

[39] Adapted from Cornelius Plantinga, *Not the Way*, 23–25.

[40] Plantinga, 25.

[41] Plantinga, 26.

[42] Plantinga, 26–27.

Recommended Resources

Bukatman, Scott. "X-Bodies: The Torment of the Mutant Superhero." Pages 92–129 in *Uncontrollable Bodies: Testimonies of Identities and Culture*. Rodney Sappington and Tyler Stallings, eds. Seattle: Bay Press, 1994.

Claremont, Chris, Suzanne Gaffney, John Byrne, Dave Cockrum, Barry Windsor-Smith, John Romita Jr. *The Essential X-Men*. 5 Vols. New York: Marvel, 2002–2004.

Claremont, Chris, Fabian Nicieza, John Bolton, and Jan Duursema. *Magneto #0*. New York: Marvel, 1993.

Ganoczy, Alexandre. "Original Sin." In *Handbook of Catholic Theology*. Wolfgang Beinert and Francis Schüssler Fiorenza, eds. New York: Crossroad, 1995.

Klock, Geoff. *How to Read Superhero Comics and Why*. New York: Continuum, 2002.

Lee, Stan. *Bring On the Bad Guys*, rev. ed. New York: Marvel Comics, 1998.

Lee, Stan. *Son of Origins of Marvel Comics*, rev. ed. New York: Marvel Comics, 1997.

Lee, Stan, and Roy Thomas. *The Essential Uncanny X-Men*. New York: Marvel, 2003.

Plantinga, Cornelius. *Not the Way It's Supposed to Be: A Breviary of Sin*. Grand Rapids: Eerdmans, 1995.

Reynolds, Richard. *Superheroes: A Modern Mythology*. Jackson: University of Mississippi Press, 1992.

Sanderson, Peter. *The Ultimate Guide to the X-Men*. Updated Edition. New York: Dorling Kindersley Publishers, 2003.

Part Three:

Heroes from Intersecting Media—Third Age and Beyond

Figure 1 Frank Miller's Dark Knight series altered the Batman into a grim character reminiscent of the hero's original status. This miniseries became a tremendously influential title for the Third or "Postmodern" Age of Comics. It also anticipated the Warner Brothers movie of Batman in 1989 (*Batman The Dark Knight* #4:6; "The Dark Knight Falls," 1986; DC Comics; Frank Miller [art]).

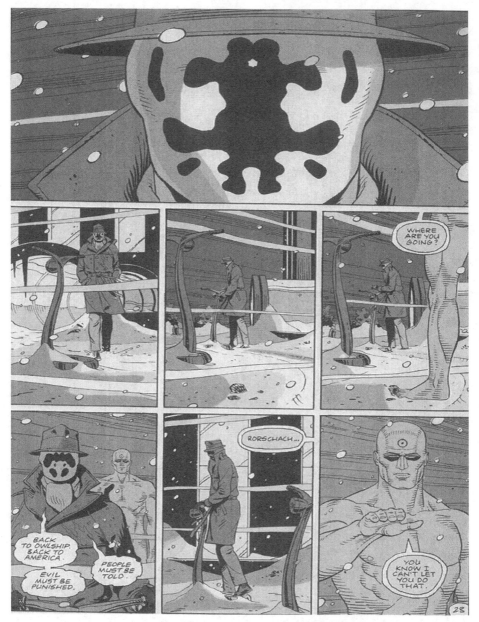

Figure 2 Alan Moore's *Watchmen* introduced a set of dysfunctional superheroes who become pivotal players in determining the fate of the world. In these panels Dr. Manhattan tries to stop Rorschach from exposing a doomsday devastation caused by Ozymandias, their former teammate. The series won over many mature readers, and it became one of the most significant comic books for the Third Age (*Watchmen* #12:23; Oct, 1987; DC Comics; Alan Moore [script] Dave Gibbons [art]).

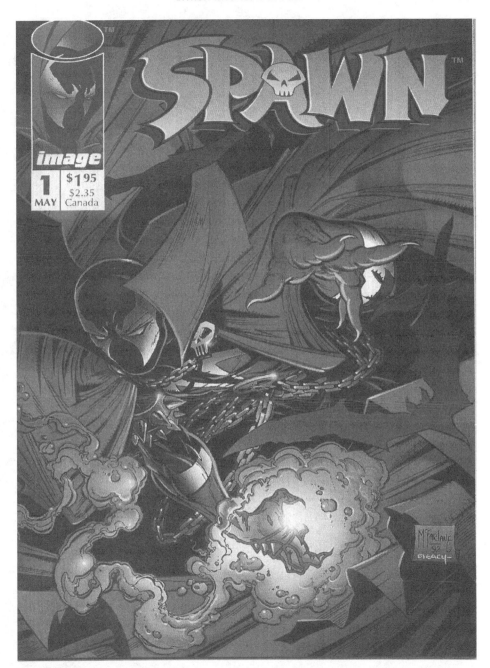

Figure 3 Todd McFarlane's Spawn epitomizes the antihero genre in the Third Age. Al Simmons dies, goes to hell, and returns to Earth as Spawn. The choices he makes will determine his eternal destiny in a world on the brink of Armageddon (*Spawn* #1 May, 1992; Image; Todd McFarlane [pencils and inks] Ken Steacy [colors]).

Figure 4 Mark Waid and Alex Ross's *Kingdom Come* portrays a futuristic JLA (Justice League of America) that faces an apocalyptic crisis when a new generation of superheroes fail to live up to traditional moral standards and thus threaten the world's safety. A Christian minister by the name of Norman McCay—a character inspired by Ross's father—plays a major role in the series (*Kingdom Come* graphic novel version; 1997:55; DC Comics; Mark Waid [script] Alex Ross [art]).

Figure 5 This cover of Warrior Nun Areala exemplifies an eclectic blend of "good girl" posing, superheroism, religious imagery, and *manga* artwork. Such elements are commonplace in many Third Age comic books (*Warrior Nun Areala and Glory* #1; "God and Country," Sept. 1997; Antartic Press; Ben Dunn [pencils and inks] Pat Duke [as Patrick Duke] Pat Thornton [as Patrick Thornton] [colors]).

Figure 6 Kurt Busiek's Astro City marks a reconstructive trend back to more traditional-styled superheroes. Characters in the comic include Confessor; Altar Boy; Winged Victory; Gentleman; Hanged Man; First Family; Cleopatra; Crossbreed; and in this picture, Samaritan: a hero whose name recalls the Good Samaritan parable of Jesus in the Gospel of Luke (*Astro City: Life in the Big* City; 1995 and 1996 graphic novel; Image; Alex Ross [cover art]).

10
Superheroes in Crisis: Postmodern Deconstruction and Reconstruction in Comic Books and Graphic Novels

Thom Parham

The third era of comic books cannot be understood properly without knowing something about the first two eras. As a recap the Golden Age of comics is widely held to have started with the first appearance of Superman in *Action Comics* #1 (June 1938). In his introduction to *The Greatest Golden Age Stories Ever Told*, Mike Gold calls the era "A time of exploration, an era of growth, a land of magic."[1] This age flourished until "about 1951, when the sky-soaring underwear boys went into what turned about, surprisingly, to be only a temporary nosedive," according to comics writer and historian Roy Thomas.[2] Among the contributing factors for this change of fortune were "shopping centers, television, McCarthyism, and juvenile delinquency."[3] The Silver Age revival of comics began with the appearance of a new Flash in *Showcase* #4 (Oct. 1956): "The Flash was outfitted with an entirely new approach: instead of having roots in fantasy or vengeance, the origin was of a scientific nature. The artwork was clean, clear, and highly individualized: it looked nothing like styles common to the super-heroes of the Golden Age. The entire book looked extremely modern. And it clicked."[4] This era boomed in the 1960s and heralded the revival of additional heroes from DC Comics like Green Lantern, Hawkman, the Atom, Aquaman, and others, as well as the rise of signature Marvel heroes such as the Fantastic Four, the Hulk, and Spider-Man.

Denoting the end of the Silver Age is a bit difficult. Mike Gold fixes that date at 1985, although he opines "the Silver Age ended in spirit more than a decade earlier."[5] In 1985 DC Comics' continuity-altering *Crisis on Infinite Earths* miniseries replaced the company's 50-year-old "multiverse" with a coherent *uni*verse. This enabled DC to reinvent its flagship characters for contemporary audiences. Meanwhile at Marvel Comics, the heavily hyped *Secret Wars* miniseries produced no lasting changes—save the introduction of Spider-Man's black costume, which later became the Venom symbiote when merging with reporter Eddie Brock. Clearly there was excitement in the comics industry with these two projects, as well as Alan Moore/Dave Gibbons's *Watchmen* and Frank Miller's futuristic take on Batman in *The Dark Knight Returns*.

The question arises what to call this new era. A 1991 DC Universe trading card set produced by Impel Marketing describes the third generation of superheroes as the Modern Age. Although this is a functional definition, one could argue that the current era of comic books is actually the postmodern age. There are two distinct strains of postmodern comic books, both of which can be traced to the mid-1980s. By scrutinizing these, it is possible to reflect upon the state of contemporary comic book and graphic novel heroes.

Postmodernism's Twin Strains: Deconstruction and Reconstruction

Postmodernism is not a single, cohesive theory but a group of tenets that arise as a reaction to modernism. The theologian Robert E. Webber describes six paradigms that have shaped western culture over the past millennia: biblical, ancient (Platonic), medieval (Aristotelian), nominalism, modern, and finally postmodern. He expounds, "The new revolutions in science, philosophy, and communications—in all areas of life—are shifting us toward the affirmation of new values."[6] These new standards include: opposing hierarchy, diversifying and recycling culture, questioning scientific reasoning, and embracing paradox. Other crucial traits include the fall of grand narratives, the fragmentation of society and individuals, and the challenge and changing of language.[7] An appropriate watchword for these tenets may be *deconstruction*. In layman's terms, "Everything you know is wrong; accept nothing on face value."

A valid extension of deconstruction, however, is *re*construction. As the philosopher Benedict Spinoza once said, "Nature abhors a vacuum." At the end of the day "Question questions" may be a clever catchphrase, but people still want to believe in something. Paul Crowther explains this dichotomy between deconstruction and reconstruction when he argues that "there are two fundamentally different aspects to postmodernism in the visual arts." The deconstructionist bent is "a new form of art whose very pictorial means embody a skepticism as to the possibility of high art." He continues, "However, this deconstructive approach also created a market demand which was rapidly met by Secondary (uncritical) Super Realisms and Neo-Expressionisms." This incited a reaction that reinvigorated "legitimate" art forms that tapped "traditional expectation[s] of virtuoso performances."[8]

Both the deconstructive and reconstructive trends have signified the current third age of comics that began circa 1985–1986. I will identify this age as the Postmodern Age of superheroes. In 1986 *Watchmen* and *The Dark Knight Returns* epitomize the deconstructive trend while the relaunch of flagship heroes after DC Universe's *Crisis on Infinite Earths* (such as Superman and Wonder Woman), as well as the advent of Kurt Busiek/Alex Ross's *Marvels* and Busiek's *Astro City*, reflect a "back to basics" approach pointing to reconstruction. These trends are worthy of study.

Deconstruction and Dissection of Heroes

Creature Feature: Alan Moore's Swamp Thing

A prelude to the Postmodern Age occurred when Alan Moore became the writer on *Saga of the Swamp Thing* with issue #20 (Jan. 1984), a revamped monster hero whose first series was simply entitled *Swamp Thing* (1972–76). The creature made its debut in *House of Secrets* #92 (July 1971). The Swamp Thing became a flagship monster for DC at a time when the Comic Code Authority began to loosen their standards related to the portrayal of serious content in comic books. Other grotesque characters followed the Swamp Thing's success with Marvel Comics producing a similar creature known as the Man Thing, which first appeared in *Fear* #10 (Oct. 1972).[9] During the same period Marvel's *Tomb of Dracula,* which introduced the vampire slayer named Blade, *Werewolf by Night*, and *Monster of Frankenstein* became popular remakes of old monsters.

The first Swamp Thing series did not survive the 1970s, but filmmakers brought to fruition a big screen version of the Swamp Thing directed by Wes Craven (1982) that was popular enough to produce a sequel. Previously, scientist Alec Holland thought a "bio-restorative formula" had caused him to merge with vegetation after an act of sabotage nearly killed him. In Alan Moore's inaugural story, "The Anatomy Lesson," an obscure Justice League villain named Jason Woodrue divulges the truth: "We thought that the Swamp Thing was Alec Holland, somehow transformed into a plant. It wasn't. It was a plant that thought it was Alec Holland!" (*Saga of the Swamp Thing* #20:12). Over the course of this storyline, the Swamp Thing learns he/it is an earth elemental imbued with Alec Holland's consciousness.

Noted British horror writer Ramsey Campbell calls this work "a poetic reinvention of the superhero, not only Swamp Thing but the Justice League...." The success to Moore's interpretation of this character rests in his imagining of a cosmos "where ancient gods still exist somewhere...

Heaven and Hell are demonstrably real...angels and demons alike seem to walk the earth with impunity."[10] Moore deconstructs the Swamp Thing as a creature born from science, making him rather a mystical caretaker of "The Green." In the author's own words, Swamp Thing's world may not "look much like the world we live in, but that doesn't mean it couldn't be every bit as glorious, touching, sad, or scary."[11] Here we may perceive an inverted facet of God's edict for Adam to tend the Garden of Eden, which later becomes a paradise lost.

From *The Saga of the Swamp Thing* came John Constantine (*Saga of the Swamp Thing* #37), who would later star in *Hellblazer*. Moore's success as a comic writer prompted stories in other titles: *League of Extraordinary Gentlemen, Top Ten, Tom Strong, Tomorrow Stories*, but his most influential for the third era was *Watchmen*.

Watching the Watchmen

In his next major project, Alan Moore again imbued a fictional comic book world with realism. He initially presented DC Comics with a proposal using characters from the defunct Charlton Comics line, which DC had recently acquired. Rather than allowing Moore to alter those characters—which the company planned to integrate into the post-Crisis DC Universe—Moore was allowed to proceed with characters loosely based on the Charlton ones. Thus, Blue Beetle became Nite-Owl, Captain Atom became Doctor Manhattan, The Question became Rorschach, and so forth. Moore's resulting collaboration with artist Dave Gibbons produced the seminal postmodern tome *Watchmen*. The creators set their tale in a world much like our own with several crucial exceptions: the United States won the Vietnam War (because of a godlike hero), the Keene Act outlawed unsanctioned heroes in 1977, Nixon is still president in the 1980s, and someone appears to be murdering superheroes.

Moore discussed his creative process in the "Minutes" section of the DC Comics/Graphitti Designs limited hardcover edition of *Watchmen*:

> [I]t wasn't enough to describe the particular circumstances in the life of a Rorschach or a Dr. Manhattan without considering their politics, their sexuality, their philosophy and all of the factors in their world that had shaped those things.... We couldn't discuss that world without in some way referring to our own, if only obliquely.

Although all of the characters are compelling—from the overweight and over-the-hill Nite-Owl who strikes a love affair with the embittered Silk Spectre II (Laurel Jane Juspeczyk) to the nearly omnipotent Doctor

Manhattan who has lost virtually all of his humanness—Rorschach arguably became the breakout star. This fact perturbed Moore:

> Rorschach was to a degree intended to be a comment on the vigilante super hero, because I have problems with that notion. I wanted to show readers that the obsessed vigilante would not necessarily be a playboy living in a giant Batcave under a mansion. He'd probably be a very lonely and almost dysfunctional guy in some ways.[12]

Underneath the mask, Rorschach is revealed to be an odd-looking fellow with a propensity for beating the snot out of perpetrators. In one flashback scene he discovers the remains of a kidnapped child whose bones are being devoured by German shepherds. He kills the dogs with an ax, and after immobilizing the kidnapper with a handcuff, he lights the criminal's place on fire, giving the man a hacksaw with the option to either saw off his wrist with his free hand or be burned alive in the house. In short Rorschach is not a well person.

The villain in the story turns out to be the one who was earlier considered a virtual saint. Ozymandias (Adrian Veidt), named after Pharaoh Ramses II, forces his vision of utopia upon the world by attempting to unite superpowers at the brink of Armageddon against an alien foe that he creates to kill millions of people in New York City. For Veidt, the end justifies the means, but Rorschach's allegiance to justice does not let him see it that way. The latter intends to expose the utopian scheme to the public even after the calamity takes place and apparently creates the desired effect: peace among the superpowers. The *Watchmen* story also contained a minor plot of another comic book in which a marooned mariner uses the bloated dead bodies of his companions as a float to get off the island and attempt to warn his hometown about the dangerous ship that wrecked his vessel. Richard Reynolds posits that "Just like Ozymandias/Adrian Veidt, [the mariner] hopes to stave off disaster by using the dead bodies of his former comrades as a means of reaching his goal."[13] It has been suggested that the characters point to different ideologies: Rorschach represents radical conservativism while Veidt holds to radical liberalism.[14] Societal problems may be addressed via the flaws of the superheroes: "Moore criticizes Manhattan's withdrawal from human affairs as well as Ozymandias's direct involvement and Rorschach's absolutes."[15]

Each chapter of *Watchmen* drew its name from a classic work of literature, philosophy, or pop music. Chapter III, for example, "The Judge of All the Earth" comes from Genesis 18:25; Chapter IV "Watchmaker" is derived from an Albert Einstein quote. Other chapter titles come from sources as diverse as Elvis Costello, Bob Dylan, Carl Jung, and Friedrich

Nietzsche. This blurring of high- and low-culture is quintessentially postmodern, but Moore and Gibbons never lose sight that their true focus is human nature. Though the Watchmen's world teeters on the brink of nuclear annihilation, the conflict is resolved through a unique synthesis of scapegoating and manipulation by an unlikely adversary. The authors imply that humans, no matter how godlike, are still ill-equipped to discern an equitable balance between justice and mercy when the fate of humanity is concerned.

Frank Miller Spawns a Dark and Stormy Knight

While Moore and Gibbons completed *Watchmen*, Frank Miller was redefining Batman in *The Dark Knight Returns*. Miller had formerly revitalized Marvel's *Daredevil* (#158–191; 1979–83), adding grim realism to the plot of the blind "Man without Fear" and Matt Murdock, the melancholy lawyer who played his alter ego. He also introduced the Elektra saga (*Daredevil* #168–181, 190), the story from which was derived the later *Daredevil* movie that included a female antihero whose life was tragically altered when her father was accidentally killed by the government.[16] It turned out that Daredevil and Elektra were former sweethearts in their earlier years, and Murdock rekindles his love for her only to lose her again when the villain Bullseye kills her. Miller also worked on the jaded vigilante called The Punisher in the same series (*Daredevil* #182–84; 1982), and with Chris Claremont, contributed to the mythos of Wolverine in a limited series in 1982 (*Wolverine* #1–4). His interpretation of the four superheroes is representative of the typical characters one finds in the Postmodern Age of comics. In many ways the dark tenor that would capture Miller's later work on Batman and spark a new era in comics were already seminally present in his interpretation of Daredevil. Prior to Batman he also originated *Ronin*, a series that echoed the Japanese *manga* style that later graced the pages of *Dark Knight Returns*.

The four-issue *Dark Knight Returns* miniseries became the first of what DC Comics soon branded as its *Elseworlds* line. Rather than merely label them as imaginary tales, a Silver Age *nom de plume*, the company continues to use Elseworlds as a means of transplanting heroes from their traditional settings and making them fresh. Miller's take on a futuristic Batman allowed him to get "[b]eyond the imagery, themes, and essential romance of" the Batman mythos.[17] Objecting to the humanization of Batman in recent years, Miller used the opportunity to return the Dark Knight to his mythic roots as a "god of vengeance,"[18] while commenting on increasingly topsy-turvy values in contemporary American culture. Fellow writer Alan Moore elucidates in his introduction to Miller's *Dark Knight* collected volume:

> The Batman himself, taking account of our current perception of vigilantes as a social force in the wake of Bernie Goetz, is seen as a near-fascist and a dangerous fanatic by the media while concerned psychiatrists plead for the release of a homicidal Joker upon strictly humanitarian grounds.[19]

The lack of moral clarity in Miller's Gotham City is reflected in the muted palette colorist Lynn Varley draws from. No longer can "[t]he values of the world [be] defined in the clear, bright, primary colors of the conventional comic book."[20] As in the early *Detective Comics*, Batman resembles a costumed pulp hero, intimidating in appearance and exacting out his own code of justice. Television talk shows argue about whether he is a hero or menace. The violence is graphic in the series with bloody fight scenes as Batman takes on a gang of mutants and battles Superman through brains instead of brawn when the Man of Steel intends to bring him to justice.

Pleased with Miller's work, DC commissioned him to redefine Batman's post-Crisis origin in *Batman: Year One*, a miniseries that ran in the February–May 1987 issues of *Batman* (# 404-407). Miller hoped to "surprise" readers whose "only memory of Batman [was] of Adam West and Burt Ward exchanging camped-out quips while clobbering slumming guest stars."[21] Although nowhere near as radical as the post-Crisis revisions to Superman and Wonder Woman, *Year One* focused on the Dark Knight's early encounters with then-Lieutenant James Gordon.

DC also created other epic storylines of Batman to sustain reader interest after *Dark Knight*. The Joker turned out to be a key player in several of these. The "Clown Prince of Crime" murdered the second Robin, Jason Todd, in *A Death in the Family*. He also crippled Barbara Gordon (Batgirl) in *The Killing Joke* and murdered Sarah Essen Gordon (Commissioner Gordon's wife) during the climax of *No Man's Land*. But the most intriguing supervillain storyline in Batman was *Knightfall*, in which the sadistic villain Bane broke Batman's back, necessitating his replacement by the younger, less capable Jean-Paul Valley. Dennis O'Neil, then-group editor, discusses the experiment:

> We wondered if Batman might not be passé, because for all his dark mien he will not inflict more pain than is absolutely necessary, and he will never take a life. We were looking at other heroes in other comics...in which wholesale slaughter seemed to be the qualification for a hero. So we set out to create an anti-Batman, and my greatest fear was that people would love him.[22]

Frank Miller's *Dark Knight Returns* remains an influential milestone in the history of comic books. His watchwords of "good and scary" helped inspire an entire generation of postmodern heroes like the Image Comics line, of which Todd McFarlane's grim and gritty *Spawn* is an example: After government assassin Al Simmons is murdered, he goes to hell and returns to earth as a "Hellspawn," tapped to lead demonic forces. Spawn fights unearthly, external, and internal conflicts as he makes choices that will determine his eternal fate as the world prepares for Armageddon. Like Batman, Spawn is a dark, caped vigilante who has no problem taking matters into his own hands. Unlike Batman, however, Spawn struggles to find his purpose, his past, and seems less concerned about upholding justice. His ultimate nemesis is Satan. McFarlane says that if Spawn defeats the devil, he will become the greatest hero because he has defeated the greatest bad guy of all time.[23] Some of DC's readers rejected the more violent and amoral Image Comics-type heroes. They still favored the more traditional ones. O'Neil concludes that "The idea of a moral and compassionate hero is not an outmoded one."[24]

Perchance to Dream: The Sandman

A protégé of Alan Moore created one of the most intriguing postmodern heroes, rife with spiritual implications. Neil Gaiman originally wanted to revive a fairly obscure DC hero named Sandman. Because another writer was already working with that character, Gaiman developed an entirely new character with the same name. He explains, "I wanted to write a comic for intelligent people. I don't understand why people write down. Who are they writing down to?"[25] The result of Gaiman's effort symbolizes a genre often called "dark fantasy." Hy Bender summarizes the series at the beginning of *The Sandman Companion*: "Sandman is about a being [Morpheus] who's the personification of dreams and rules the place where we spend a third of our lives. The series tells about how this godlike being comes to question his past actions, and the consequences of that questioning...."[26] One of the major themes of the series is the emphasis on the narrative paradigm itself rather than comic book talk balloons. Les Daniels elucidates, "Gaiman uses his forum as a way to assert the primacy of stories and dreams, which far from being mere diversions are presented as the devices by which we comprehend existence itself."[27]

Like the world of Moore's *Swamp Thing*, Gaiman's cosmology posits the existence of angelic and demonic beings as well as classical and Christian mythological content. In *Season of Mists,* the first Sandman storyline to be reprinted in hardcover, Lucifer Morningstar abdicates his position as ruler of

Hell, "tired of being the Adversary."[28] Like Dante's Satan, Gaiman's Lucifer is a fascinating, complex character. He expresses his frustration with humanity: "'The Devil made me do it.' I have never made one of them do anything. Never. They live their own tiny lives. I do not live their lives for them."[29] Lucifer gives Morpheus the key to Hell fully knowing that beings from diverse world mythologies—Egyptian, Norse, Japanese, and so on— will want to wrest it from him. The author resolves the storyline with an elegant *deus ex machina*; God sends two angels to take over Hell because "Hell is Heaven's shadow" and "without Hell, Heaven has no meaning."[30] Alluding to Voltaire's quote, "If God did not exist, it would be necessary to invent him," Frank McConnell expresses his affinity for Gaiman's cosmos in the preface to *The Sandman: Book of Dreams*:

> We need gods—Thor or Zeus or Krishna or Jesus or, well, God—not so much to worship or sacrifice to, but because they satisfy our need— distinctive from that of all the other animals—to imagine a meaning, a sense to our lives, to satisfy our hunger to believe that the muck and chaos of daily existence does, after all, *tend* somewhere.[31]

The entire *Sandman* series, then, affirms postmodern humanity's search for transcendence through the mystical, the divine, or even the occult.

Apocalypse, Wow! The Justice League of Mark Waid and Alex Ross's Kingdom Come

Perhaps a final trend in deconstructionist comic heroes is to place familiar heroes in a dark, alternate future. In the DC Elseworlds miniseries *Kingdom Come*, Mark Waid and Alex Ross imagine the DC Universe where the older superheroes have "slipped out the limelight and been replaced by an amoral, bloodthirsty younger generation."[32] In a reversal of Jesus' famous words, "The meek shall inherit the earth" (Matthew 5:5), the strong and violent "heroes" are possessing it to the dismay of regular humans. Emerging from retirement (a type of Second Coming), Superman and Wonder Woman issue an ultimatum to these newer superheroes: join a resurrected Justice League or face incarceration in a rehabilitation camp. This leads to escalating conflicts that threaten to hasten Armageddon as Superman struggles in a brawl with a confused Captain Marvel. The United Nations decide to drop a nuclear bomb on the battlefield where the Justice League is fighting the new generation of superbeings. James Cleaveland points out that *Kingdom Come* works on several levels. In addition to rebutting "Alan Moore's scathing condemnation of the shallow clichés of the superhero genre, *Watchmen*," it also contrasted "the amoral killers that 1990s comics held up as heroes with the more staid and virtuous characters of yesteryear."[33]

Mark Waid, with Alex Ross, clarifies his intent with the series. "Alex's story, we decided, was about the sin the super-heroes committed the day they divorced themselves from their own humanity, and the struggle they would encounter in trying to restore their human souls."[34] The character who facilitates the heroes' journey is Norman McCay, a Christian minister who develops a relationship with them (given the assistance of the Spectre). Clark Ross, the visual inspiration for the character, notes "[McCay] grows through all the trials and tribulations that follow. Instead of simply observing the fallible super-heroes, he actually becomes a pastor to them, encouraging them to yield to their truer, better selves."[35] The creators appropriate religious images and text citations from the biblical book of Revelation. One of the characters is even named Magog (and is a thinly veiled version of the gun-toting Marvel character Cable) after the wicked power that attacks God's people in Revelation 20 and Ezekiel 38–39. Battling in the middle of Kansas, Magog cuts through Captain Atom who then detonates with the effects of a giant nuclear bomb that essentially wipes out the heartland state, America's Eden and the early home of Clark Kent.

Shortly after the completion of *Kingdom Come*, Alex Ross collaborated with writer Jim Krueger on *Earth X*, a similar project set in the Marvel Universe. This series, which includes follow-ons *Universe X* and *Paradise X* has a simple premise: "[I]n the future, the mutant gene will have manifested in everyone on earth. And the world is falling apart."[36] Although both *Earth X* and *Kingdom Come* focus on dystopian futures rooted in the respective continuities of the Marvel and DC Universes, each uses deconstruction as a means to affirm classical heroics. Joss Whedon lauds, "[*Earth X*] not only reassesses every tenet of Marvel mythology, but in the process explains a lot of them as well."[37]

Reinvention: Daughter of Necessity

Reality Check: Kurt Busiek's Astro City *and* Marvels

Deconstruction is a tricky business and can sometimes ruin a person's affinity for the subject that is being dissembled. Although *Watchmen* pointed out inherent flaws and absurdities in standard superhero fare, it could not exist without its numerous antecedents. Writer Kurt Busiek discusses this dilemma:

> For the past decade...the prevalent mode for "serious" superhero creators
> has been deconstruction. The superhero has been dissected, analyzed and
> debunked...it's almost become impossible to present a superhero who does
> what he does without being emotionally unstable, incapable of dealing with
> reality without "acting out" his psychoses and obsessions. But it strikes me
> that the only real reason to take apart a pocket watch, or a car engine, aside
> from the simple delight of disassembly, is to find out how it works. To
> understand it, so you can put it back together again better than before, or
> build a new one that goes beyond what the old model could do.[38]

Busiek clearly delineates his current interest in writing superheroes; he
presents a "back to basics" approach. This philosophy undergirds the
recontructionist approach to postmodern heroes. DC, Marvel, and other
companies have used this approach to reinvent classic heroes as well as to
develop new ones. As Marv Wolfman summarizes in his introduction to the
Crisis on Infinite Earths collected edition, "Every generation of comic-book
readers deserves to have the comics belong to them, not to their older
siblings and parents."[39] The key, then, is to recapture the original spirit of
classic heroes, yet somehow make them relevant for contemporary
audiences.

Busiek helped define the reconstructionist approach to heroes by
bristling at the notion that he makes superhero stories "realistic." He clarifies
that making "a hermetically-logical alternate reality in which all the pieces
make sense and work logically" strikes him "less as a superhero story per se,
and more as science fiction...."[40] If *Watchmen* and *The Dark Knight Returns*
prompt us to ponder what life would be like if super characters lived in the
real world, Busiek helps us see what it would be like for us to live in the
superhero's world.[41]

In *Marvels*, Busiek's 1994 groundbreaking collaboration with Alex Ross,
the duo examine pivotal events in the Marvel Universe through the lens of
photographer Phil Sheldon. Rather than create a new world or deconstruct an
old one, their stated purpose was to examine the Marvel heroes "from the
perspective of an ordinary human, and what effect their presence had on his
workaday world."[42] Busiek is especially concerned with the love-hate
relationship Americans have with celebrities. Book Three "Judgement Day"
ends with Sheldon admonishing his peers for turning against the heroes, who
have just stopped Galactus from destroying Earth: "You people! What do
you need—the world to actually end? Are you so busy digging for garbage
you can't even admit to yourselves that you're grateful? Look up. Why don't
you—look up for once in your lives—!" The photographer retires at the end
of *Marvels*, shaken by Spider-Man's inability to prevent Gwen Stacy's death.

Sheldon realizes humanity cannot always depend on superbeings to prevent Earth's calamities.

Although Busiek has excelled in creating tales within a preexisting continuity, his storytelling skills proverbially soar in his series *Kurt Busiek's Astro City*. Unfettered by the constraints of operating within the Marvel or DC Universe, he has subcreated a world with heroes and back stories that seem familiar yet can diverge in fascinating and compelling ways.[43] Thus readers witness the first date between Samaritan and Winged Victory, this world's most powerful man and woman. Though the relationship seems doomed, "You're a God, pretending to be normal. I'm a normal woman trying to live up to the role of a god," Busiek leaves a glimmer of hope for the two superheroes to connect.[44] The second collected edition, *Astro City: Confession*, focuses on complications that arise when Altar Boy, faithful sidekick to a dark avenger, learns his mentor is a vampire. After The Confessor sacrifices himself to thwart an alien invasion, his protégé must process the events. A member of the Crossbreed informs the young hero, "Regardless of what [The Confessor] was, he was doing God's work—he was saving innocents and serving truth. And in the final judgment, what is more important? The burdens we bear—or the way we bear them?"[45] Writing within the confines of the superhero genre, Busiek creates stories that are about something worthwhile. Science fiction author Harlan Ellison praises, "There is a reality to Astro. Realer than Metropolis or Gotham City or the New York of *Spider-Man*. Realer, perhaps, than many of the places in which you now sit, reading this."[46] And Busiek achieves this reality by his observation of (and insight into) human behavior.

Last Son of Krypton, First Son of Earth

DC Comics chose to revamp the very first superhero as their first "reboot" after *Crisis on Infinite Earths*. Popular comics writer/artist John Byrne was hired to rework Superman. His purpose was "[t]o try to pare away some of the barnacles that have attached themselves to the company's flagship title" and "make Superman of today as exciting in his own right as was that primal Superman of yesterday."[47] His approach was simple. Superman was the *sole* survivor of Krypton—no more Supergirl, Superdog, Super-Monkey, and so on. Spared from the tragic fate of their Silver Age counterparts, Jonathan and Martha Kent are alive and well in the post-Crisis DC Universe. In fact their presence is arguably the wisest decision of the revision. "Byrne decided," writes comic book historian Les Daniels, "that the real personality was not Superman but Clark Kent, a kid who grew up in the heartland and embraced its ethics."[48] The sixth issue of Byrne's *Man of Steel* miniseries (1986) ends with Superman thinking, "Krypton bred me, but it was Earth that gave me all I am. All that matters. It was Krypton that made me Superman.... But it is the Earth that makes me Human!!"[49]

Byrne stayed with Superman slightly more than two years and managed to create renewed interest in the character. However, an inherent problem with Superman may be that "He's just not cool."[50] *Time* magazine writer Lev Grossman theorizes postmodern audiences like their heroes "dark and flawed and tragic." He continues, "Look at the Punisher (wife and kids dead), or Hellboy (born a demon), or Spider-Man (secretly a nerd). Look at Batman: his parents were killed in front of him, and he dresses like a Cure fan."[51] To remedy the "coolness factor," DC Comics has initiated radical storylines such as *The Death of Superman*, his transformation into an energy being, and the long-awaited marriage of Clark Kent and Lois Lane. More recently (June 2004) DC placed new creative teams on the Superman comics to make him more flawed and less super in order to increase the character's appeal. Ray Bradbury disagrees with the notion that Superman is too "square" for today's readers. The noted science fiction author feels the character helps readers cope with the rapid onslaught of new technology. "If he is the Man of Steel, then we are his steel compatriots, trying to figure out how in blazes to make do with yet another and another invention that careens into our world to knock us off the walls."[52] Bradbury's thesis seems to contradict Grossman's assertion that "Americans don't want to be told what to aspire to anymore, who we should be."[53]

My Big, Strong Greek Heroine: The New Wonder Woman

The last of DC's "Big Three" heroes to be revamped was Wonder Woman (1987). Although she survived the near collapse of superhero comic books in the early 1950s, and was temporarily revised in the late 1960s to fit in better with the changing times, the amazing Amazon has never been as popular as Superman or Batman. DC struggled with how to create a new Wonder Woman for contemporary readers. George Pérez recounts the situation.

> The problem was, however, that while [DC Comics] wanted a new Wonder Woman, it wasn't quite set on what exactly "new" meant. Several creators had come in with concepts that retained little but the Wonder Woman name. DC may have wanted a new Wonder Woman, but it still wanted to keep its iconic character recognizable.[54]

Pérez's approach was to "get back to the mythology" and "purify the concept."[55] Bothered by an indiscriminate mixture of classical mythology,

Pérez (with collaborators Greg Potter and Len Wein) focused exclusively on Greek mythology, excising all traces of Roman influence. This created interesting challenges. Why is Wonder Woman named Diana when the Greek goddess of the hunt is named Artemis? How can there be "W"s on her costume when there is no such letter in the Greek alphabet? And where on earth did Amazons on an isolated island get a handgun to play "bullet and bracelets"? The creative team's answers were simple yet credible.

The new Wonder Woman was a stirring success. Taking a cue from her 1940s origin by William Moulton Marston in which she first became an emissary to "Man's World," Pérez and company had Ares clarify Princess Diana's mission in issue #6. After her golden lasso shows the god of war the projected outcome of his machinations, Ares admonishes, "There is a difference between destruction and oblivion, Child—and it falls to you to teach it to man—to save man from himself! We shall see if you are equal to it!"[56]

Since *Wonder Woman* comics have never sold as well as DC's male flagships, the company inevitably tried to lure new readers with storylines ironically resembling those of her male counterparts. Diana was briefly replaced by Artemis, a rival Amazon; she died and ascended to Olympus as a goddess of truth. Her mother, Queen Hippolyta, died in the company-wide crossover *Our Worlds at War*. The current creative team, led by writer Greg Rucka, has grounded the series by making Diana the U.N. ambassador from Themiscyra (Paradise Island). The publication of Wonder Woman's book of essays and speeches has caused her to run afoul of conservatives who oppose her neo-pagan, Amazonian ideals. Rucka explains, "She's an entirely political figure. She has a political office, and she's the only superhero who does. She has a political title, she has a place in the world in a way that Superman doesn't."[57] The writer hopes the mixture of politics, super-heroics, and mythology will return Wonder Woman to her core roots yet make her revolutionary and fresh.

Conclusion

There are several lessons to be learned from examining postmodern comic books, both the deconstructionist and reconstructionist strains. First, contemporary audiences are reasonably sophisticated. They desire psychologically rich stories that reflect contemporary reality. Second, the superhero genre is not passé. Although traditional standards of morality may be difficult to adhere to in a post-1985 world, readers still find solace in the absolute heroics of masked or caped "good guys." Third, science no longer holds a privileged position for postmodern audiences. People are willing to explore the spiritual, the mystical, the neo-pagan, and even traditional religion as a means of deriving a semblance of order in the chaos of twenty-first century life. Finally, and perhaps most importantly, the primacy of story can never be overestimated. Because the three great monotheistic faiths (Christianity, Judaism, Islam) all share the biblical book of Genesis in which God speaks the world into existence, storytelling inevitably serves a religious function. Narrative thus becomes a chief means by which human beings describe reality.

Notes

[1] Mike Gold, "The Roots of Magic," in *The Greatest Golden Age Stories Ever Told* (New York: DC Comics, 1990), 10.

[2] Roy Thomas, "One Man's God Is Another Man's Copper Pyrite," in *The Greatest Golden Age Stories Ever Told* (New York: DC Comics, 1990), 6–7.

[3] Mike Gold, Introduction, *The Greatest 1950s Stories Ever Told* (New York: DC Comics, 1990), 6.

[4] Gold, *1950s*, 9.

[5] Gold, Introduction, *The Greatest Flash Stories Ever Told* (New York: DC Comics, 1991), 12.

[6] Robert E. Webber, *Ancient-Future Faith: Rethinking Evangelicalism for a Postmodern World* (Grand Rapids: Baker Books, 1999), 14–15.

[7] Cf. Richard Campbell, Christopher R. Martin, and Bettina Fabos, *Media and Culture: An Introduction to Mass Communication* (4th ed., New York: Bedford Books, 2003), 24–25; Julia T. Wood, *Communication Theories in Action* (3rd ed., Belmont, Calif.: Wadsworth Publishing Company, 2003), 290, 293, 299.

[8] Paul Crowther, "Postmodernism in the Visual Arts," in *Postmodernism: A Reader* (Ed. Thomas Docherty; New York: Columbia University Press, 1993), 188–89.

[9] Howard the Duck also made his first appearance in a Man-Thing episode (*Fear* #19; Dec. 1973).

[10] Ramsey Campbell, Foreword, *Saga of the Swamp Thing* (New York: Warner Books, 1987), iv, viii.

[11] Alan Moore, Introduction, *Saga of the Swamp Thing* (New York: Warner Books, 1987), viii.

[12] Les Daniels, DC Comics: Sixty Years of the World's Favorite Comic Book Heroes (Boston: Bulfinch Press, 1995), 196.

[13] Richard Reynolds, *Super Heroes: A Modern Mythology* (London: B. T. Batsford Ltd., 1992), 111.

[14] Matthew Wolf-Meyer, "The World Ozymandias Made: Utopias in the Superhero comic, Subculture, and the Conservation of Difference," *Journal of Popular Culture* 36/3 (2003), 508.

[15] Matthew Pustz, *Comic Book Culture: Fanboys and True Believers* (Jackson: University of Mississippi, 1999), 138. Pustz adds that "Moore's answer is some kind of middle ground in which average people come to the aid of their

neighbors not out of devotion to a philosophical ideal or to fulfill some sort of psychological need but rather out of human concern and empathy."

[16] Elektra's name comes from the Greek mythological daughter of Agamemnon, who was determined to avenge her murdered father.

[17] Alan Moore, "The Mark of Batman: An Introduction." *The Dark Knight Returns* (New York: DC Comics, 1986), 6.

[18] Les Daniels, *DC Comics,* 190.

[19] Moore, "The Mark of Batman," 6.

[20] Moore, 6.

[21] Frank Miller, "Introduction," *Batman: Year One* (New York: DC Comics, 1988), 2.

[22] Daniels, *DC Comics,* 234.

[23] New Line Cinema's movie, *Spawn* (Director's Cut); Todd McFarlane Interview (1997).

[24] Daniels, 235.

[25] Daniels, 206.

[26] Hy Bender, *The Sandman Companion* (New York: Vertigo Books, 1999), 2.

[27] Daniels, 207.

[28] Bender, 95.

[29] Neil Gaiman, et al., *The Sandman: Season of Mists* (New York: DC Comics, 1992), Ep. 2:18.

[30] Gaiman, Ep. 6:8.

[31] Frank McConnell, "Preface," *The Sandman: Book of Dreams* (Ed. Neil Gaiman and Ed Kramer; New York: HarperPrism, 1996), 2.

[32] James Cleaveland, Rev. of *Kingdom Come* by Mark Waid and Alex Ross. [Cited 21 May 2004] Online: www.amazon.com/exec/obidos/tg/detail/ /1563893304/qid=1088124354/sr=1-1/ref=sr_1_1/104-0180506-5367108?v =glance&s=books.

[33] Cleaveland.

[34] Mark Waid, "From Here to Kingdom Come: Mysteries Unveiled, Secrets Revealed," *Kingdom Come: Revelations* (New York: DC Comics, 1997), 6.

[35] Clark Norman Ross, "Witness to the End," *Kingdom Come* (Limited Hardcover Edition; New York: DC Comics, 1997), 7.

[36] Joss Whedon, "Preface," *Earth X* (Limited Hardcover Edition; Anaheim, Calif.: Graphitti Designs, 2001), 8.

[37] Whedon, 9.

[38] Kurt Busiek et al. *Kurt Busiek's Astro City: Life in the Big City* (La Jolla, Calif.: Homage Comics, 1996), 9.

[39] Marv Wolfman, "Introduction," *Crisis on Infinite Earths* (New York: DC Comics, 1998), 7.

[40] Busiek, *Life in the Big City,* 9.

[41] Cf. Geoff Klock, *How to Read Superhero Comics and Why* (New York/London: Continuum, 2002), 77.

[42] Kurt Busiek and Alex Ross, *Marvels* (Limited Hardcover Edition; Anaheim, Calif.: Graphitti Designs, 1994), 6.

43 Klock notes similarities between the heroes in Astro City (named after a Jack Kirby hero) and Marvel and DC heroes: "Fantastic Four (the First Family), Superman (Samaritan), Iron Man (Mock Turtle), Batman (the Confessor), Captain America (the Old Soldier), the Flash (M.P.H.), Spider-Man (Crackerjack), Wonder Woman (Winged Victory), and the X-Men (The Astro City Irregulars)" (Klock, 87–88).

44 Busiek, *Life in the Big City*, 164.

45 Kurt Busiek, *Kurt Busiek's Astro City: Confession* (La Jolla, Calif.: Homage Comics, 1997), 155.

46 Harlan Ellison, "Introduction," *Kurt Busiek's Astro City: Family Album* (La Jolla, Calif.: Homage Comics, 1998), 12.

47 John Byrne, "Superman: A Personal View," *The Man of Steel* (New York: DC Comics, 1987), 8.

48 Daniels, *DC Comics*, 193.

49 John Byrne and Dick Giordano, "The Haunting," *The Man of Steel* #6 (New York: DC Comics, 1986), 22.

50 Lev Grossman, "The Problem with Superman," *Time* (17 May 2004), 71.

51 Grossman, 71.

52 Ray Bradbury, "Why Superman? Why Today?" *The Man of Steel* (New York: DC Comics, 1987), 5.

53 Grossman, 72.

54 George Pérez, "Introduction," *Wonder Woman: Gods and Mortals* (New York: DC Comics, 2004), 4.

55 Daniels, *DC Comics*, 194.

56 George Pérez et al., "Powerplay," *Wonder Woman* #6 (second series; New York: DC Comics Inc., 1987), 21.

57 Cited from Mike Cotton, "Wonder Bred," *Wizard* (Oct. 2003), 78.

Recommended Resources

Bender, Hy. *The Sandman Companion*. New York: VertigoBooks, 1999.

Bongco, Mila. *Reading Comics: Language, Culture, and the Concept of the Superhero in Comic Books*. New York: Garland, 2000.

Busiek, Kurt. *Kurt Busiek's Astro City: Life in the Big City*. La Jolla, Calif.: Homage Comics, 1996.

Busiek, Kurt, and Alex Ross. *Marvels* (Limited Hardcover Edition). Anaheim, Calif.: Graphitti Designs, 1994.

Byrne, John. "Superman: A Personal View." In *The Man of Steel*. New York: DC Comics, 1987.

Campbell, Richard, Christopher R. Martin, and Bettina Fabos. *Media and Culture: An Introduction to Mass Communication*. 4th ed. New York: Bedford Books, 2003.

Cotton, Mike. "Wonder Bred." *Wizard* Oct. 2003: 76–80.

Crowther, Paul. "Postmodernism in the Visual Arts." Pages 180–93 in *Postmodernism: A Reader*. Edited by Thomas Docherty. New York: Columbia University Press, 1993.

Daniels, Les. *DC Comics: Sixty Years of the World's Favorite Comic Book Heroes.* Boston: Bulfinch Press, 1995.

Grossman, Lev. "The Problem with Superman." *Time* (17 May 2004): 70–72.

Klock, Geoff. *How to Read Superhero Comics and Why*. New York/London: Continuum, 2002.

Miller, Frank. *The Dark Knight Returns*. New York: DC Comics, 1986.

Moore, Alan. *Watchmen* (Limited Hardcover Edition). New York: DC Comics, 1988.

Moore, Alan, Stephen Bissette, and John Totleben. *Saga of the Swamp Thing*. New York: Warner Books, 1987.

Pérez, George et al. "Powerplay." *Wonder Woman* #6 (second series). New York: DC Comics Inc., 1987.

Rothschild, D. Aviva. *Graphic Novels: A Bibliographic Guide to Book-Length Comics*. Englewood, CO: Libraries Unlimited, 1995.

Schmitt, Ronald. "Deconstructive Comics." *Journal of Popular Culture* 25 (Spring 1992): 153–61.

Waid, Mark and Alex Ross. *Kingdom Come*. New York: DC Comics, 1997.

Webber, Robert E. *Ancient-Future Faith: Rethinking Evangelicalism for a Postmodern World*. Grand Rapids: Baker Books, 1999.

Weiner, Stephen, and Keith R. A. Decandido. *The 101 Best Graphic Novels*. New York: Nantier Beall Minoustchine Publishing; 2001.

Wiater, Stanley, and Stephen R. Bissette. *Comic Book Rebels: Conversations with the Creators of the New Comics*. New York: Donald I. Fine, 1993.

Wolfman, Marv. Introduction. Pages 5–7 in *Crisis on Infinite Earths*. New York: DC Comics, 1998.

Wolf-Meyer, Matthew. "The World Ozymandias Made: Utopias in the Superhero Comic, Subculture, and the Conservation of Difference." *Journal of Popular Culture* 36/3 (2003): 497-517.

Wood, Julia T. *Communication Theories in Action* 3rd ed. Belmont, Calif.: Wadsworth Publishing Company, 2003.

Wright, Bradford W. *Comic Book Nation: The Transformation of Youth Culture in America*. Baltimore: Johns Hopkins University Press, 2003.

11
Pulp Heroes in the Shadow of God

Gregory Pepetone

The Old Testament chronicles a curious event in the *Heilsgeschichte* or "salvation history" of ancient Israel during the period of time recorded in the books of Judges, Ruth, and 1 Samuel. This period involved a transitional era after the Hebrews moved from Egypt into Palestine (probably somewhere from the thirteenth century B.C.E. to the establishment of the Davidic monarchy towards the end of the eleventh century B.C.E.). The nation became a decentralized people known as the Tribal Confederacy after it lost great leaders like Moses and Joshua. The era of the book of Judges is self-described as a time in which "everyone did as he saw fit" (Judges 21:25). The tribes lapsed into repetitive cycles of apostasy and deliverance. According to this book God would raise up *shopheṭiym*, a Hebrew term often translated as "judges" or "ones who bring justice," to deliver ancient Israel from oppressive enemy states that bordered it. Depending on how much these deliverers relied on the moral authority of God instead of themselves or patriotic nationalism, they would either become vigilantes who took the law into their own hands, or charismatic rulers who reigned not by dynastic entitlement but by a divinely conferred spiritual grace. In other words they were faced with a choice of first allegiance. They could either be led ultimately by God's moral direction or trust in themselves and their national pride.

What does Hebrew history have to do with American pulp fiction heroes of the 1930s and 1940s, such as Lester Dent's *Doc Savage* or Walter Gibson's *The Shadow*? Ancient Israel during the Judges era and America during the heyday of pulp fiction were both characterized by a struggle between faith and culture. As I hope to show, they both give rise to parallel concepts of heroism related to their own respective histories. The Jesus of biblical tradition will be considered as an alternative kind of cultural hero.

Violence and the Gothic Strain in
Pulp Fiction Heroes and the Book of Judges

In many ways, Israel's ancient tribal legends associated with the judges from Othniel to Samuel contain all the elements of the pulp fiction thrillers. We find a melodramatic universe inhabited by victims, good guys, and sheer baddies, a plethora of sensational incident, and a fast-paced narrative that maximizes action at the expense of ethical or psychological nuance. Above all, we find an implicit code of vigilante justice premised on the heroic deeds of individuals who have no qualms about using violent and sometimes treacherous means in the service of noble ends. The Arnold Schwarzenegger-like Samson, for example, metes out exactly the kind of punishment to the Philistines that Doc Savage ("The Man of Bronze") or The Shadow (a.k.a. Lamont Cranston/Kent Allard) dispense to their villains. That Samson does so with jawbone flailing rather than guns blazing is inconsequential. Similarly, Jael in the *Song of Deborah* wields a tent stake (to kill a Moabite oppressor) as effectively as the pulp heroes wield a .45 automatic in the hard-broiled detective stories.

Another intriguing connection between Judges (and 1 Samuel) and pulp fiction is the sensationally Gothic element inherent in both: angels, demons, precognitive dreams, visions, political intrigues, and miracles in the one; and ghouls, vampires, mystical powers, werewolves, time anomalies, political and criminal conspiracies in the other. The lurid titles of pulp episodes created by Dashiell Hammett, Raymond Chandler, Robert E. Howard, Lester Dent, Walter Gibson and others tell the tale. In Doc Savage and the Shadow, for instance, one could read "The Land of Terror," "The Squeaking Goblin," or "The Sargasso Ogre" (Doc Savage); and "Isle of the Dead," "Tomb of Terror," or "When the Grave Is Open" (The Shadow).[1] There is definite overlap between the religious and the paranormal.[2] In the Shadow, the mystical power to assume a cloak of invisibility by clouding men's minds is conferred on Lamont Cranston by a Tibetan *tolku*. This holy man is bent on Cranston's redemption from a life of crime and self-indulgence. In short, the Shadow's ability to perceive and thwart the "evil that lurks in the hearts of men" is a conditional power conferred by a supernatural agency. Just as Samson's phenomenal strength is a divinely conferred bulwark against the wickedness of the Philistines, so the Shadow's mysterious powers are a barricade against official corruption and organized crime.

However, the Shadow is not a character of unalloyed virtue. Repeatedly he takes the law into his own hands and is perceived as meddlesome and officious by Commissioner Weston. In the Russell Mulcahy film *The Shadow*, for instance, Commissioner Weston at one point threatens to place a task force on the Shadow in order to curb his interference. Indeed, one of the persistent messages of the Gothic strain in pulp fiction found in the pages of *The Spider*, *The Phantom*, *The Black Bat*, and *The Whisperer*, to cite only a handful, is the dualistic yet inseparable nature of good and evil. While presented as embodiments of right and righteousness (and no doubt perceived as such by the bulk of their readers), the pulp heroes frequently use ethically questionable means such as violence and deception to achieve virtuous ends. In some cases—the Shadow a prime example—their commitment to fighting evil is grounded in their own prior corruption, and they mirror some of their dark qualities. Likewise, Samson, Jephthah, Jael, Gideon, Saul, and other heroes from the books of Judges and 1 Samuel protected the Hebrews, yet at the same time, their methods and character were far from exemplary. To name a few examples, Samson fights more for vengeance and his sexual appetite than for God, Jephthah sacrifices his daughter to secure a battle victory, and Saul, already influenced by demons, consults a witch before going to war.

What both the official and unofficial representatives of justice have in common is a tendency to confuse righteousness with official zeal. They mix up patriotism with loyalty to a private or tribal agenda rather than to the will of God. Just ends are served by questionable or even criminal means. Indeed, the tragedy of the Samson tale in the book of Judges (i.e., he loses his hair and is blinded), according to Bernard Anderson, is "what happens to a man filled with *charisma* when he disregards the guidance of Yahweh [God] in a time of crisis to pursue his own passions."[3] But as the narrator of the weekly Shadow radio dramas might have paraphrased it, "Crime [read "sin"] does not pay."

The heroes of the Gothic imagination in classical as well as pulp fiction not only exhibit latent antisocial tendencies, but also become complementary opposites of their enemies, representing a metaphysical dyad. While at a conscious level, pulp heroes seem impervious to the villainy they oppose, at a deeper level they are bound to their villainous nemeses in almost a symbiotic relationship (e.g., Hamlet/Horatio, Jane Eyre/Bertha Mason, Holmes/Moriarty, Lamont Cranston/Shiwan Khan, and similarly, Batman/The Joker). A specter known as the *Doppelgänger*, an inverted mirror image of one's self, stalks the pages of late eighteenth- and nineteenth-century German Romantic literature. Albert Chamisso's *Peter Schlimihl* is a classic example. This intriguing but neglected Gothic novella concerns a young man who forfeits his soul to the forces of darkness by agreeing to surrender his own shadow. Many unanticipated consequences result from such a folly.

Not long after this story, Charles Dickens contemplated the creation of serialized magazine character, identified as "the Shadow." This character would escort his readers undetected into a variety of disreputable settings in order to issue a cautionary warning or expose blatant Victorian humbug. A similar character actually appears as a ghostly image of unrepentant death in Dickens's *A Christmas Carol:* The Ghost of Christmas Yet to Come. This book presented many of the elements that would later define pulp fiction, such as the intervention of supernatural agencies and a melodramatic juxtaposition of good and evil characters, domestic and sublime settings, humorous incident, and pathos.[4]

The Shadow Side of God

In the early decades of the twentieth century, Swiss psychoanalyst C. G. Jung appropriated the Romantic/Gothic tradition to his own clinical purposes. He rehabilitated myth and religious symbolism, including Christian Gnosticism, as legitimate areas of scientific enquiry. In the process, he postulated a conception of the Deity as a Faust-like duality within which the properties of good and evil, God and Satan, coexist. This deity's task, and by extension that of his human creatures, is to achieve psychic integration between these conflicted (though potentially energizing) forces: "The message typically conveyed by these Gothic dualisms is that we are sane, individually and collectively, to the extent to which we have assimilated and balanced our internal contradictions. Conversely, to the extent that we have denied them or projected them unto others, we are not."[5]

Jung's elaboration of this thought is found in his monograph, *Answer to Job* (based on the Book of Job in the Old Testament). In contrast to the more orthodox view of God ("God is light, and in him is no darkness at all" 1 John 1:5), the God of Jung's monograph is a flawed tribal deity who failed to integrate his own dark or "evil" side. Accordingly this God suffers a "reversal into the [evil] opposite" when he inflicts the baffled and unsuspecting man named Job with intense suffering. Jung calls this transformation *enantiodromia*, a type of Dr. Jekyll/Mr. Hyde process that Jung regards as "a fundamental law of life."[6] "Evil," claims Jung, with regard to the gentleman's agreement between God and Satan over Job's torment (Job chapter 1) "is by no means fettered, even though its days are numbered. God still hesitates to use force against Satan. Presumably he still does not know how much of his own dark side favors the evil angel."[7] The later incarnation and crucifixion of Christ, according to Jung's interpretation, represents an act of divine atonement for the undeserved suffering of Job. This involves a symbolic act of healing through self-awareness.[8]

When moving the discussion from God to humanity, Jung comments that "Healing may be called a religious problem.... In the sphere of social or national relations, the state of suffering may be civil war, and this state is to be cured by the Christian virtue of forgiveness." He goes on to ask, "How is he [man] to reconcile himself with his own nature—how is he to love the enemy in his own heart and call the wolf his brother [?]"[9] Given the prominent role played by werewolves in the Gothic strain of popular culture, it is a question still germane; maybe "the shadow" has the answer.

In the Jungian system, "the shadow" is a recurrent Gothic archetype of those untamable, violent, or sinister components of the human psyche with which we are able to cope only by denying their very existence and subsequently projecting them onto an external "enemy." This enemy is then pursued with obsessive zeal, but this delusion often ends tragically for pursuer and pursued alike. It does so for the obvious reason that the conscious target of such zeal is, in reality, a discarded aspect of the vigilante's own disintegrated psyche. In consequence, he often ends by destroying that which, at the subconscious level, he most cherishes, including his own spiritual or physical well-being. "Who knows what evil lurks in the hearts of men?" asks a disconcertingly maniacal voice at the beginning of each week's live radio broadcast of *The Shadow*. Jung's theology concludes that the evolved, self-actualized God of the New Testament embodied in Christ knows that evil (as does the Shadow of course), because at an earlier stage of God-consciousness it lurked within God's own heart! It follows that all humans, who are made in God's image, must take up the cross of their own discarded shadow side in order to tread a path toward psychic integration and wholeness. This necessary but painful journey is unique to each individual.

So then, how precisely do the Jungian concept of God and the recurrent themes in the book of Judges concerning loyalty to God's moral authority versus loyalty to the State figure into the mythology of American pulp fiction? What can these themes tell us about the collective national psyche during a period when pulp magazines and radio dramas flourished? The answer to these questions lies in what might be termed the *Heilsgeschichte* or "salvation history" of the American experience.[10]

American *Heilsgeschichte*

The colonial root of the American experiment is a world explored imaginatively by Gothic writers such as Hawthorne and Melville. It is a world that was rigidly run by God, a theocracy of sorts.[11] America was to be the New World Eden, a land untainted by the sins of forefathers; i.e., by the nationalistic sins of European history. Like the Israelites of old, American settlers believed themselves to be a chosen people, representatives of a sacred covenant. By implication, the North American continent, according to this view, was transformed into a latter-day Canaan flowing with milk and honey. In this sense the settlers could continue their own "salvation history" as God's chosen.

Within the American dream, however, there rested an unaddressed contradiction between a utopian commitment to equality for all and yet a growing problem of racism, paternalism, jingoism, and predatory capitalism. America's original commitment to an international "brotherhood" of man sustained by an open political process was shadowed by its *Doppelgänger*—a covertly fascist, quasi-religious belief system that was later to find its most virulent expression in the German National Socialism of the 1930s and 1940s.

In the early twentieth century the United States had expanded both in population and economy. Ideological factors that had assisted along the way included Social Darwinism in the private sector, coupled with a bellicose doctrine of Manifest Destiny in the public sector. With the advent of a large and growing urban population of impoverished and disenfranchised immigrants came the rise of organized blue-collar crime (officially unsanctioned though largely ignored). Furthermore, the advent of organized white-collar crime was spawned by the industrial elite. This growing problem made things twice as difficult to situate within the authentic American dream.

The Great Depression with its snaking bread lines, massive unemployment, rumors of impending war, and rampant crime punctuated this long chronicle of a decline of democracy. Meanwhile the authoritarian conception of nationhood that characterized colonial America found expression in post-World War I ideologies such as populism and religious fundamentalism. The American dream reversed into a society that was in many respects the antithesis of the New World Eden it had originally hoped to be.

It was into this political arena, this "Jekyll and Hyde" *enantiodromia,* that pulp heroes were born. They comprised an imaginative phalanx against a rising tide of official and unofficial corruption. These pop culture *shopheṭiym* ("ones who bring justice") welled up from America's unconscious, yearning for a renewal of faith in a dysfunctional democracy. Such pulp champions of the people as the Shadow, Doc Savage, the Spider, Operator #5, and others provided weekly reassurance to an increasingly anxious public that the cause of justice was not irretrievably lost. They offered hope that the vindication of right would ultimately triumph over the rule of might, however improbable such an outcome must have appeared in the cold light of the latest headlines and bread lines. Moreover, the idiom of those who created these fantasy figures was that of the people.

Not unlike the heroic exploits chronicled in the Old Testament, the pulps offered America's huddled masses a brief but affordable respite from the misery and disappointment of a society ruled by cosmopolitan "Philistines" such as Al Capone, Henry Ford, and Adolph Hitler. For a mere coin, a reader could purchase multipaged adventures printed on cheap paper (hence, "pulp"); they could seek temporary refuge from a menacing reality in a pop-culture dream world where justice is truly meted out and criminals really do pay for their crimes. Moreover, these heroes were not allied with an establishment that seemed incapable of preventing sinister forces from alienating those they had relegated to the status of a disenfranchised peasantry.[12]

The current resurgence of interest in the mythology of pulp fiction in the Western world may suggest that public confidence in the ability of the legal/political systems to offer protection against criminality, in or outside of public office, is once again at a low ebb. Given the increasingly Gothic quality of life that has characterized the West for some decades now, it would seem that most, if not all, revolutions whether sacred or secular, begin in freedom but end in tears.

Vigilantism and the Return of the Shadow

The unarticulated rub in the American experience and pulp heroes is vigilantism. The assumption that the cause of justice can best be served by matching the ruthlessness of one's enemies goes to the heart of both pulp culture and the tribal culture ancient Israel encountered in the book of Judges. Jung warns that giving the Devil his due is not the same thing as adopting the devil's methods. This same warning, unheeded by pulp heroes, was sounded during the pulp era by American writer Sinclair Lewis. In his 1935 novel, *It Can't Happen Here*, he writes a parable about the coming to America of a homegrown variety of German fascism. Lewis quotes Romain Rolland to the effect that "a country that tolerates evil means...for a generation, will be so poisoned that it will never have any good end."[13] The appeal of the pulp fiction heroes partially involves the fact that while the heroes' motives are sincere, their methods are often difficult to distinguish from those of their opponents. Accordingly, these heroes serve as mythic embodiments of a national mood in favor of a rough-hewn justice unconcerned about the "legal niceties" and ethical qualms enshrined by Geneva conventions or the Amendments to the Constitution of the United States.

Like "God's chosen" leaders in the books of Judges and Samuel, they smite their enemies with a voracious appetite, regardless of the consequences. The pulp heroes surrendered to the compulsion of their shadow side, and they were subsequently delivered to the evil that lurked within their own hearts. In a sense they seemed to prefigure top-secret government and outlaw agencies with names that sound like alphabet soup, who were licensed not only to kill, but also to further their own agenda by implementing a lengthy catalog of covert, violent, and unsanctioned methods.[14] Again, the end does not justify the means.

DC Comics revived *The Shadow* in a 1986 update written and illustrated by Howard Chaykin. In a miniseries entitled "Blood & Judgment," the Shadow returns to the Western world after a long hiatus in Shambala, a technologically futuristic Shangri-La. His mission is to enlist former comrades to fight a former Russian turned American entrepreneur. Referred to as "the Pres" by his cohorts (short for Preston Mayrock), this crazed and crippled old man is obsessed with returning to Shambala and settling the score with his old enemy, the Shadow (Kent Allard). Bound for life to a frustrating existence in a wheelchair, Mayrock nevertheless has built an empire of crime and engineered a physically perfect relic of himself. The "Pres" has the Shadow's former friends systematically murdered in order to flush Allard out of hiding. As an added incentive, this criminal menaces the world with nuclear annihilation. Mayrock's ultimate objective is to have the technicians of Shambala transfer his brain into the super body of his genetic clone.

In a revealing interview with Howard Chaykin, Joe Orlando (DC Comic's vice president–creative director) says to Chaykin, "In your story, The Shadow is very unapologetic about his attitudes and his methods." Chaykin responds, "Yeah. The Shadow is an arrogant S.O.B. He's taken it upon himself to say, 'Hey! I kill 'em! I kill 'em as see 'em!' In the context of comic books we were raised to believe that Batman didn't use a gun, and Superman always played fair. The Shadow *never* played fair in that context—he perceived himself as the law, and when necessary, *above* the law."[15] Essentially Chaykin's Shadow makes explicit the cynicism and criminality that were implicit in the original version, a cynicism that permeated American culture from the lowliest mob hit-man to the highest in the land, including "the Pres" himself.

Occasionally, even in the radio version (e.g., "The Little Man Who Wasn't There," April 8, 1995), Police Commissioner Weston suspects the Shadow of criminal activity, saying, "He's always been a potential danger to law and order. Now the potential has turned real." The difference between earlier and later incarnations of the Shadow is that the original in the pulp magazines never doubts his own rectitude (and neither did his fans). The moral absolutism of his worldview, and by extension that of the pre-1960s America he represents, makes such introspection unthinkable. As a result, this earlier Shadow reflects the hypocrisy of a culture torn between its respect for lawfulness and its fantasies about vigilantism.

The Shadow had appeared in a number of B-films produced in the 1930s and 1940s, such as *The Shadow Strikes* and *International Crime* starring Rod La Rocque, and a weekly film serial produced by Columbia Pictures with Victor Jory in the lead role. In 1994, however, Universal Pictures released under the direction of Russell Mulcahy, a slick, special-effects-laden feature film starring Alec Baldwin as the pulp hero.[16] In this version, Lamont Cranston is once again tied to an Oriental drug ring in Tibet. Notorious as "the Butcher of Lhasa," he is redeemed by a Tibetan holy man and sent back to the United States to complete his penance by fighting crime and preventing his evil counterpart, Shiwan Khan, descendant of Ghengis Khan, from reducing New York City to a pile of atomic rubble. What it lacked in bite, it compensated for in humor as well as glamour. In my view the film successfully synthesized the more Gothic elements of Walter Gibson's original conception of the crime fighting and comedic emphasis of the radio drama and earlier film versions. It added a touch of tongue-and-cheek parody to the mixture in keeping with the sophistication of its post-Cold War audience. Conceived as family entertainment, the movie's characterization is undoubtedly innocuous when compared to DC Comics' hard-edged, New-World-Order cynicism. Nevertheless, the Jungian implications are deftly presented even if America's schizoid commitment to just ends by criminal means is considerably softened in the film version.

Nemesis from Nazareth

The issue between the kind of heroism displayed by Samson or the Shadow and the martyrdom of Jesus Christ is essential to understanding the differences between older conceptions of God and *New Testament* conceptions sanctified by the example and teachings of Christ. In the Gospels, rejection toward Jesus is largely explicable in terms of disappointed Messianic expectations. Jesus was *not* a militant action hero like Gideon, Samson, Saul, or the later Judas Maccabeus. Instead of promoting patriotic nationalism, Jesus taught his followers to love their neighbors and forgive their enemies. He replaces the vigilante "eye for an eye, tooth for a tooth" with "turn the other cheek" (Matthew chaps. 5–7). This teaching must have sounded contrary to the agenda of those of his era possessing a mixture of religious and patriotic zealotry exhibited by Jihadists of our own era.

In the words of cultural historian Benjamin Barber, "The language most commonly used to address the ends [and means] of the reinvented and self-described tribes waging Jihad—whether they call themselves Christian fundamentalists or Rwandan rebels or Islamic holy warriors—remains the language of nationalism."[17] Jesus understood that violence only begets more violence. The political absolutism, hostility, and racial bigotry that sustained the kingdom of Caesar were to have no place in the kingdom of God. Jesus himself made that clear by separating the two systems (Matthew 22:15–22; Mark 12:13–17; Luke 20:20–26; John 18:36).

Lost in denial, the violent nationalists of Jesus' day pretend to themselves that Jesus is there auditioning for the lead in *Nemesis from Nazareth, or How the Hick Messiah Kicked Roman Butt*—the latest action-packed installment of that ever popular ancient pulp serial in the tradition of the book of Judges: "Tribal *Heilsgeschichte*"! No doubt expecting Jesus to pander to their nationalistic zeal by passing judgment against Israel's oppressors, they engaged in civilized exchange designed to make theological mincemeat of this upstart carpenter's son from the boonies. Imagine their surprise when instead he passes judgment on, you guessed it...*them*. No doubt relying on the novelty of this strategy to carry the day, Christ proclaims for all to hear that he is the exact o-p-p-o-s-i-t-e of everything they represent. The Boris Karloff *New Gothic Paraphrase of King James* reads as follows: "You in bondage, me free. You proud, me humble. You no follow God, me Son of God; me show the way!"[18]

The serious point of this pulp parody is that by any conceivable measure, the Christ of the *New Testament* presents a radical alternative to the Messianic expectation that Israel would be saved by a Jewish Doc Savage dealing death and mayhem to the enemies of Yahweh their God. Clearly Christ was not interested in being a nemesis to anyone but those who confused loyalty to a tribal code with loyalty to God. He came not as a dispenser of divine retribution, but as a savior intent on role-modeling, among other things, an alternative to the "idolatrous power of nationalism." "The weed of crime," as the narrator of *The Shadow* affirms, "bears bitter fruit"; and as Christ proclaims of the false teachers, "Ye shall know them by their fruits" (Matthew 7:15–20). I suspect that self-righteous zealots on behalf of misguided causes are a breed we will always have with us. Moreover, zeal that leads to senseless violence can take place in many forms, whether in a government system or a faction within Christianity, Judaism, Islam, secularism, or something else.

The melodramatic universe to which the Shadow and the other heroes of pulp fiction belong resembles our own world in certain respects. Vigilantism in the pulp stories functions as a parable addressing violent fervor for nationalism in the real world. In my opinion I also suspect that, charming, well intentioned, and entertaining though they were, it would be harder for self-appointed vigilantes of pulp narrative to pass through the gates of heaven than it would be for a man as rich as Lamont Cranston to pass through the eye of a needle. Both zealous nationalism and vigilantism see life in terms of an unambiguous *physical* battle between irreconcilable forces or nations categorized as right or wrong, good or evil, on God's side or Satan's. Frankly, this worldview is not consistent with the Gospel of Jesus that emphasizes love more than justice, and forgiveness instead of vengeance. "God alone is king" and his ways are not our ways, as the example of God's son clearly illustrates. It follows that the responsibility of those who would faithfully serve the King of Kings is to shun nationalism's infernal means, however tempting, when it presumes to usurp heaven's transcendent authority.

Notes

[1] Don Hutchison, *The Great Pulp Heroes* (Buffalo, N.Y.: Mosaic Press, 1995), 26–27, 44

[2] See an excellent exploration of this issue in John J. Heaney, *The Sacred & The Psychic: Parapsychology and Christian Theology* (New York: Paulist Press, 1984).

[3] Anderson, *Understanding,* 154.

[4] Cf. Jim Harmon, *The Great Radio Heroes* (London: MacFarland & Company, 1992), 40.

[5] Gregory G. Pepetone, *Gothic Perspectives on the American Experience* (New York: Peter Lang, 2003), 115.

[6] C. G. Jung, *Modern Man in Search of a Soul* (New York: Harcourt, Brace, Jovanovich, 1933), 238.

[7] C. G. Jung, *Answer to Job* (Princeton, N.J.: Princeton University Press, 1958), 72.

[8] As author Madeleine L'Engle points out, "It is no coincidence that the root word of whole, health, heal, holy, is hale (as in *hale and hearty*). If we are healed we become whole; we are hale and hearty; we are holy." Madeleine L'Engle, *Walking on Water: Reflections on Faith & Art* (New York: Bantam Books, 1980), 57.

[9] Jung, *Modern Man,* 237.

[10] For a more nuanced presentation of this thesis, see Pepetone, *Gothic Perspectives.*

[11] Not unlike ancient Israel during the time of Judges; albeit, the flowering of U.S. democracy that incongruously sprang from this root was nurtured in the skeptical soil of Enlightenment rationality. Arguably, that soil proved too acidic for so delicate a shrub.

[12] Until compelled to do so by the Justice Department of the Kennedy brothers in the 1960s, America's longtime crime fighter *par excellence*, J. Edgar Hoover, refused to acknowledge either the extent or influence of organized crime in America.

226   *The Gospel According to Superheroes*

[13] Sinclair Lewis, *It Can't Happen Here* (New York: Signet Classic, 1935), 212.

[14] Anyone who wishes to explore this matter will find ample documentation of illegal activities engaged in by the CIA and the FBI during the 1950s and 1960s in the conclusions issued by governmental committees such as the House Select Committee on Assassinations and the Rockefeller Commission. For the ties between the CIA and the Nazi intelligence apparatus, see David Wise and Thomas B. Ross, *The Invisible Government* (New York: Random House, 1964).

[15] Howard Chaykin in Joe Orlando, *The Light Behind The Shadow: An Interview with Howard Chaykin* (New York: DC Comics, 1987), 8.

[16] Seen as a less biting and trenchant spin-off of the 1989 Warner Bros. Release, *Batman*, it was mostly panned by critics and pulp fiction aficianados and ignored at the box office—unjustly so in my opinion.

[17] Benjamin R. Barber, *Jihad vs. McWorld* (New York: Ballantine Books, 1995), 165.

[18] Actually better renditions of Jesus' confrontations with his adversaries are found in the Gospel of John 8 and Matthew 22. It is important to note that Jesus' words should not be considered anti-Semitic. Jesus the Jew denounced a proud faction within his own people, much the same way the Old Testament Israelite prophets denounced proud people among their kin in their own time. Unfortunately, the violent, religious nationalism of Jesus' day is the very type of wrongheaded zeal seen among some of the Christians in later history who twisted the Gospel words of Jesus into a misguided justification for hatred toward the Jews.

Recommended Resources

2222éééé
Anderson, Bernard W. *Understanding the Old Testament.* Englewood Cliffs, N.J.: Prentice Hall, 1975.

Barber, Benjamin R. *Jihad vs. McWorld.* New York: Ballantine Books, 1995.

Bloesch, Donald G. *Faith & Its Counterfeits.* Downers Grove, Ill.: InterVarsity Press, 1981.

Daniels, Les. "At the Corner Newsstand." In *Marvel: Five Fabulous Decades of the World's Greatest Comics.* New York: Harry N. Abrams, Inc., Publishers, 1991.

Harmon, Jim. *The Great Radio Heroes.* London: MacFarland & Company, 1992.

Heaney, John J. *The Sacred & The Psychic: Parapsychology and Christian Theology.* New York: Paulist Press, 1984.

Horn, Maurice, Editor. *100 Years of American Newspaper Comics: An Illustrated Encyclopedia.* New York: Gramercy Books, 1996.

Hutchison, Don. *The Great Pulp Heroes.* Buffalo, N.Y.: Mosaic Press, 1995.

Jewett, Robert, and John Shelton Lawrence. *Captain America and the Crusade Against Evil: The Dilemma of Zealous Nationalism.* Grand Rapids: Eerdmans, 2003.

Jung, C. G. *Answer to Job.* Princeton, N.J.: Princeton University Press, 1958.

Jung, C. G. *Modern Man in Search of a Soul.* New York: Harcourt, Brace, Jovanovich, 1933.

Lewis, Sinclair. *It Can't Happen Here.* New York: Signet Classic, 1935.

McAllister, Matthew P., Edward H. Sewell, and Ian Gordan, Editors. *Comics & Ideology*. New York: Peter Lang, 2001.

Orlando, Joe. *The Light Behind The Shadow: An Interview with Howard Chaykin*. New York: DC Comics, 1987.

Pepetone, Gregory G. *Gothic Perspectives on the American Experience*. New York: Peter Lang, 2003.

Phillips, Kevin. *American Dynasty*. New York: Viking Press, 2004.

Server, Lee. *Danger Is My Business: An Illustrated History of the Fabulous Pulp Magazines*. San Francisco: Chronicle Books, 1993.

Steranko, Jim. *The Steranko History of Comics*. Vol. 1. Reading, Penn.: Supergraphics, 1970.

12
Superheroes in Film and Pop Culture: Silhouettes of Redemption on the Screen

Leo Partible

T he excitement and fervor that usually precedes the opening of the latest superhero film is comparable to that of Elvis Presley or the Beatles arriving on the scene. The tenor of the times in an era of uncertainty and global economic downturn seems to have laid the groundwork for this cultural phenomenon. The opening voice in 1978's *Superman The Movie* perfectly describes the climate: "In the decade of the 1930s even the great city of Metropolis was not spared the ravages of the worldwide depression. In a time of fear and confusion the job of informing the public was a responsibility of the Daily Planet, the metropolitan newspaper whose reputation for clarity and truth had become a symbol of hope for the city of Metropolis." This describes *today's* world, similar to the late 1930s and early 1940s, where in place of World War II, the new battle involves global terrorism; and once again, the superhero has captured the imagination of a new generation, this time through motion pictures.

In addition to the effects of the social climate, when people need to make sense of uncertain times, the popularity of the superhero can be attributed to the dominance of youth culture and the rise of spirituality. If we investigate further, we find there is a definite, observable pattern that merges various forms of popular culture and points us to the comic book superhero.

Comic Books and Youth Culture in the 1940s and 1950s

Damien Cave remarked, "Before movies and rock 'n' roll, comic books invented youth culture."[1] In the 1940s the popularity of comic books reflected the mood of a nation hungry for escapist entertainment, particularly among young people and GIs as World War II dominated the headlines. Superheroes captured the imagination of young people everywhere, and Hollywood quickly responded by adapting *Superman*, *Batman*, *Spy Smasher*,

Captain America, and *Captain Marvel* into low-budget serials that were hugely popular. The special effects of these serials were crude and the plots simplistic; but *The Adventures of Captain Marvel*, arguably the best of the bunch, featured interesting visual effects such as flying sequences. Max Fleischer's animated Superman was more superior to the live-action serial of Superman (with Kirk Alyn). It overcame the limitations of technology with spectacular animation as the series successfully re-created the Man of Steel's most amazing feats, even so far as to add superpowers such as flight and heat vision. The serial also featured groundbreaking animation with art deco futurist designs and over-the-top villains that laid the groundwork for future superhero stories. The robots in the episode "Superman and the Mechanical Monsters" became the progenitors of today's shape-shifting mech robot designs popularized by the Transformers and most of Japanese *anime*. Afterward *Mighty Mouse* parodied the animated tradition of Superman, with cats as villains, of course.

The serials faded out after television sets graced family living rooms, but the Man of Steel would continue to soar in the 1950s with a television series called *The Adventures of Superman.* It was second in popularity only to series like *I Love Lucy* and competed with another hero on TV: *The Lone Ranger.*

Religion played a subtle role in the development of the superhero. A large segment of comic book creators were either Jewish or Roman Catholic Italians, and like their Hollywood counterparts they were influenced by the dominant Judeo-Christian culture of Americans. A number of Jewish creators changed their names to avoid discrimination and to "fit in" better with the American ethos. Thus Jack Kurtzberg became Jack Kirby and Stanley Lieber became Stan Lee. Other prominent Jewish comic book creators were Gil Kane, Will Eisner, Batman creator Bob Kane, Superman creators Jerry Siegel and Joe Shuster, and EC Comics co-founder Harvey Kurtzman.

The superhero genre in comic books experienced a decline in the 1950s as postwar audiences preferred the realism of crime stories, horror, and romance. The influential book *The Seduction of the Innocent* by psychologist Dr. Frederic Wertham made the charge that comic books caused juvenile delinquency. In addition to the McCarthy hearings against the entertainment industry, the Senate investigated claims against the comic book industry. Dr. Wertham's book, for example, made the charge that the relationship between Batman and Robin was a homoerotic fantasy. In response DC Comics' superheroes became whimsical; and Batman and Robin were given a dog, Ace the Bat-Hound, as well as girlfriends, Batwoman and Batgirl. Meanwhile many youths turned to a new music craze.

The advertising campaign for the RCA CD collection, *Elvis #1 Hits*, proclaimed, "Before anyone did anything, Elvis did everything."[2] Elvis played the prototypical hero, the rock and roll equivalent of Superman. In an excerpt from his acceptance speech for the Ten Outstanding Young Men of the Nation award, Elvis gave some insight into his diverse influences as an artist: "When I was a child, ladies and gentlemen, I was a dreamer. I read comic books, and I was the hero of the comic book. I saw movies, and I was the hero in the movie. So every dream I ever dreamed has come true a hundred times..."[3] Elvis's genius lay in his ability to take disparate strains of Western culture, synthesize those strains, and reinvent them into something fresh and exciting. He became the conflation of every aspect of youth culture: rebellion, controversy, sexuality, Hollywood stardom, and comic books. He nevertheless upheld the traditions of his Bible-belt upbringing, displaying faith in God, a respect for his parents, and a love for his country. He was the "American David" as U2 frontperson Bono called him.

Elvis also changed fashion almost overnight. Men dressed in suits in the 1950s, but Elvis preferred a more relaxed, casual wear that seemed to be a statement of independence. Elvis' hairstyle—jet black with falling bangs and punctuated with a semi-spit curl—was inspired by his matinee idol, Tony Curtis, and his comic book hero, Captain Marvel Jr. In the 1970s Elvis would go as far as wearing a jumpsuit with a half-cape, gold trim, and a sash that were obviously influenced by Captain Marvel; even his belt bore the famous lightning bolt symbol! Elvis also imitated the sultry look of Marlon Brando and James Dean's brooding figure. He appeared ahead of his time as a movie star, anticipating the rise of the action hero by incorporating the martial arts in his fight scenes (now the staple of today's action films), playing a racecar driver in a few films (predating the NASCAR phenomenon), a boxer (*Kid Galahad*), an adventurer in the Middle East (*Harum Scarum* had nothing on Indiana Jones), and a western hero (Clint Eastwood's Man-with-no-name influenced *Charro*, but Elvis was more convincing in his earlier effort, *Flaming Star*). In real life, Elvis followed another one of his heroes, James Bond, whose lifestyle he emulated in his revolving door of relationships with famous starlets and Vegas showgirls. Elvis even paid a visit to President Nixon in 1973 to secure an honorary FBI badge and strengthen his secret agent credentials.

Beatle-Mania, Bat-Mania, and Marvel-Mania: The 1960s and Early 1970s

Elvis Presley's immediate impact on American culture coincided with the revival of the superhero genre in 1956. That year the Flash, a reinvention of the Golden Age superhero, made his debut in the pages of *Showcase* #4. Subsequently the success of the Flash prompted editor Julius Schwartz to continue reinventing old heroes. The Green Lantern soon returned and the Justice League replaced the Golden Age Justice Society. Marvel Comics publisher Martin Goodman noticed the tremendous sales of DC's Justice League and asked his editor Stan Lee to create a team book. Along with artist Jack Kirby, Lee created the Fantastic Four. Lee and Kirby did what Schwartz had done with the new breed of hero: they injected a sci-fi twist. However, the Marvel efforts did not stop there; Lee explored deep emotions in the characters and gave insights into the human condition by introducing flaws to which the audience could relate. The Fantastic Four argued among themselves, Spider-Man was a teen-age geek with a guilt complex, and Bruce Banner turned into a green monster (the Hulk) whenever his emotions got out of control.

The Bible also gave depth to its characters—the most beloved heroes in Scripture, such as Abraham, David, Noah, Moses, Samson, Peter, and Paul all had major flaws, yet God used them anyway. Classic literature likewise presented complex heroes. Apparently, Stan Lee was well versed in both. As he affirms, "With Thor, I was influenced by Shakespeare and the Bible as I turned to 'Wither goest thou?' and similar phrases.... I've always been a nut about the poetic flavor of the Bible and the sentence structure and lilt of Elizabethan writing, and this was my chance to play with it."[4] The influence of the Bible and Shakespeare may have been an outgrowth from Lee's cultural Judaism or Western culture or both, but he also desired to follow the tradition of classic mythology. Lee goes on to say, "[With Dr. Strange] my correspondents would explain the relationship of Raggador to Ragnarok, or trace the origin of the eternal Vishanti right back to the Book of Genesis."[5]

By the mid-1960s the tide of Marvel mania swept through the college campuses. College students and academics began to take comic books seriously. Lee and Kirby presented monthly tales along with their cohorts in the Marvel bullpen such as Steve Ditko, John Romita, Gene Colan, and Roy Thomas. Lee's catchy phrases such as "true believer," "no-prize," "'nuff said," and "Excelsior!" became a new vocabulary for early Marvel "zombies." Comic books also influenced the pop art craze epitomized by Andy Warhol and Roy Lichtenstein. The latter adapted his famous work of art *Drowning Girl* from DC Comics' *Secret Hearts* #83 (Tony Abruzzo did the original splash panel). At the same time, J. R. R. Tolkien's *Lord of the Rings* trilogy became a college phenomenon. The Tolkien trilogy drew from the same classic heroic archetypes that influenced the superhero genre in comic books. In turn, the *X-Men* comic books featured a villain who took his name from the antagonist of *The Lord of the Rings*: Sauron.

Television networks quickly capitalized on the new hero craze in the 1960s. Marvel characters came to the cartoon world with Spider-Man, the Hulk, Iron Man, Thor, and others. Hanna-Barbera presented quality animation with their adaptation of the Fantastic Four (1967). The networks also presented a stampede of original animated heroes watered down for young viewers: *Space Ghost, Underdog, Atom Ant, The Mighty Mightor, Frankenstein Jr., Samson and Goliath,* and the goofy, slapstick *Mighty Heroes* (with Strong Man, Rope Man, Tornado Man, Cuckoo Man, and their leader, Diaper Man!).[6] Japanese *anime* contributed to the entourage with titles like *Astro-Boy, Marine Boy, Speed Racer,* and *Tobor, the Eighth Man.* Long before there was He-Man and his Masters of the Universe, *The Herculoids* invaded the airwaves on Saturday morning. And CBS introduced *The Impossibles,* a superhero team who secretly doubled as a mop-top music band after the tradition of the British Pop Invasion. That music icons could become children's heroes was amply evident—the Beatles had their own animated series on Saturday morning too.

Beatle-mania was in full bloom during the mid-1960s. The Beatles were the rock and roll equivalent of the Fantastic Four. Parallels with the Fab Four and the Fantastic Four were not lost on Stan Lee, as he humorously depicted in a story from *Strange Tales* #130. The cover features a panel exclaiming "in this issue, the Thing and the Human Torch meet the Beatles!" with the two superheroes wearing Beatle mop tops! From an aesthetic standpoint the Beatles all wore the same hairstyle and dressed in distinctive tailored suits that emphasized the unified group rather than the individual, much the way the Fantastic Four emphasized the team concept. The Fantastic Four revitalized comic books by inaugurating the Marvel Age much like the Beatles revitalized rock and roll and started the British Pop Invasion. Like their idol Elvis, the Beatles read comic books, and in addition, they praised Tolkien's *Lord of the Rings*. They wanted to do their own movie version of the Tolkien classic with John Lennon as Gollum, Paul McCartney as Frodo, George Harrison as Gandalf, and Ringo Starr as Sam Bombadil! Coming full circle in the early 1970s the X-Men and Iron Man inspired Paul McCartney when he wrote the song, "Magneto and Titanium Man," and performed it with his band, Wings. Marvel, Tolkien, and the Beatles symbolized the counterculture of the time, as youth movements experienced turbulence fueled by the Vietnam War, the civil rights movement, student protests, the sexual revolution, hippies, drug culture, and psychedelic rock. The Baby-Boom generation had arrived.

The European filmmakers also showed a love for comic books. The James Bond films starring Sean Connery pit the British secret agent against powerful villains bent on taking over the world. DC Comics adapted Ian Fleming's *Dr. No*, featuring James Bond, in one issue of *Showcase* (#43; 1963). Marvel Comics created its own spy hero with Nick Fury, Agent of S.H.I.E.L.D. (*Strange Tales* #135; 1965) as did television with *The Man from U.N.C.L.E.* and then *The Girl from U.N.C.L.E.* Italian director Mario Bava made his stab at the comic book genre with *Danger: Diabolik*, as did Roger Vadim with his cinematic adaptation of *Barbarella*, starring Jane Fonda. (Later on, pop music group Duran Duran would derive their name from a character in the movie.) Future Superman villain Terrance Stamp starred in the film version of the comic strip *Modesty Blaise*. In a sense they were not superheroes, but they did capture the campy essence of comic books at the time—most superhero stories outside of Marvel Comics were fairly innocent and simplistic. On the flip side of the coin, the climax of Russ Meyer's X-rated cult satire of Hollywood excess, *Beyond the Valley of the Dolls*, explored the homoerotic nature of the hero in a script written by future film critic Roger Ebert.

The *Batman* TV series debuted in 1966 on ABC and enjoyed unprecedented success, starring Adam West as Batman and Burt Ward as Robin. The following year it was showing twice a week (Tuesdays and Fridays) when Batgirl made her appearance. Die-hard comic book fans were embarrassed by its camp approach, yet it stayed much in line with the character's incarnation from the 1950s with gimmicky plots (i.e., Batman travels through time, Batman rockets to space, and so on), animal sidekicks (like Ace, the Bat-Hound), and colorful villains with kitschy names like Mad Hatter, Kite-Man, Egghead, and Crazy Quilt. The program opened with a slick Batman go-go tune and typically ended with a cliff-hanger as Batman and Robin struggled to free themselves from their opponents' diabolical traps. As the program ended with a cheesy question about the Caped Crusader's survival, the viewers were told to "stay tuned" for next week's show, "same Bat-time, same Bat-channel." Batman merchandise and trading cards soared. It seemed that overnight 1960s culture was overwhelmed by Bat-mania.

As quickly as *Batman* rocketed to the top of the Nielson ratings, the show died out after two seasons. *The Green Hornet*, starring Van Williams, another TV show adapted from comic books (and a radio program), died out the same time after one season. Even so, Bruce Lee, who played Kato, the Green Hornet's sidekick (with an emphasis on *kick*), went on to instigate a martial arts craze in the early 1970s with movies such as *Enter the Dragon*. During the heyday of *Batman* on television, science fiction programs such as *Lost in Space* and *Star Trek* enjoyed success. The latter, of course, would develop into a pop cultural phenomenon in the decades that followed, complete with movies, television spin-offs, and a multitude of "Trekkies." Starting in 1968, Stanley Kubrick's *2001: A Space Odyssey* premiered in theaters, a special effects forerunner to *Star Wars*.

The social turmoil of the 1960s and early 1970s inspired comic book creators to tackle more mature themes. Under writer Denny O'Neil and artist Neal Adams, Batman became a somber adventurer who dressed as a frightening creature of the night while his stories mixed elements of the James Bond films and the pulp stories of the 1930s' *The Shadow*. The Batman rogues gallery evolved from the brightly colored villains to a more timely threat such as the environmental terrorist, Ra's Al-Ghul, whose name according to Batman scribe Denny O'Neil translates into "the Demon's Head." The new villains were portrayed as misunderstood people who saw flaws in established systems and wanted to replace them with systems of their own.

Superhero references became more common in film. In *Easy Rider* (1969), Peter Fonda's character Wyatt nicknamed himself "Captain America." The film turned into a watershed for cinema as it combined the elements of youth culture: rock music, comic books, and the familiar themes of rebellion and the search for freedom. Not surprisingly, each of these aspects at one time or another endured criticism for contributing to juvenile delinquency. The peace-loving Silver Surfer went on his own *Easy Rider*-type quest as he questioned societal problems while himself trapped in a violent world not of his own making. Spider-Man's stories were set against the backdrop of student unrest on the college campuses, the specter of the Vietnam War, and the growing problem of drug addiction as Peter Parker's best friend, Harry Osborn, struggled to cope with his drug habit. Even the Justice League fought villains that posed a threat to the sociological and environmental landscape, and it turned out that the Green Arrow's sidekick Speedy became a drug addict.

Comic books fell in line with the evolving youth culture as new characters came out to capitalize on the popularity of Kung Fu films, Blaxploitation movies, and post-apocalyptic science fiction. Bruce Lee inspired *Shang-Chi, Master of Kung Fu*; Jack Kirby's post-apocalyptic *Kamandi: The Last Boy on Earth* drew heavily from *The Planet of the Apes*; Len Wein and Bernie Wrightson's *Swamp Thing* reinvented the horror genre with a sympathetic monster as the protagonist; and *Luke Cage: Hero for Hire* (later *Powerman*) mirrored *Shaft* as a superhero. Actor Nicolas Cage, a rabid comic book fan, took his surname from the African American crime fighter.

While America's Watergate scandal headlined the news, Hollywood had yet to embrace the comic book superhero as a legitimate source material for cinematic adaptation. There were high hopes for the 1973 George Pal production of *Doc Savage* starring Ron Ely (who played Tarzan in the 1960s television series), but the effort turned out to be just another exercise in camp. Perhaps out of ignorance Hollywood producers and executives felt that the simplistic black-and-white view of good and evil often portrayed in superhero adventures was not in vogue with the moral ambiguity that marked the high-brow films of the 1970s. Even so, the blockbusters of the time touched upon a theme that comic book superheroes had already been addressing—that somehow our established systems contain frightening flaws. While Nixon resigned from the White House, disco made its humble entry into the music scene; and as disco would soon take the record industry by storm, so also the temperament in the film industry would change by the late 1970s.

Star Wars: The Force versus Evil

George Lucas made it clear where his inspiration for filmmaking came from during an interview with his then mentor and producer, Francis Ford Coppola. He revealed to Coppola, "When I was a kid I was influenced by comic books."[7] Lucas took the model of *Easy Rider*, with its emphasis on the questioning youth culture and wall-to-wall soundtrack, and put his own spin on the genre in his ode to high school life, *American Graffiti*. As a follow-up, Lucas wanted to bring to life one of his favorite heroes on the silver screen: Flash Gordon. He tried to get the rights for a film version of the character in 1973 only to be turned away because another director had the rights (Frederico Fellini).

The Flash Gordon disappointment did not deter Lucas from creating something that unexpectedly turned into a cultural phenomenon: *Star Wars*. The 1977 film combined many elements: it took the best from mythology, mixing the King Arthur saga with sci-fi, with a nod to E. E. Doc Smith's *Lensmen* and the Silver Age version of the superhero Green Lantern. It likewise echoed the Samurai films of Akira Kurosowa, particularly *Hidden Fortress*, which along with his other Samurai films were in turn influenced by John Ford's westerns. Lucas merged these parallels into a hybrid epic. His epic even has, though not intentionally, a vague Christian spirituality. The conflict between the Empire and the Rebellion resembled the first-century struggle between the Roman Empire and, as Han Solo might call it, the "hokey religion" of Christianity. It made respectable again the classic motif of archetypal good versus evil. The Jedi salutation "May the Force be with you" sounds much like "May the Lord be with you"; albeit, strains of Eastern mysticism also resonate with the Force.

To make the world of *Star Wars* more believable, Lucas gathered a crew of young and talented people to develop state-of-the-art special effects. The effort paid off as the movie went on to break box office records and was nominated for an Academy Award for Best Picture.[8] *Star Wars* made it possible for sci-fi, fantasy, and superhero movies to be taken seriously. Screenwriter/ director Paul Schrader said, "Star Wars was the film that ate the heart and the soul of Hollywood. It created the big-budget comic book mentality."[9] This new mentality was dubbed "high-concept," a type of film that has now become the staple of cinema.

Superman at the Movies, *Raiders of the Lost Ark,* and Television Superheroes

On the heels of the success of Lucas's *Star Wars* and Steven Spielberg's *Close Encounters of the Third Kind*, the first big-budget superhero epic made its debut on the silver screen in December 1978—Richard Donner's *Superman: The Movie*. It became the model for the superhero film and elevated the genre from B-movie status to the A-list. Working from a script by Academy Award–winning screenwriters David and Leslie Newman (*Bonnie and Clyde*), James Bond screenwriter/director Tom Mankiewicz, and the Pulitzer Prize–winning author of *The Godfather*, Mario Puzo, Donner took Superman seriously. The movie combined the scope of David Lean and the quick wit of classic Cary Grant films.

Donner's epic, starring Christopher Reeve, played up the biblical nature of the Superman mythology: His origin as an alien refugee from a dying planet hints at the Moses story; his childhood, raised by Christian parents Jonathan and Martha Kent ("The Good Lord saw fit to give us a child, Jonathan"), underlines Superman's Christ-like mission sent to be a savior from another star.[10] A draft of the screenplay for the Superman film describes Jonathan and Martha Kent in this way: "Two people are seated in the truck cab, dressed in their shiny, patched 'Sunday best' clothes. The man is in his 50s, the woman in her 40s. 'Private' people who mind their business, Christian folk whose morals are as basic as the soil they till: Jonathan and Martha Kent."[11] Elliot S. Maggin's novel *Superman: Last Son of Krypton* was a tie-in to the Superman movie that gave additional religious insight into the character of the Man of Steel. Maggin describes Martha Kent as being careful to filter Clark's influences: "[She] held, for example, that stories of cutthroats and street urchins of the type Dickens wrote were not the sort of things Clark should be exposed to. She put the *Bible* and lots of *Horatio Alger* on his reading list."[12]

For a period of time Superman was the lone superhero to receive respectable treatment in movies. The highly acclaimed *Superman II* was released in the summer of 1981, a successful mixture of action, romance, and special effects. Outstanding ticket sales at the box office ensued, yet it was overshadowed by another comic book–inspired blockbuster. Steven Spielberg and George Lucas tapped into their childhood love for serials and comic books, this time mixing it with Old Testament Judaism in *Raiders of the Lost Ark*. On a retreat in Hawaii, Lucas and Spielberg compared notes, and Lucas told Spielberg of a character he had been working on called Indiana Smith. After a few adjustments with the story, they finally came up with Indiana Jones (named after Lucas's dog)—a professor-archaeologist who goes on a quest to find the lost Ark of the Covenant that housed the original Ten Commandments given to the children of Israel, according to the Bible (Exodus 25:10–22; 37:1–9). Spielberg's inspiration for the look of Raiders came from comic books. "I wanted to go with a comic art style...I was... inspired by comic books like The Green Lantern, Blackhawk, and Sgt. Rock."[13]

During the same period Spielberg, Lucas, and Donner were creating their sci-fi/hero movies, superheroes experienced a small renaissance on television. The Wonder Woman series debuted to good ratings, followed by Spider-Man, Captain Marvel, Dr. Strange, Captain America, the Hulk, and a mythological heroine named Isis. The Hulk and Wonder Woman made for popular viewing, but Spider-Man faltered with less than a season under his belt. Captain America had two special made-for-TV films that disappointed, and Dr. Strange did not make it past the pilot episode. The shows failed due to a lack of respect for the source material and woefully inadequate special effects that could not capture the grandeur of the comic books. Too many people still regarded superheroes as juvenile, and the material reverted back to embarrassing camp. Hanna-Barbera's live action *Challenge of the Super-Heroes* and the follow-up *Roast of the Super-Heroes* featured Ed McMahon hosting a superhero celebrity roast while the DC Comics superheroes were portrayed as buffoons; even so far as to have Adam West and Burt Ward (from the 1960s Batman TV show) reprise their roles. ABC's campy *The Greatest American Hero* continued to show Hollywood's lack of respect for the genre.

Bombs and Blockbusters from Hollywood:
The Transitional 1980s

While *Superman II* was a respectable achievement for its time, the technology still was not advanced enough to fully realize the cosmic grandeur of superhero comics on the silver screen. *Superman III* did not improve things, even with comedian Richard Pryor as the co-star of this third sequel that hit the big screen in 1983. That same year Richard Gere devotedly read Silver Surfer comic books in *Breathless* and debated with a youth after hearing the boy blurt out, "The Silver Surfer sucks!" If the Superman movies, *Star Wars*, and *Raiders of the Lost Ark* made progress toward the acceptance of comic books in Hollywood, Wes Craven's low-budget and unintentionally tacky adaptation of the brilliant *Swamp Thing* comic book (1982) and George Lucas's foray into the comic book genre, the surprisingly bad *Howard the Duck* (1986), momentarily set back those gains. Moreover the charm of the earlier Superman films could not be repeated in the *Supergirl* movie (1984). Instead the films of Arnold Schwarzenegger and Sylvester Stallone became the formula for many of the action films of the 1980s. The landscape was replete with Rambo knock-offs and heavy accented, monosyllabic musclemen like Jean Claude Van-Damme and Dolph Lundgren. The films were mostly low-budget efforts that featured highly athletic kung fu protagonists, close to being superheroes, even though they did not possess superpowers.

Five films from this period would influence the direction of the comic book movies. First, John Milius' R-rated vision of *Conan the Barbarian* (with a script co-written by Oliver Stone) took the comic book movie to a new level of ultra-violence and sexuality. Marvel Comics' sensational barbarian was an anti-hero driven not by a moral code but survival. Second, James Cameron's *Terminator*, a film that owed much to Harlan Ellison's short story *Demon with a Glass Hand* (adapted as an episode of the *Outer Limits* in the early 1960s) introduced a terrifying cyborg that resembled comic book supervillains and Marvel's killing cyborg named Deathlok. Cameron's film influenced a slew of imitators in years to come, inspiring even the look of comic books. It would later become a comic book itself, published by Dark Horse Comics. *The Terminator* spawned a sequel almost a decade later, and then a third installment a decade after that; and somehow the star in all three, Arnold Schwarzenegger, did not seem to age in the process. Two more significant films were the futuristic Tokyo-inspired neon cityscape of Ridley Scott's *Bladerunner*, and the post-apocalyptic punk fashion of George Miller's *The Road Warrior*. They would influence the art design in later films, especially in Tim Burton's *Batman*, Japanese *anime* such as *Akira*, and the Wachowski Brothers' *Matrix* trilogy. The final influential film of this period was Terry Gilliam's *Brazil*. Gilliam brought together various influences to create a unique aesthetic for the hybrid film that mixed humor, social commentary, dark fantasy, and superhero undertones. Gilliam paid tribute to his former mentor Harvey Kurtzman (co-founder of *Mad* magazine) and EC Comics luminary Bill Elder in *Brazil* with characters named after them.

In 1987 Paul Verhoeven's *Robocop* became a cinematic superhero that did not originate from a comic book; he seemed to be heavily influenced by Frank Miller's Batman epic, *The Dark Knight Returns*. Together with Alan Moore's *Watchmen, The Dark Knight Returns* started a trend toward the gritty antihero, taking superhero comic books to a new level of sophistication, and portraying a cynical vision of the Reagan-era political climate. The world of Dark Knight and the Watchmen offered a dark revisionist history (Richard Nixon wins the Vietnam War in *Watchmen*) where the superheroes were devoid of a moral compass and no better than the villains they fought. Even though the superhero was going through this renaissance in the comic books, the superhero in film was going nowhere, apart from *Robocop*. (A bright but fleeting moment came when director Chris Columbus, a Steven Spielberg protégé, paid tribute to his comic book roots with a reference to the Marvel Comic superhero Thor in his teen comedy, *Adventures in Babysitting*.) The fourth Superman film, *The Quest for Peace*, succumbed to last-minute budget changes resulting in a mediocre performance under the aegis of low-budget producers Golan and Globus. Even more disheartening was the duo's plan to bring Spider-Man and Captain America to the silver screen with much lower budgets than their failed Superman effort. The Hollywood studios started seeing comic book superheroes as box-office poison.

The dismal response to fantasy and comic book films at the time caused Terry Gilliam to lament:

> I think people are confused about what they want to make comments about because there's no Big Picture anymore. They tend to deal with mundane little relationships—does he love her, does she love him? The world is reduced to that now and the Gods have all gone away somewhere.... The old myths, the Greek myths, are so complicated and wonderful—and incredibly human, that's what's nice about them.... A few hundred years ago people understood all the references: you talked about the labours of Hercules and other great stories, and people knew what you were talking about. I don't know what the stories are that people know about now.[14]

Toward the end of the 1980s, Western culture had turned to VCRs and video game players for entertainment, which became standard household items and fierce competitors against comic books. It seemed just as easy for many people, especially youths, to play the Nintendo Entertainment System, watch MTV, the Fox channel, or pop in a favorite movie video as it was to read the latest comic book. And for the superhero on film, things could not have looked worse. Then, though, came the summer of 1989.

Batman Movies and the 1990s

Tim Burton's cinematic treatment of the Caped Crusader, *Batman*, premiered the month of the hero's fiftieth anniversary in June 1989. The dark and serious retelling of Batman placed the character back to his roots as a gothic adventurer. The motion picture became a phenomenal success and opened the door for more superhero films. If *Superman: The Movie* laid the foundation for the genre, *Batman* took the superhero film to another level in terms of potential merchandising, as the profits from the tie-ins soared to new heights, making billions of dollars as no other film had done before with the exception of *Star Wars*. The new Batman craze eventually birthed three sequels. Jack Nicholson had played a compelling Joker, and afterward top stars were cast to play supervillains in the sequels: Michelle Pfeiffer (Cat-Woman), Danny DeVito (the Penguin), Jim Carrey (the Riddler), Tommy Lee Jones (Two-Face), Uma Thurman (Poison Ivy), and Arnold Schwarzenegger (Mr. Freeze).

The Hollywood studios started to take the comic book more seriously as a possible source for material. The studios capitalized on the craze with Sam Raimi's *Darkman* film, Alex Proyas's *The Crow*, Jim Carrey's first blockbuster hit *The Mask,* and the lucrative cash cow *Teenage Mutant Ninja Turtles*, which was based on the cult black-and-white comic book and popular animated series. On television the *The Flash* series lasted no more than a season, but the *Moonlighting*-inspired Superman TV series *Lois & Clark: The New Adventures of Superman* did much better.

Nevertheless the film industry had its share of misguided attempts to bring the Marvel superheroes to the big screen with *The Punisher* (1989 version), Albert Pyun's *Captain America,* and the never-released *Fantastic Four* film produced by Roger Corman. The comic book genre took further hits when a succession of bad movies again threatened its viability: Sylvester Stallone's outing as the superhero *Judge Dredd, Tank Girl, Steel, Barbwire, The Shadow,* and *The Phantom* all had less-than-stellar results at the box office. The films failed, again due to a lack of respect for the characters or budget restraints. Legal complications made it even more difficult to make any more attempts to bring the Marvel superheroes to the big screen until the late 1990s. As a result, one highly anticipated project never got off the ground: James Cameron's *Spider-Man*. More than this, the concept of the hero itself seemed to take a beating at the hands of the disappointing *Last Action Hero* (1993). To add insult to injury—in a repeat of the *Superman IV* debacle a decade before—the 1997 release of Joel Schumacher's universally reviled *Batman & Robin* returned the character to its campy '60s incarnation and introduced a gay subtext that realized some of Dr. Wertham's 1950s accusations about the characters. Schumacher's film seemed to kill the progress of the superhero film, causing many Hollywood observers to again spell doom for the genre, even though *Spawn*, another comic book movie also released that year, was a minor hit.

On a positive note the decade saw the emergence of new filmmakers whose vision was an outgrowth of the 1970s mavericks. They cut their teeth in small, character-driven indie films like their predecessors Scorsese,

Copolla, and Friedkin, but they also embraced the high-concept blockbuster filmmaking of Spielberg and Lucas. Most were marked by an encyclopedic knowledge of motion picture history, yet they equally respected the art-house movements and trashy cinema. This group included M. Night Shyamalan, Peter Jackson, Quentin Tarantino, Robert Rodriguez, Sam Raimi, Christopher Nolan, Ang Lee, and the Wachowski Brothers. They joined Tim Burton and Chris Columbus, along with 1970s and 1980s wunderkinds George Lucas, Steven Spielberg, and James Cameron, as a group of filmmakers with one thing in common: a love for comic books.

Independent filmmaking came into its own, particularly in 1994, the year when the small films generated excitement and water-cooler talk: Quentin Tarantino's *Pulp Fiction*, Robert Rodriguez's *El Mariachi*, and Kevin Smith's *Clerks*. The filmmakers exhibited a fierce independence and raw talent not unlike their predecessors of the 1970s. Sam Raimi created a cult fan following with his earlier *Evil Dead* films, and the Wachowski brothers began their careers writing comic books for Marvel Comics, scripting Clive Barker's *Ektokid* series, before generating heat on their spec screenplay, *Assassins*. They embraced pop culture in all its forms and spread the comic book gospel like fervent Baptists looking for converts. Tarantino's script doctored the film *Crimson Tide* and added a reference to the Silver Surfer by having two characters fight over who did the better rendition of the character, Jack Kirby or Moebius? Denzel Washington's answer settled it: "Why Jack Kirby, of course." Kevin Smith's second film, *Mallrats*, was replete with comic book references, going so far as to include Stan Lee in a cameo. *The Simpsons* animated series frequently featured references to comic books and even introduced a character, a pugnacious and puerile comic shop owner simply known as "The Comic Guy," who would show up every now and then. Moreover, in a preview of things to come, Ang Lee's film adaptation of the novel *The Ice Storm* featured a pre-Spider-Man Tobey McGuire reading an issue of the Fantastic Four!

Recent Developments and the
Resurgence of the Superhero Genre in Film

The comic book superhero genre revitalized beginning in the late 1990s with the successive release of three films based on Marvel Comics properties: *Men in Black* continued Will Smith's summer box-office dominance post-*Independence Day*. *Blade,* an obscure Marvel character in the 1970s, scored surprising box-office returns. Blade creator Marv Wolfman says, "When I did things like *Tomb of Dracula* [where *Blade* made his first appearance] the Christian feel was most evident since vampirism is a literal reversal of

Christianity. I've used the Moses story a lot and as someone who is Jewish I've always had those thoughts in the back of my mind. Jewish tradition always tells of the underdog who rises up. Great myth-making stories."[15] A third Marvel movie was Bryan Singer's *X-Men*. Fraught with pre-release controversy due to aesthetic changes of the beloved Marvel icons, it ultimately won over die-hard fans and opened to big numbers. Professor Xavier, Cyclops, and Jean Grey (Marvel Girl) from the original mutants teamed up with Wolverine, Rogue, and Storm from the newer X-Men to take on Magneto and his team of villain mutants. The sequel added Night Crawler and ended with Jean Grey's apparent death. While Marvel was beginning to enjoy big screen success, a lesser-known debut took place with the film *Mystery Men*, which portrayed a group of superhero wannabes derived from Dark Horse comics.

Television started adding new wrinkles to the superhero story: Joss Whedon's *Buffy the Vampire Slayer* had plots that echoed some of the best of Marv Wolfman's *Tomb of Dracula*. Even the character co-opted Wolfman's designation of his Blade character—vampire slayer! The Buffy stories also contained underlying themes that played up a subtle Christian spirituality. The Sam Raimi-produced series *Hercules,* and its spin-off, *Xena: Warrior Princess* (1995–2001), were successful in syndication and featured plots that could have been lifted from the 1970s Marvel Comics. He went on to direct the film *Spider-Man.* Superman continues in his current successful incarnation as a teenager in the WB Network's *Smallville*, and at the same time is poised to make another cinematic comeback.

M. Night Shyamalan's *Unbreakable* was structured like a comic book, and with a dour and deliberate resolve, it placed the concept of the superhero squarely in a realistic world without the window dressing of costumes. The superhero-like plot in *Unbreakable* makes it appear as though the story were adapted from a comic book. The same is true with *The Matrix*. That latter film, according to Michael Uslan, is "the best comic book movie ever made even if it's not from a comic book."[16] The Wachowski brothers created a successful trilogy centering on a computer hacker turned into a Christ-like superman, complete with incredible powers, flight, and ability to raise the dead. The superhero genre continues to inspire original film projects that did not originate as a comic book or graphic novel. First-time director Kerry Conran's *Sky Captain and the World of Tomorrow* pays homage to the Max Fleischer *Superman* serials, the Wally Wood EC comics of the 1950s, Japanese *anime*, as well as *Raiders of the Lost Ark* and *Star Wars*. Pixar Entertainment continues its streak of excellence with its own spin on the superhero genre, *The Incredibles*—a family whose powers recall those of the Fantastic Four. The movie was a runaway success in 2004.

The development of sophisticated special effects had a tremendous impact on the explosion of most recent superhero movies. What could not be done in the days of the early serials could now be achieved and began with George Lucas's Industrial Light & Magic (ILM) that pioneered with *Star Wars* and then continued with the groundbreaking special effects for *Terminator 2* and *Jurassic Park.* Michael France, the screenwriter of *The Hulk* and James Bond's *Goldeneye*, observes that "Larger than life heroes have always been popular." In his view, "The first comic book was painted somewhere on a cave wall with berry juice. These are the same stories. It's just that the technology of movies has caught up to the scale of the stories. The fact that these massive stories can now be told on film is a relatively new thing for movie audiences."[17]

When it is done extremely well, the superhero film can achieve mega box office success and critical acclaim like the crown jewel of the genre, *Spider-Man.* The public was ready for the return of the old-fashioned hero in a post-9/11 world when the highly anticipated *Spider-Man* was released in May of 2002. The film became the biggest grossing superhero movie to date. Two years later the sequel *Spider-Man 2* successfully mixed human drama with spectacular special effects. With a script by Academy Award winner Alvin Sargent (*Ordinary People*), and a story by Pulitzer Prize–winning author Michael Chabon (*The Adventures of Kavalier and Clay*), and *Smallville* creators Alfred Gough and Miles Millar, *Spider-Man 2* became the quintessential superhero adaptation, duplicating the first Superman movie by gathering a team of high-caliber writers with similar award-winning credentials. Comic book creators are now so highly respected that director Robert Rodriguez, for example, insisted that he share directing chores on *Sin City* with the graphic novel's creator, Frank Miller.

However, as with all genres, there can be missteps such as the Batman spin-off *Catwoman, Elektra, The Punisher* (2004), and the mixed reception of Ang Lee's *The Hulk.* Faithfulness does not always guarantee great box-office results, as attested by the modest box office performances of Guillermo Del Toro's *Hellboy*, and *Daredevil* starring Ben Affleck. Other dark renditions from the comic world included *League of Extraordinary Gentlemen,* starring Sean Connery, and *Road to Perdition,* starring Tom Hanks. Keanu Reeves starred in *Constantine,* an adaptation of *Hellblazer.* The comic book is about a self-seeking magician and exorcist from London who likes to double-cross demons. The movie version has him in Los Angeles attempting to earn his way to heaven by fighting against the forces of hell. Both *Constantine* and *Sin City* became box office hits in 2005.

The next superhero icon to make the leap to the big screen is the highly anticipated *Fantastic Four*, with *Barbershop* director Tim Story, the first African American to helm a big-budget superhero picture. Ralph Winter, the producer on the Fantastic Four, is also prepping another sequel to the popular X-Men series. Warner Bros. is once again launching the Batman franchise; this time they are guided by critical favorite Christopher Nolan from a screenplay by David Goyer and starring Christian Bale. Batman is returning to his roots, combining the James Bond films with *Raiders of the Lost Ark*-style action and featuring less flamboyant but no less menacing villains in Ra's Al-Ghul and the Scarecrow. This seems to indicate the beginning of a DC Comics renaissance in film as Bryan Singer helms a relaunch of *Superman,* which promises updated special effects and an all-star cast featuring relative unknown Brandon Routh in the title role, Kevin Spacey as Lex Luthor, and Kate Bosworth as Lois Lane. The list of comic book films continues to grow with *Spider-Man 3, Wonder Woman, The Flash, Ghost Rider,* starring Nicolas Cage, and a duo of Alan Moore creations: the long-awaited *Watchmen* and *V For Vendetta* (written and produced by the Wachowski Brothers).

The comic book superhero shows no signs of losing popularity. The *New York Times* reported that comics are enjoying a renaissance and a newfound respectability. It speculates that "someday the novel will go into decline and will become, like poetry, a genre treasured and created by just a relative few" while "the comic book will be the next literary form to replace it."[18] The once reviled comic book culture that created the high-concept film can now be counted among the trendsetters of Hollywood. The new generation of filmmakers demonstrated that the superhero film is most successful when the source material is given proper respect. When the superhero is given a campy treatment, the material often fails to draw in an audience. The superhero concept demands a certain amount of dignity because it presents a story with sophisticated themes that mirror the human condition. The hero motif itself taps into the very soul of our beings where grand archetypes of fantasy reside.

The Lord of the Rings and Popular Fantasy: A Legacy of the Inklings

At the same time as the current superhero trend made its way back on film, director Peter Jackson turned his attention to a film version of J. R. R. Tolkien's classic trilogy, *The Lord of the Rings.* Three pictures later, and billions of dollars from the worldwide box office, *The Lord of the Rings: The Return of the King* won 11 Academy Awards, including Best Picture. The promise of *Star Wars* and *Raiders of the Lost Ark* was fulfilled. The current influence of fantasy on culture traces back to an unassuming group from the early part of the twentieth century that changed the face of science fiction and fantasy. During their heyday C. S. Lewis and J. R. R. Tolkien led a group of writers and other creative types in frequent discussions and fellowship called the Inklings. They were marked by their devout Christian faith and a sincere love for storytelling.

The influence of this extraordinary group can be felt today from comic books and children's stories to motion pictures. Many best-selling fantasy writers cite Tolkien and Lewis as an influence. The *Dungeons and Dragons* craze and the fantasy aspects of Japanese *anime* received their inspiration from *The Lord of the Rings*. The *Star Wars* trilogy was certainly a science fiction version of Tolkien. The influence of the Inklings, along with Pre-Inkling Christian authors G. K. Chesterton, George MacDonald, and others, is also evident in the work of acclaimed comic book author Neil Gaiman, creator of the postmodern *Sandman* (DC Comics).[19]

Lately their biggest impact rests in the popular children's book that began with J. K. Rowling's *Harry Potter* series. Rowling's work was highly influenced mainly by Lewis and Tolkien; in turn, her success has rekindled interest in Lewis's *Chronicles of Narnia* series, featuring his most famous work from the series, *The Lion, Witch, and the Wardrobe*. Rowling not only owes a huge debt to these novels, as well as Tolkien's *Lord of the Rings*, she even shares a common spiritual trait. Syndicated columnist Terry Mattingly writes:

> Rowling remains a member of the Church of Scotland and keeps saying, "I believe in God, not magic." She also has stated that the magical elements in her books come from her studies in British folklore. This means she is trying to tap some of the same wellsprings as C. S. Lewis, J. R. R. Tolkien and even Charles Dickens... Rowling told a Canadian reporter that she is a Christian and that this "seems to offend the religious right far worse than if I said I thought there was no God. Every time I've been asked if I believe in God, I've said, 'yes,' because I do. But no one ever really has gone any more deeply into it than that.... If I talk too freely about that, I think the intelligent reader—whether 10 or 60—will be able to guess what is coming in the books."[20]

Though Harry Potter does not officially make the cut to be named a superhero, the boy wizard holds many of the same traits that characterize the superhero. He is an orphan boy who possesses powers beyond the average mortal, has great moral clarity, and is destined for greatness as he struggles with evil forces that attempt to drive him to mediocrity. Not every Christian will agree on the displaying of Potter's power. Some see it as glamorizing witchcraft; others see it as pure fantasy and relatively harmless. Potter does bear some similarities to another—the biblical prophet Daniel. In the Old

Testament, the Jewish hero happens to be an orphan boy made "the chief of magicians" by King Nebuchadnezzar of Babylon (Daniel 5:11–12).

The works of Rowling and the Inklings also share with the modern superhero myth common archetypes in biblical literature and the person of Jesus Christ. There is an obvious connection with the rise of the superhero movie and Christ in pop culture. Western superheroes are the reinvention of old myths and biblical characters for our generation. Superman is a combination of the Old Testament figures of Moses and Samson with the New Testament Jesus. Although Batman as the dark avenger of the night may be re-imagining Zorro and the Scarlet Pimpernel, ultimately this mythos goes all the way back to the *gō'ēl* or "avenger of blood" mentioned in the Old Testament books of Deuteronomy 19, Numbers 35, and Joshua 20.

In late 2003, Internet gossip guru (turned Hollywood producer) Harry Knowles screened Tolkien's *Return of the King* and Mel Gibson's *Passion of the Christ* to an enthusiastic audience at his BNAT film festival in Austin.[21] Both films portrayed aspects of the Christ story: Gibson's film depicts an actual retelling of the crucifixion of Christ and Tolkien's version tells a symbolic representation that is an outgrowth of the author's Christian worldview. The movie poster for *Lord of the Rings: Return of the King* features a frontal shot of the majestic Aragorn riding toward us on a white steed as he leads an army, resembling the depiction of Christ's return in the book of Revelation (Revelation 19). Gibson's *Passion* relies on the power of the visual to communicate iconic images to tell a story in a way similar to comic books. His film turned out to be a controversial yet wildly successful effort, a seminal work that will influence the direction of films for years to come because it taps into the central theme of Christianity—the universal story of the sacrificial god who came down to Earth as a man. Many would affirm it is the greatest love story about the greatest hero.[22] Variations of the Christ story are retold in many genres, from science-fiction films such as *The Day the Earth Stood Still* and *ET: The Extraterrestrial* to superhero films such as *Superman* and the *Matrix*. No wonder a *New York Times* headline declared Jesus Christ as "Box-Office Superhero"![23]

What Superheroes Tell Us about Ourselves

The success of the superhero story in this age suggests that it has placed its finger on the pulse of the cultural *zeitgeist* or spirit of the times. With the convergence of art, literature, and pop culture, superheroes have become an artistic vehicle that conveys the collective hopes and dreams of humankind. They answer very important questions about life and can explore the human condition, oftentimes better than stories grounded in reality. The genre restores the biblical tradition of the grand spectacle, the marriage of the heroic traditions of Athens and Jerusalem. Terry Gilliam observes:

> I think maybe I would have liked the Middle Ages. There was a very rich tradition, the Church passed on these great images and great stories. Those things were a much more important part of people's lives and now I think people have forgotten all of that stuff…. You can look back on the text of an education and feel angered at all the gaps: the world of the visual, the worlds of mythology. The paradox being that children are especially open to these things—witness their delight in even dodgy movies that exploit these areas…[24]

As a result of the Internet, globalization creates a demand for stories with universal messages. These stories are widely received and provide a key to creating bridges between cultures. They are paramount to a greater understanding of humanity because fantasy and myth play on very broad themes. A look at the worldwide box-office grosses of the top 50 films of all time reveals an enormous acceptance for comic book–style movies. The superhero deals with universal themes that transcend cultural particulars, such as life and death, good and evil, peace and calamity: "Beneath what seem to be purely commercial considerations, the need to mentally prepare for disasters is precisely what prompts the creation of…action adventure and post-apocalyptic tales. People have always used storytelling to try to make sense of life and death."[25] The common themes that appeal to us in Superman, Spider-Man, Batman, Harry Potter, and other heroes are that of the search for significance and the guidance of a good parent. Both carry with them a missing social dimension, as does the need to have a fellowship group. Likewise we find a savior, a pure Christ-like deliverer, in many heroes. These motifs give us something to trust in and a way to interpret our world.

The superhero story acts as an allegory of the human struggle as seen from the eyes of heaven. The insignificant matter, the mediocre human existence so seemingly mundane—small compared to grand events of a planetary scale in the universe—is in truth of great cosmic significance. It is important enough for the entire host of heaven to watch the unfolding epic of humanity defined in the microcosm of the every human experience. Such stories address the questions, "What are we here for?" "Why?" and "Where are we going?" We all hope that somehow we may be heirs to something greater; like the orphan Harry Potter or the neglected Cinderella, our destiny somewhere awaits us, ready to bestow us to our rightful place, to rescue us from insignificance. According to C. S. Lewis, the nature of Christ answers our longings and big questions: "Whatever may have been the powers of unfallen man, it appears that those of redeemed Man will be almost unlimited. Christ, re-ascending from His great dive, is bringing up Human Nature with Him. Where He goes, it goes too. It will be made 'like Him.'"[26] The Gospel points us to a time when frail humanity, like the superhero, will have "greater abilities."[27] Commenting on his film *Signs*, Mel Gibson adds, "The humanity in the film comes from the spiritual element because all of us have within us an instinctual thing that wants to reach for a higher place...a suspicion that there is a higher realm outside ourselves that exists and influences who we are. We all ask that question: 'Why the hell am I here?' That's human nature."[28]

We want to be significant but not alone. The absent parent is common in the Western world, and in the shadow of financial uncertainty, the possibility of losing a loved one, or the stable life, carries with it emotions that might not occur otherwise. Depending on the region and economic conditions, the family unit has been broken up in various ways: by wars, plagues, natural disasters, or by divorce and reckless ambition. Add to this the increasingly advanced technology and the result is a world of extremities where underprivileged people lose much or never experience "the good life" at all. A deep sense of longing remains that oftentimes is best captured and resolved in fantasy. The superhero story is full of subplots about relationships in the midst of crisis. Perhaps this explains why the orphan story is so successful.

"You are here for a reason," says Jonathan Kent to his frustrated super-son in the first Superman movie. Clark Kent esteems his foster father as a parent so worthy of respect and honor that when he dies, Clark laments, "All these powers...and I couldn't even save him." There is a searching for the supportive parent, one who resembles our heavenly Parent, or in New Testament metaphor, "God the Father." The superhero story asks for the missing ideal parent or mentor; one who is morally strong and can instill solid values in a world that pressures a person to make immoral choices in the name of survival. The archetypes are many: Jor-El and Lara, who sacrifice their lives for their only son Kal-El; Jonathan and Martha Kent, who possess a nurturing wisdom and humility that helps Clark fulfill his destiny; Uncle Ben Parker and Aunt May who are longsuffering, standing with a silent strength that gives Peter a reason to live. We want an Obi-Wan Kenobi to mentor and train us, to stand as a surrogate for the parent who abandoned us. This is why there is also a desire to bring a wayward parent to a place of redemption by destroying the dark force in the world that influenced them, much like Luke Skywalker saw in his father a spark of good that justified saving him from his Darth Vader persona.

Another social aspect in the superhero genre that resonates with the audience is that of friendship. We see the group dynamic, the fellowship of friends, as a key element in *The X-Men*, *The Matrix*, *Star Wars*, and *The Lord of the Rings*. There is a sense that, with so many crises in the world, no one wants to face the problems alone. Among the orphan superheroes, Superman leaned on his friends in the Justice League, Wolverine joined the X-Men, Aragorn and Frodo had the fellowship of the Ring, Arthur Pendragon sat with the knights of the roundtable, King David had his mighty men, and Jesus had the twelve disciples. From the same dynamic also appears the close friend who ultimately betrays. The Judas story in the Gospels has become essential to modern superhero mythology. He may be Clark Kent's boyhood friend Lex Luthor or Spider-Man's arch nemesis the Green Goblin, who was the father of his best friend, Harry Osborn, and then Harry himself. Again this speaks volumes in relation to our need to belong.

A comparison between films featuring an anti-hero in contrast to the films featuring a virtuous Christ-like hero demonstrates that the current *zeitgeist* desires to see purity in a protagonist. The grosses for *The Lord of the Rings*, *Harry Potter*, *Spider-Man*, and *Star Wars* franchises are staggering, earning billions of dollars in revenue. Compare them to the grosses of films like the Hannibal Lecter franchise or the recent comic book adaptation of the violent *Punisher* ($34 million domestic gross)—the preference is for a pure hero who does not abuse his or her powers. Stan Lee's oft-quoted words, "With great power comes great responsibility" (*Amazing Fantasy* #15) is not too far from Christ's teaching that "Unto whomsoever much is given, of him shall much be required" (Luke 12:48). The desired quality we want in the superhero, then, is a Christ-like purity that refuses to abuse great power. In Madeleine L'Engle's opinion:

> Children don't like anti-heroes. Neither do I. I don't think many people do, despite the proliferation of novels in the past decades with anti-heroes for protagonists. I think we all want to be able to identify with the major character in a book—to live, suffer, dream, and grow through vicarious experience. I need to be able to admire the protagonist despite his faults, and so be given a glimpse of my own potential.... We don't want to feel *less* when we have finished a book; we want to feel that new possibilities of being have been opened to us. We don't want to close a book with a sense that life is totally unfair and that there is no light in the darkness; we want to feel that we have been given illumination."[29]

In the new millennium the unstable nature of the world, with continuing wars, increasing terrorism, and environmental catastrophes creates a need for stories that help us make sense of the chaos. There still looms the threat of a madman who, by accessing computer codes, could take over nuclear systems internationally, plunging the world into nuclear catastrophe. For many, the evil in this world seems to be superpowerful, as potent as the villains in the comic books. The audience in the dangerous post-9/11 world wants to feel that they can trust in *someone*.

Hence a major theme in the superhero genre is that of the god-person, the Christ archetype, the ultimate deliverer: a remarkably common concept found in virtually every culture around the world. However, the New Testament story is distinguished from some other ancient stories by replacing the whimsical gods with the God of love, and the relentless law of karma with the emancipating principle of grace. Whereas the god heroes of old were petty, cruel, or indifferent, the traditional superheroes try to mirror Christ. They stand against injustice and offer us a moral example to follow. The superheroes do not boast about their exploits like the gods who demanded worship, but rather they do their good deeds in secrecy, as Christ teaches. They sacrifice their own needs and desires for the betterment of humankind, while the gods of old demanded a sacrifice from their worshipers. Western culture in this age has reinvented the messianic story in various forms. As to why this story is so popular and keeps recurring with different variations lies in the central theme of the human struggle—the story of humanity's need for redemption by a powerful and exemplary savior. As *X-Men* producer Ralph Winter points out:

> The strong hero is certainly a paradigm in our American culture. We idolize our movie hero, from Indiana Jones, James Kirk, to Luke Skywalker. Those mythic heroes take on a status that is compelling. They have flaws. They're not perfect. But somehow they get thrust into these extraordinary circumstances, and do the right thing. And it's those values of what we track with them that is interesting. To me it's what draws me in. I want to go live in that world. The best [heroes] are the ones that teach us a little bit how to live. How do we get through this life? How do we negotiate through this life?"[30]

Conclusion

By conflating the various forms of youth culture, the superhero film has been able to fulfill a function of great art—the preservation of culture. The themes of the *Matrix* trilogy encourage political and religious public discourse, the Superman films exemplify classic mythology and biblical narrative, and the plot of *Spider-Man 2* draws from the timeless romantic sensibilities of Jane Austen. The superhero saga will continue to flourish because it has a universal appeal with symbols that create a bridge of cultural understanding through stories of good versus evil. It is a vehicle for cultural exchange as the story transcends the local region and finds a commonality for all people of the world. The superhero myth is timeless, the shadow of the greatest story ever told in all its variations, grand and earth shattering. The audience will never lose interest in the story because, at its heart, it is a fairy tale come true: the wish of all of humanity is for victory over the oppressor and peace on earth where all just beings truly live happily ever after.

Notes

[1] Damien Cave, "'Comic Book Nation by Bradford W. Wright'" [Cited 1 Sept. 2004] Online:dir.salon.com/books/review/2001/05/25/wright/index.html?sid=1032052.

[2] *Elvis #1 Hits*, RCA Records, 2003.

[3] Elvis Presley, Acceptance speech for the 1970 Ten Outstanding Young Men of the Nation Award ceremony (16 January, 1971).

[4] Stan Lee, *Origins Of Marvel Comics* (New York: Simon & Schuster, 1975), 183.

[5] Lee, *Origins,* 225–226.

[6] DC had their own slapstick heroes at the time with *The Inferior Five,* and Marvel created a spoof of their flagship heroes in *Not Brand Echh.*

[7] *Easy Riders & Raging Bulls*, documentary (Kenneth Bowser, dir.; Sony Music Distribution: DVD Release date: 11 May, 2004).

[8] Unfortunately, movie voters were not quite ready to give accolades to what they perceived as lowbrow entertainment and bestowed the honor to Woody Allen's *Annie Hall.*

[9] Peter Biskind, *Easy Riders and Raging Bulls: How the sex-drugs-and-rock 'n' roll generation saved Hollywood* (New York: Simon & Schuster, 1998), 316.

[10] See Tom Mankiewicz's comments from *Superman* DVD version.

[11] Tom Mankiewicz, *Superman* Shooting script, April 6, 1977.

[12] Elliot S. Maggin, *Superman: The Last Son of Krypton* (New York: Warner Bros., 1978), 73.

[13] David Hutchison, "The Making of *Raiders of the Lost Ark.* Interview with Steven Spielberg." *Starlog Magazine* 50 (Sept. 1981), 44 cf. 41–45.

[14] Ian Penman, "The Big Picture" (Terry Gilliam interview), *The Face* magazine (Feb. 1989) [Cited 1 Sept. 2004] Online: www.smart.co.uk/dreams/tgface.htm.

[15] Marv Wolfman, interview by Leo Partible, electronic correspondence [retrieved] 19 April 2004.

[16] Quote from Geoff Boucher, *Los Angeles Times* (March 25, 2001), as cited from "Comic Books Influence Culture" [Cited 1 Sept. 2004] Online: www.bluecorncomics.com/cominflu.htm.

[17] Michael France, interview by Leo Partible, electronic correspondence [retrieved] 16 April 2004.

[18] Charles McGrath. "Not Funnies," *New York Times Magazine* (11 July , 2004); [Cited 1 Sept. 2004] Online: www.nytimes.com/2004/07/11/magazine/11GRAPHIC.html.

[19] G. K. Chesterton became a devout Roman Catholic after converting from Anglicanism and wrote the perpetual Christian classic *Orthodoxy*. Chesterton flourished in writing novels such as *Napoleon of Notting Hill, The Everlasting Man,* and *The Ball and the Cross,* which interacted with theological and psychological subtexts. Oppositely, George MacDonald was a Scottish clergyman for the Congregationalists before converting to Anglicanism. He wrote in many genres including fantasy, poetry, Scottish country life, and children's stories.

[20] Terry Mattingly, "Hot quotations about Satan to grab readers' attention," *Central Florida Episcopalian* 103/12 (Dec. 2001) [Cited 1 Sept. 2004] Online: www.cfdiocese.org; Cf. Scripps-Howard News Service (21 Nov. 2001) Online: tmatt.gospelcom.net/column/2001/11/21/.

[21] Harry Knowles, Butt Numb-A-Thon (8 Dec. 2003) [Cited 2 Sept. 2004] Online: www.aintitcool.com/display.cgi?id=16625.

[22] Cf. Jesus equated with heroism, for instance, in Elizabeth Lev, "Mel Gibson's Ultimate Hero Movie: An Arts Historian's View of 'The Passion'," [Cited 1 Sept. 2004] Online: www.nfcym.org/v3/resources/passion_news.html.

[23] A. O. Scott, "Jesus as Box-Office Superhero," *New York Times* (7 Mar. 2004) [Cited 1 Sept. 2004] Online: www.nytimes.com/2004/03/07/movies /07SCOT.html.

[24] Ian Penman, "The Big Picture," Online: www.smart.co.uk/dreams/tgface.htm.

[25] Quote attributed to Mary McNamara and Reed Johnson, *Los Angeles Times* (12 September, 2001) as cited from Robert V. Schmidt, "Why Write About Superheroes?" [Cited 1 Sept. 2004] Online: www.bluecorncomics.com /whyhero.htm>.

[26] C. S. Lewis, *Miracles*, Miracles of the Old Creation, in *The Best of C.S. Lewis* (Harold Lindsell, ed.; Grand Rapids: Baker, 1977/New York: The Inversen-Norman Associates, 1969), 333.

[27] Madeleine L'Engle, *Walking on Water: Reflections on Faith and Art* (New York: North Point Press, 1980), 72.

[28] Glenn Whipp, "The Edge of Night," *Los Angeles Daily News* (July 28, 2002), 4/ "Rotten Tomatoes Forum/View Thread: Interview with M. Night Shyamalan, Mel Gibson on Religious Subtext of 'Signs'" [Cited 1 Sept. 2004] Online: www.rottentomatoes.com/vine/archive/index.php/t-160512.

[29] Madeleine L'Engle, *Walking on Water*, 116.

[30] Ralph Winter, interview by Leo Partible, electronic correspondence [retrieved] 20 April 2004.

Recommended Resources

Anchors, William E. *The Superhero Illustrated Guidebook: A Review of Superhero Series on Television.* Dunlap, Tenn.: Alpha Control Press, 1995.

Biskind, Peter. *Easy Riders and Raging Bulls: How the Sex-Drugs-and-Rock 'n' Roll Generation Saved Hollywood.* New York: Simon & Schuster, 1998.

Borgmann, Albert. *Power Failure: Christianity in the Culture of Technology.* Grand Rapids: Brazos Press, 2003.

Carrier, David. *The Aesthetics of Comics.* University Park: Pennsylvania State University Press, 2001.

Clements, Jonathan, and Helen McCarthy. *The Anime Encyclopedia: A Guide to Japanese Animation Since 1917.* Berkeley, Calif.: Stone Bridge Press, 2001.

Ellis, Robert. "Movies and Meaning." *Expository Times* 112/9 (2001): 304–308.

Goulart, Ron. *Comic Book Culture: An Illustrated History.* Portland, Ore.: Collectors Press, 2000.

Harvey, Robert C. *The Art of the Comic Book: An Aesthetic History.* Jackson: University Press of Mississippi, 1996.

Hurley, Neil P. "Hollywood's New Mythology." *Theology Today* 39 (Jan. 1983): 402–408.

Johnston, Robert K. *Reel Spirituality: Theology and Film in Dialogue (Engaging Culture).* Grand Rapids: Baker Academic, 2000.

L'Engle, Madeleine, *Walking on Water: Reflections on Faith and Art.* New York: North Point Press, 1980.

Lyden, John C. *Film as Religion: Myths, Morals, and Rituals.* New York: New York University Press, 2003.

Martin, Joel W., and Conrad E. Ostwalt, Jr., eds. *Screening the Sacred: Religion, Myth and Ideology in Popular American Film.* Boulder, Colo.: Westview Press, 1995.

McCloud, Scott. *Reinventing Comics: How Imagination and Technology Are Revolutionizing an Art Form.* New York: Perennial, 2000.

Misiroglu, Gina, and David A. Roach. *The Superhero Book: The Ultimate Encyclopedia of Comic-Book Icons and Hollywood Heroes.* Canton, Mich.: Visible Ink Press, 2004.

Montgomery, John Warwick, ed. *Myth, Allegory, and the Gospel: An Interpretation of J. R. R. Tolkien/C. S. Lewis/G. K. Chesterton/Charles Williams.* Minneapolis: Bethany Fellowship, 1974.

Neal, C. W. *The Gospel According to Harry Potter: Spirituality in the Stories of the World's Most Famous Seeker.* Louisville, Ky.: Westminster John Knox Press, 2002.

Reinhartz, Adele. *Scripture on the Silver Screen.* Louisville, Ky.: Westminster John Knox Press, 2003.

Ross, Alex, Chip Kidd, and Geoff Spear. *Mythology: The DC Comics Art of Alex Ross.* New York: DC Comics, 2003.

Shutt, Craig. *Baby Boomer Comics: The Wild, Wacky, Wonderful Comic Books of the 1960s!* Iola, Wis.: Krause Publications, 2003.

Walsh, Robert. *Reading the Gospels in the Dark: Portrayals of Jesus in Film.* Harrisburg, Penn./ London: Trinity Press International/SCM, 2003.

Wood, Ralph C. *The Gospel According to Tolkien.* Louisville, Ky.: Westminster John Knox Press, 2003.

13
Neo: Messianic Superhero of *The Matrix*

James F. McGrath

To what extent does the description "superhero" fit Neo or any other character from the *Matrix* films? It cannot be denied that these movies have created quite a sensation and that they have made important, pioneering innovations, both in special effects and in the integration of philosophy into contemporary storytelling. Nevertheless, it remains to be seen whether they will stand the test of time and become simultaneously classics told for decades, as has been the case with most of the best known superheroes. All this being said, the inclusion of some discussion of these films is crucial for a number of reasons, not the least of which is that, in them, one finds a unique integration of comic book themes and motifs on the one hand, and explicit religious ideas and symbolism, on the other.

The Matrix and sequels are firmly rooted in, and are essentially cinematic expressions of, the graphic novel genre. This will come as no surprise to those familiar with the background of the Wachowski brothers, creators of the *Matrix* films, who found much of their inspiration in comic books. In addition, it is no surprise for those fans who know that comic book spin-offs from the films have long been planned. Does this mean Neo deserves to be classified as a superhero? He certainly has superpowers and clothes that could pass for a costume. On one occasion his flying is associated with doing that "superman thing" (*Matrix Reloaded*). His dual identity as Thomas Anderson/Neo also resembles a superhero. What is more, he is both empowered and commissioned for an important task that will protect many people.

More often than not, classic superhero origins also find their basis in science fiction. With most flagship superheroes of Marvel Comics, for instance, it is often the case that the individual gets his or her powers from a source that is "scientific" (although not always plausibly so). This seems especially true of the most popular superheroes, such as Superman, Spider-Man, Batman, the Hulk, Daredevil, and the X-Men. Whether their powers come from radiation, mutation, superior gadgetry, or something else, these heroes fall on the side of the sci-fi rather than the magic spectrum. (Wonder

Woman and Dr. Strange are two examples that fall more toward the other end.) Hence, although the more recent graphic novels frequently involve mythical and magical characters or themes, the roots of the superhero genre seem more closely centered on the sci-fi rather than the magic side of the spectrum. The same is true of *The Matrix* and sequels. Although the story incorporates werewolves and other such entities, their existence in the world of the Matrix is ultimately explained in a "scientific" rather than a supernatural way.

The reason for this characteristic of the superhero is not hard to find. Those of us who grew up reading comic books also grew up in the scientific age and the heyday of science fiction. Of course, comic book heroes are not renowned for their realism, but they are conceived in such a manner as to involve either a lesser measure of suspension of disbelief than in the case of fantasy, or at the very least a different sort. We could wish or imagine that we were a great wizard like Gandalf, but we can hardly aspire to have powers like his. In the case of a superhero such as Batman, however, we can easily envisage ourselves possessing various gadgets, and this concept involves no gigantic stretch of the imagination—except when they happen to be on Batman's utility belt at just the right moment, of course!

Neo's powers depend on his connection with computers, and to the unreality of the world in which he does his amazing feats. The Wachowski brothers specifically sought to create a world in which a superhero can fly like Superman, yet without as much suspension of disbelief as comic books normally require. Superman can fly because of the radiation from our sun. Okay...we are not told exactly how it works, because presumably it does not—but the story is not spoiled because of this. The Wachowskis, however, sought to create a world in which all these things can be "real," precisely because *nothing* is real: the world of virtual reality. One reason Neo is so appealing to our generation is that virtual reality resonates with us as a realistic technological possibility. It represents something genuinely within the realms of what we may achieve in the future, because first steps in developing it have already been made in our time.

It was therefore to be expected that we would see a convergence of the hacker, whose strength is superior knowledge and computer skill, and the superhero. Indeed, the sci-fi subgenre of cyberpunk had already begun to explore these similarities prior to *The Matrix*, which is considered a cyberpunk film. This idea ties in to another feature of superhero comics and shared by the *Matrix* films: an anti-establishment tendency.[1] Superheroes fight for good, and this trait can at times mean upholding society's values, but even when they do so, they operate essentially outside and apart from the law. Neo, the main character of the *Matrix* films, is a hacker, and apparently he had distinguished himself enough in the realm of hacking to attract the attention of both Morpheus and the authorities.

Another point is that there tends to be a certain type of ambiguity about superheroes. They wear masks rather than white hats, and they are often seen wrestling with temptation, particularly regarding whether to use their powers for selfish ends or for the benefit of others. The powers themselves regularly have an inherent vagueness about them. The X-Men and the Hulk have been transformed in ways that make them more powerful, but these abilities can be dangerous to themselves or others. Of course, historically there have been many superheroes that stood for stereotypical cultural values such as "truth, justice, and the American way," but the trend since the Silver Age has been to make the heroes more complex, with greater psychological depth. Neo is no exception: He wrestles to find the courage to learn what the Matrix is, then to accept what he has learned; then he struggles to decide whether he believes he is the One; and finally he deals with uncertainties about what ultimate role he must play.

Therefore we see that several common features—his dual identity, struggles with ambiguity, costume, commission and powers, and the desire to make his powers realistic—all point to the genre of the *Matrix* films as being that of the superhero comic. When this is coupled with the religious and philosophical issues raised in the movies, the legitimacy of examining the *Matrix* trilogy becomes clear.

Neo as "The One": Messianic Parallels

Neo is clearly a messianic figure in the *Matrix* films. In a broad sense he is the long-awaited savior and coming "One" expected to bring the present dominion of evil forces to an end, with Morpheus functioning as his forerunner prophet or John the Baptist. The name "Neo" itself means "new," which may be suggestive of the new era of peace the coming One would usher in. The name can also be short for "neophyte," a religious term signifying a new convert or proselyte. Neo certainly plays this role in the first film.

In a more specific sense there are regular reminiscences to the story of Jesus in connection with his character. Also it is in connection with Neo that the name "Jesus" appears in the script (albeit as a swearword), and when he gives a client illegal software at the beginning of the first film, the buyer associates him with Jesus in a facetious manner. More significantly, in the first film, Neo gets killed by Agent Smith, a representative of "the establishment," but then he rises again from the dead more powerful than ever. The last scene has him flying heavenward. These portrayals recall Jesus

Christ being killed by the establishment of his day but rising again in a glorified body and ascending to heaven after commissioning his disciples. In the second film many people in Zion recognize Neo as their savior, and he raises Trinity from the dead. This sequence echoes Jesus' ministry in Galilee and Judea, where multitudes followed him as he healed their sick and raised Lazarus from the dead. The final film ends with Neo sacrificing his life to save his people in Zion from destruction caused by an all-out attack from the machines. Here Neo reflects the crucified Christ who dies for the sins of the world so as to protect them from the wrath to come and Armageddon. Other similarities between Neo and Jesus have been noted and discussed on Web pages and in several recent books and articles. [2]

There are differences between Neo and the Messiah as well, and they make clear that these films do not simply attempt to update the traditional Christian story of Jesus. Throughout the trilogy, Neo wrestles with self-doubt. "I only wish I knew what I'm supposed to do," he says. In contrast, the canonical Gospels increasingly eliminate any hint of a slow process of self-discovery on the part of Jesus. The Gospel of Mark has Jesus beginning to speak about his rejection and death after John the Baptist is imprisoned and in connection with Peter's identification of him as the Messiah. In the Gospel of John (written later than Mark) Jesus knows from the beginning of his ministry who he is, where he has come from, and what he must do. Of course, there is the agonized prayer of Jesus in the garden of Gethsemane, but this prayer is still presented in the Gospels as a struggle to *follow* the path, not to *find* it. The Gospel portraits show a lack of interest in what might be called the "psychology of Jesus," with his upbringing and influences, with his inner wrestling. This has more to do with different interests on the part of ancient versus modern biographers and readers than anything else. Nevertheless, the lack of importance given to such details in the Bible often leaves modern readers either with unanswered questions, or with the impression that Jesus is not quite human. Not surprisingly, filmmakers often add precisely such elements to the story of Jesus if they feel comfortable taking liberties with the text.

Contemporary readers feel the need to understand the thinking behind the main character's actions and expect there to be inner conflict along the way. *The Matrix* thus seems to provide a messianic storyline that sits more comfortably in our age than its ancient parallels and paradigms. That Neo is a messianic sort of figure is quite recognizable, but this does not get us very far beyond the surface level of the film. The really interesting questions are whether Neo is connected to any particular God or gods, and what sort of victory or salvation Neo is understood to bring. It is to these questions that we now turn.

God in the Matrix

The idea of a messiah is not completely distinct from a wider spectrum of stories about heroes found in many cultures, but in the Western religious traditions one cannot normally think of a messiah without also thinking about God. In the world of the Matrix, then, who is God? There is no obvious God in the spiritual sense; however, there are a number of characters whose names or whose dialogues suggest some sort of identification. Indeed, there are so many that one could only with great difficulty argue that there is anything remotely resembling monotheism in the films. Be that as it may, we have the following candidates to consider for divinity:

- Trinity, whose name is derived from the historic Christian concept of God.
- Morpheus, who is sometimes felt to represent God the Father, forming a "trinity" together with Neo and Trinity. Others, however, suggest that Morpheus is more closely akin to John the Baptist.
- The Architect, who created the Matrix, clearly recalls stereotypical depictions of God (white hair, beard, throne). His role most closely resembles the demiurge in Gnostic mythology, in which the creator god of the Bible is not the Highest God.
- *Deus ex machina*, who appears toward the end of the trilogy, is precisely that—a "god" or supreme ruler of the machines who appears "out of the machine" at the film's end to help bring resolution.
- The Trainman in *Revolutions* says, "Down here, I'm God," and recalls the boatman on the river Styx from Greek mythology.
- Agent Smith responds to the word "God" (used as an expletive) by saying "Smith will suffice." In the video game *Enter the Matrix* he describes himself in words recalling the portrait of God in the book of Revelation: "I am the Alpha of your Omega; I am the beginning of your end..."

With such a plethora of deities and demigods, the world of *The Matrix* seems more closely akin to Greek mythology than the Bible. Indeed, there is a great deal that is derived from ancient Greek sources, including the Oracle and her motto "Know thyself."

However, most scholars of early Judaism and Christianity are aware that these faiths were not monotheistic in the same sense that they are for many of their adherents today. There was indeed one God who was above all, alone worthy of worship, the Creator; but beneath him was a vast array of beings who, although they might preferably be called angels, could also be called gods in ancient Jewish texts. It was, among other things, primarily the question of whom one should *worship* that was the make-or-break issue in observing God's first commandment: "You shall have no gods besides me." Thus, if we wish to explore the question of God in the Matrix, we must not ask simply how many gods or god-like figures appear on the screen, but whether there is a transcendent being or reality of some sort, above all others.

In the first movie, we learn that human beings believe themselves to be free, while they are in fact enslaved by being kept connected to a computer simulation while they are unknowingly used as a power source. In the second film, we learn that there is another level of control: The rebels themselves are not really being allowed to rebel, but rather the Architect of the Matrix allows the existence of Zion, the One, and the human rebels, as a way of stabilizing the Matrix. As Neo puts it toward the end of *Reloaded*, "It was just another system of control." By the end of the final film, we have followed the lines of control and manipulation as far as we can. They lead, as does the path of the One, to the elusive Source. The Source, like the God of Western monotheism, seems to be at once aloof, all-knowing, and in control. Moreover, the Source appears to be a power that transcends not only the Matrix and the machine city, but the whole of the "real world." The power of the Source extends from the machine world into the world of humans, we are told. It enables Neo's mind to be in the Matrix and at the same time not completely disconnected from his body. It enables Neo to stop sentinels and see the "souls" of artificial intelligences in the "real world." The possibility thus arises that the Source actually transcends what appears to be the "real world," or in other words, this world is just another level of simulation.

The writings of Jean Baudrillard, which are one of the main sources of inspiration for *The Matrix* and sequels, focus on the fact that once reality can be perfectly simulated, the very notion of reality loses all meaning. In view of this important aspect of the Wachowski brothers' outlook, we should not think of the "real world" as simply another illusion from which Neo or someone else will eventually wake up. Rather than "reality" being simply another layer of simulation, it is something about which one can no longer be certain, *ever*, and so the *Matrix* films are closer to the movie *Total Recall* in that they leave us guessing. From the standpoint of the films, the existence of the Source can be perceived, but one can never know whether it is the ultimate reality, and indeed whether the ultimate reality is human, machine, spirit, or something else.

Therefore one important difference between Neo and the Christian idea of messiah is that Neo does not speak for God. Rather, he has to find his way through interaction with many god-like figures, some of whom seem to desire to help him, while others are determined to hinder him. In this respect

Neo is closer to the hero of classical Greek and other literature than to the Judeo-Christian concept of the messiah. Neo reminds us of a Gnostic redeemer, who brings new revelation. The Gnostic knows that the world we see around us is not the ultimate reality, that there is a God beyond god. Neo's revelation, however, is that the god who is the architect of the visible world has deceived and manipulated people. Nevertheless the Baudrillardian perspective of the films undermines any and all claims to certain knowledge about the nature of reality. The question remains unanswered as to whether Neo is simply a human being who achieves more than his contemporaries, or if he has been made able to become the One by code that was placed in him at some point. If he had this special code from birth, then he might closely parallel the Jesus of Christian orthodoxy. If it is given to him later (some have suggested it was in the cookie and/or candy that the Oracle gives him), then this messiah needs to be understood along adoptionist lines: Adoptionism is an early Christian viewpoint, eventually declared heretical, which regarded Jesus as a human being chosen by God and empowered at his baptism with God's Spirit, so that he is not by nature the Son of God, but is adopted as such at a given point in time. Orthodox Christianity rejected this view, as it did Gnosticism, but both views were popular (and many times combined) among some circles in the early church.[3]

The Victorious Messiah

At any rate Neo is not simply the Gnostic Jesus. Inasmuch as he sacrifices his life at least once in the course of the trilogy, he is more akin to the Jesus of orthodox Christianity. This in turn raises an important point. Toward the end of the first film, Neo closely paralleled the story of Jesus: he died and returned to life in a form that now transcended the bounds of human existence, then at the very end ascended, presumably to return again. However, in the second film we find Neo to perhaps be a pawn of manipulative powers, and in the final installment, we find him called upon to put his life on the line yet again, possibly for good. What are we to make of this? Another question is whether, and in what sense, Neo defeats evil (which is usually what messiahs are expected to do). He defeats Agent Smith, but he does so in collaboration with the machines that he once thought were his enemy. This dynamic merits further attention.

One way of interpreting the meaning of the climactic finale of the *Matrix* trilogy is as follows. Our real enemies are not the others who are different from us, with whom we vie for power, over whom we seek control. If we are to have a future, we must forge alliances with them and learn to coexist. What Neo does, at the end, is forge an alliance against a common foe, which is the first step toward peace and potential reconciliation. The true enemy is Smith. He represents those forces that wish not just to dominate others, but to obliterate all individuality. Such forces, whether fundamentalist or nihilist in character, are the real danger to all our survival.

However, whereas this interpretation of the finale in the trilogy makes for a nice happy ending, it is not entirely unproblematic. The creation of the virus Smith as a result of Neo returning from the dead may have been inevitable. "It is happening exactly as before," one Smith says to the other, although this is met with the reply "Well, not *exactly*." Precisely what is different is uncertain, but Smith seems to state already in *Reloaded* that his new form as a self-replicating virus is not a newfound freedom. He became what he is against his will, and the path he follows is one of compulsion rather than freedom. It can be speculated that, had Neo chosen the other door (toward the end of the second film, *Reloaded*), he would have gone immediately to confront Smith, enabling Smith's deletion and the rebooting of the system. As Neo says at the end of *Revolutions*, "It was inevitable." He was now where he would have been, even if he had chosen the other door: connected to the Source, stabilizing the system, allowing the Matrix to be rebooted. While one can state this positively as fulfilling his destiny, a more negative way of looking at it is also possible: he could not escape his fate. Nevertheless, even if one feels the latter is closer to the truth, by following the lengthier route that he does, Neo's delaying of his fate allows him to bargain for peace.

Nonetheless, it still seems that the machines were in control from the very beginning. Things moved forward as though fate were in control, some obscure higher power, but in actual fact the hands of fate may be simply a contrivance of the machines themselves. However, the very name of the machine city, 01 (Zero-One), foresaw the need for balance and reciprocal forces. This would later be expressed in the existence of Neo (the One) and Cypher (one meaning of which is "zero"), and then in Neo and Smith, the latter being described as Neo's negative. The Architect had the function of creating the Matrix and balancing the equation, while the Oracle had the function of unbalancing it. All these sets of reciprocal roles were given to them from above, one might say, presumably from the Source.

Good vs. Evil

The concept of a messiah who brings victory and salvation presupposes notions of good and evil. The assessment of good and evil in the *Matrix* films, however, is not without ambiguity. During the first film, things seem pretty black and white: the machines are bad, the humans are good. In

Reloaded and *Revolutions*, and in *Animatrix* as well, such simplistic views are challenged. According to the "The Second Renaissance" storyline, we are told that the current domination of machines is a result of a continued series of injustices carried out by humans against the artificial intelligences they created. It is when they try to wipe them out by going to the extreme measure of scorching the sky that the machines finally strike back hard, enslaving humans and using them to replace the sun as their power source. To say, though, that the humans in the film are getting their just deserts is too simplistic also—although one might be tempted to say that they have inherited some bad karma.

A key development in the plot of the trilogy is when Neo begins to see that things are not black and white, and in particular when he sees beyond the outer appearance of the machines. To human eyes, the sentinels and the machine city are ugly, but Neo looks beyond these external appearances and beholds a city made of light. Humans also consistently refer to the machines in insulting (one might say "racist") terms: "squiddies" and "calamari," for example. Humans are still inclined toward prejudice, and until these human characteristics that caused this mess in the first place can be overcome, there can be no hope for a better future. Neo, at least, seems to have taken a step in that direction. This is a key feature in the life of any religious leader or messianic figure who has a profound and beneficial impact on the whole world: the recognition that one's own national perspective, one's own limited horizon of culture and belief, is not the whole story. Hence whether we think of Jesus saying that many will come from other nations and join the Israelites at the messianic banquet, or the teachings of Gandhi or of the Islamic Sufi mystics, these positive forces all recognize that the divine plan includes many people that have been thought of as enemies (from a political perspective at least). The aim then becomes not victory, but reconciliation, and in this, the *Matrix* seems particularly close to key emphases of early Christianity.

Assuming that comics and other media will continue the storyline, what will happen next in the *Matrix* universe? It is a question we are compelled by the story to ask because although the final installment of the trilogy has a degree of resolution, it is nonetheless in many ways strikingly open-ended. My own view is that Sati is the next One, and unlike previous Ones (as far as we know), she comes from the machine world rather than the human. She clearly has the most obvious characteristic a One needs to have: At the end she paints a beautiful sunrise, and so she clearly can manipulate the Matrix according to her will, which we are told from the outset is a (perhaps *the*) defining feature of the One. *Sati*, it should be noted, is a term from Hinduism denoting a righteous woman, which traditionally meant a wife who was willing to throw herself on her husband's funeral pyre. Sati, like Neo and all other Ones, will presumably be called upon to offer herself up in self-sacrifice. She also represents a new step in the evolution of machines, uniquely produced by the love between two programs. The Oracle sacrificed her own life (in its previous form at least) to save Sati because she knows her to be important to the future of both humans and machines. Because things have changed, perhaps the next time balance needs to be restored, it will be the machines who need a savior. While the Matrix represents a prison for the mind of many humans, it represents a safe haven for programs whose purpose in the machine world is ended.

Unlike Western traditions, the *Matrix* films envisage not a static paradise that can be maintained free from evil, but a cycle of conflicting forces which ideally need to be kept in balance. As the Oracle puts it, the only future for humans and machines is together. One of the striking features of *Revolutions* is the way it brings Hinduism more explicitly into the foreground. At the beginning of the film, we have Neo's discussion about karma with Rama-Kandra. As the final credits roll, we have choral music with Hindu text from the Upanishads. Given these references, one might appropriately watch *Revolutions* with the teaching of another famous Hindu text, the Baghavad Gita, in mind. This work teaches that the battles we fight have been fought before and will be fought again, that neither the one who kills nor the one who is killed truly does so. The showdown between Neo and Smith is simply the latest incarnation of a conflict that is fated to be repeated in every Matrix. Although at the end of the first film, we had a Christ-like death and resurrection, by the end of the final installment, even though Neo looks as though he might be dead, the Oracle can still expect that they may see him again someday.

One question that the films do not answer explicitly is whether there is reincarnation within the world of the Matrix. The Oracle said, "Everything that has a beginning has an end." What does this mean, though? Did this conflict have a beginning, or is it an ongoing cycle without beginning or end? The latter interpretation might explain why the Oracle's words spoken through Smith bring about in Neo the realization of how the battle is to be won. More likely, however, there is a cross-reference to the Oracle's earlier statement to Neo that the Source is where the path of the One ends, and Neo has ended up connected to the Source and carrying out his destiny. The path of the One has a beginning and an end, but the role of the One seems to be persistent across the various instances of the Matrix. So are we to think (as Morpheus hints in the original *Matrix* film) of Neo as a *return* of the One, like the latest incarnation of the Buddha? If everything in the world of the *Matrix* films is information, then one can see how that could indeed survive death. I have always been struck by the parallels between the way the terminology of saved and lost is used in computing and in Evangelical

Christianity. Neo, and perhaps everyone in the world of *The Matrix*, can be saved and may (as the Oracle suggests at the end of the trilogy) be seen again someday. Certainly the case of the Oracle being deleted but not completely erased by the Merovingian, suggests that this is part of the worldview of the *Matrix* films.

Moreover, the fact that at the end the Oracle, Seraph, and Sati have survived being taken over by Smith suggests that what matters is not whether one lives or dies, but whether one is "saved"—in other words, one might say, whether a backup copy has been made. Whereas this development can be viewed positively, as a sort of eternal life, it also has a shadow side. As long as programs like the Merovingian can be backed up and restored, can evil ever be eliminated? Once again, the idea of salvation in the *Matrix* films does not perfectly correlate with traditional Christianity, which envisages a final victory over evil. This concept, however, has always been a problematic one in those branches of Christianity that accept some form of free will. How can the absence of evil be guaranteed as long as there are free beings who can choose wrongly? The Architect sought to create a perfect world, and it was a disaster—no one would accept the program! It seems that choice *is* a reality in the world of the *Matrix* films, and for those who accept the reality of freedom, a world where peace and/or balance is achieved is a more realistic ideal than one in which static perfection is attained.

Simulated Jesus

For Christians, while the religious elements of the story of Neo are interesting, and the Christ parallels are perhaps even inspiring, this is still a fictional story, whereas Jesus is a real historical figure. No serious historian would deny this last statement. Nevertheless, these films raise the question of how one knows about previous eras, taking their lead from the writings of French philosopher Jean Baudrillard (in whose book *Simulacra and Simulations* Neo hides illicit computer disks in the original film). When it comes to the past, as Morpheus puts it, "We have only bits and pieces of information." Religious believers are often surprised at how different a historian's way of reading the Gospels is from the way the Bible tends to be read in church. Historical study is genuinely trying to reconstruct past events as accurately as possible. However, as in the case of a court of law, it can never truly be about "what really happened," so much as about what we can demonstrate "beyond reasonable doubt" based on the available evidence. No one genuinely thinks that Jesus said only the things attributed to him in the Gospels: The real Jesus inevitably said and did much more than the Jesus historians can recover.[4] In the case of Jesus, as in the case of any historical figure from long ago, our knowledge is partial and piecemeal. It thus follows that any historical reconstruction, any cinematic depiction of his life, requires creativity—similar to a work of historical fiction. Whether we look at the Gospels or modern historical reconstructions of Jesus' life, there are many glimpses of the real Jesus in them, but there are also things that may obscure the real Jesus from view. This is the problem of simulacra that Baudrillard highlights. Once reality can be simulated, the word "real" loses all meaning. This idea is powerfully illustrated by the *Matrix* films on a general level: If we can simulate the experience of the world by our senses, then we can experience "reality" that isn't there except in our minds or in a computer. However, the same point is also made about religious figures. We catch a glimpse briefly of a table full of statues and icons when Neo visits Chinatown to meet Seraph. These are images primarily of Jesus and Buddha, images that are hardly likely to accurately depict the historical figure of either Jesus of Nazareth or Siddhartha Gautama, but which are so part of our perception that we can hardly escape them. In the world of the Matrix, though, do these images point to real figures from humanity's past, or are they figures that point to other simulated "realities"? While we may presume (indeed hope!) that the reality we perceive is not merely simulated, when it comes to our perceptions of the past we cannot be so certain.

The *Matrix* films thus raise the question as to the importance of history, of actual past events, and to the meaning we find in our present-day lives. If we cannot know for certain about the past, if our information is always (from a historical perspective) partial and provisional, does it really matter? If all we can know for certain are the stories, and not the precise extent to which those stories correspond to historical reality, is the meaning found in the narratives sufficient? Confronted with the question in these terms, we find ourselves forced with the challenge of one of the characters in *The Animatrix*: perhaps what matters most is indeed not what is "real," but how we live our lives. This philosophical debate continues. If we conclude that it is legitimate to focus on narrative stories as a source of inspiration, then the superhero genre becomes all the more important.

One final thought. The *Matrix* films began with Baudrillard, Buddhism, Christianity, and Greek mythology, continued with Gnosticism and Taoism, and concluded with Hinduism. In Hinduism and Buddhism, there is in reality no existence of distinct entities. Enlightenment means the realization that all things are fundamentally one. This point of view provides us with an interesting question to put to these movies that at times seem like a web of incompatible ideas that can never be disentangled. Is everything ultimately one in the Matrix universe? Could everything (Neo, the Architect, Zion, the Matrix, the agents, the Oracle, and everyone and everything else) all be part of one reality, perhaps one might say a single *program*, one whose aims may not be clear to anyone else, but which somehow ties everything together? If so, then presumably nothing will ever truly be lost, and the meaning of Neo's sacrifice and of the lives of all inhabitants of the world is clear only if one recognizes that nothing is real and that everything is ultimately one. This is one way of reading the *Matrix* films, but ultimately the film's philosophical starting point forces one to acknowledge that only one answer can be given: we do not know. Morpheus' fervent beliefs turn out to be an illusory dream at the end of *Reloaded*, and part of the films' message is that, while it may take courage to believe, it takes even greater courage to accept uncertainty. Even so, precisely because of this postmodern uncertainty that is characteristic of our age and of the *Matrix* films, it is unclear whether these stories will have the resources not only to entertain and to make us think, but also to inspire us to emulate the story's main character. Only when it has passed this test will we know Neo's real superhero potential.

Notes

[1] Frank Miller, in an interview published as "Batman and the Twilight of the Idols: An Interview with Frank Miller," in *The Many Lives of The Batman*, ed. Roberta E. Pearson and William Uricchio (New York: Routledge, 1991), 39. Cf. Richard Reynolds, *Super Heroes: A Modern Mythology* (Jackson: University Press of Mississippi, 1992), 74–77.

[2] For parallels see Chris Seay and Greg Garrett, *The Gospel Reloaded* (Colorado Springs, Colo.: Pinon Press, 2003), chs. 6 and 15; and also the references in my "Conflicting Visions of the Real: Christianity, Buddhism & Baudrillard in *The Matrix* films and popular culture," in *Visions of Humanity in Cyberculture, Cyberspace and Science Fiction*, ed. Marcus Leaning and Birgit Pretzsch (Amsterdam/New York: Rodopi, forthcoming). For more information on the Matrix, see web site: www.tlfc.net. See also the Recommended Resources on the next page.

[3] For more information on these views as well as other orthodox and heretical doctrines in the early church, see J. N. D. Kelly, *Early Christian Doctrines,* rev. ed. (San Francisco: Harper & Row, 1978). Gnostic texts are translated in James M. Robinson, ed., *The Nag Hammadi Library in English* (San Francisco: HarperCollins, 1990).

[4] Conversely, it is difficult for historians to distinguish what Jesus actually said from what the Gospel writers interpret him as saying. For example, the words attributed to Jesus in John's Gospel differ from those recorded in the other Gospels both in terms of vocabulary and in terms of style, while they are essentially identical to the style of the author himself. The earliest sources that we have stem from communities committed to certain beliefs about Jesus. How much of what we have in our earliest sources has been transformed by that

perspective remains an open question. The distinction between the historical Jesus and the "real" Jesus is derived from John P. Meier's book, *A Marginal Jew: Rethinking the Historical Jesus* (New York: Doubleday, 1993), ch. 1.

Recommended Resources

Cohen, Stanley. "Messianic Motifs, American Popular Culture and the Judeo-Christian Tradition." *Journal of Religious Studies* 8 (Spring 1980): 24–34.

Detweiler, Craig, and Barry Taylor. *A Matrix of Meanings: Finding God in Pop Culture.* Grand Rapids: Baker, 2003.

Ford, James L. "Buddhism, Christianity, and *The Matrix:* The Dialectic of Myth-Making in Contemporary Cinema." *The Journal of Religion and Film* 4/2 (Oct. 2000) [Cited 20 May 2004] Online: www.unomaha.edu/~wwwjrf/thematrix.htm.

Gresh, Lois H., and Weinberg, Robert. *The Science of Superheroes.* Hoboken, N.J.: John Wiley & Sons, 2003.

Haber, Karen. *Exploring the Matrix: Visions of the Cyber Present.* New York: St. Martin's Press, 2003.

Irwin, William, ed. *The Matrix and Philosophy.* Chicago: Open Court, 2002.

Meier, John P. *A Marginal Jew: Rethinking the Historical Jesus.* New York: Doubleday, 1993.

Seay, Chris, and Greg Garrett. *The Gospel Reloaded: Exploring Spirituality and Faith in the Matrix.* Colorado Springs, Colo.: Pinon Press, 2003.

Yeffeth, Glenn, ed. *Taking the Red Pill: Science, Philosophy, and Religion in The Matrix.* Dallas: BenBella, 2003.

Conclusion
Superheroes in God's Image

B. J. Oropeza

> Creation is not a hurdle on the road to God, it is the road itself. (Martin Bucer[1])

We have observed through this anthology that superheroes tell us much about our own dreams, aspirations, and fantasies. Not everything in the superheroes is redemptive or points to religious inclinations. As in many human creations, we have found or noticed elements of the sacred and secular (and sacrilegious). However, enough thematic content related to theology has made such an investigation a worthwhile venture. Comic book and movie fans often see a better image of themselves through the superhero. As Les Daniels affirms, "The comics show us ourselves and our attitudes in a funhouse mirror, the images exaggerated but still recognizable."[2] Perhaps we long for the "super-self" because it really does exist as the *imago Dei,* the "image of God" or imprint of God's very nature that every one of us has. It is described in Genesis when God first created humankind: "Let us make *adam* in our image, after our likeness" (Genesis 1:26–27). Whatever else this may mean, if we are made in God's own likeness, this would seem to include rationality, creativity, social communion with God and others, the capacity for goodness or moral virtues, and taking responsibility for the life and resources on Earth.[3]

Through abuse, wrongful acts, pride, hurt, and distrust, humanity has distorted this image, some individuals more than others. Ultimately, though, we retain some knowledge of right and wrong, we hunger for meaning in life, and we desire communion with what is transcendent. Why? Our Creator seems to have "wired" us that way. As J. W. Montgomery affirms, it is as though every human heart is built upon a puzzle with one piece missing that causes it unrest. That piece is a "God-shaped blank," resembling the form of a cross.[4] In St. Augustine's famous words, "Thou hast made us for Thyself and our heart is restless until it rest in Thee" (*Confessions* 1.1). Montgomery continues to make a connection between the studies of religious patterns and human need for God:

> Suppose that the fallen race had kept a primordial realization of its separation from God through sinful self-centeredness and of its specific need for redemption through the divine-human conquest of the evil powers arrayed against it. Suppose within each human heart this realization were etched beyond effacement.... This darkening of the heart would quite naturally take the form of a repression of the natural knowledge of God's redemptive plan to the subconscious level, where it could be ignored consciously; but its eradication from the psyche could never occur. Under these circumstances, redemptive knowledge would surface not in a direct fashion but by way of symbolic patterns.[5]

This view maintains that our higher nature longs to be rejoined with its creator and cries out to be fed through spiritual words and symbols. What the superhero myths do is repackage segments of these symbols in a form that removes it from a religious setting into popular cultural context. The divine image described in the Eden story is indirectly nurtured in the hearts of humans who embrace the superhero myths. They echo the Gospel's redemptive story in faint colors. They whisper of a human plight back to God and paradise through a medium that is able to reach audiences who might otherwise remain unable or unwilling to hear, see, or read the message and thoughts behind biblical texts. We see a nobler and more adventurous self through the heroes, a better self that directs us heavenward. But we also see the flaws in heroes, which make them humans rather than gods, creatures instead of Creator. Their shortcomings in fact make them like us: humans in God's image.

St. Paul writes about having this treasure, the illuminating story of redemption imprinted in the human heart, housed within a frail clay pot that he interprets as the human body (2 Corinthians 4:4–7, 10). As a follower of Christ, he looks forward to the day when he can dwell in God's presence and when this mortal exterior will be entirely transformed by eternal life—"the One who raised the Lord Jesus will raise us also" (2 Corinthians 4:14a). Christ, the perfect god-man, is our ultimate hero and forerunner to the restored paradise. Perhaps it is not too profane to suggest also that some of the classic superheroes and their theme of restoring paradise make them resemble a "funhouse mirror" version of the Gospel—in this sense they become little Christs in tights.[6] Onward and upward!

Notes

[1] Martin Bucer in M. Ellison, "Sexuality and Spirituality: An Intimate—and Intimidating—Connection," in A. Thatcher and E. Stuart (eds.), *Sexuality and Gender* (Leominster, Herefordshire: Gracewing/Fowler Wright, 1996), 221.

[2] Les Daniels, *Marvel: Five Fabulous Decades of the World's Greatest Comics* (New York: Harry N. Abrams, 1991), 14.

[3] I realize that my interpretation is rather eclectic and inclusive; I simply do not agree that the *imago Dei* has to boil down to only one of these aspects or be defined in such a way that it becomes exclusive of some of these aspects.

[4] John Warwick Montgomery, "Introduction: The Apologists of Euchatastophe," in *Myth, Allegory, and the Gospel: An Interpretation of J. R. R. Tolkien, C. S. Lewis, G. K. Chesterton, Charles Williams* (Minneapolis: Bethany Fellowship, 1974), 23.

[5] Montgomery, 25–26.

[6] Term adopted from Peter Ross, "Caped Crusader," (Interview with Mark Millar), *Sunday Herald* (July 11, 2004), 17 [Cited 1 Sept. 2004] Online: www.sundayherald.com/43205.

Contributors

Elizabeth Danna ministers at Crossroads Christian Communications in Ontario, Canada, and was a tutorial assistant at the University of Hawaii at Manoa, Department of European Languages. She has a Ph.D. in New Testament from the University of Durham. Some of her academic articles include "Intertextuality, Verbal Echoes, and Characterisation in the Gospel of John" from *Revue Biblique* (April 1999), and "Looking Out for No. 1: Concepts of Good and Evil in *Star Trek* and *The Prisoner*," a chapter submitted for *Religion and Science Fiction* (edited by James McGrath).

Robin J. Dugall is Executive Director of the Youth Leadership Institute at the C. P. Haggard Graduate School of Theology. Reverend Dugall earned a Master of Divinity degree at the Graduate Theological Union, Berkeley, California, and is currently working on a Doctor of Ministry Degree at Azusa Pacific University. Dugall is a 30-year veteran of professional ministry and author of *Worship Experiences,* which is one of the "Fresh Ideas" Series of Student Ministry resources published by Gospel Light/Regal Books.

James F. McGrath is Assistant Professor of Religion at Butler University in Indianapolis, Indiana. He also worked as Assistant Professor of New Testament at Emanuel University and University of Oradea in Romania. His many publications and writings include *John's Apologetic Christology* (SNTS Monograph Series, 111; Cambridge University Press, 2001), "Religion, But Not as We Know It: Spirituality and Sci-Fi," in *Religion as Entertainment,* ed. C. K. Robertson (Peter Lang, 2002). McGrath is editor of the forthcoming collection of essays, *Religion and Science Fiction* (SUNY Press). His Ph.D. is from the University of Durham, England.

B. J. Oropeza is a professor at the C. P. Haggard School of Theology at Azusa Pacific University (Azusa, California) and an internationally acclaimed author whose many publications include *99 Answers to Questions about Angels, Demons, and Spiritual Warfare* (IVP, 1997), *99 Reasons Why No One Knows When Christ Will Return* (IVP, 1994), *Paul and Apostasy* (Mohr-Siebeck, 2000), and *A Time to Laugh* (Hendrickson Publishers, 1996). He also worked as a professor of religion at George Fox University in Newberg, Oregon, and was formerly an associate researcher for the Christian

Research Institute and *Christian Research Journal.* He received his Ph.D. from the University of Durham, England.

Thom Parham, Ph.D., is a professor in communication studies at Azusa Pacific University. He has written for CBS's hit drama *JAG* and the Family Channel sitcom *Big Brother Jake*, and he has worked on *Touched By an Angel.* He is listed in the 2002 and 2004 editions of *Who's Who Among America's Teachers.* He recently finished co-writing *Steeple Chasers*, an original "dramedy" that will go on tour. Parham made his directorial debut on the APU stage with Thornton Wilder's Pulitzer Prize–winning play *The Skin of Our Teeth.*

Leo Partible is a principal partner at Great Rift Entertainment in Los Angeles, California. He was previously vice-president of Creative Affairs at Takoma Entertainment where he set up and developed products such as *Shadowman* for New Line Cinema; *Harbinger*, in association with Jan De Bont's Blue Tulip Productions; and *Magnus: Robot Fighter* for Warner Brothers. He is also co-founder of TPG Visions, a productions and comic company.

Gregory Pepetone is a professor of music and interdisciplinary studies at Georgia College and State University, as well as a concert pianist. Having spent several years living and studying in Great Britain, Pepetone has spent considerable time studying the life and works of Charles Dickens. His is also the author of *Gothic Perspectives on the American Experience* (Peter Lang, 2002).

Tim Perry is Associate Professor of Theology, Division of Biblical and Theological Studies, at Providence College and Seminary in Neville, Canada. He edits *Didaskalia: The Journal of Providence College and Seminary* and is a columnist for *Faith Today Magazine.* His many publications include *Radical Difference: A Defense of Hendrik Kraemer's Theology of Religions* (Waterloo, ON: Wilfred Laurier University Press, 2001), and *Our Lady, Too: Toward an Evangelical Mariology* (Downers Grove, Ill.: InterVarsity Press, forthcoming). He received his Ph.D. from the University of Durham.

C. K. Robertson is Canon for Congregational Development in the Diocese of Arizona and Adjunct Professor of Pastoral Theology at the Virginia Theological Seminary. Holding a Ph.D. from Durham University and a Fellowship from the Episcopal Church Foundation, Robertson has written and edited several books and articles, e.g., *Religion and Sexuality: Conflicts* *and Controversies* (Peter Lang, 2005), *Religion as Entertainment* (Peter Lang, 2002), and "Sorcerers & Supermen: Old Mythologies in New Guises" (in the upcoming *Religion and Science Fiction,* ed. James McGrath).

Scott Rosen is Assistant Professor and a reference librarian at Azusa Pacific University. He holds an M. A. in History from UCLA and an M.L.S. from San Jose State University. He has assembled an extensive collection of comic books with an emphasis on religiously themed comic books—the most significant of which were recently exhibited as part of the Fullerton Museum Center's show "Gotta Have It Too: Collecting in the Internet Age." He is currently working to document and describe every religiously themed comic book published in the United States.

Ken Schenck is Associate Professor of Biblical Studies at Indiana Wesleyan University, and has taught at the University of Notre Dame and Asbury Theological Seminary. In addition to many articles, he has written *Understanding the Book of Hebrews* (Westminster John Knox), *Jesus Is Lord: An Introduction to the New Testament* (Triangle), and *A Brief Guide to Philo* (forthcoming, Westminster John Knox). He has been elected as a Fulbright Scholar to lecture and research in Tübingen, Germany, on afterlife traditions in Second Temple Judaism. He received his Ph.D. in New Testament from the University of Durham.

Robert G. Weiner is past president of the Southwestern/Texas Popular Culture Association and chaired the Marvel Comics and Popular Culture area. He has published articles on the history of popular music, film, and library-related topics including "Graphic Novels in Libraries" for the *Texas Library Journal* and the book, *The Grateful Dead and the Deadheads: An Annotated Bibliography*. His graduate degrees are from Texas Tech University (in history) and North Texas University (in information services). He is currently a reference librarian at the Mahon Library in Lubbock, Texas.

Index

ABOUT THE EDITOR

 **B. J. Oropeza** earned his Ph.D. in New Testament theology at the University of Durham, England. He is Assistant Professor of Biblical Studies at the C. P. Haggard School of Theology at Azusa Pacific University in Azusa, California, and an internationally acclaimed author whose many publications include *Paul and Apostasy* (2000), *A Time to Laugh* (1996), and *99 Answers to Questions about Angels, Demons, and Spiritual Warfare* (1997).